D1756314

THE CONSTITUTIONAL FOUNDATIONS
OF JUDICIAL REVIEW

The Constitutional Foundations
of Judicial Review

MARK ELLIOTT

MA PhD (Cantab)
University Assistant Lecturer in Law, University of Cambridge
Fellow, Director of Studies and Richard Fellingham Lecturer
in Law, St. Catharine's College, Cambridge

·HART·
PUBLISHING
OXFORD – PORTLAND
2001

Hart Publishing
Oxford and Portland, Oregon

Published in North America (US and Canada) by
Hart Publishing c/o
International Specialized Book Services
5804 NE Hassalo Street
Portland, Oregon
97213-3644
USA

Distributed in the Netherlands, Belgium and Luxembourg by
Intersentia, Churchillaan 108
B2900 Schoten
Antwerpen
Belgium

Hart Publishing is a specialist legal publisher based in Oxford, England.
To order further copies of this book or to request a list of other
publications please write to:

Hart Publishing, Salter's Boatyard, Folly Bridge,
Abingdon Road, Oxford OX1 4LB
Telephone: +44 (0)1865 245533 or Fax: +44 (0)1865 794882
e-mail: mail@hartpub.co.uk
WEBSITE: http//www.hartpub.co.uk

British Library Cataloguing in Publication Data
Data Available
ISBN 1–84113–180–6 (hardback)

Typeset by Hope Services (Abingdon) Ltd.
Printed and bound in Great Britain on acid-free paper by
Biddles Ltd, www.biddles.co.uk

Foreword

Dr Mark Elliott's aim is to examine Judicial Review within our constitutional order and to provide a justification for the power that it permits the Judiciary to exercise. However, because judicial review is the medium through which disputes between the branches of Government are fought, he is able, through his examination of the constitutional basis of the supervisory jurisdiction, to give an insight into a crucial issue of public law: the relationship between the Judiciary, the Executive and the Legislature.

His choice of this subject is timely: we are in the midst of a major programme of constitutional reform. These reforms will have important consequences for judges and for the relationship between the branches of Government. As the author concludes, those consequences are more of a progression than a seismic shift. The message, then, is that we need not fear the changes that are taking place, because they are firmly grounded in our constitutional traditions—they are, in the terminology of the book, legitimate.

Much of the commentary on judicial review of recent years has focussed on the desirability of a power of judicial review and its proper scope. This work, however, warns us that there is a logically prior question: that of the constitutional legitimacy of the power, the answer to which we must understand if we are to achieve the correct balance between the branches of Government. The glossary says of constitutional legitimacy that, "Judicial Review in any given area enjoys constitutional legitimacy if there exists a satisfactory constitutional warrant and legal basis." In other words, the existence of the power and the way in which it is exercised must be in line with the principles, both political and legal, on which our Constitution is based. That statement may appear to be a truism—and indeed, it is accepted from the start that Judicial Review in the United Kingdom is legitimate. What this work seeks to do is to demonstrate that legitimacy by reference to the sovereignty principle.

I have written before that the principles of Judicial Review in the United Kingdom rest upon the constitutional imperative of judicial self-restraint. There are at least three bases for this imperative. First, a *constitutional imperative*: public authorities receive their powers from Parliament which intends, for good reason, that a power be exercised by the authority to which it is entrusted. This is because each and every authority has, within its field of influence, a level of knowledge and experience which justifies the decision of Parliament to entrust that authority with decision-making power. Secondly, *lack of judicial expertise*: it follows that the courts are, in relative terms, ill-equipped to take decisions in place of the designated authority. This is all the more true where the decision in question is one of "policy"; and the further into the realm of "policy" an issue lies, the more reluctant a court should be to interfere with the authority's decision. Thirdly, the *democratic imperative*: it has long been recognised that elected authorities, and particularly local authorities, derive their authority in part from their electoral mandate. The electoral system also operates as an important safeguard against the unreasonable exercise of public powers, since elected authorities have to submit themselves, and their decision-making records, to the verdict of the electorate at regular intervals.

The author focuses on the constitutional imperative in his re-evaluation of the ultra vires principle. Ultra vires has its basis in parliamentary sovereignty: it implies that the courts do nothing more than adjudicate on whether the public authority has followed the intention of Parliament. But the truth is more complex: to say that the courts will only adjudicate on whether a public authority has acted within its powers tells us nothing about how they will interpret the scope of those powers.

It is the scope for interpretation to which some critics of the Human Rights Act point in order to argue that the European Convention should not have been incorporated. However, the legislation has been carefully framed to preserve the traditional constitutional restraints on judicial interpretation of the law, particularly the sovereignty of Parliament. The Human Rights Act will lead the courts to exercise a more intensive form of scrutiny over Government and public authorities. The judges will have to deploy such concepts as proportionality and necessity, permitting human rights to be cut down only if in response to a pressing social need. The courts *will* be, as they were before the Act, drawn into politically controversial issues. But they will not as a result be enabled to strike down Parliamentary legislation, although they will be able to declare it incompatible with the European Human Rights Convention.

The author comments that a declaration of incompatibility has "no impact upon the validity, continuing operation or enforcement of the offending legislation". Under the Act, however, Ministers are required to sign a statement on the compatibility of any new legislation with the Convention provisions. If contradicted by the courts, that statement will put a powerful political pressure on Government as a whole (and on an individual Minister) to have the legislation amended as soon as practicable.

As the author says, opinions vary on the extent to which the Act will bring about a new culture of respect for human rights. He writes of the experience in Canada, where it has been observed that a commitment to human rights by judges, politicians and public servants is essential if any "Bill of Rights" is to have meaning. My own belief is that in this country it will only be achieved over time by a partnership between the Government and the Judiciary. The Human Rights Act should be seen not as an obstacle to good administration but as an essential element on the path to achieving it. Successful challenges in the human rights area should be seen, not as defeats, but as steps on the road to ensuring that our laws, our institutions and the procedures they apply are really compliant.

The advent of the Human Rights Act makes no material difference to the position of the judiciary. To the author, the Human Rights Act is a "legislative signal that, henceforth, [substantive human rights] review is constitutionally acceptable, notwithstanding that this entails a reordering of the Constitution in terms of the manner in which the three branches of Government interrelate". Although this intensity of review is new, the judges in this country are used to interpreting the law in controversial cases in a way which might be represented as bringing them into conflict with the executive, but which respects our constitutional settlement. Judges in the House of Lords, and below, have traditionally made decisions, under the law, which were highly controversial—in landmark cases on civil liberties; on trade union immunities; on citizens' rights in times of war; on natural justice; on freedom of expression and freedom of the press; on contempt of court; and on the whole modern development of judicial review under which the judges have from time to time struck down executive decisions as contrary to law. The most the reforms will do is make a difference of degree, not kind; and one which will enhance the role and standing of the judiciary.

The Human Rights Act preserves the orthodoxy of parliamentary sovereignty, while changing the political context within which the legislative process occurs. It deepens the constitutional role of the judiciary but, in doing so, builds upon the powers of judicial review which the courts have traditionally exercised and the libertarian ethos which the common law has for so long reflected. The Human Rights Act does not, therefore, signal a wholly novel approach to public law in the United Kingdom; rather, it should be understood as a crucial stage in the ongoing evolution of our system of public law. The author concludes that the power assumed by the courts under the Human Rights Act is not only desirable, but constitutionally legitimate. I agree: we should embrace, not fear, the future it promises.

Irvine of Lairg
Lord Chancellor

Preface and Acknowledgements

The constitutional justification for judicial review of administrative action has, in recent years, been a keenly debated issue. This is unsurprising. Although the discourse has, at times, appeared to revolve around largely technical—if not semantic—issues, the way in which we approach questions concerning the justification of judicial review reveals a great deal about how we think, at the most fundamental level, about the foundations of the constitutional order.

The importance of the issues involved has made the debate an extremely lively one; but it has, at times, tended to be somewhat divisive. The contributors to the discussion are habitually separated into different camps, and the various theories on offer are presented as competitors. It is impossible to write about this subject without taking account of the fact that the debate has come to be structured in this manner, and the "competing" theories are therefore, inevitably, assessed in this volume. However, this should not be allowed to detract from the fact that the polarised nature of much of the literature concerning the foundations of judicial review obscures a very substantial measure of consensus. It is hoped, therefore, that the approach which is advocated in this book will be perceived not simply as another competing model of judicial review but, rather, as an attempt to construct a foundation which embraces the strongest features of what, hitherto, have been viewed as irreconcilably different theories of judicial review.

It is appropriate to indicate, at the outset, the questions which this book does not seek to answer. It is not directed towards an evaluation, in normative terms, of the exact content of the controls to which the courts should subject administrative agencies. That is, in itself, an immense subject which could not be done justice to as a mere facet of the present work. Rather, the focus of this volume is on how the law of judicial review is accommodated, at a structural level, by the unwritten constitutional order of the United Kingdom. Attention is therefore directed towards such matters as how judicial review and parliamentary sovereignty may co-exist, and the manner in which different forms of public power raise diverse challenges of justification. The impact of the Human Rights Act 1998 on the constitutional foundations of judicial review is also considered at length.

The research on which this book is based was funded principally by the Arts and Humanities Research Board of the British Academy, and also by the University of Cambridge's Wright Rogers Studentship Fund, to both of which I am very grateful. I also wish to thank my family and friends for their support while I researched and wrote this book. Special thanks are due to my parents and to Vicky; the book is dedicated to them. I would like to record my gratitude to Lord Irvine of Lairg for writing the foreword; to Trevor Allan and Jack Beatson for their helpful comments on drafts of this work, and to Richard Hart for handling its publication. Finally, I am greatly indebted to Christopher Forsyth for his stimulating supervision of the doctoral research on which this book is based, his detailed comments on drafts of this work, and the unstinting encouragement and support which he has provided during the course of this project.

MARK ELLIOTT
Cambridge
October 2000

Contents

Detailed Contents

Table of Cases

European Court of Human Rights

European Union

UNITED KINGDOM

OTHER JURISDICTIONS

Australia

New Zealand

South Africa

United States of America

Table of Legislation

COUNCIL OF EUROPE

EUROPEAN COMMUNITIES

UNITED KINGDOM

OTHER JURISDICTIONS

Glossary

A number of expressions which are frequently used in this book are set out below, together with the meaning which is ascribed to them.

Active artificiality

The traditional ultra vires model suffers from active artificiality because it is unable to explain the approach of the courts to ouster provisions: review is supposedly justified by recourse to parliamentary intention, but lies even when an apparently contrary intention is actively stated. Cf the related concept of *passive artificiality*.

Common law model

This theory of judicial review holds that, in requiring discretionary powers to be exercised consistently with principles of good administration, the courts are applying rules of the common law which bear no relation whatever to the legislative intention of Parliament. *Cf traditional ultra vires model and modified ultra vires model*.

Constitutional justification

Judicial review in any given area is constitutionally justifiable when it enjoys *constitutional legitimacy* (which, in turn, requires a satisfactory *constitutional warrant* and *legal basis* for review). Constitutional justification must be distinguished from *normative justification*.

Constitutional legitimacy

Judicial review in any given area enjoys constitutional legitimacy if there exists a satisfactory *constitutional warrant and legal basis*.

Constitutional warrant

There exists a constitutional warrant for judicial review in any particular area when such review can be justified by recourse to constitutional principle. This requires examination and evaluation of the role of the judiciary and its interrelationship with the other branches of government. The existence of a satisfactory constitutional warrant for judicial review in any given area is a prerequisite of *constitutional legitimacy*.

Internal coherence

A theory of judicial review possesses internal coherence when it provides a satisfactory explanation of the operation of review, in relation to such matters as the derivation of the grounds of review. *Cf* the distinct concept of *structural coherence*.

Legal basis

The legal basis of review refers to the legal location of the grounds of review which the courts apply. The existence of a legal basis which is coherent and constitutionally acceptable is a prerequisite of *constitutional legitimacy*.

Limited competence model

The limited competence model refers to a framework within which it is held that there exist substantive limits on the legislative competence of Parliament.

Moderate solution

A moderate solution to the justification of judicial review, while recognising that the *traditional ultra vires doctrine* is problematic, preserves a connection between legislative intention and judicial review. *Cf radical solution*.

Modified ultra vires model

This justification for judicial review holds that the courts, in requiring discretionary powers to be exercised in accordance with principles of good administration, are giving effect to Parliament's general intention that, when it creates decision-making powers, it only intends to grant such power as is consistent with the rule of law. *Cf traditional ultra vires model* and *common law model*.

Normative justification

Normative justification of judicial review involves evaluation of the normative foundations of the supervisory jurisdiction in terms of its scope and the principles which it vindicates. The evaluation is directed towards the desirability of review in policy terms. Normative justification must be distinguished from *constitutional justification*.

Passive artificiality	The *traditional ultra vires model* suffers from passive artificiality because it provides an explanation of the derivation of the grounds of review which is implausible: Parliament's intention is invoked as the foundation of review, yet Parliament, in reality, is usually silent, and hence appears to be passive, about this matter. *Cf active artificiality.*
Radical solution	A radical solution to the justification of judicial review involves wholesale departure from ultra vires theory, so that no relationship is postulated between legislative intention and judicial review. *Cf moderate solution.*
Rule-based model	Within a rule-based model of review, the courts' control of discretionary power is conceptualised as the application of autonomous rules which have nothing to do with the original scope of the power conferred upon the decision-maker. The *common law model* is rule-based. *Cf vires-based model.*
Strong critic	Strong critics argue that there are certain matters over which Parliament does not enjoy legislative competence; they therefore challenge the doctrine of parliamentary sovereignty and postulate a *limited competence model. Cf weak critic.*
Structural coherence	A theory of judicial review possesses structural coherence when it furnishes an account which is consistent with the framework of the constitution generally, and the doctrine of parliamentary sovereignty in particular. *Cf* the distinct concept of *internal coherence.*
Traditional ultra vires model	This justification for judicial review is founded on the idea that the principles of good administration which decision-makers are required to respect are specifically intended by Parliament when it creates discretionary powers. *Cf modified ultra vires model* and *common law model.*
Vires-based model	Within a vires-based model of review the courts' control of discretionary power is

conceptualised as the identification and enforcement of the limits which mark the scope of the power and which were inherent in the original grant. Judicial review therefore lies on the sole ground that administrative action is ultra vires. The *traditional ultra vires model* and the *modified ultra vires model* are vires-based. *Cf rule-based model.*

Weak critic

Weak critics argue that the ultra vires doctrine should be discarded as the justification for judicial review in favour of a *common law model*. It has been argued that every weak critic is also a *strong critic* because to challenge ultra vires is implicitly to challenge parliamentary sovereignty.

1

Justifying Judicial Review

1. THE RISE OF JUDICIAL REVIEW

" 'UNTIL AUGUST 1914,' it has been said, 'a sensible, law-abiding Englishman could pass through life and hardly notice the existence of the state, beyond the post office and the policeman.' " So begins Sir William Wade's text on administrative law.[1] As Wade goes on to point out, "This worthy person could not, however, claim to be a very observant citizen", since by 1914 "there were already abundant signs" of the growth of the governmental function.[2] At the beginning of the twenty-first century, even the least observant citizen cannot fail to notice the immense regulatory power which is now wielded by government. This interventionist trend has effected a social and political revolution over the last hundred or so years which, in turn, has raised difficult questions concerning the supervision and accountability of the burgeoning state. The way in which these issues have been addressed has led to a corresponding transformation in the spheres of constitutional and administrative law.[3]

The supervision of the executive was traditionally a matter largely for Parliament. However, while this task has become ever more complex as the exposure of individuals to governmental regulation has steadily grown, the legislature has become increasingly dominated by organised political parties. Taken together, these two factors have significantly undermined Parliament's capacity to provide an adequate check on the administration.[4] It is the courts which have sought to fill this accountability deficit by requiring—through judicial review—that the executive exercises its power fairly, reasonably and consistently with the scheme which Parliament, in the first place, prescribed in

---

[1] H W R Wade and C F Forsyth, *Administrative Law* (Oxford: Oxford University Press, 2000) at 1, quoting A J P Taylor, *English History, 1914–1945* (Oxford: Clarendon Press, 1965) at 1.

[2] Wade and Forsyth, above n. 1, at 1.

[3] See generally Lord Diplock, "Administrative Law: Judicial Review Reviewed" (1974) 33 *CLJ* 233; T Koopmans, "Legislature and Judiciary—Present Trends" in M Cappelletti (ed.), *New Perspectives for a Common Law of Europe* (Boston, Mass.: Sijthoff, 1978) at 313–16; M Cappelletti, *The Judicial Process in Comparative Perspective* (Oxford: Clarendon Press, 1989) at 11–24; Sir Stephen Sedley, "Governments, Constitutions, and Judges" in G Richardson and H Genn (eds.), *Administrative Law and Government Action* (Oxford: Clarendon Press, 1994); Sir Stephen Sedley, "The Sound of Silence: Constitutional Law Without a Constitution" (1994) 110 *LQR* 270.

[4] For an interesting perspective on the ability of Parliament (and, in particular, Select Committees) to hold the executive to account, together with suggestions for reform, see the recent report of the Liaison Committee of the House of Commons, *Shifting the Balance: Select Committees and the Executive* (London: 2000).

the enabling legislation.[5] The manner in which the courts have grown into this constitutional role was made clear by Lord Mustill in the *Fire Brigades* case:

> To avoid a vacuum in which the citizen would be left without protection against a misuse of executive powers the courts have had no option but to occupy the dead ground [left by Parliament] in a manner, and in areas of public life, which could not have been foreseen 30 years ago.[6]

These interconnections between the expansion of the governmental function, the reduction in the legislature's ability to hold the executive to account and the rise of judicial review are captured well by Sir Gerard Brennan, who comments that "we can perceive an increment in the scope of judicial review responding to a diminution in legislative control over executive power".[7] Moreover, the comparative lawyer Mauro Cappelletti emphasises that these phenomena are not peculiar to the United Kingdom: he perceives a general trend, according to which the rise of "welfare-oriented legislation" tends to lead to the courts "becoming themselves the 'third giant' to control the mastodon legislator and the leviathan administrator".[8]

It would be misleading, however, to suggest that these developments have occurred suddenly, and that judicial review ought therefore to be regarded as a recent innovation. As Sir Stephen Sedley remarks, "It is typical of the ahistoricism of lawyers that they treat as a landmark the *Wednesbury* case . . . in which the Master of the Rolls . . . rehearsed a number of doctrines which had been perfectly familiar to the Victorian judges".[9] Nevertheless, it is clear beyond doubt that, during the past fifty years, the growth of administrative law has been at its most rapid.[10] As Sedley puts it, "in recent years something has stirred in the judicial bowels . . . [T]he judiciary . . . has secured a commanding position from which it can now direct withering fire on executive and local government".[11]

Such developments are to be welcomed. The scrutiny of governmental action and the capacity of individuals to challenge abuses of executive power are non-negotiable prerequisites of a civilised, democratic society. It is not, therefore, the purpose of this book to question the *desirability* of the courts' exercising a judicial review jurisdiction. However, the development of English administrative law at what has been called "breakneck speed"[12] creates the risk that it is "built

---

[5] The most frequently cited summary of the controls which the courts apply to the executive on judicial review is found in Lord Diplock's speech in *Council of Civil Service Unions* v. *Minister for the Civil Service* [1985] AC 374 at 410–11.

[6] *R* v. *Secretary of State for the Home Department, ex parte Fire Brigades Union* [1995] 2 AC 513 at 567.

[7] "The Purpose and Scope of Judicial Review" in M Taggart (ed.), *Judicial Review of Administrative Action in the 1980s* (Auckland: Oxford University Press, 1986) at 19.

[8] Cappelletti, above n. 3, at 14–19.

[9] "Governments, Constitutions, and Judges" in G Richardson and H Genn (eds.), *Administrative Law and Government Action* (Oxford: Clarendon Press, 1994) at 38.

[10] See generally B Schwartz, *Lions over the Throne: The Judicial Revolution in English Administrative Law* (New York: New York University Press, 1987), ch. 1.

[11] Sedley, above n. 9, at 37–8.

[12] P Cane, *An Introduction to Administrative Law* (Oxford: Clarendon Press, 1996) at p. v.

on a foundation with too much sand and not enough rock".[13] The desirability of judicial review within the modern British polity does not obviate the need to establish its *constitutional legitimacy*. In developing their contemporary supervisory jurisdiction, the courts have arrogated to themselves considerable powers over the executive and have assumed constitutional functions which, traditionally, have been exercised by the legislative branch. It is, therefore, the purpose of the present work to investigate the basis of these developments by examining the constitutional and legal foundations on which the superstructure of modern administrative law rests.

This chapter deals with three issues which are necessary precursors to that investigation. First, the *specific justificatory challenges* which arise in this area are considered. Secondly, a *model of constitutional legitimacy* is articulated which furnishes the analytical framework that is applied later in the book in order to evaluate the existing justifications for review and develop a more satisfactory constitutional foundation for the supervisory jurisdiction. Finally, section four considers *why it is important to address these matters*, and why public lawyers—in contrast to private lawyers—sometimes appear to be more preoccupied with the broad, constitutional legitimacy of their discipline than with the substantive content of the principles which it prescribes.

2. THE CHALLENGE: JUSTIFYING JUDICIAL REVIEW

The challenges which inhere in any attempt to articulate a constitutional justification for judicial review are myriad, but may broadly be grouped under three headings.

2.1. Ultra Vires and Statutory Power

The first challenge quickly becomes apparent when the traditional constitutional rationalisation of judicial review is considered. Review is centrally—albeit not exclusively—concerned with the control of administrative powers which are conferred by legislation. According to orthodox theory, the constitutional legitimacy of such review is vouchsafed by the ultra vires doctrine which provides that, when a court reviews an exercise of statutory power, this entails nothing more than judicial enforcement of the express and implied limits which Parliament attaches to grants of such power.

The perceived strength of this approach is its capacity to reconcile the supervisory jurisdiction with the doctrine of parliamentary supremacy.[14] However, ultra vires has been subjected to a great deal of criticism in recent years, and its

---

[13] J G McK Laws, "The Ghost in the Machine: Principle in Public Law" [1989] *PL* 27.
[14] See further below, Ch. 3.

ability to provide a convincing justification for judicial review of power conferred by statute has been seriously doubted. That there is considerable force in some of these criticisms is undeniable, and it is therefore necessary to consider afresh the legitimacy of review in this core area while taking full account of the constitutional framework which determines the proper relationship between the three branches of government. These matters are addressed at length in the following three chapters.

2.2. Judicial Review and the Human Rights Act 1998

A novel justificatory challenge arises in the context of the Human Rights Act 1998, section 6 of which places public authorities under a duty to act in accordance with the fundamental rights set out in the European Convention on Human Rights. Clearly, this implies that public authorities are amenable to judicial review on the ground that they have unlawfully breached one or more of the Convention rights. Questions therefore arise concerning precisely how, if at all, this new rights-based mode of judicial review fits into the traditional theoretical model which is rooted in notions of vires, intention and statutory construction.

In particular, the clear statutory duty to respect human rights which section 6 introduces arguably places rights-based review on a distinct and altogether more straightforward constitutional footing than that which the ultra vires principle prescribed for the existing law of judicial review, thus obviating the need—within the context of human rights review—to have recourse to the often tortuous and unconvincing implication-based methodology of the conventional ultra vires theory.

These ideas are explored in detail in Chapter 6, which evaluates competing theoretical models by reference to which judicial review, under the Human Rights Act, may be constitutionally justified, and which develops a model that attempts to reconcile human rights review with a broader constitutional framework which is characterised by parliamentary sovereignty and the explicitly non-entrenched nature of the Human Rights Act.

2.3. Beyond Statutory Power: New Vistas of Judicial Review[15]

The justificatory challenge outlined in the foregoing section derives from the Human Rights Act's expansion of the grounds of judicial review, such that they now encompass a broad range of substantive fundamental rights (as distinct from the largely process-oriented rights conferred by the pre-existing law of

---

[15] This phrase is Wade's (see H W R Wade, "New Vistas of Judicial Review" (1987) 103 *LQR* 323).

judicial review). In contrast, the third, and final, challenge is posed not by the expansion of the heads of judicial review but, rather, by the widening of the scope of review. A fundamental part of the modern expansionist tendency in the field of judicial review is the extension of the supervisory jurisdiction beyond its traditional concern with the control of statutory powers. Prerogative and other non-statutory powers are now—at least to some extent—amenable to review. These important developments raise two particular questions. First, can the ultra vires doctrine provide a coherent constitutional justification for review of non-statutory powers? Secondly, if not, how may judicial control of such power be rationalised in constitutional terms?

The answer to the former question is firmly, and self-evidently, in the negative. Even if the ultra vires principle is perceived as an adequate justification for review of statutory power, it is meaningless to refer to it outside that context. As Professor Paul Craig correctly observes, ultra vires was developed as "an institution to police the boundaries [of public power] which Parliament had stipulated"[16] and therefore constitutes "the vehicle through which the courts effectuate the will of Parliament".[17] Consequently ultra vires can be of no relevance in situations where the courts control the exercise of powers which are not granted by parliamentary legislation, since this "cannot be rationalised through the idea that the courts are delineating the ambit of Parliament's intent".[18] The point is, ultimately, a very simple one. If judicial review of statutory power is justified by reference to the notion that the courts are enforcing the express and implied limits contained in enabling legislation, that justification cannot be extended into spheres in which enabling legislation is absent and in which, *a priori*, the courts cannot be engaged in the enforcement of any express or implied statutory restrictions.

Elias must therefore be correct when he asserts that "the theory that all principles of judicial review have their basis in the presumed intentions of Parliament . . . has been exploded by the *GCHQ* case[19] [which authoritatively confirmed that, in principle, prerogative power is amenable to judicial review] . . . Since . . . [prerogative] powers are not derived from Parliament, the justification for reviewing them cannot be based upon the presumed intentions of Parliament."[20] The same point applies, with precisely the same force, to review of other non-statutory powers.[21] It follows that any attempt to apply the language of ultra vires outside the context of review of statutory power would constitute only a semantic exercise, since it would "transform the ultra vires

---

[16] *Administrative Law* (London: Sweet and Maxwell, 1999) at 5.

[17] *Ibid.* at 16.

[18] *Ibid.*

[19] *Council of Civil Service Unions* v. *Minister for the Civil Service* [1985] AC 374.

[20] P Elias, "Legitimate Expectation and Judicial Review" in J Jowell and D Oliver (eds.), *New Directions in Judicial Review* (London: Stevens, 1988) at 45. See also F Wheeler, "Judicial Review of Prerogative Power in Australia: Issues and Prospects" (1992) 14 *Sydney Law Review* 432 at 461–6.

[21] See, *e.g.*, D Oliver, "Is the Ultra Vires Rule the Basis of Judicial Review?" [1987] PL 543 at 545–8.

concept".[22] As a result, as De Smith, Woolf and Jowell conclude, "The doctrine of ultra vires, to the extent that it implies that all administrative power is derived from a specific statutory source, can no longer be considered the sole justification for review".[23]

The force of this point is recognised even by those who continue to propound the utility of ultra vires in relation to the review of statutory power. Lord Steyn, for instance, has remarked that ultra vires is the "essential constitutional underpinning of the *statute based* part of our administrative law".[24] The clear subtext to this statement is that, while ultra vires can—in Lord Steyn's opinion— explain judicial review of statutory power, curial supervision of other forms of power must necessarily be justified by different, and more appropriate, means. Similarly, Christopher Forsyth—a leading exponent of ultra vires as the constitutional basis of judicial review of statutory power—readily acknowledges that an alternative justification must be found for review of non-statutory forms of power.[25]

In light of this—and given that the courts habitually accept ultra vires as the justification for review of statutory power—it is natural to look to the judiciary for an exposition of the constitutional theory which underpins judicial review of non-statutory power. Perhaps the most surprising feature of the expansionist jurisprudence is that no such explanation is forthcoming. Indeed the leading decisions which have affirmed that judicial review transcends the control of statutory power disclose a good measure of reluctance to deal with questions of legal and constitutional justification. As Wheeler notes, the courts have provided "a minimum of accompanying explanation or analysis",[26] preferring instead to concentrate on the desirability, from a normative standpoint, of subjecting a broader range of powers to curial supervision. Denis Galligan, arguing that Sir William Wade's leading text on administrative law shares this defect, complains that, "It is never suggested that there are limits to the effective and legitimate exercise of judicial review; the general message is 'the more review the better' ".[27]

This judicial attitude is exemplified by the case of R v. *Panel on Take-overs and Mergers, ex parte Datafin plc*[28] in which the courts clearly stated their willingness to review the exercise of certain public powers which derive from

---

[22] P P Craig, *Administrative Law* (London: Sweet and Maxwell, 1999) at 16.

[23] S A de Smith, Lord Woolf and J Jowell, *Judicial Review of Administrative Action* (London: Sweet and Maxwell, 1995) at 250.

[24] *Boddington* v. *British Transport Police* [1999] 2 AC 143 at 172 (emphasis added).

[25] C F Forsyth, "Of Fig Leaves and Fairy Tales: The Ultra Vires Doctrine, the Sovereignty of Parliament and Judicial Review" (1996) 55 *CLJ* 122 at 122–7.

[26] F Wheeler, "Judicial Review of Prerogative Power in Australia: Issues and Prospects" (1992) 14 *Sydney Law Review* 432 at 463.

[27] D J Galligan, "Judicial Review and the Textbook Writers" (1982) 2 *OJLS* 257 at 267, reviewing H W R Wade, *Administrative Law* (Oxford: Clarendon Press, 1977). C Harlow and R Rawlings, *Law and Administration* (London: Butterworths, 1997), ch. 2, describe this approach as a "red light theory" which emphasises the importance of judicial (rather than political) control of governmental power.

neither statute nor prerogative. The approach adopted by Sir John Donaldson MR was heavily policy-oriented: eschewing any analysis of the constitutional justification for applying judicial review outside the context of statutory power (and, in particular, largely failing to deal with the patent inapplicability of the traditional ultra vires justification), he characterised the main issue in the case as being whether the Take-over Panel "is above the law".[29] His remark that he "should be very disappointed" if the court was forced to reach such a conclusion underscores his concentration on the desirability of subjecting the Take-over Panel to judicial review, and the consequent subjugation of the equally important question concerning the implications of asserting supervisory power in a context outwith the legitimising reach of the established ultra vires justification. A similar emphasis on policy is discernible in Lloyd LJ's judgment.[30] Professor Wade thus appears to be correct when he says that:

> The judicial instinct is to fight on all fronts against uncontrollable power; and although there will always be a great deal of power in human affairs which no law will ever control, that is no reason for not annexing new territory wherever possible, and for not protecting against public abuse.[31]

This judicial concentration on the desirability, from a policy-based perspective, of widening the ambit of judicial review finds expression, in some cases, as a de facto presumption in favour of expanding the supervisory jurisdiction. *R v. Criminal Injuries Compensation Board, ex parte Lain*[32] is a case in point. It concerned the amenability to review of a body which the Court of Appeal treated as having been established under prerogative powers.[33] Both Lord Parker CJ and Diplock LJ seemed to adopt as their starting point a presumption that review ought to lie. The Lord Chief Justice was persuaded by the fact that he could "see no reason" why the body should *not* be amenable to review,[34] while Diplock LJ noted that, "No authority has been cited which . . . compels us to

---

[28] [1987] QB 815.

[29] *Ibid.* at 827.

[30] *Ibid.* at 845–6.

[31] H W R Wade, "New Vistas of Judicial Review" (1987) 103 *LQR* 323 at 324. The *desirability* of "annexing new territory" does not, however, detract from the importance of articulating a constitutional theory which establishes the *legitimacy* of such expansionism. L Hilliard, "The Take-over Panel and the Courts" (1987) 50 MLR 372 at 377 makes substantially the same point as Wade, albeit in more cynical language. She writes that the court in *Datafin* was simply seeking to "attach one more acquisition to its supervisory empire".

[32] [1967] 2 QB 864.

[33] Characterising the Criminal Injuries Compensation Board as the product of prerogative power is correct only if the broad definition of the prerogative, propounded by A V Dicey, *An Introduction to the Study of the Law of the Constitution* (London: Macmillan, 1959) at 425, is accepted. If a narrower definition, such as that which was advocated by Sir William Blackstone, *Commentaries* (Oxford: Clarendon Press, 1768), vol. 1 at 239, is adopted, then *Lain* may more accurately be viewed as having involved non-statutory non-prerogative power. This point was taken by Lloyd LJ in *R v. Panel on Take-overs and Mergers, ex parte Datafin plc* [1987] QB 815 at 848. See further below at 172–4.

[34] *R v. Criminal Injuries Compensation Board, ex parte Lain* [1967] 2 QB 864 at 881.

decline jurisdiction".[35] Thus it seems that the courts do not generally feel obliged to articulate any *positive* constitutional justification for the extension of the supervisory jurisdiction. The importance (and, very often, the patent desirability) of extending the protective reach of the courts' public law jurisdiction seems to obscure the more esoteric—but nevertheless important—question of what constitutional theory underpins judicial review of non-statutory powers.

In those rare cases when some judicial attention has been paid to matters of this nature, the results have generally been superficial and unsatisfactory, as the decision of the House of Lords in *Gillick* v. *West Norfolk and Wisbech Area Health Authority*[36] usefully illustrates. The case concerned, *inter alia*, the question whether a government circular relating to the provision of contraceptive advice to minors could be subjected to judicial review.[37] Although their Lordships expressed, obiter, their willingness in principle to review such circulars, the reasons which were advanced in support of this innovation were contradictory and largely unconvincing.[38] Lords Fraser and Scarman thought that the guidance was issued pursuant to a statutory power,[39] so that review was justified by the ultra vires doctrine.[40] Lord Bridge, however, disagreed, opining that the guidance had "no statutory force whatever" and did "not purport to be issued in the performance of any statutory function"; ultra vires was therefore of no relevance.[41] Nevertheless, his Lordship said that review was justified because ministerial guidance had been treated as susceptible to review in *Royal College of Nursing of the United Kingdom* v. *Department of Health and Social Security*,[42] unfortunately overlooking the fact that the constitutional justification for such amenability had not been discussed in that case. This willingness to reason purely from authority is the natural corollary of the courts' general reluctance in this field to engage with questions of constitutional principle. Lord Templeman did not attempt to expound any justification as such, preferring instead merely to state that review was possible, albeit that the ultra vires principle was inapplicable.[43] Lord Brandon simply did not address the question of amenability. This case epitomises the typology of judicial reasoning in this area. The clear judicial tendency is to concentrate on the raw, pragmatic imperatives which often pull in favour of the expansion of judicial review, in preference to

---

[35] *R* v. *Criminal Injuries Compensation Board, ex parte Lain* [1967] 2 QB 864 at 888 (emphasis added).

[36] [1986] AC 112.

[37] The case was, in substance, one of judicial review, notwithstanding that the Order 53 application for judicial review procedure was not used.

[38] For a succinct critique of the reasoning in *Gillick*, see H W R Wade, "Judicial Review of Ministerial Guidance" (1986) 102 *LQR* 173.

[39] See National Health Service Act 1977, s. 5(1)(b).

[40] *Gillick* v. *West Norfolk and Wisbech Area Health Authority* [1986] AC 112 at 166, *per* Lord Fraser, and 177, *per* Lord Scarman.

[41] *Ibid.* at 192.

[42] [1981] AC 800.

[43] *Gillick* v. *West Norfolk and Wisbech Area Health Authority* [1986] AC 112 at 206.

undertaking any thoroughgoing analysis of the constitutional and legal foundations on which such expansionism may be based.

Indeed, the authorities indicate that this judicial attitude has now been elevated to the status of principle. Numerous dicta indicate that whether the exercise of a particular power is vulnerable to review depends on its nature, not its source.[44] It is this type of thinking which has prompted the growth of judicial review, replacing the simplistic formula which equated statutory underpinning and amenability to review with a more nuanced approach to the scope of review which is rooted primarily in considerations of justiciability and, more fundamentally still, the underlying function of the review jurisdiction.

There are two aspects to the courts' assertion that amenability now turns on the nature, not the source, of the power in question. As a matter of empirical fact it is largely accurate: given that the courts are now willing to review a number of different types of governmental power, sources are of little importance to intending litigants who wish to know whether a particular power is amenable to review.[45] Amenability is, instead, revealed only upon a more thorough analysis of the nature of the power and the role which it occupies within public life. However, the fact that the question of sources is now irrelevant in this *practical* sense should not be allowed to obscure its continuing and pivotal relevance to the *theoretical* basis of review. For example, many of the issues which arise when considering the legitimacy of the review of statutory power are specific to that context, because it is necessary to construct a foundation for review which reconciles the courts' jurisdiction with the principle of legislative supremacy; this idea is elaborated in Chapters 2 to 4. Different issues, however, arise in relation to other types of power. For instance, it will be argued in Chapter 5 that, as regards action taken under neither statutory nor prerogative powers, the justification for review must take account of the fact that no legal power as such is in play so that, in cases of this type, it is theoretically significant that the relevant power derives from a factual rather than a legal source.

Sources therefore continue to be highly relevant on the plane of constitutional theory. One of the central arguments advanced in this book is that, while judicial review of all forms of power possesses a common constitutional impetus and heritage, the detailed manner in which review is justified must ultimately be approached in a way which is sensitive to the distinct constitutional and legal issues that arise in each context. It is for that reason that this book distinguishes

---

[44] See, *e.g., R v. Panel on Take-overs and Mergers, ex parte Datafin* [1987] QB 815 at 838, *per* Sir John Donaldson MR, 846–8, *per* Lloyd LJ; *Council of Civil Service Unions v. Minister for the Civil Service* [1985] AC 374 at 399, *per* Lord Fraser, 407, *per* Lord Scarman, 410, *per* Lord Diplock. For comment, see C F Forsyth, "The Scope of Judicial Review: 'Public Function' Not 'Source of Power'" [1987] *PL* 356.

[45] Subject to the proviso that the courts will not supervise powers which derive solely from contract: see, *e.g., R v. Panel on Take-overs and Mergers, ex parte Datafin* [1987] QB 815 at 838; *R v. Disciplinary Committee of the Jockey Club, ex parte Aga Khan* [1993] 1 WLR 909 at 924. For criticism, see J Alder, "Obsolescence and Renewal: Judicial Review in the Private Sector" in P Leyland and T Woods (eds.), *Administrative Law Facing the Future: Old Constraints and New Horizons* (London: Blackstone Press, 1997) at 167–8.

between different types of public power in seeking to articulate legally workable and constitutional coherent foundations for the modern law of judicial review—a task which the courts have largely omitted to undertake.

3. THE NOTION OF CONSTITUTIONAL LEGITIMACY

References have been made, thus far, to the importance of examining the *constitutional legitimacy* of judicial review. It is appropriate, at this point, to explain what is meant by this term. A useful starting point is the theory of ultra vires. The justificatory power which has traditionally been ascribed to that theory derives from the fact that it addresses—or at least seeks to address—two fundamental issues.

First, it attempts to furnish an ultimate constitutional rationale for judicial review. It does this by relating the courts' supervisory endeavour to the implementation of Parliament's sovereign will, thereby clothing judicial review with a constitutional legitimacy which—if the theory of legislative supremacy is accepted—is beyond question. This follows straightforwardly from the fact that, if the orthodox view of parliamentary sovereignty is embraced, the courts' paradigm constitutional duty is the ascertainment and implementation of the legislature's legally unquestionable intention.[46]

Secondly, the ultra vires concept deals with the legal basis or location of the principles which the courts apply on judicial review; importantly, it identifies a location—*viz.* express and implied statutory provisions—which renders the operation of the supervisory jurisdiction manifestly reconcilable with the theory of legislative sovereignty.[47]

At this juncture, two points must be emphasised. On the one hand, as discussed above in section two, the justification offered by ultra vires logically cannot be extended to prerogative and other non-statutory forms of governmental power. On the other hand, as is explained below in Chapter 2, even within the core area of review of statutory power, the justification which the ultra vires principle furnishes suffers from a number of very significant weaknesses. Nevertheless, it is submitted that the *issues* which the ultra vires doctrine addresses are of potentially substantial relevance to any attempt to articulate a convincing justification for judicial review, and that this is so notwithstanding that the *answers* which ultra vires provides are neither convincing in themselves nor applicable to non-statutory powers. Viewed in this manner, the ultra vires

---

[46] It will be argued below, in Ch. 2, that this one-dimensional view of sovereignty, and the model of judicial review to which it gives rise, ignore the rich set of constitutional principles which lie at the heart of the British polity. The present discussion, however, is concerned simply with the traditional models of sovereignty and ultra vires.

[47] For detailed analysis of how the manner in which the legal location of the rules applied on review impacts upon the ability of constitutional theory to reconcile judicial review with the principle of parliamentary sovereignty, see below, Chs. 3 and 4.

principle points towards two considerations which are of general relevance to any examination of the legitimacy of review.

First, ultra vires demands the existence of a satisfactory *constitutional warrant* for judicial review. This necessitates consideration of whether judicial supervision of any given form of power is consistent with and therefore justifiable by reference to the proper constitutional role of the courts. As regards statutory power the ultra vires model seeks to accommodate this criterion by providing that the courts' intervention is necessitated by legislative intention. As explained above, by clothing review with the constitutional imprimatur of the sovereign will of Parliament, the ultra vires principle purports to establish the *a priori* legitimacy of review in this area given that, within the prevailing constitutional framework, effectuation of legislative intention is the highest touchstone of legitimacy for the judiciary. However, distinct aspects of the role of the courts, together with broader considerations of constitutional theory, must be engaged if review in other areas is to be legitimate in the present sense.

Secondly, the ultra vires doctrine demonstrates that it is necessary to identify the specific *legal basis* or location of the grounds of review applied by the courts. This is a matter which can have important constitutional implications. For example, a number of contemporary commentators suggest that some of the rules which the courts apply when reviewing the use of statutory power should be viewed as subsisting in the common law rather than, as the ultra vires doctrine maintains, in implied statutory provisions. As Chapter 3 explains, this raises very difficult constitutional problems in light of the doctrine of parliamentary sovereignty. The new substantive grounds of review which operate now that the Human Rights Act 1998 is in force raise comparable issues which are addressed in Chapter 6. Moreover, little attention has been paid to the legal location of the rules which are applied to exercises of prerogative and de facto power (which, self-evidently, cannot subsist in legislation given the absence, in the first place, of any statutory grant of power): Chapter 5 seeks to demonstrate that this issue can sensibly be approached only after careful analysis of the conceptual differences between those two forms of power.

Thus it can be seen that, in relation to judicial review, the notion of constitutional legitimacy possesses two facets. It requires a broad, contextual investigation of the constitutional principles which may justify curial supervision of a particular form of power, as well as a narrower, more technical examination of the legal basis of review in order to ensure that judicial control can be rationalised in a legally coherent and constitutionally acceptable manner.

The examination of these issues is the central concern of this book.[48] It is worth pointing out, however, that this work is *not* directed towards an

---

[48] It should be noted at this point that the distinction between the two facets of constitutional legitimacy identified above will not be rigidly maintained in the following Chs. In particular, in the discussion of the basis of judicial review of statutory power in Chs. 2–4 below, questions of constitutional warrant and legal basis are inextricably linked to one another. Nevertheless, it is important to bear in mind these two constituent elements of constitutional legitimacy.

evaluation, in normative terms, of the content of the controls to which the courts subject—or ought to subject—administrative agencies. That is, in itself, an immense subject which could not be done justice to as a mere facet of the present work. The focus of this book is on how the law of judicial review is accommodated, at a *structural* level, by the unwritten constitutional order of the United Kingdom, rather than on the *substantive* content of the grounds of review deployed by the courts.

4. THE IMPORTANCE OF EXAMINING CONSTITUTIONAL LEGITIMACY

4.1. Introduction

Before embarking on that task, it is worth considering further precisely *why* it is being undertaken. The need to justify the investigation in this way derives from the suggestions made by some commentators that enquiring into the constitutional legitimacy of public law at a structural level is either unnecessary or relatively unimportant. Professor Craig, for instance, criticises what he perceives to be the undue preoccupation of administrative lawyers with questions concerning the constitutional legitimacy of their discipline, arguing that they should instead (like private lawyers) concentrate their attention on issues of substance.[49] That argument will be considered below.

First, however, it is necessary to deal with a more radical contention advanced by Sir John Laws which, if accepted, would render wholly otiose any examination of the legitimacy of judicial review. He has written that:

> [F]or every body other than the courts, legal power depends upon an imprimatur from an external source; but this is not true of the High Court and its appellate hierarchy. In point of theory, there exists no higher order law for them. It follows that any analysis of their jurisdiction, if it is not to be confined to the simplest statement that the court reviews what it chooses to review, must consist in a description of the nature and extent of judicial review in practice . . . [T]he ultimate freedom of movement which on my analysis the judges enjoy needs to be understood in order to appreciate that the court, if it decides in effect to push out the boundaries of judicial review in the particular case, is not guilty of any constitutional solecism.[50]

This argument consists of two central propositions: first, that the British *constitution* prescribes no limits on judicial power and, secondly, that the only true limits to the powers of the other branches of government are those which the *courts* recognise. This implies that any evaluative analysis of the legitimacy of judicial review is both unnecessary and impossible. While the courts' jurisprudence in this area can be described empirically, its legitimacy cannot be assessed:

---

[49] "Ultra Vires and the Foundations of Judicial Review" (1998) 57 *CLJ* 63 at 86–7.
[50] Sir John Laws, "Illegality: The Problem of Jurisdiction" in M Supperstone and J Goudie (eds.), *Judicial Review* (London: Butterworths, 1991) at 69–70.

there exists no constitutional yardstick against which it can be measured, since English courts "have, in the final analysis, the power they say they have".[51] Truly, this is, in Sir Stephen Sedley's words, a "trailer for a constitutional theory of judicial supremacism" which demands the closest inspection.[52]

4.2. Allocation of Governmental Power: An Unregulated Matter of Fact?

Laws's thesis is imbued with the notion that power is ultimately a question of fact. At root, the veracity of this proposition is undeniable. In primitive and undemocratic societies, governmental power is exercised by those who are best able to arrogate it to themselves at any particular time. However, as communities develop, power-distribution by naked arrogation is replaced with more refined power-allocation methodologies which tend to be based on some form of consensus concerning the way in which society should be governed. Ultimately, a written constitution may be adopted in order to embody and record such consensus, thereby conferring greater formality and transparency on the mechanics of power-allocation.[53]

Of course, if the vision of government enshrined in a constitution ceases to be underpinned by consensus support, this may eventually lead to the abandonment of the constitution and the reallocation of governmental power. Once a constitution is discarded, subsequent redistribution of power can be analysed and explained only in factual terms and can consist only of empirical description: the post-constitutional re-emergence of unregulated public power precludes any evaluative study of the legitimacy, in constitutional terms, of the new arrangements.

However, so long as constitutional power-allocation prevails in a community, the position is very different. Since the constitution imposes a framework which regulates the distribution of power, claims of public power may be analysed evaluatively rather than merely described empirically. This follows because they are legitimate only to the extent that they can be reconciled with society's consensus view, embodied in the constitution, of the proper functions of the different branches of government.

Laws argues that, in the British context, the courts' power does not derive from any "external" imprimatur, in which case its existence must be purely factual and its scope unlimited. In turn, the powers of the other branches of government exist only to the extent that the constitutionally unregulated courts permit. Hence, according to this view of the British constitution, the incidence of public power is determined by factual arrogation and not by constitutional allocation.

---

[51] Sir John Laws, "Illegality: The Problem of Jurisdiction" in M Supperstone and J Goudie (eds.), *Judicial Review* (London: Butterworths, 1997) at 4.1.

[52] Sir Stephen Sedley [1993] PL 543 at 544 (commenting on Laws, above n. 50).

[53] See, *e.g.*, the first three arts. of the US Constitution which set out, in clear terms, the respective powers and functions of the three branches of government.

Professor Craig strongly disagrees with this interpretation of Laws's thesis,[54] arguing that Laws's approach is, in essence, simply a repetition of the classic doctrine of sovereignty articulated by Sir William Wade.[55] It is necessary to consider whether this is so. The central argument which Professor Wade advances in his seminal article on parliamentary sovereignty is that the principle ultimately lies "in the keeping of the courts",[56] so that the legislative power of Parliament is, in one sense, dependent on the willingness of the judiciary to recognise parliamentary enactments as valid law. The implications of Wade's conception of sovereignty are myriad; for present purposes, however, it is necessary to consider two specific points.

On the one hand, Wade's argument properly captures the truth that power is, at root, a factual phenomenon. In pragmatic terms it is, therefore, possible for judges—just as it is possible for administrators and citizens—to refuse to recognise legislation as law. On the other hand, however, Wade recognises that, within the United Kingdom's political order, this raw conception of power as fact has been overlaid by a set of constitutional precepts. Consequently, to use Professor Hart's terminology, a "rule of recognition"[57] has emerged which constitutionally requires the courts to acknowledge Parliament's sovereignty by accepting its enactments as valid law. It is the connections which he draws between these two facets of power—one factual, one constitutional—which is one of the defining features of Wade's thesis. Crucially Wade argues that, if the courts were to refuse to apply primary legislation, they would be acting extra-constitutionally by disregarding the established rule of recognition. It is for precisely this reason that Wade refers to such situations as "revolutionary". Thus, for Wade, so long as the existing constitutional order subsists, there clearly *does* exist a constitutional framework by reference to which judicial review—and all other assertions of judicial power—must be justified. This much is apparent from his text on administrative law which strongly advocates the use of the ultra vires doctrine as the mechanism by which the judicial review jurisdiction's legitimacy is established by reconciling it with the constitutional order generally and the notion of parliamentary sovereignty in particular.[58]

Laws's approach, however, is quite different. In contradistinction to Sir William Wade, he omits, in the passage quoted above, to embrace the implications of the fundamental distinction between power in its two guises—as a factual phenomenon and as a constitutionally regulated phenomenon. Wade

---

[54] P P Craig, "Competing Models of Judicial Review" in C F Forsyth (ed.), *Judicial Review and the Constitution* (Oxford: Hart Publishing, 2000) at 384–6, responding to the critique of Laws's views set out in M C Elliott, "The Ultra Vires Doctrine in a Constitutional Setting: Still the Central Principle of Administrative Law" (1999) 58 *CLJ* 129 at 131–4.

[55] Craig also disputes the suggestion that Laws's approach, if accepted, would make it unnecessary—and, indeed, impossible—to justify judicial review.

[56] H W R Wade, "The Basis of Legal Sovereignty" (1955) 13 *CLJ* 172 at 189.

[57] H L A Hart, *The Concept of Law* (Oxford: Clarendon Press, 1994) at 100 ff.

[58] H W R Wade and C F Forsyth, *Administrative Law* (Oxford: Oxford University Press, 2000), ch. 2.

merely contends that the judges may play a pivotal role in an extra-constitutional—or "revolutionary"—reallocation of power, given the ulti-mately pragmatic nature of power. For Laws, however, the courts are free to assert fresh powers and redefine their relationship with the other institutions of government in the absence of any discontinuity, revolution or extra-constitutionality. Laws therefore differs from Wade because he elides the nature of the present constitutional settlement (under which the courts' powers are constitutionally limited) with the fact that that settlement may—extra-constitutionally—change. He thus conflates the role which Wade ascribes to the judges in the context of a dynamic extra-constitution resettlement with the nature and implications of the theory of sovereignty which the existing constitutional order embodies and which limits the constitutional powers of the judges so long as that constitutional order continues to apply.[59]

4.3. The British Constitution, Power-Allocation and the Courts

If, as argued above, Laws's thesis does not derive support from Wade's theory of sovereignty, it is necessary to evaluate his argument on its own terms. The central difficulty with his approach is that it does not convincingly explain why the courts find themselves in such a pivotal and privileged position: after all, like the judiciary, the legislature and the executive also exercise a great deal of public power and, although their adjudicative function places the courts in a powerful position, it is not clear why their competence to interpret the law is somehow superior to Parliament's ability to change it or the administration's capacity to enforce it. No satisfactory explanation is forthcoming of why the powers of the other branches are precarious in the sense that they must rely ultimately on judicial recognition, in contradistinction to the courts' power which appears to be certain and assured. If, as Laws contends, power is a matter of unregulated fact within the British system, it is unclear why, for example, the courts' adjudicatory powers are not themselves dependent on legislative and administrative acquiescence in the current distribution of functions between the three branches.

The essential point, however, is that if Britain is not to be likened to primitive and undemocratic societies in which power belongs only to those who are strong enough to claim it for themselves, then it must follow that the existing allocation of power prevails due to some measure of consensus underlying those arrangements. Once this is recognised, it becomes apparent that it is incorrect to

---

[59] Once this distinction between Wade and Laws is appreciated, it also becomes clear that Professor Craig, above n. 54, at 384–6, is incorrect when he says that there is nothing in Laws's thesis which makes the justification of judicial review unnecessary or impossible. The fact that, for Laws, judicial power is—*within the present constitutional order*—ultimately unregulated by that constitutional order logically implies that there exists no constitutional yardstick by reference to which the constitutional legitimacy of judicial review may be evaluated.

claim that the power of one branch of government is dependent upon the unregulated co-operation of another. Although in practical terms the courts' recognition of legislation as law is necessary for the efficacious fulfilment by Parliament of its legislative role, this does not mean that Parliament's power is precarious in the sense that its existence is dependent upon the co-operation of the courts. Within the British system of governance—like that of other developed democracies—constitutionalism displaces, or overlays, the conception of power as a nakedly factual phenomenon. The courts are not, therefore, competent to deny the powers of the other branches, because the courts' powers are themselves derived from and regulated by the constitution. In fairness to Sir John Laws, this is a point which, elsewhere, he has acknowledged:

> Ultimate sovereignty rests, in every civilized constitution, not with those who wield governmental power, but in the conditions under which they are permitted to do so. The constitution . . . is in this sense sovereign.[60]

Once this is appreciated, questions arise about the nature and scope of the powers which are ascribed to the different branches of government. Empirical description of the powers which the various organs exercise becomes insufficient: evaluative analysis of the legitimacy of claims of public power is both necessitated and facilitated once it is recognised that governmental institutions can act with propriety only so long as they remain within the powers granted to them by the constitution. This is true for Parliament and the executive and it is equally true for the courts.[61] This proposition is a widely accepted constitutional truth. As Michael Beloff pithily remarks:

> . . . I am not persuaded that in the new millennium the rule of law will be superseded by the rule of Laws. It was not the purpose of the constitutional battles, ideological, political and military of the Stuart era, to confirm the judges as the makers and shakers of the nation's affairs.[62]

Lord Woolf makes a similar point, albeit in rather different terms, explaining that the constitution devolves only limited powers to the courts and that they are, therefore, required to remain within their demarcated province:

---

[60] Sir John Laws, "Law and Democracy" [1995] *PL* 72 at 92. However, it is difficult to see how this comment can be reconciled with his other views, discussed above.

[61] Even if the traditional view of the legislative omnicompetence of Parliament is accepted, this does not negate the argument that the constitution allocates power to the different branches: there is no reason why the consensus embodied in the constitution should not ascribe to Parliament legislative competence over all matters. The fact that the constitution devolves absolute legislative power to Parliament should not be taken to indicate that the administrative capacity of the executive and the adjudicative competence of the courts are also unlimited.

[62] M J Beloff, "Judicial Review—2001: A Prophetic Odyssey" (1995) 58 *MLR* 143 at 147–8. See J A G Griffith, "The Brave New World of Sir John Laws" (2000) 63 *MLR* 159 for a comprehensive survey of the writings of Laws, and a critique of the relationship between the courts and the other branches of government which Laws sets out.

Our parliamentary democracy is based on the rule of law . . . [T]he courts derive their authority from the rule of law . . . and can not act in manner which it involves its repudiation.[63]

4.4. The Expansion of Judicial Review and Questions of Constitutional Propriety

Once it is accepted that the legitimacy of judicial decision-making and claims of judicial power need to be evaluated, it becomes necessary to address a more specific point: why are administrative lawyers, as distinct from private lawyers, apparently preoccupied with these broad, structural questions concerning the constitutional justifiability of their discipline? What, if anything, is there about administrative law which requires particular attention to be paid to such issues? The answer to this question is revealed upon consideration of the nature and implications of the judicial endeavour which has produced the modern corpus of English administrative law. Two particular features of that endeavour merit attention.

First, the courts have exercised a substantial law-making function by creating a set of principles of good administration which they require administrators to obey, and by extending those principles to powers, such as prerogative and other non-statutory powers, which until recently were largely unfettered. This raises questions concerning the extent to which the constitution confers on the courts the power to make law in this manner. Although it has been remarked that "it was [n]ever an important discovery that judges are in some senses lawmakers",[64] it is clear that the constitution does not ascribe to the courts an unfettered discretion to develop and make law. As Cappelletti observes, "Every civilized legal system has . . . tried to design and enforce some *limits of judicial freedom*, both procedural and substantive".[65] Such limits are required partly because judicial law-making is beset by a number of practical difficulties,[66] and also because judge-made law lacks democratic legitimacy. This view was expressed with particular force by Lord Devlin, who warned that if the courts fail to exercise their law-making function with caution, they risk creating a "totalitarian state".[67] Although he regards this as something of an exaggeration, Cappelletti agrees that a "continuous effort should be made to preserve as much

---

[63] Lord Woolf, *"Droit Public—English Style"* [1995] PL 57 at 68. Lord Woolf also suggests that the rule of law constrains the powers of the legislature; for discussion of this point see below, Ch. 3.

[64] Lord Radcliffe, *Not in Feather Beds* (London: Hamilton, 1968) at 271. For a more recent perspective, see A Lester, "English Judges as Law Makers" [1993] PL 269.

[65] M Cappelletti, *The Judicial Process in Comparative Perspective* (Oxford: Clarendon Press, 1989) at 7 (original emphasis).

[66] E.g. the retrospectivity and opaqueness of judge-made law and the institutional incompetence of the judiciary as law-makers: *ibid.* at 35–9.

[67] Lord Devlin, "Judges and Lawmakers" (1976) 39 MLR 1 at 16.

democratic legitimacy and representativeness as realistically possible in any form of law-making".[68]

In light of this, the propriety of any judicial law-making—whether in the area of public or private law—requires careful evaluation. However, a superadded consideration enters into play in the public law sphere. Judicial law-making in this area raises particularly resonant power-allocation issues, given that, historically, the supervision of the executive has primarily been a legislative function. The assertion by the courts of the contemporary review jurisdiction and its ongoing expansion therefore represent an important shift in the distribution of judicial and legislative functions. Such a fundamental shift in the constitutional settlement merits particularly close scrutiny.

Secondly, the existence of judicial review and its expansion into new territories raise questions concerning the justifiability of the courts interfering with the business of government. As the reach and intensity of the review jurisdiction grow, so the need to assess its legitimacy becomes increasingly pressing. In particular, there arises a need to evaluate the propriety of those developments in the light of what the constitutional order prescribes concerning such matters as the role of the courts and the separation of powers.

Thus it becomes apparent that the existence and growth of the supervisory jurisdiction raise important issues *vis-à-vis* the constitutional balance of power: as it involves judicial law-making and a shift in emphasis (from Parliament to the courts) concerning responsibility for oversight of the executive, the courts' expansionist jurisprudence calls into question the proper demarcation of *legislative* and *judicial* functions; moreover, since review is concerned with judicial control of the administration, it requires consideration of the proper relationship between the *judicial* and *executive* branches and the extent to which the former can properly interfere with the latter.

It is these peculiar features of public law adjudication which, it is submitted, supply the answer to the conundrum posed by Professor Craig, which was alluded to above. He observes that when legitimacy is considered in public law, the primary focus is not on the content of the grounds of review but, rather, on the structural compatibility of judicial review with the constitutional framework.[69] He goes on to argue that public lawyers should learn from private lawyers by shifting their focus to a normative evaluation of the content of the principles which the courts apply. However, while public lawyers should certainly be concerned with such matters, to suggest, by analogy with private law, that broader, structural issues of constitutional legitimacy are relatively unimportant is to overlook a fundamental difference between public and private law: the latter involves judicial supervision of another branch of government and therefore raises far more sensitive issues concerning the constitutional balance of power than does private law adjudication. It is for this reason that questions

---

[68] Cappelletti, above n. 65, at 42.
[69] See P P Craig, "Ultra Vires and the Foundations of Judicial Review" (1998) 57 *CLJ* 63 at 86–7.

of constitutional justification rightly assume a much higher profile in the public law sphere.

Notwithstanding their general reluctance to deal explicitly with justificatory matters in this context,[70] the courts are clearly aware that public law adjudication possesses this special dimension.[71] Lord Scarman, for example, observed that:

> Judicial review is a great weapon in the hands of the judges: but the judges must observe the constitutional limits set by our parliamentary system upon their exercise of this beneficent power.[72]

Lord Mustill has also remarked that the development of judicial review raises important issues regarding the proper position of the courts within the constitution:

> As the judges themselves constantly remark, it is not they who are appointed to administer the country. Absent a written constitution much sensitivity is required of the parliamentarian, administrator and judge if the delicate balance of the unwritten rules [of judicial review] evolved . . . in recent years is not to be disturbed, and all the recent advances undone . . . [T]he boundaries [between the proper functions of the different branches of government] remain; they are of crucial significance in our public and private lives; and the courts should I believe make sure that they are not overstepped.[73]

5. CONCLUSION

The British constitution, like the constitutions of all developed societies, clothes naked power with constitutional methodologies of allocation. The authority of the courts—like that of the other institutions of government—derives from a societal consensus embodied in the constitution which operates both to empower the courts and to demarcate the limits of their power. The courts do not, therefore, "have the power they say they have".[74] Once this is recognised, it becomes apparent that enquiring into the constitutional legitimacy of the expanding judicial review jurisdiction is a meaningful and useful endeavour. As Sir Stephen Sedley comments:

---

[70] See above at 6–10.

[71] The judges have acknowledged the sensitive power-allocation issues which administrative law raises by, *inter alia*, ensuring that the supervisory jurisdiction has not assumed an appellate character; reviewing only administrative, not legislative, action; invoking the ultra vires doctrine as the basis of review in order to vouchsafe its constitutional legitimacy, and refusing to institute a substantive, rights-based jurisdiction without legislative intervention. These ideas are developed in greater detail below in Chs. 3 and 6.

[72] *Nottinghamshire County Council* v. *Secretary of State for the Environment* [1986] AC 240 at 250–1.

[73] *R* v. *Secretary of State for the Home Department, ex parte Fire Brigades Union* [1995] 2 AC 513 at 567–8.

[74] Sir John Laws, "Illegality: The Problem of Jurisdiction" in M Supperstone and J Goudie (eds.), *Judicial Review* (London: Butterworths, 1997) at 4.1.

[Judicial review] is a constitutional development which needs to be understood and evaluated. Instead, a combination of popular legitimism and common law interventionism is offering us the open-ended syllogism that because the law is by definition what the judges say it is, so is the constitution.[75]

Sir Gerard Brennan captures the same point when he remarks that:

the judicial *ipse dixit* is [not] sufficient to expand the scope of judicial review . . . If the Courts simply declare that the common law authorizes intervention on conditions that have not previously been held sufficient to authorize intervention, the declaration adds no patina of historical authority to what is a modern extension of judicial review.[76]

Thus it is necessary to embark upon the task of examining the constitutional justification for judicial review of the various forms of power to which it now extends. In each case it will be necessary to identify both the constitutional warrant for review and the legal basis of the principles which the courts apply in effecting review. By distinguishing between different sorts of power in this manner, it will be possible to confine context-specific justificatory devices like ultra vires to their proper sphere and to enquire into the legitimacy of judicial review of administrative action in a more open manner; this, in turn, obviates the need to stretch established doctrine beyond breaking point. In the absence of a sovereign constitutional text, this exercise cannot be conducted by the construction of any written instrument, and must therefore consist in an examination of the unwritten principles of the British constitution which are relevant to the nature and scope of judicial power and to the interrelationship of the various organs of government.

Cappelletti observes that "the unprecedented growth of judicial power in many modern countries"[77] has led to a growing awareness of the need to enforce limits on that power by recourse to notions of judicial responsibility. The lack of any effective machinery for enforcing the limits which the constitution imposes on judicial power may be perceived as a weakness of the British legal order. However, this does not detract from the importance of determining and articulating such limits. In the absence of any formalised institutional arrangements aimed at securing judicial accountability, it can be realised only through judicial self-restraint.[78] Thus the more clearly the constitutional limits of judicial power are determined, the more likely it is that they will be observed in this

---

[75] "Governments, Constitutions, and Judges" in G Richardson and H Genn (eds.), *Administrative Law and Government Action* (Oxford: Clarendon Press, 1994) at 43.

[76] "The Purpose and Scope of Judicial Review" in M Taggart (ed.), *Judicial Review of Administrative Action in the 1980s* (Auckland: Oxford University Press, 1986) at 23. Although this comment relates to the development of new grounds of review, it is equally applicable to the extension of the principles of review to exercises of power formerly exempt from judicial supervision.

[77] M Cappelletti, *The Judicial Process in Comparative Perspective* (Oxford: Clarendon Press, 1989) at 61.

[78] This is not a plea against judicial creativity. Rather, it is submitted that such judicial behaviour must be justifiable by reference to constitutional theory; and, where such theory does not support judicial interventionism, self-restraint must be exercised.

manner.[79] Although this is a very broad issue, it is one which crystallises in the context of judicial review. The closest inspection of the constitutional legitimacy of the courts' activity in this area is therefore required, and it is that task with which the remainder of this book is concerned.

[79] The reverse side of this coin is that the more clearly the justification for judicial review is articulated, the healthier it will be within its constitutionally defined province.

2

The Traditional Ultra Vires Principle

1. STRUCTURAL COHERENCE AND INTERNAL COHERENCE

1.1. Introduction

Orthodox theory holds that judicial review of the exercise of statutory power involves nothing more than the enforcement of parliamentary intention. Review lies on the sole ground that administrative action is ultra vires, or beyond the powers granted by Parliament, so that the familiar obligations which are incumbent upon the executive—to observe the rules of natural justice; to take all relevant (but no irrelevant) considerations into account; to make only reasonable decisions, and so on—all spring from unwritten legislative intention. Sir William Wade, long regarded as the leading exponent of this view, has thus written that, "The simple proposition that a public authority may not act outside its powers (ultra vires) might fitly be called the central principle of administrative law".[1] Recent House of Lords authority indicates that there is "no reason to depart from . . . [this] orthodox view",[2] and that "the juristic basis of judicial review is the doctrine of ultra vires".[3] In light of this, an evaluation of ultra vires theory must form the logical starting point for any discussion of the constitutional foundations of judicial review of statutory power.

1.2. Structural Coherence

Baxter explains that the great strength of ultra vires is its capacity to reconcile judicial review with the doctrine of parliamentary sovereignty:

> The ultra vires doctrine was adopted at the Cape almost as soon as the Supreme Court was established. This is not surprising because the logic behind the doctrine provides an *inherent* rationale for judicial review . . . The self-justification of the ultra vires doctrine is that its application consists of nothing other than *an application of the law itself*, and the law of Parliament to boot.[4]

---

[1] H W R Wade and C F Forsyth, *Administrative Law* (Oxford: Oxford University Press, 2000) at 35.

[2] *Boddington v. British Transport Police* [1999] 2 AC 143 at 171, *per* Lord Steyn.

[3] *Ibid.* at 164, *per* Lord Browne-Wilkinson. Lord Irvine LC, at 158, also spoke in favour ultra vires.

[4] L Baxter, *Administrative Law* (Cape Town: Juta and Co., 1984) at 303 (original emphasis). Judicial review in South Africa now takes place in the context of a written constitution.

Similarly, Wade insists that the principle of ultra vires is constitutionally imperative:

> Having no written constitution on which he can fall back, the [English] judge must in every case be able to demonstrate that he is carrying out the will of Parliament as expressed in the statute conferring the power. He is on safe ground only where he can show that the offending act is outside the power. The only way in which he can do this, in the absence of an express provision, is by finding an implied term or condition in the Act, violation of which then entails the condemnation of ultra vires.[5]

Supporters of the ultra vires principle therefore claim that it possesses what may be termed *structural coherence*: that, in other words, it furnishes a theoretical model of judicial review which is consistent with the structure of the constitutional order generally and with the principle of parliamentary sovereignty in particular (which, at least in orthodoxy, is regarded as a key feature of that constitutional structure).

Given that structural coherence, thus defined, is the principal claim which proponents of ultra vires make in favour of its retention as the justification for review of statutory power, it is imperative that the nature of the claim is clearly understood. The importance of ensuring clarity on this point is underscored by Nicholas Bamforth's recent contribution to the debate concerning ultra vires in which, it is respectfully submitted, he fundamentally misrepresents the claim which ultra vires theorists make about the doctrine.[6] The core of Bamforth's argument can be resolved into two component elements.

He begins by describing the goal which, he maintains, supporters of ultra vires ascribe to that theory:

> Given that defenders of ultra vires often characterise the protection of sovereignty— or at least, preservation of the appearance of deference to Parliament—as the normative goal or goals of their theory, proof that ultra vires fails in such a task must force us to conclude that there is an inconsistency between the theory's aims and its outcome. Such a conclusion *must* fatally undermine the theory's claims to be seen as substantively attractive, given that its appeal—for supporters—rests on the normative goal or goals claimed for it.[7]

Having thus contended that, according to ultra vires theorists, the goal of the theory is the "protection of sovereignty", Bamforth then goes on to assess whether it secures that objective. He does so by reference to the theory of parliamentary sovereignty elaborated by Sir William Wade.[8] That theory provides

---

[5] Wade and Forsyth, above n. 1, at 37.

[6] See N Bamforth, "Ultra Vires and Institutional Interdependence" in C F Forsyth (ed.), *Judicial Review and the Constitution* (Oxford: Hart Publishing, 2000). For further criticism of Bamforth's argument, see C F Forsyth, "Heat and Light: A Plea for Reconciliation" in C F Forsyth (ed.), *Judicial Review and the Constitution* (Oxford: Hart Publishing, 2000) at 404, n. 39.

[7] Bamforth, above n. 6, at 115–16 (original emphasis).

[8] H W R Wade, "The Basis of Legal Sovereignty" (1955) 13 *CLJ* 172. For further discussion of Wade's views on sovereignty see below at 44–9.

that the sovereignty principle ultimately lies "in the keeping of the courts".[9] As discussed in Chapter 1, this reflects the idea that, in pragmatic terms, if the judiciary refused to countenance parliamentary legislation as enforceable law, this may prompt the demise of the existing constitutional order and, hence, of the sovereignty principle which it embodies.[10] The extra-constitutional character which such a development would possess is reflected by the "revolutionary" epithet which Wade would attach to it.[11]

In light of this characterisation of sovereignty theory, Bamforth concludes that the acid test of the efficacy of the ultra vires doctrine must be whether it is capable of vouchsafing the sovereignty principle when it is placed under pressure. In other words, is ultra vires able to safeguard sovereignty in potentially revolutionary situations? Bamforth firmly concludes that ultra vires is not able to do so, and therefore reasons that the theory is a failure because it does not achieve the goal which, he asserts, ultra vires theorists claim that it achieves.[12] This prompts two responses.

In one sense, it is perhaps somewhat simplistic to suggest that ultra vires is of no relevance whatsoever in potentially revolutionary situations. It is clear that the *legal* doctrine of ultra vires cannot absolutely guarantee the sovereignty of Parliament given that—as Wade explains—the latter is a quasi-*political* feature of the constitution. However, it is possible to argue that one of the virtues of the ultra vires concept is that it reflects and reinforces those dynamics of institutional interrelation which the British constitution presently prescribes.[13]

There is, however, a second—and more fundamental—response to Nicholas Bamforth. His central criticism of ultra vires is that it fails to protect parliamentary sovereignty which, he asserts, is the doctrine's *raison d'être*. This, however, merely begs the question what precisely is meant by the "protection of parliamentary sovereignty". There are, in fact, two principal competing meanings which this expression may bear in the present context.

One possibility is that it may refer to the protection of parliamentary supremacy against a constitutional revolution: as discussed above, this is the

---

[9] *Ibid.* at 189.

[10] See above at 14–15.

[11] Wade, above n. 8, at 189.

[12] N Bamforth, "Ultra Vires and Institutional Interdependence" in C F Forsyth (ed.), *Judicial Review and the Constitution* (Oxford: Hart Publishing, 2000) at 121–3.

[13] As C F Forsyth, "Of Fig Leaves and Fairy Tales: The Ultra Vires Doctrine, the Sovereignty of Parliament and Judicial Review" (1996) 55 *CLJ* 122 at 136–7 notes, "[Ultra vires theory maintains that] judicial review does not challenge but fulfils the intention of Parliament. By their ready acceptance of ultra vires the judges show that they are the guardians, not the subverters, of . . . [the] existing constitutional order. This fact is not a 'fig-leaf' nor is it a 'fairy tale'; it marks the maintenance of the proper balance of powers between the elected and non-elected parts of the constitution. Adherence to ultra vires is a gentle but necessary discipline." On this view, ultra vires exerts a symbolic influence which locates public law principles within a constitutional framework that requires judicial deference to parliamentary enactment. In this way it can be argued that adherence to ultra vires embodies a mode of constitutional practice which reinforces the idea of sovereignty, thereby militating—albeit indirectly—in favour of respect for Parliament's supremacy in potentially revolutionary situations.

goal which Bamforth ascribes to ultra vires, and this is clearly what he means by the protection of parliamentary sovereignty in this context. However, saying that ultra vires protects, or aims to protect, parliamentary sovereignty may mean something entirely different. When a commentator who supports the ultra vires theory refers to its capacity to uphold parliamentary sovereignty, he is alluding to the doctrine's claimed capacity to effect a constitutional reconciliation which permits the co-existence of the judicial review jurisdiction and the principle of legislative supremacy. In this sense the purpose of ultra vires theory is not to guarantee the existence of parliamentary sovereignty in the face of potential constitutional change. Rather, its function is to vouchsafe the legitimacy of judicial review—by furnishing the theoretical means by which to explain its existence in a manner which is consistent with the principle of parliamentary supremacy—so long as the present constitutional order, and the supremacy doctrine which it embodies, continue to subsist.

Bamforth therefore fundamentally misunderstands the claims of those commentators who support the ultra vires principle: their contention is merely that it reconciles judicial review with the constitutional framework (and, specifically, with the sovereignty principle). This is the notion which the concept of structural coherence attempts to capture—the idea that, if a theoretical model of judicial review is to be constitutionally legitimate, it must be compatible with the framework of the constitutional order. Whether the ultra vires doctrine is actually structurally coherent in this sense—and, equally importantly, whether any other models of judicial review possess structural coherence—will be considered in detail in Chapter 3. However, it is important, at the outset, to be clear about the nature and extent of the claim which ultra vires theorists make. They assert that ultra vires renders judicial review compatible with the structure of the constitution—but it is no part of their argument that it preserves that structure against external forces of constitutional (or extra-constitutional) change. One of the principal purposes of this book is to evaluate the ultra vires doctrine, and it is crucial that any such assessment should be founded on an accurate understanding of the goals which it claims to secure. It is submitted, with respect, that Nicholas Bamforth's assessment of ultra vires does not rest on such a foundation.

1.3. Internal Coherence

As is apparent from the comments of Baxter and Wade, set out above,[14] the claim that ultra vires is structurally coherent is made frequently and boldly; and it will be argued in Chapter 3 that the claim is correct. However, arguing that ultra vires provides a rationalisation of judicial review which achieves a good fit with the constitutional order at the structural level does not, on its own, estab-

---

[14] See text to nn. 4 and 5.

lish the efficacy of the principle as a justification for the courts' powers of review.

In spite of its claimed structural coherence, the ultra vires principle manifestly lacks *internal coherence*: that is, it is not capable of providing a convincing explanation of the source of the principles which the courts apply on review. Although ultra vires neatly fits into the broader constitutional structure, once we peer into the internal workings of the theory we do not find a satisfying explanation of how judicial review operates in practice. The nature of internal coherence, and the argument that the ultra vires principle lacks such coherence, are elaborated in the following paragraphs.

First, however, it is worth emphasising the present discussion's terms of reference. Perhaps the most frequently levelled of all the charges made against the ultra vires concept is its inability to legitimate the extension of the supervisory jurisdiction beyond the realm of statutory power. As Chapter 1 explained, given that the essence of the doctrine is its insistence that the basis of review is found in the implied provisions of enabling legislation, the logic of this argument is undeniable.[15] The juridical foundations of review of *non-statutory power* are discussed later in this book. However, the concern of the present chapter is to evaluate ultra vires on its own terms, by considering whether it provides a coherent and sustainable account of the operation of judicial review *vis-à-vis statutory power*. Even within this core area, the doctrine of ultra vires suffers considerable shortcomings; it is these which collectively deprive it of internal coherence, and which are of present concern.

2. THE ARTIFICIALITY OF THE ULTRA VIRES PRINCIPLE

Roger Cotterell correctly observes that the ultra vires principle, taken at face value, relegates the courts to the role of "modest underworkers" which merely "fulfil Parliamentary sovereignty".[16] Consequently, as Mauro Cappelletti points out, judicial review becomes but a "logical consequence of the fact that it is the very function of judges to interpret the law".[17] However, legislation which creates discretionary powers generally has nothing to say about how they should be exercised. It is, therefore, extremely implausible to assert that the courts divine from Parliament's legislative silence the complex rules to which administrators must adhere. This may be described as the problem of *passive artificiality*: the very fact that the legislature is silent—and, hence, apparently passive—*vis-à-vis* the conditions which apply to the exercise of statutory power makes it very difficult indeed to contend that the sophisticated

---

[15] See above at 5–6.

[16] R Cotterell, "Judicial Review and Legal Theory" in G Richardson and H Genn, *Administrative Law and Government Action* (Oxford: Clarendon Press, 1994) at 16.

[17] M Cappelletti, *The Judicial Process in Comparative Perspective* (Oxford: Clarendon Press, 1989) at xv.

controls applied by the courts derive in any straightforward sense from the will of Parliament.

When courts review executive action even though this is (prima facie, at least) forbidden by a preclusive provision, a second type of artificiality emerges. Naturally, once the court comes to apply the principles of good administration, the problem of passive artificiality, described above, arises. However, at a logically prior stage we are faced with the problem of *active artificiality*. Before the court can apply the grounds of review, it must conclude that review can lie notwithstanding the ouster clause. In such cases the legislation, far from being apparently neutral (or passive) about the limits which apply to the exercise of the power, actively says something which appears to impose a blanket prohibition on judicial control of the decision-maker. Thus such cases expose in especially clear terms the artificiality of the ultra vires principle: it purports to explain judicial review *in terms of* the enforcement of legislative intention, yet the courts at least appear to effect review *in spite of* Parliament's will.

It is necessary to address these two forms of artificiality in turn, beginning with the problem in its passive form.

3. PASSIVE ARTIFICIALITY

The grounds on which the courts review executive action may be grouped under two general headings. On *narrow review* the courts are concerned to ensure the presence of those "things which are conditions precedent to the tribunal having any jurisdiction to embark on an enquiry".[18] Professor Craig explains that this ensures that "the relevant agency [has] . . . the legal capacity to act in relation to the topic in question: an institution given power by Parliament to adjudicate on employment matters should not take jurisdiction over non-employment matters".[19] The basis of this form of review is therefore simple since, as Lord Wilberforce pointed out in the *Anisminic* case, the limits which the courts impose on narrow review are "to be found from a consideration of the legislation" which marks out the scope of the delegate's competence.[20]

Consequently, so far as narrow review is concerned, the relationship between the legislative scheme (and the intention underlying it) and the endeavour of the courts is transparent and straightforward: the courts clearly *are* policing those boundaries which Parliament intended should apply to the discretionary power created by the enabling legislation. For this reason, the ultra vires doctrine—which holds that review involves precisely such judicial enforcement of the statutory scheme—adequately and convincingly justifies judicial review in its

---

[18] *Anisminic Ltd.* v. *Foreign Compensation Commission* [1969] 2 AC 147 at 195, *per* Lord Pearce.
[19] P P Craig, "Ultra Vires and the Foundations of Judicial Review" (1998) 57 *CLJ* 63 at 65. See, e.g., *White and Collins* v. *Minister of Health* [1939] 2 KB 838.
[20] *Anisminic Ltd.* v. *Foreign Compensation Commission* [1969] 2 AC 147 at 207, *per* Lord Wilberforce.

narrow form. It is therefore entirely unsurprising that critics of ultra vires, like Lord Woolf, accept that it "can readily be applied" to explain narrow review.[21]

It is the courts' *broad review* jurisdiction—which entails the application of principles of good administration to the decision-making process—that poses severe problems for the ultra vires doctrine. It is extremely difficult to maintain that the broad grounds of review derive straightforwardly from the will of Parliament, particularly in light of the detailed and complex nature of certain grounds (such as the rules of natural justice). As Cotterell observes, "judicial review of administration obviously entails much more" than the ultra vires doctrine suggests.[22] Hence Forsyth comments that "[n]o-one is so innocent as to suppose that judicial creativity" does not centrally underpin the development of administrative law.[23] That the problem of passive artificiality exists is not, then, in doubt.[24] The live issue is how it should be responded to.

One way of avoiding the difficulties raised by the problem of passive artificiality is to embrace a theory of judicial supervision which postulates no relationship whatsoever between review (on broad grounds, at least) and legislative intention. Sir John Laws (*inter alios*) has advocated just such an approach, which reduces to a *common law model* of judicial review:

> In the elaboration of these principles [of good administration] the courts have imposed and enforced judicially created standards of public behaviour . . . [T]heir existence cannot be derived from the simple requirement that public bodies must be kept to the limits of their authority given by Parliament. Neither deductive logic nor the canons of ordinary language . . . can attribute them to that ideal . . . [I]n principle their roots have grown from another seed altogether . . . They are, categorically, judicial creations. They owe neither their existence nor their acceptance to the will of the legislature. They have nothing to do with the intention of Parliament . . .[25]

Similarly, Lord Woolf doubts whether it is possible:

> to justify the courts demanding fairness and reasonableness in the performance of a public duty by reading into a statute which contains no such requirement an implied requirement [to that effect] . . . I am far from sure whether in these circumstances the court is fulfilling an intention Parliament actually possessed or, by seeking to justify the need to achieve fairness on this basis, indulging in a fondness for fairy tales.[26]

---

[21] Lord Woolf, "*Droit Public*—English Style" [1995] *PL* 57 at 65.

[22] R Cotterell, "Judicial Review and Legal Theory" in G Richardson and H Genn, *Administrative Law and Government Action* (Oxford: Clarendon Press, 1994) at 17.

[23] C F Forsyth, "Of Fig Leaves and Fairy Tales: The Ultra Vires Doctrine, the Sovereignty of Parliament and Judicial Review" (1996) 55 *CLJ* 122 at 136.

[24] See H W R Wade and C F Forsyth, *Administrative Law* (Oxford: Oxford University Press, 2000) at 37.

[25] Sir John Laws, "Law and Democracy" [1995] *PL* 72 at 78–9.

[26] Lord Woolf, "*Droit Public*—English Style" [1995] *PL* 57 at 66. Lord Woolf CJ and Laws LJ express markedly more orthodox views in their judicial capacities. See, *e.g.*, *R v. Secretary of State for the Home Department, ex parte Fayed* [1998] 1 WLR 763 at 766–7, *per* Lord Woolf MR; *R v. Lord Chancellor, ex parte Witham* [1998] QB 575 at 585–6, *per* Laws J.

Superficially, at least, this approach—which may be termed the *radical response* to the problem of passive artificiality—is attractive in its simplicity and openness. Moreover, it coincides (unlike the traditional ultra vires doctrine) with the modern tendency to emphasise the constitutional autonomy and creativity of the judicial function. It thus seems to fit well with contemporary conceptions of constitutionalism.

However, notwithstanding the arguments of the radical critics, a number of factors—which will be considered in detail in later chapters—suggest that it is more satisfactory to preserve *some* form of relationship between legislative intention and the broad grounds of judicial review. The most compelling argument, set out in Chapter 3, is that to divorce review from intention altogether is to render the supervisory jurisdiction unworkable in terms of constitutional theory. There also exist more immediately tangible reasons for preferring an approach which maintains some form of linkage between the statutory scheme and the broad grounds of review: for example, the courts attach weight to the statutory context in determining the intensity and impact of the principles of review,[27] and, on many occasions, have stated in terms that they are concerned with effectuating the implied will of Parliament in judicial review cases.[28]

In truth, the difficulty which lies at the core of the problem of passive artificiality is not that the traditional ultra vires doctrine accords *some* relevance to parliamentary intention. The real problem is that it postulates intention as the *exclusive*, *comprehensive* and *sufficient* explanation for the existence and application of the principles of good administration.

A more *moderate response* to the problem of passive artificiality might therefore be to suggest that it can be overcome without going so far as to abandon altogether the role of legislative intention. Instead, it may be argued that, while intention is relevant, the courts are not merely giving effect to it in a straightforward sense: rather, they are drawing also upon other constitutional principles in order to help them to determine what limits should be imposed on discretionary powers. On this view legislative intention is a part, but certainly not the whole, of the story. This idea will be developed in Chapters 3 and 4 where it will be argued that, for a series of conceptual and pragmatic reasons, this more moderate response should be preferred.

4. ACTIVE ARTIFICIALITY

English courts traditionally adopt a very robust attitude towards statutory provisions which purport to interfere with the operation of their supervisory jurisdiction. In doing so they often effect judicial review in spite of a legislative enjoinder which, on a literal reading, is to the contrary. Thus the problem of

---

[27] See below at 138–40.
[28] See, *e.g.*, above, nn. 2 and 3, and accompanying text.

artificiality arises in its active form and suggests, in even starker terms than its passive counterpart, that review cannot satisfactorily be explained in terms of the straightforward implementation of legislation. As Craig points out, "If the rationale for judicial review is that the courts are thereby implementing legislative intent this leads to difficulty where the legislature has stated in clear terms that it does not wish the courts to intervene with the decisions made by the agency".[29]

This problem can be observed nowhere more clearly than in the House of Lords' decision in *Anisminic Ltd. v. Foreign Compensation Commission.*[30] The Foreign Compensation Act 1950, which established the Foreign Compensation Commission, provided in section 4(4) that, "The determination by the Commission of any application made to them under this Act shall not be called in question in any court of law". Their Lordships nevertheless held that a decision of the Commission based on a misapprehension of the scope of its legal powers could be quashed. The preclusive provision, said the House of Lords, prevented review only of valid determinations, which meant determinations reached within jurisdiction. By misconstruing its powers, the Commission had acted outwith its jurisdiction, so that no valid determination had been made. Section 4(4) therefore presented no bar to review.

Even if this interpretation of the statutory language is regarded as tenable, it undoubtedly constitutes a strained construction. In no sense can it be maintained that the House of Lords simply gave effect to the plain meaning of the preclusive provision in *Anisminic*. As with passive artificiality, there is no question that the problem of active artificiality exists: the important issue concerns how it should be dealt with.

It may be that the only possible explanation of the courts' attitude to ouster clauses is that they refuse to apply them. Such an approach is favoured by Sir William Wade:

> In order to preserve this vital policy [of access to justice] the courts have been forced to rebel against Parliament . . . In refusing to enforce [the Foreign Compensation Act 1950, section 4(4)] . . . the court was applying a presumption which may override even their constitutional obedience, namely that jurisdictional limits must be legally effective. This is tantamount to saying that judicial review is a constitutional fundamental which even the sovereign Parliament cannot abolish . . .[31]

On this view, any attempt to characterise judicial treatment of ouster provisions as a form of interpretation is rejected as untenably artificial. This may be termed

---

[29] P P Craig, "Ultra Vires and the Foundations of Judicial Review" (1998) 57 *CLJ* 63 at 68. See also D Dyzenhaus, "Reuniting the Brain: The Democratic Basis of Judicial Review" (1998) 9 *Public Law Review* 98 at 101–2.

[30] [1969] 2 AC 147.

[31] H W R Wade and C F Forsyth, *Administrative Law* (Oxford: Oxford University Press, 2000) at 708. On this argument, however, not only is Parliament incompetent to *abolish* judicial review in its entirety; it is also unable to *suspend* the operation of the principles of good administration in a particular context. This is an important distinction, since the latter makes far greater inroads than the former into the sovereignty principle. For further discussion see below at 78–9.

the *radical response* to the problem of active artificiality. However, it is important that the implications of this approach are fully understood. If the radical response is adopted, it necessarily follows that the supervisory jurisdiction must stand on altogether different foundations from those which the ultra vires doctrine envisages: if the courts are entitled, by ignoring an ouster clause, to effect review contrary to Parliament's will, it makes no sense to say that the vindication of legislative intention forms any part of the constitutional justification for review. The radical responses to passive and active artificiality are thus inextricably connected.

It is worth emphasising this point, for it is submitted, with great respect, that it is one which eludes Sir William Wade. This is clear when his treatment of ultra vires is compared with his discussion of ouster clauses. So far as the former is concerned, he contends that ultra vires is the "central principle of administrative law", and that judicial review is constitutionally legitimate only to the extent that the courts can demonstrate that they are enforcing the express or implied will of Parliament.[32] Wade thus explicitly connects the justificatory capacity—and necessity—of ultra vires with the notion that Parliament is sovereign. However, he goes on to argue that, in certain hard cases, such as those involving ouster provisions, it is necessary to rely on the "deeper constitutional logic" that review is a fundamental which is prior even to the sovereignty of Parliament.[33]

A problem with this stance becomes immediately apparent. It is simply impossible, as a matter of logic, to advance both of these propositions. If review is justified by reference to intention, it cannot be legitimate for the courts to effect review when Parliament directs to the contrary. Conversely, if it is constitutionally acceptable for judicial review to occur in spite of parliamentary intention, it is unnecessary and ultimately meaningless to postulate the effectuation of such intention as the foundation of the legitimacy of review. Parliament is either sovereign, in which case the ultra vires doctrine is arguably necessary in order to justify judicial review, or it is not, in which case the *raison d'être* of ultra vires is swept away. Parliament cannot simultaneously be sovereign for some purposes and non-sovereign for others.

A radical response to the problem of active artificiality therefore logically compels a radical response to the problem of passive artificiality. It characterises the courts' treatment of preclusive provisions as a "policy of . . . total disobedience to Parliament",[34] thereby stretching the ultra vires doctrine's putative connection between intention and the legitimacy of review beyond breaking point, so that the implementation of legislation can logically form no part of the theoretical model by reference to which judicial review is justified.

---

[32] H W R Wade and C F Forsyth, *Administrative Law* (Oxford: Oxford University Press, 2000) at 35–40.
[33] *Ibid.* at 706–10.
[34] *Ibid.* at 707.

However, a second, more *moderate response* is possible. As T R S Allan points out, "The *Anisminic* decision can . . . be readily explained as the result of a rule of construction, whereby clauses excluding the courts' jurisdiction should be narrowly interpreted".[35] This view derives a good deal of support from the speeches in *Anisminic*. For example, Lord Reid sought to justify the bold approach of the majority by emphasising that it turned on the construction of the preclusive clause:

> No case has been cited in which any other form of words limiting the jurisdiction of the court has been held to protect a nullity . . . Undoubtedly . . . a provision [such as section 4(4) of the Foreign Compensation Act 1950] protects every determination which is not a nullity. But I do not think that it is necessary or even reasonable to construe the word "determination" as including everything which purports to be a determination but which is in fact no determination at all.[36]

Similarly, Lord Wilberforce maintained that the court was "carrying out the intention of the legislature, and it would be misdescription to state it in terms of a struggle between the courts and the executive".[37] He underscored his view that the court was searching for, and applying, Parliament's intention by asking, "What would be the purpose of defining by statute the limit of a tribunal's powers if, by means of a clause inserted in the instrument of definition, those limits could safely be passed?"[38]

However, if one seeks to present the courts' jurisprudence on preclusive clauses as an exercise in statutory construction—rather than non-application—it is necessary to acknowledge the special character of the interpretative process which is in play. Cases like *Anisminic* can be accommodated within an interpretative framework only if it is accepted that the process of construction involved entails a great deal more than an attempt to give effect to the natural and plain meaning of the words which Parliament employs. An explanation must be provided of the factors which induce courts to hold that ouster clauses actually mean something different from that which they appear to mean. It will be argued below that such an explanation is forthcoming once the interpretative process to which preclusive clauses are subjected is understood within its proper constitutional setting.[39]

Unlike the radical response to the problem of active artificiality, the moderate response is compatible with the orthodox view of the dynamics of the relationship between the judiciary and the legislature. It is consistent with, rather than an affront to, the theory of parliamentary sovereignty, and thus it is also compatible with the core contention of the ultra vires concept—that judicial

---

[35] T R S Allan, "Parliamentary Sovereignty: Law, Politics, and Revolution" (1997) 113 *LQR* 443 at 447. See also R Mullender, "Parliamentary Sovereignty, the Constitution, and the Judiciary" (1998) 49 *NILQ* 138 at 142.

[36] *Anisminic Ltd.* v. *Foreign Compensation Commission* [1969] 2 AC 147 at 170.

[37] *Ibid.* at 208.

[38] *Ibid.*

[39] See below at 121–5.

review takes place consistently with, and is, in some sense, justified by reference to, the effectuation of Parliament's sovereign will. It will be argued in Chapters 3 and 4 that this moderate response is the better—and constitutionally right— reaction to the undoubted problems which beset the ultra vires doctrine in its traditional form.

5. THE EMPTINESS OF THE ULTRA VIRES PRINCIPLE

A shortcoming of ultra vires which is closely related to its artificiality is its emptiness. Sir John Laws comments that:

> [The ultra vires doctrine has] nothing to say as to what the court will *count* as a want of power in the deciding body; and so of itself it illuminates nothing. It amounts to no more than a tautology, *viz.* that the court will strike down what it chooses to strike down.[40]

While the problem of passive artificiality holds that it is impossible for the courts to divine the complex principles of good administration purely from legislative silence, the problem of emptiness represents the other side of that coin: if the grounds of review do not straightforwardly derive from intention, where do they spring from? As Galligan remarks:

> [W]e still want to know, but are never told, what deeper principles the courts are invoking in giving meaning and content to their discretion; we also want to know whether the courts are justified in using these principles whatever they are.[41]

Craig thus points out that the ultra vires doctrine is "indeterminate": it is so flexible that it can purport to legitimate any sort of judicial intervention by reference to presumptions of legislative intention, but cannot "provide any independent *ex ante* guidance" on the grounds on which the courts should intervene.[42] Thus, on this view, ultra vires is a purely formalistic concept which is normatively barren.

---

[40] Sir John Laws, "Illegality: The Problem of Jurisdiction" in M Supperstone and J Goudie (eds.), *Judicial Review* (London: Butterworths, 1991) at 52 (original emphasis). See also J G McK Laws, "The Ghost in the Machine: Principle in Public Law" [1989] *PL* 27 at 29.

[41] D J Galligan, "Judicial Review and the Textbook Writers" (1982) 2 *OJLS* 257 at 264, criticising the exposition of ultra vires in H W R Wade, *Administrative Law* (Oxford: Clarendon Press, 1977).

[42] P P Craig, "Ultra Vires and the Foundations of Judicial Review" (1998) 57 *CLJ* 63 at 66–7. See also J Beatson, "The Scope of Judicial Review for Error of Law" (1984) 4 *OJLS* 22 at 24–9. It is perhaps something of an exaggeration to suggest that ultra vires reasoning is wholly devoid of content. In some situations, the statutory scheme *does* provide the courts with a certain amount of guidance concerning how the administrator ought to use the power in question—for instance, it may provide for a certain procedure to be followed, or it may set out the purposes for which the power may legitimately be used. Viewed thus, the ultra vires principle need not be regarded as wholly empty (see further below at 138–40). Nevertheless, it must be conceded that recourse simply to the legislation clearly cannot adequately explain the derivation of the full range of controls which courts apply to administrators. The problem of emptiness does, therefore, exist, even if not in quite such an extreme form as some critics of ultra vires suggest.

However, it is important to note that the issues highlighted by the problem of emptiness arise whether or not intention is thought to be of any relevance to the justification of review. If intention is felt to be wholly irrelevant, it is necessary, in articulating an alternative basis for review, to explain how courts decide what to strike down. Maintaining that the common law—rather than the ultra vires doctrine—forms the foundation of judicial review says nothing in itself about the source of the normative principles which the common law model of review enforces. Equally, if it is contended (pursuant to a moderate response) that there exists some connection between legislative intention and judicial review, such that reviewing courts are involved in a form of statutory construction, it is necessary to explain (as the ultra vires doctrine does not) how they decide which particular limits should be read into statutory powers. Consequently, the problem of emptiness is one which both moderate and radical critics of the ultra vires doctrine must confront.

6. THE RADICAL AND THE MODERATE

It was suggested in Chapter 1 that a fully satisfactory justification for review must explain both the constitutional warrant for curial supervision of the executive and the legal basis of the principles of good administration. In approaching these issues, it is crucial to avoid the shortcomings which afflict the ultra vires doctrine. Two possibilities therefore arise.

The *radical response* provides that the connection between review and the implementation of legislative intention which the ultra vires principle postulates should be severed altogether. This is the solution preferred by those who argue in favour of a common law model of judicial review. Alternatively, it is possible to adopt a more *moderate response* by advocating that *some* relevance should be ascribed to legislative intention: that parliamentary will is a part, but not the whole, of the story.

The focus has, thus far, been on identifying the internal artificialities which beset the ultra vires doctrine. A convincing response to these problems—which collectively deprive ultra vires of *internal coherence*—must be central to any attempt to articulate a satisfactory juridical basis for review. However, it must be recalled that *structural coherence* is also essential to a proper theory of the foundations of review, in order that judicial supervision may be reconciled with the constitutional framework.

It is this imperative of securing both forms of coherence which, it will be argued, dictates the necessity of adopting moderate, rather than radical, responses to the problems identified above. Chapter 3 seeks to substantiate this proposition by showing that any attempt to articulate an autonomous theory of review which is wholly unrelated to the effectuation of legislative intention is fundamentally unworkable because it runs directly counter to the established constitutional order. Chapter 4 then sets out an approach which at once enjoys both internal and structural coherence, by overcoming the internal tensions which beset the ultra vires doctrine in a manner which is consistent with, rather than an affront to, the constitutional order generally and the doctrine of parliamentary sovereignty in particular.

3

Legislative Frameworks and the Control of Discretionary Power

1. INTRODUCTION

ALTHOUGH THE DEBATE regarding the juridical basis of judicial review engages a broad range of issues, it is, at root, concerned with one central question—*viz.* whether a relationship ought to be acknowledged between the controls which the courts apply to discretionary powers and the legislation which gives rise to those powers. That question forms the focus of this chapter and the one which follows.

As is apparent from the discussion in the foregoing chapters, commentators are divided on this fundamental question. Orthodoxy—articulated by such writers as Sir William Wade[1] and Christopher Forsyth[2]—provides that judicial review can be constitutionally justified only if the courts' endeavour is rationalised in terms of the enforcement of parliamentary intention; hence the claimed importance of the ultra vires doctrine. However, those who, for reasons outlined in Chapter 2, support a common law model of review—notably Paul Craig,[3] Dawn Oliver[4] and Sir John Laws[5]—contend that judicial review takes effect independently of legislative intention: on this view, ultra vires is merely a dogma which obscures the true provenance of modern administrative law.

An assessment of these competing views is essential to any attempt to determine how the juridical basis of judicial review ought properly to be conceptualised. The writing of Christopher Forsyth furnishes a helpful starting point in this regard.[6] The core of his argument is that it is constitutionally imperative to maintain the kernel of the ultra vires theory, which provides that judicial review is related to the implementation of legislative intention. His thesis therefore

---

[1] H W R Wade and C F Forsyth, *Administrative Law* (Oxford: Oxford University Press, 2000) at 35–40.

[2] C F Forsyth, "Of Fig Leaves and Fairy Tales: The Ultra Vires Doctrine, the Sovereignty of Parliament and Judicial Review" (1996) 55 *CLJ* 122 and "Heat and Light: A Plea for Reconciliation" in C F Forsyth (ed.), *Judicial Review and the Constitution* (Oxford: Hart Publishing, 2000).

[3] P P Craig, "Ultra Vires and the Foundations of Judicial Review" (1998) 57 *CLJ* 63 and "Competing Models of Judicial Review" in C F Forsyth (ed.), *Judicial Review and the Constitution* (Oxford: Hart Publishing, 2000).

[4] D Oliver, "Is the Ultra Vires Rule the Basis of Judicial Review?" [1987] *PL* 543.

[5] Sir John Laws, "Law and Democracy" [1995] *PL* 72 and "Illegality: The Problem of Jurisdiction" in M Supperstone and J Goudie (eds.), *Judicial Review* (London: Butterworths, 1997).

[6] Above n. 2.

forms a useful focus for assessing the central question whether a relationship needs to be articulated between the supervisory jurisdiction and the enforcement of legislation. The essence of Forsyth's reasoning is captured in the following extract from his work:

> [W]hat an all powerful Parliament does not prohibit, it must authorise either expressly or impliedly . . . [Therefore] if Parliament grants a power to a minister, that minister either acts within those powers or outside those powers. There is no grey area between authorisation and prohibition or between empowerment and the denial of power. Thus, if [for example] the making of vague regulations is within the powers granted by a sovereign Parliament, on what basis may the courts challenge Parliament's will and hold that the regulations are invalid? If Parliament has authorised vague regulations, those regulations cannot be challenged without challenging Parliament's authority to authorise such regulations.[7]

An example may help to unpack this reasoning. Many statutory provisions confer decision-making power on administrators without saying very much (if anything) about the conditions which attach to the exercise of that power. For instance, a statutory power to grant licences may well say nothing about the procedure which must be followed by the decision-maker as he assesses the applications of those who seek a licence. Nevertheless, administrative law would almost certainly require applicants to be accorded at least a rudimentary measure of procedural fairness[8]: typically, this would demand that they be given an adequate opportunity to present their claim, and that, in turn, the claim be assessed in an impartial manner, taking account of the particular circumstances and merits of the specific applicant. Given that our hypothetical (but typical) statutory provision is silent as to these conditions which apply to the exercise of the power, it is necessary to enquire into their provenance. Forsyth's argument is that there exist only two possible sources of those conditions.

On the one hand it may be argued that, although Parliament's grant of power is prima facie unlimited by reference to any obligation of procedural fairness, the legislation is to be read as including implied provisions requiring the decision-maker to act fairly and so on. Consequently, when the court insists that the administrator acts in accordance with the principles of natural justice, it is simply articulating and giving effect to those limits on power which represent the outer perimeter of the authority which Parliament is taken to have conferred as a matter of empirical fact. Review therefore lies on the sole ground that the donee has acted ultra vires, or beyond the power which Parliament granted. Understood thus, review is constitutionally legitimate because it fulfils Parliament's sovereign will. This account of judicial review, which is represented diagrammatically in Figure 1, accords with the explanation which is traditionally furnished by the ultra vires principle.

---

[7] (1996) 55 *CLJ* 122 at 133–4.

[8] Unless, of course, the legislation made sufficiently clear contrary provision.

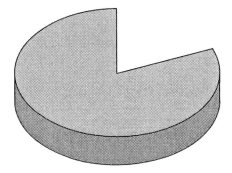

FIG. 1. The ultra vires principle: The shape of the conferred power

The shaded part circle represents the power which Parliament is taken to have granted to the agency. The missing part of the circle shows that Parliament never gave to the administrator the power to contravene the principles of good administration. Thus the powers of the administrator are inherently limited from the outset, and review lies on the sole ground that the agency has acted beyond the powers thus conferred.

On the other hand it might be that Parliament's grant of power is subject to no requirement of fair decision-making. On this view there is—self-evidently—no explicit enjoinder that the decision-maker should act fairly, but—crucially— nor is there taken to be any implicit legislative direction to that effect. It is Forsyth's contention that, in this scenario, Parliament has not prohibited unfair decision-making and must, therefore, have permitted it. As Figure 2 illustrates, if this is so, it must lie within the decision-maker's derived competence to act unfairly.

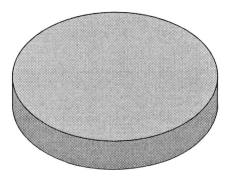

FIG. 2. The common law model: The shape of the conferred power

The circular shaded area represents the scope of discretionary power granted by Parliament to the agency. If, pursuant to the common law model, the methodology of statutory implication is rejected, then, when Parliament initially confers power on administrators, it must be an ample power unfettered by any obligation to abide by the principles of good administration. The circular shaded area therefore includes the power to act contrary to those principles.

If a court were then to impose a requirement of fair decision-making, this would produce two important and related consequences. First, this requirement would, quite clearly, be enforced *independently of* legislation. Secondly, the courts' quashing of administrative action adopted pursuant to an unfair procedure would occur *in spite of* the legislation, given that, on the present view, Parliament must be taken to have granted an ample power unfettered by any requirement of procedural fairness. Explained thus, judicial enforcement of broad limits on discretionary power involves interference with administrative action which is intra vires in the sense of being within the power which Parliament has chosen to grant. As Figure 3 shows, the courts, within this model, prevent administrators from exercising powers that Parliament gave them. Conflict thus arises between the courts' jurisprudence and the enabling legislation. The difficulty with this conclusion is that—so far as the orthodox conception of parliamentary supremacy is concerned—judicial review becomes unconstitutional because, conceptualised thus, it runs counter to Parliament's legislative framework.

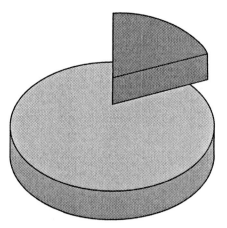

FIG. 3. The common law model: The shape of the power once common law rules of good administration are applied

The darker area represents the power to act contrary to the principles of good administration. Within the common law model, courts remove this power from the administrator (which, as figure two shows, it originally possessed pursuant to Parliament's ample, unfettered grant). The agency's remaining competence is represented by the lighter portion of the diagram. In this manner, the courts take away from agencies powers which they originally possess according to the scope of Parliament's grant.

The conclusion which Forsyth draws from this analysis is straightforward:

> The upshot of this is that . . . to abandon ultra vires is to challenge the supremacy of Parliament. "Weak" critics [who purport to criticise only the ultra vires doctrine, and

not the sovereignty of Parliament], whether they intend it or not, are transmuted into "strong" critics [who challenge parliamentary sovereignty].[9]

If Forsyth is correct, then a moderate approach must be adopted to the justification of review.[10] This follows ineluctably from his argument, according to which judicial review *either* constitutes enforcement of those (express and implied) limits which Parliament is taken to intend should apply to statutory discretionary powers (in which case review is constitutionally legitimate) *or* involves judicial contradiction of the legislative scheme (in which case it is unconstitutional). Thus it is clear that Forsyth's argument, if it is correct, has important implications for how the juridical basis of judicial review must—of constitutional necessity—be constructed. It is therefore necessary carefully to evaluate the correctness of this argument. In order to do so, the two distinct points which collectively form Forsyth's thesis must be distinguished and analysed in turn.

First, he contends that it is constitutionally illegitimate for the courts to act in a manner which is incompatible with parliamentary legislation. This is consistent with traditional conceptions of legislative supremacy, and the dynamic which it dictates *vis-à-vis* the manner in which judicial and legislative power interrelate. However, it is well known that there exists growing evidence in some academic and judicial circles of dissatisfaction with sovereignty theory. It is therefore necessary to consider whether Forsyth's argument—that ultra vires is essential if judicial review is to be constitutionally justified—holds true even if parliamentary sovereignty, in its orthodox sense, is rejected as an accurate statement of the legislature's contemporary role within the British polity. This matter is considered below.[11]

Secondly, Forsyth argues that, when Parliament creates a power, it must *either* include *or* omit the competence, for example, to adopt an unfair decision-making procedure. This, it is said, follows *a priori*: because the official's competence derives from and owes its existence to the parliamentary grant, the limits of his competence must logically be coterminous with the scope of that grant. Thus, when Parliament confers a power, it must—as a matter of empirical fact—either grant or withhold the competence to act unfairly. On this view, the concepts of ultra vires and intra vires are collectively exhaustive and mutually exclusive: one cannot be *both* within the power granted by Parliament and outside it; and, at the same time, one must be *either* inside or beyond the power which was actually conferred. Since the court can interfere only with executive action which is outwith the scope of the power (assuming that Parliament is

[9] Above n. 7 at 134.

[10] It will be recalled from Ch. 2, above, that a moderate approach to the justification of judicial review is one which embraces a connection between the controls applied through the supervisory jurisdiction and the effectuation of the legislative scheme which gives rise to the relevant discretionary power. In contrast, radical approaches divorce review from the implementation of legislative intention.

[11] At 73–87.

sovereign such that its will cannot legitimately be disregarded by the judiciary), it follows (once the second part of the argument is taken into account) that review of statutory power, if it is to be constitutionally legitimate, must ultimately be about identifying the limits of the authority conferred by enabling legislation.

It is clearly imperative to Forsyth's thesis that *both* of these propositions are correct. Thus it is possible to establish the constitutional necessity of connecting judicial review with the legislative framework that creates discretionary power only if ultra vires and intra vires are mutually exclusive and collectively exhaustive concepts *and* if the courts are constitutionally prohibited from holding unlawful that which lies within the powers conferred by Parliament. The purpose of the remainder of this chapter is to assess the validity of each of these propositions.

2. THE CONSTITUTIONAL STATUS OF LEGISLATIVE INTENTION

2.1. Introduction

For the purpose of assessing the correctness and implications of Forsyth's first proposition, it will be assumed that his second is correct. Whether this assumption is justified will be considered below.[12] For the time being, therefore, it is taken for granted that a decision-maker acts either inside or beyond his conferred powers. Within this framework, the operation of judicial review can be divorced from the implementation of legislative intention only if it is constitutionally legitimate for the courts to hold administrative action sanctioned by Parliament to be unlawful. The reasoning which produces this conclusion is straightforward. If Parliament is sovereign, and if ultra vires and intra vires are collectively exhaustive and mutually exclusive concepts, then it is *a priori* unconstitutional for the courts, on judicial review, to do anything other than declare the illegality of that executive action which lies *outside* the powers conferred by the enabling legislation.

Consequently, if judicial review is to be justified otherwise than by reference to ultra vires theory, it must be shown that it is constitutionally legitimate for the courts to strike down that which lies within the competence conferred by Parliament through primary legislation. Orthodox constitutional theory teaches that this is impossible: legislation is the supreme form of law, and is legally unchallengeable. It follows that, if the role of the courts in judicial review cases is to be rationalised other than in terms of the identification of ultra vires administrative action, it must be shown that Parliament is not sovereign in the traditional sense. Thus it is necessary to consider the meaning and role of the principle of parliamentary sovereignty, viewed from a contemporary perspective. Three caveats should, however, be entered.

[12] At 87–95.

First, this book is not primarily about sovereignty theory and, as is argued later in this chapter, the contemporary validity of orthodox conceptions of sovereignty is not as central to the correctness of the arguments of ultra vires theorists as may at first appear. For these reasons, it is unnecessary to examine the issue of parliamentary sovereignty in exhaustive detail.

Secondly, the purpose of the following discussion is not to evaluate the correctness or otherwise of the various theories regarding parliamentary sovereignty. Rather, the objective is to provide a survey of the principal theoretical approaches to sovereignty as a necessary precursor to the argument advanced below that, whichever view of sovereignty is adopted, the core methodology of the ultra vires principle remains central to the constitutional justification of judicial review.

Thirdly, British membership of the European Union has had a major impact on how the issue of parliamentary sovereignty is approached. However, before assessing the implications of EU membership for the sovereignty doctrine,[13] it is necessary to consider the different ways in which we think, at a fundamental level, about sovereignty. The order of the following analysis—in which the implications of EU law are considered at the end—may seem to sit uncomfortably with the fact that EU membership has impacted significantly on our thinking about sovereignty. However, there are two principal reasons for ordering the analysis in this way.

In the first place, the implications of EU law can be rationalised properly only against the background of the pre-existing modes of thought about legislative supremacy: if membership of the EU has changed the sovereignty principle, or at least our conceptualisation of it, it is first necessary to be clear about what that principle meant—or what we thought it meant—before the consequences of EU membership became apparent.

The second reason for considering the implications of EU law at the end of the analysis is specific to the line of argument advanced in this book. It is suggested below that the contention that ultra vires is constitutionally essential holds true even if it is acknowledged that parliamentary sovereignty has been qualified. For purposes of clarity, the analysis first substantiates that argument, and explains how it operates in terms of principle, by reference to the suggestions of some commentators that Parliament's legislative authority is, or ought to be regarded as, limited by substantive normative values based on democracy and human rights. That discourse is dealt with first because it is within that context that the relevance of ultra vires theory has been most openly questioned. Once the argument has been advanced that challenges to sovereignty within that discourse do not displace the necessity of ultra vires theory, it then becomes possible to explain why similar reasoning applies within the EU context. It is against this background that the following discussion of sovereignty theory should be read.

---

[13] See below at 80–6.

As every student of British constitutional law quickly learns, the traditional conception of Parliament's role within the constitutional order was classically stated by Professor Albert Venn Dicey. Parliament, he said, has "the right to make or unmake any law whatever", so that "no person or body is recognised by the law of England as having a right to override or set aside" primary legislation enacted by Parliament.[14] Dicey described this as "the dominant characteristic of our political institutions"[15] and as "the very keystone of the law of the constitution".[16] Given this centrality which Dicey ascribes to parliamentary sovereignty, it is surprising that so much controversy surrounds it. As well as disagreement on whether, from a normative perspective, Parliament ought to be regarded as sovereign, there is further tension, amongst those who accept that sovereignty is a feature of the British constitution, about precisely what that means.

Any attempt to categorise the various schools of thought will necessarily involve a degree of generalisation and will fail to capture and accommodate the nuances of every model which writers have proposed. Nevertheless, for the purposes of the arguments advanced in this book, it is useful to separate the views which have been expressed on the issue of parliamentary sovereignty into three broad groups. The following account begins, in section 2.2, by examining that approach to legislative supremacy which is generally regarded as orthodoxy; it then moves on to consider, in section 2.3, what has been termed the "new view", before addressing, in section 2.4, the contemporary school of thought which holds that Parliament is not—or should not be regarded as—sovereign. Sections 2.5 and 2.6 then consider the implications of these different perspectives for the argument that the constitutional framework—and, specifically, Parliament's place within it—dictate that ultra vires theory is the only acceptable means by which judicial review may be justified.

2.2. The Orthodox Account

Dicey's view of sovereignty has traditionally been regarded as the orthodox account of the principle. However, the implications and conceptual foundations of that orthodoxy were articulated pre-eminently by Sir William Wade in his article, "The Basis of Legal Sovereignty".[17] It is unnecessary here to set out and evaluate Wade's theoretical approach comprehensively. However, it is useful to outline three of the principal characteristics of the model of legislative supremacy which he developed.

---

[14] A V Dicey, *An Introduction to the Study of the Law of the Constitution* (E C S Wade, ed.) (London: Macmillan, 1964) at 40. Although Dicey's formulation consisted of these two limbs—one positive, one negative—Jeffrey Goldsworthy points out that they are "merely different formulations of the same principle": see *The Sovereignty of Parliament* (Oxford: Clarendon Press, 1999) at 10.

[15] Above n. 14 at 39.

[16] Above n. 14 at 70.

[17] H W R Wade, "The Basis of Legal Sovereignty" (1955) 13 *CLJ* 172. See also H W R Wade, *Constitutional Fundamentals* (London: Stevens, 1980), ch. 3.

The first important point to note is that for Wade, as for Dicey, Parliament is sovereign in the sense that it enjoys the competence to legislate over all matters.[18] Primary legislation is thus the supreme form of law within the legal order: since the subjects on which Parliament may legislate are unlimited, no legislation may be "unconstitutional". This has important implications for the relationship between the courts and the legislature: in particular, the former are constitutionally incompetent to strike down the enactments of the latter.

Secondly, Wade's model supplies a particular explanation of the provenance of the sovereignty which it ascribes to Parliament. Crucially, it provides that Parliament may not itself legislate so as to change its own powers. It is for this reason that, within the present model, sovereignty is said to be "continuing": Parliament's unfettered legislative competence over all matters is a constant, and cannot therefore be changed by Parliament. It follows that it is impossible, on this view, for one Parliament to bind its successors by entrenching legislation. Consequently, according to the continuing view of sovereignty, Parliament's competence *is* "limited" in one important respect, because it is incapable of attenuating the scope of its own legislative competence.

This is said to follow because Parliament could not, in the first place, have conferred sovereign (or any other) legislative power upon itself, so that the constitutional principle which accords supreme law-making power to Parliament must lie beyond Parliament's legislative reach. As Wade observes:

> The rule of judicial obedience [to primary legislation] is in one sense a rule of common law, but in another sense—which applies to no other rule of common law—it is the ultimate *political* fact upon which the whole system of legislation hangs. Legislation owes its authority to the rule: the rule does not owe its authority to legislation. To say that Parliament can change the rule, merely because it can change any other rule, is to put the cart before the horse.[19]

Hence the constitutional principle which ascribes sovereignty to Parliament is said to be *sui generis*: it is ultimately a political principle of the constitution which is neither statutory nor, in the normal sense, a common law construct (given that Parliament is capable of changing or abrogating ordinary principles of the common law).

The two aspects of continuing sovereignty theory thus far discussed are relatively uncontroversial. The first proposition—that Parliament enjoys legislative competence over all matters—accurately captures orthodox thinking regarding

---

[18] Professor Wade has now modified his view, in light of the implications for the sovereignty principle of British membership of the European Union as revealed in the decision of the House of Lords in *R v. Secretary of State for Transport, ex parte Factortame Ltd. (No. 2)* [1991] 1 AC 603. See H W R Wade, "Sovereignty—Revolution or Evolution?" (1996) 112 *LQR* 568. However, it is Wade's original thesis, as set out in "The Basis of Legal Sovereignty" (1955) 13 *CLJ* 172, which is presently under consideration: the way in which developments prompted by EU membership have impacted upon traditional perceptions of sovereignty and sovereignty theory is examined below at 80–6.

[19] H W R Wade, "The Basis of Legal Sovereignty" (1955) 13 *CLJ* 172 at 188 (original emphasis).

the role of the legislature within the British polity[20]: as Detmold puts it, the doctrine "has become a constitutional commonplace".[21] Similarly, the second proposition, according to which the principle of sovereignty is ultimately a political construct, enjoys a relatively broad measure of support: it is widely accepted that the supremacy doctrine constitutes the legal expression of a broader conception of political sovereignty.[22]

However, the third aspect of the continuing theory of sovereignty which falls to be discussed is rather more contentious. This relates to the mechanisms by which the role of the legislature within the constitutional order may change. Specifically, the third proposition which inheres in Wade's theory of sovereignty seeks to explain how the first proposition—that Parliament enjoys unfettered competence—may alter, bearing in mind what the second proposition maintains *vis-à-vis* the provenance of Parliament's sovereignty. It is on this point that the greatest divergence opens up among those writers who may be categorised as supporters of the core orthodoxy which the first two aspects of the continuing theory embody.

For Wade, the issue is straightforward:

> What Salmond calls the "ultimate legal principle" is therefore a rule which is unique in being unchangeable by Parliament—it is changed by revolution, not by legislation; it lies in the keeping of the courts, and no Act of Parliament can take it from them. This is only another way of saying that it is always for the courts, in the last resort, to say what is a valid Act of Parliament; and that the decision of this question is not determined by any rule of law which can be laid down or altered by any authority outside the courts. It is simply a political fact.[23]

Thus, according to Wade, any judicial refusal to recognise the legal validity of an Act of Parliament would have to be explained by reference to a shift in judicial allegiance amounting to a constitutional "revolution".[24] The use of the language of "revolution" clearly signals that, for Wade, such a step would involve a discontinuity: one legal order (in which Parliament was sovereign) would be replaced by a new legal order (in which Parliament was not sovereign). For Wade, this follows because the principle from which Parliament's sovereignty

---

[20] Although, as explained in section 2.4, below, this view is certainly not shared by all writers, it has—at least until recently—enjoyed very broad support. As Allan—a leading critic of sovereignty theory—concedes, "it is hard to question . . . [the sovereignty] doctrine without appearing to lose touch with practical reality. Until very recently, it was almost unthinkable that the courts would ever refuse to apply an Act of Parliament . . .". See T R S Allan, *Law, Liberty, and Justice: The Legal Foundations of British Constitutionalism* (Oxford: Clarendon Press, 1993) at 16.

[21] M Detmold, *The Australian Commonwealth: A Fundamental Analysis of its Constitution* (Sydney: Law Book Company, 1985) at 253.

[22] Although the *conclusions* which Dicey and Wade draw from this are contested by some writers. See, *e.g.*, the work of T R S Allan, discussed below in section 2.4.

[23] H W R Wade, "The Basis of Legal Sovereignty" (1955) 13 *CLJ* 172 at 189.

[24] Wade applies this analysis in order to explain how directly effective European Union law may now take priority over incompatible domestic primary legislation. See H W R Wade, "Sovereignty—Revolution or Evolution?" (1996) 112 *LQR* 568. For further discussion see below at 80–6.

springs is, in one sense, external to the *legal* system: it is, rather, the *political* "peg" from which the system hangs.

It is unnecessary to analyse the merits of Wade's approach in detail. However, it is worth noting that there are substantial problems with his influential theory. The main difficulty concerns the reasoning which purports to connect the second and third propositions. He asserts that the sovereign legislative authority enjoyed by Parliament derives ultimately from the political reality of the constitution. It is, however, unclear why this necessarily renders the courts uniquely pivotal in the continued existence of Parliament's sovereignty.[25] The point is expressed well by Professor Jeffrey Goldsworthy. He observes that, "Parliament's sovereignty was not created by the judges alone, and its continued existence depends only partly, and not solely, on their willingness to accept it".[26] This is a telling criticism of Wade's approach. Viewed in a contemporary setting, the normative legitimacy of parliamentary sovereignty derives from the fact that it gives legal expression to a political consensus concerning the form of governance which is felt appropriate in the United Kingdom.[27] In particular, it expresses a political commitment to a particular (majoritarian) conception of democracy, as Lord Irvine points out:

[The reforms, during the nineteenth and early twentieth centuries, of the electoral franchise] demonstrate the emergence of representative and participatory democracy as the primary principle of constitutional and political theory in Britain. They evidence a paradigm shift in how the relationship between the state and the individual is conceptualised in UK. In this way, the process of electoral reform has fundamentally changed the environment within which parliamentary sovereignty subsists, transforming the doctrine into the vehicle by which the modern commitment to democracy is institutionalised. Thus the legal sovereignty exercised by Parliament is now viewed as deriving its legitimacy from the fact that Parliament's composition is, in the first place, determined by the electorate in whom ultimate political sovereignty resides.[28]

[25] This point becomes even clearer in light of the conceptual foundations of Wade's approach. It was explained above, at 14–15, that his thesis is that, in legal terms, the courts are constrained by the constitution and are therefore required to apply parliamentary enactments as law. However, Wade recognises that, from a pragmatic perspective, if the courts were to refuse to apply legislation as law, this may prompt an extra-constitutional "revolution" which would result in the abandonment of the old constitutional order and the adoption of a new order (within which the relationship between the judiciary and the legislature would be redefined). In light of the fact that the mode of change is extra-constitutional, and therefore essentially reduces to a question of practical politics, it is much more likely that a judicial refusal to apply legislation would succeed in prompting an extra-constitutional "revolution" if the other branches of government supported such change.

[26] J Goldsworthy, *The Sovereignty of Parliament* (Oxford: Clarendon Press, 1999) at 240.

[27] Of course, not all commentators agree that sovereignty possesses an "inherent legitimacy". Nevertheless, the democratic argument is clearly the strongest weapon in the armoury of those who argue in favour of the legitimacy of the sovereignty principle. This is not, however, an appropriate forum in which to assess the desirability of sovereignty in normative terms. For contrasting perspectives, see Goldsworthy, above n. 26, ch. 10; T R S Allan, *Law, Liberty, and Justice: The Legal Foundations of British Constitutionalism* (Oxford: Clarendon Press, 1993), especially ch. 11; P P Craig, "Public Law, Political Theory and Legal Theory" [2000] *PL* 211 at 212–30.

[28] Lord Irvine, "Sovereignty in Comparative Perspective: Constitutionalism in Britain and America" (the James Madison Memorial Lecture, New York, 2000).

The ultimate principle of legislative supremacy is thus characterised as an expression (and consequence) of the political sovereignty of the electorate: it represents the means by which the constitution reflects the primacy of representative, majoritarian democracy. In light of this, it is strongly arguable that Wade is wrong to contend that sovereignty is secure only so long as the judiciary assents to its continued existence. The normative foundations on which parliamentary sovereignty—within this account—rests suggest that its constitutional basis is altogether richer than that which Wade elaborates. Goldsworthy—following Professor Hart[29]—advances a more convincing approach:

> The authority of either Parliament, or the judges, or both, must be based on laws that neither was solely responsible for creating. Those more fundamental laws are what H L A Hart called the "secondary rules" of the legal system, comprising rules of recognition, change and adjudication. A necessary condition for the existence of such rules is a consensus among the most senior legal officials of the legal system, in all three branches of government, legislative, executive and judicial. This avoids the question-begging that is implicit in any one branch of government purporting to confer law-making authority on itself.[30]

Although it is submitted that this is a more satisfactory approach than that which Wade articulates, it is still open to criticism. In particular, Goldsworthy's argument does not draw a clear connection between the existence of sovereign legislative power and the normative foundations on which it rests. The non-positivist[31] response to theses such as those advanced by Wade and Goldsworthy would therefore be to argue that the consensus among senior officials—which, in practical terms, determines whether Parliament may effectively exercise its legislative competence—ought to be shaped by broader societal attitudes concerning the proper role of the institutions of government. In this manner, appropriate weight may be attached to the democratic imperative which is said to furnish the normative justification for the constitutional principle of legislative supremacy. The competence of Parliament is thus rendered a function of that conception of governance which society chooses to embrace. The implications of this approach—which seeks to connect the principle of sovereignty with

---

[29] See H L A Hart, *The Concept of Law* (Oxford: Clarendon Press, 1994).

[30] Goldsworthy, above n. 26, at 240. This approach is clearly more consistent with Hart's theory than is Wade's approach. Although Wade embraces Hart's notion of the "rule of recognition", he contends that "it lies in the keeping of the judges and it is for them to say what they will recognise as effective legislation": H W R Wade, *Constitutional Fundamentals* (London: Stevens, 1980) at 26. However, it is clear that Hart envisaged that the rule of recognition should represent a consensus among senior legal officials across all three branches of government: see Hart, above n. 29, ch. 6. See further J W F Allison, "Parliamentary Sovereignty, Europe and the Economy of the Common Law" in M Andenas (ed.), *Judicial Review in International Perspective: Liber Amicorum in Honour of Lord Slynn of Hadley* (Kluwer: The Hague, 2000), vol. 2.

[31] In this ch., the term "positivism" is applied to theories of sovereignty which accept the existence of unlimited law-making power simply as a matter of fact. In contrast, the labels "non-positivism" and "normativism" are applied to those perspectives which hold that legislative authority can legitimately exist only to the extent that it is supported by an underlying, principled justification.

the democratic ideal which, it is now widely accepted, underpins Parliament's law-making power—are considered in section 2.4, below.

The orthodox view of Parliament's role is, in many senses, straightforward. In particular, its central message—that Parliament enjoys legislative competence over all matters[32]—is clear. However, as the foregoing discussion demonstrates, even within the "orthodox" view, there exist various shades of opinion about how Parliament's legislative power and its relationship with the courts may change. Detailed evaluation of the competing conceptions of the orthodox theory lies beyond the scope of the present work. Rather, for the purposes of the argument developed below, concerning the juridical basis of judicial review, it is necessary simply to distinguish broadly between the various models of sovereignty which commentators have articulated. In particular, the orthodox view, which ascribes to Parliament competence over all matters and an inability unilaterally to bind its successors,[33] must be contrasted with two other theories, *viz.* the "new view" and what may be termed the "limited competence" model. It is to those other conceptions of legislative authority that we now turn.

2.3. The "New View"

The factor which distinguishes the "new view" of sovereignty from the orthodox view, discussed above, is that proponents of the former—unlike proponents of the latter—hold that, in some respects, legislation may be entrenched such that Parliament may bind its successors. This conception of sovereignty is most closely associated with the work of Heuston.[34] He refers to it as:

> a doctrine which has the attraction of being couched in the calm, hard, tightly knit style of the common lawyer rather than in the vague and emotional language of the political scientist. The concept of sovereignty, as a result of a cautious and subtle re-examination from within its own four corners, as it were, has been shown to be at once more complex and less terrifying than had been thought. It appears that the lawyer can, without reservation or evasion, subscribe not only to the unlimited power of Parliament, but also to the possibility of legal restraints upon (at least) the mode of user of that power.[35]

Heuston's argument thus consists of two central propositions: that Parliament is sovereign, in that it possesses "unlimited power", but that there may, without contradiction, exist legal constraints on the "mode of user" of that power.

---

[32] Subject to European Union law, which is discussed below at 80–6.

[33] Irrespective of whether one follows, on the one hand, Wade or, on the other hand, Goldsworthy and Hart, it is correct to assert that, within the orthodox model, Parliament cannot *unilaterally* bind its successors. For Wade, any attempt by Parliament to entrench legislation would be dependent upon judicial acquiescence while, for Hart and Goldsworthy, such an attempt would be successful only if it secured broad support within all three institutions of government.

[34] R F V Heuston, *Essays in Constitutional Law* (London: Stevens, 1964), ch. 1.

[35] *Ibid.* at 6.

Importantly, it is the contention of those who support the new view of sovereignty that those legal constraints on the "mode of user" of Parliament's legislative power may be imposed by Parliament upon itself by means of ordinary legislation. Sir Ivor Jennings explained the point in the following terms:

> "Legal sovereignty" is merely a name indicating that the legislature has for the time being power to make laws of any kind in the manner required by the law. That is, a rule expressed to be made by the Queen, "with the advice and consent of the Lords spiritual and temporal, and Commons in this present Parliament assembled, and by the authority of the same", will be recognised by the courts, *including a rule which alters this law itself*. If this is so, the "legal sovereign" may impose legal limitations on itself, because its power to change the law includes the power to change the law affecting itself.[36]

The distinction between, on the one hand, the *manner and form* in which legislation is enacted and, on the other hand, the *substantive content* of legislation is thus central to this argument. Its relevance is two-fold: it defines the extent to which legally enforceable constraints may apply to the legislative process, and it is central to Heuston's claim that the notion of "sovereignty" is compatible with the existence of such constraints.[37] The arguments for and against this conceptualisation of sovereignty are well rehearsed,[38] and it is unnecessary to repeat them here. It is sufficient to mention three specific problems which the new view encounters.

The first two difficulties may both be characterised as internal tensions within the theory, relating to the distinction which it draws between limitations of manner and form and limitations of substance. The new view holds that Parliament may, by enacting legislation in accordance with the normal procedure (such as it exists at any given time), change the formal requirements which apply to the legislative process. Subsequently, all legislation would have to be passed in accordance with the manner and form requirements as enacted. However, Heuston contends that the same is not true of substantive limits. He remarks that, "There is no need to rehearse here the familiar examples which prove that there is no restriction on the area or ambit of the power of Parliament [in a substantive sense]".[39] It is therefore not open to Parliament, according to the new view, to mark any substantive subjects as being entirely off limits. This raises two important and related issues.

---

[36] Sir Ivor Jennings, *The Law and the Constitution* (London: University of London Press, 1959) at 152–3.

[37] Jennings, on the other hand, was less concerned with reconciling his view with a notion of "sovereignty". He argued that, rather than focussing on an abstract idea of "sovereignty", the courts are simply concerned to determine what constitutes "the established law", and that this task is to be undertaken by reference to any definitions enacted by Parliament of what constitutes valid legislation: *ibid.* at 152.

[38] For useful overviews, see C C Turpin, *British Government and the Constitution: Text, Cases and Materials* (London: Butterworths, 1999) at 32–40; C R Munro, *Studies in Constitutional Law* (London: Butterworths, 1999) at 154–66.

[39] R F V Heuston, *Essays in Constitutional Law* (London: Stevens, 1964) at 9.

First, it is unclear why it is either necessary or appropriate to draw such a distinction: if Parliament is able to impose legal limitations upon itself *vis-à-vis how* it enacts legislation, why should it not also be able to impose limitations concerning the substance of *what* it enacts? The answer to this question lies in Heuston's concern to reconcile his argument with the view that Parliament is "sovereign". His contention is that there exists no contradiction between, on the one hand, allowing a legislature to entrench manner and form limitations and, on the other hand, holding that the legislature is "sovereign". Goldsworthy finds this reconciliation convincing:

> The power of a legislature to change its procedure, or form of legislation, is consistent with its possessing continuing sovereignty provided that it must always remain free to change the substance of the law however and whenever it chooses. Consider, for example, a procedural law requiring bills of a certain kind to be introduced and passed in the House of Commons before being considered in the House of Lords, or a law as to form providing that some existing statute can be amended or repealed only by express words, and not mere implication. If the courts were prepared to enforce those laws, by invalidating any statute enacted contrary to them, Parliament might no longer be fully sovereign in Dicey's sense. But it would still be fully sovereign in the more important sense of being free to change the substance of the law however and whenever it should choose.[40]

Ultimately, however, this reduces to a matter of semantics: it reflects a particular choice concerning the precise meaning which ought to be ascribed to the term "sovereignty". If it is viewed—as Goldsworthy and Heuston view it—in terms of a legislature's substantive ability to legislate on any subject which it chooses to regulate, then it does become at least arguable that the new view may be espoused while, at the same time, maintaining that Parliament is "sovereign".

This supplies a neat, but ultimately formal, solution to the first problem, by furnishing an intelligible justification for the distinction between manner and form limitations (which, according to the new view, can be entrenched) and substantive limitations (which, it is said, cannot). However, this putative justification for the distinction tends to break down once the second internal tension within the new view is taken into account. Even if, as Goldsworthy contends, the term "sovereignty" describes an omnicompetence to legislate on matters of substance, this merely begs the question what, precisely, is meant by "substance". The focus thus shifts from the *reason* for the distinction between form and substance to the *nature* of that distinction. The difficulty which arises is that the dividing line between matters of form and matters of substance is highly nebulous.

---

[40] J Goldsworthy, *The Sovereignty of Parliament* (Oxford: Clarendon Press, 1999) at 15. Goldsworthy's reference to Parliament's ability, in the face of manner and form limitations, to change the law "however" it chooses reads rather curiously, given that the very purpose of such limitations is that they dictate precisely how legislation is to be enacted. It follows that, when Goldsworthy refers to Parliament's continued ability to legislate "however" it chooses, he is referring to its capacity freely to select the substantive matters with which legislation deals, notwithstanding that the manner in which the legislation is enacted, and the form which it takes, may be subject to specific requirements imposed by earlier legislation.

This point is best illustrated by example. Assume that Parliament enacts legislation which confers upon all British citizens a given right. There are many ways in which attempts may be made to entrench such legislation; three examples, however, will suffice. First, the legislation may provide that it can be repealed or derogated from only by the use of express language. If Parliament later enacted legislation which, on any reading, was irreconcilable with the protected right but which did not expressly repeal or derogate from the earlier Act, then—according to the new view—the courts would refuse to enforce it on the ground that the earlier legislation was entrenched and could be departed from only following compliance with the prescribed formal requirement (*viz.* express words of repeal). This example is unproblematic: on any reasonable view the limitation is formal rather than substantive and, according to Heuston's theory, should therefore be accorded binding force.

Secondly, the Act conferring the right may state that it cannot be repealed in any circumstances and that no future Parliament may legislate so as to interfere with or remove the right in question. Just as the first example clearly concerned a limitation of form, so this is self-evidently a limitation of substance. The protected right is marked off-limits in a substantive sense, such that the original legislation purports to prevent any future legislative incursions into the area which it seeks to protect. An attempt at entrenchment in this substantive sense would fail, according to the new view: if the position were otherwise then, to express the point in Goldsworthy's language, Parliament would not be "fully sovereign in the . . . sense of being free to change the substance of the law however and whenever it should choose".[41]

The problem, of course, is that not all attempts at entrenchment can be characterised so easily as "formal" (and, hence, permissible) or "substantive" (and, therefore, impermissible). For instance, the legislation conferring the given right may provide that it can be repealed or derogated from only by primary legislation which commands the support of 90 per cent of each parliamentary chamber. Equally problematic would be provisions making repeal or derogation conditional upon, say, 95 per cent support in a referendum or unanimous parliamentary assent. In technical, or semantic, terms it can be argued that such preconditions relate to form rather than substance, given that they do not absolutely preclude legislative intervention in relation to the relevant matter. To adopt such a characterisation would, however, be to overlook the reality of the situation. The impossibility (or near impossibility) of securing unanimity (or something approaching unanimity) in a referendum or a parliamentary vote means that such requirements are, in all practical senses, substantive rather than formal in nature.[42]

---

[41] J Goldsworthy, *The Sovereignty of Parliament* (Oxford: Clarendon Press, 1999) at 15.

[42] This difficulty is alluded to by Professor Wade. He asks, "Would it really be possible . . . for the United Kingdom Parliament to make an Act *virtually unrepealable* by requiring any repealing Act to be approved by, say, ninety per cent of the electors in a referendum?" (emphasis added). See H W R Wade, "The Basis of Legal Sovereignty" (1955) 13 *CLJ* 172 at 181.

Thus it becomes clear that the distinction between "manner and form" limitations and "substantive" limitations is highly nebulous. This is particularly problematic in light of the dual relevance which is attached to the distinction by those theorists—predominantly Heuston—who support this conception of sovereignty. It was noted above that the load which the distinction needs to bear is substantial: as well as supplying the criterion for determining, in a pragmatic sense, whether a particular attempt at entrenchment is legally binding, it is further claimed that the division between form and substance provides the conceptual means by which the new view may be rendered compatible with the orthodox proposition that Parliament is sovereign. The fact that that distinction cannot be drawn with clarity thus represents an important drawback of the new view, and inhibits its ability to provide convincing practical guidance *vis-à-vis* the perimeter of Parliament's competence and a satisfactory conceptual explanation of what "sovereignty" actually means.

In addition to the internal tensions which affect the new view, a significant external tension is revealed when attempts are made to make the theory fit with the way in which the sovereignty of Parliament is traditionally characterised. Given that the manner and form theory is, in essence, about how the relationship between Parliament and the courts should be conceptualised—and, in particular, the circumstances in which judges may refuse to enforce legislation which fails to comply with pre-existing formal requirements imposed by earlier enactments—it is natural to look to the case law in order to test the theory. It is therefore significant that, in two key respects—one positive, one negative—the courts' jurisprudence does not support the view that Parliament may impose binding requirements of manner and form on its successors. Since this criticism of the "new view" is well documented in the literature,[43] it is necessary here to provide only an overview of the critique.

Viewed in negative terms, the "new view" is directly contradicted by certain judicial dicta. The most famous examples are the cases of *Vauxhall Estates*[44] and *Ellen Street Estates*.[45] Both cases concerned the Acquisition of Land (Assessment of Compensation) Act 1919, which set out a scheme for assessing the compensation to be awarded in respect of the compulsory purchase of land. Crucially, it provided, in section 7(1), that other legislation relating to compulsory purchase "shall, in relation to the matters dealt with in this Act, have effect subject to this Act, and so far as inconsistent with this Act those provisions shall cease to have or shall not have effect". Counsel contended that this subsection effected a partial entrenchment of the Act of 1919, such that it could be repealed only by the use of express language: in other words, it was argued that Parliament, in 1919, had imposed a binding formal limit on its successors. Maugham LJ, in *Ellen Street Estates*, found himself:

[43] See, *e.g.*, Wade, above n. 42.
[44] *Vauxhall Estates Ltd.* v. *Liverpool Corporation* [1932] 1 KB 733.
[45] *Ellen Street Estates Ltd.* v. *Minister of Health* [1934] 1 KB 590.

quite unable to accept that view. The Legislature cannot, according to our constitution, bind itself as to the form of subsequent legislation, and it is impossible for Parliament to enact that in a subsequent statute dealing with the same subject-matter there can be no implied repeal. If in a subsequent Act Parliament chooses to make it plain that the earlier statute is being to some extent repealed, effect must be given to that intention just because it is the will of the Legislature.[46]

Scrutton LJ,[47] in the same case, and Avory and Humphrys JJ in the Divisional Court in *Vauxhall Estates*,[48] advanced similar views. Heuston responded by saying that the "particular arguments" which he made "were not brought to the attention of Maugham LJ" in the *Ellen Street Estates* case.[49] Similarly Colin Turpin rightly comments that these cases "are not necessarily conclusive of the matter. In each of them the 'manner and form' question arose in a specific and narrow context and in neither case was the nature of parliamentary sovereignty examined in depth."[50] Nevertheless, the dicta in the *Vauxhall* and *Ellen Street* cases do at least suggest that the new view does not accurately capture how sovereignty is traditionally conceptualised.[51]

The difficulty encountered by the argument advanced by writers such as Heuston is perhaps revealed more clearly when one considers whether the case law furnishes any positive support for the new view. Writers who advance that view point to a number of cases in which legislative bodies have been held to be subject to preconditions of manner and form. For instance, in *Harris v. Minister of the Interior*,[52] *Attorney-General for New South Wales v. Trethowan*[53] and *Bribery Commission v. Ranasinghe*,[54] the legislatures of South Africa, New

---

[46] *Ellen Street Estates Ltd. v. Minister of Health* [1934] 1 KB 590 at 597.

[47] *Ibid.* at 595–6.

[48] [1932] 1 KB 733. Avory J, at 743, expressed the clearest disagreement with the submission that legislation could be entrenched. It is also implicit in the judgment of Humphrys J, at 746, that he disagreed with the submission, given that he was willing to conclude that Parliament, in later legislation, could be taken to have *implicitly* repealed the relevant provisions of the Act of 1919. Macnaughten J did not express an opinion on the point.

[49] R F V Heuston, *Essays in Constitutional Law* (London: Stevens, 1964) at 27.

[50] C C Turpin, *British Government and the Constitution: Text, Cases and Materials* (London: Butterworths, 1999) at 38. A more sophisticated—and, it is submitted, more convincing—approach to the question whether Parliament may entrench legislation is advanced by Trevor Allan. He argues that it is too simplistic to hold that Parliament can never bind its successors (according to the continuing view) or can bind its successors whenever it chooses to (as the new view maintains). Rather, Allan contends that the question whether a particular provision may be entrenched is a political question which must be answered by reference to the specific factual and political matrix within which it arises. There is, therefore, no universally applicable rule which determines whether entrenchment is possible; rather, the question falls to be answered in a context-sensitive manner. See T R S Allan, "Parliamentary Sovereignty: Lord Denning's Dexterous Revolution" (1983) 3 *OJLS* 22, especially 32–3.

[51] Sir William Wade, unsurprisingly, places considerably more weight on the *Vauxhall Estates* and *Ellen Street Estates* cases. He says that "since questions of 'manner and form' . . . figure so prominently in this subject it is worth emphasising that the question of form was squarely before the courts" in those cases. See H W R Wade, "The Basis of Legal Sovereignty" (1955) 13 *CLJ* 172 at 176.

[52] 1952 (2) SA 428.

[53] [1932] AC 526.

[54] [1965] AC 172.

South Wales and Ceylon (as it then was) were respectively held to be bound by requirements of manner and form. Exponents of the new view of parliamentary sovereignty argue that it follows from these cases that the United Kingdom's Parliament may also subject itself to formal limits of a legally binding nature.[55]

However, the legislatures which featured in the *Harris*, *Trethowan* and *Ranasinghe* cases differed fundamentally from the Westminster Parliament. For instance, as Turpin observes, the South African Parliament—at the time *Harris* was decided[56]—"owed its existence to the South Africa Act [1909], which therefore had a special status as the constituent instrument of that Parliament. Only when functioning in accordance with the procedural requirements of the constituent Act could it be said that the Union Parliament existed at all."[57] The Privy Council's decisions in *Trethowan* and *Ranasinghe* similarly turned on the existence of specific instruments which constituted the legislatures in question.

It is unsurprising that the courts have been willing to hold that the requirements of manner and form which derive—or whose authority derives—from instruments which are constitutive of the relevant legislature's power are binding upon the legislature. However, as the Privy Council pointed out in *Ranasinghe*, "in the Constitution of the United Kingdom there is no governing instrument which prescribes the law-making powers and the forms which are essential to those powers".[58] Thus it does not necessarily follow that, because manner and form requirements have been held to be enforceable in situations where they—or their authority—derive from an instrument which constitutes a legislature, such requirements are also enforceable *vis-à-vis* the United Kingdom Parliament in relation to which no constitutive instrument exists.[59]

Further evaluation of the new view is unnecessary for present purposes. It is, however, useful to draw one central conclusion from the foregoing discussion. Although the "manner and form" school differs in important respects from the orthodox—or "continuing"[60]—view of sovereignty outlined above, the two theories of sovereignty share one important characteristic. Each ascribes to Parliament an uncircumscribed legislative competence in substantive terms. Notwithstanding that "manner and form" theorists argue that Parliament may place formal limits on the exercise of its legislative powers, and in spite of the

---

[55] See, *e.g.*, R F V Heuston, *Essays in Constitutional Law* (London: Stevens, 1964) at 10–16; Sir Ivor Jennings, *The Law and the Constitution* (London: University of London Press, 1959), ch. 4.

[56] The South African legislature now operates within a framework supplied by the Constitution of the Republic of South Africa.

[57] C C Turpin, *British Government and the Constitution: Text, Cases and Materials* (London: Butterworths, 1999) at 37.

[58] [1965] AC 172 at 195.

[59] For a powerful critique of the arguments of Heuston and Jennings that the Commonwealth cases can readily be applied in the British context see H W R Wade, "The Basis of Legal Sovereignty" (1955) 13 *CLJ* 172.

[60] Of course, some commentators would argue that the "new view" *does* accord a "continuing" sovereignty to Parliament, given that they argue that "sovereignty" relates to omnicompetence over matters of substance, and is not therefore displaced by restrictions of a formal nature. See above at 51 and J Goldsworthy, *The Sovereignty of Parliament* (Oxford: Clarendon Press, 1999) at 14–15.

fact that the distinction between "manner and form" and "substance" is somewhat nebulous, it is nevertheless important that proponents of the continuing and new views agree that there exists no legally binding limit to the substantive matters on which Parliament may legislate, and that Parliament may not unilaterally create such limits.[61] The implications of this common feature of the continuing and new views *vis-à-vis* the constitutional foundations of judicial review will be addressed below. First, however, it is necessary to consider a rather different school of thought.

2.4. The Limited Competence Model

2.4.1. *The background to the anti-sovereignty discourse*

In recent years a prominent literature has developed which challenges the core orthodoxy—that Parliament enjoys legislative competence over all substantive matters—to which continuing theorists and proponents of the new view subscribe. It is helpful to begin by considering what may lie behind this trend.

It is clear that the United Kingdom's membership of the European Union goes some way towards accounting for the fundamental re-evaluation of sovereignty theory which is evident in the literature. However, while EU membership is perhaps the most tangible explanation for the heightened scrutiny in recent years of parliamentary sovereignty, a number of other catalysts are of at least equal importance. Three, in particular, stand out.

First, a growing emphasis on human rights as legally enforceable constructs is increasingly apparent, both domestically and internationally.[62] This, in turn, has placed sovereignty theory's ascription to Parliament of unlimited legislative power under growing strain, given the common perception that human rights can be afforded adequate protection only by means of judicial review of the constitutionality of legislation.[63] In this sense, the model adopted in the United States, within which legislative action is constrained by judicial enforcement of a constitutional catalogue of fundamental rights, is widely perceived as human rights protection operating in its paradigmatic form.[64] This mode of argument

[61] As explained above, the manner in which EU membership is to be accommodated by sovereignty theory is discussed below at 80–6.

[62] See below at 197–200.

[63] *Cf* Lord Irvine, "Sovereignty in Comparative Perspective: Constitutionalism in Britain and America" (the James Madison Memorial Lecture, New York, 2000), who argues that there is no necessary contradiction between parliamentary sovereignty and human rights protection. See further T R S Allan, "Legislative Supremacy and the Rule of Law: Democracy and Constitutionalism" (1985) 44 *CLJ* 111 for an explanation of how the principles of parliamentary sovereignty and the rule of law are reconciled within the British constitutional order.

[64] It is beyond the scope of the present work to evaluate the correctness or otherwise of this perception. For general discussion, see M Zander, *A Bill of Rights?* (London: Sweet and Maxwell, 1997). For contrasting perspectives on whether constitutional review is a desirable feature of constitutionalism in the United States, compare R Dworkin, *Law's Empire* (London: Fontana Press, 1991), ch. 10 (especially at 356) and R Dahl, *Democracy and Its Critics* (New Haven, Conn.: Yale University Press, 1989) at 189–91.

has thus been a powerful weapon in the armoury of those who have, in recent years, been in the vanguard of the challenge to parliamentary sovereignty. The point is illustrated with particular clarity by the work of Sir John Laws. As one of the leading advocates of the replacement of sovereignty theory with a model of limited legislative competence, he evidently draws his inspiration from a belief that a society can properly secure respect for human rights only if they are placed beyond legislative interference by the adoption of a higher order of law which is enforced by the courts.[65]

However, it may be noted in passing that the Human Rights Act 1998 *does* seek to create a framework within which human rights protection is reconciled with sovereignty theory.[66] The extent to which it succeeds in this endeavour will become apparent only when the Act has been in operation for a substantial period of time. However, the fact that, prior to its activation, the Act's balancing of rights protection with sovereignty was welcomed by a broad range of commentators[67]—including some who had previously expressed concern *vis-à-vis* parliamentary sovereignty—suggests that the critique of legislative supremacy from a human rights perspective is largely on hold, at least for the time being.[68]

Secondly, the growth in opposition to the idea of uncircumscribed legislative power is, at least in part, a reflection of the increasing tendency of public lawyers to view their discipline within a broader context that takes account of political theory.[69] This trend within public law scholarship has shifted the focus away from the somewhat formalistic questions—such as whether Parliament may bind its successors to the manner and form of legislation—with which sovereignty theorists have traditionally been preoccupied[70] and has, instead, prompted greater concentration on how any given model of legislative power

---

[65] See principally "Judicial Remedies and the Constitution" (1994) 57 *MLR* 213, "Law and Democracy" [1995] *PL* 72 and "The Constitution: Morals and Rights" [1996] *PL* 622. However, in his judicial capacity Laws LJ recognises that—in light of the principle of parliamentary sovereignty—this approach is not open to English judges. See, *e.g.*, *R v. Lord Chancellor, ex parte Witham* [1998] QB 575.

[66] The mechanisms by which the Act seeks to strike this balance are explained below at 200–2.

[67] For positive responses to the Human Rights Act's attempt to reconcile rights protection with sovereignty theory, see the comments of, *inter alios*, Sir Stephen Sedley, *Freedom, Law and Justice* (London: Sweet and Maxwell, 1999) at 15–16; Lord Lester, HL Debs., 18 November 1997, col. 521; Lord Bingham, "The Way We Live Now: Human Rights in the New Millennium" [1998] 1 *Web Journal of Current Legal Issues*; S Kentridge, "The Incorporation of the European Convention on Human Rights" in Cambridge Centre for Public Law, *Constitutional Reform in the United Kingdom: Practice and Principles* (Oxford: Hart Publishing, 1998) at 69.

[68] See also C F Forsyth, "Heat and Light: A Plea for Reconciliation" in C F Forsyth (ed.), *Judicial Review and the Constitution* (Oxford: Hart Publishing, 2000) at 393–5 on "the vanishing of the 'strong' critics"—a phenomenon which he attributes to, *inter alia*, the scheme of the Human Rights Act.

[69] See, *e.g.*, M Loughlin, *Public Law and Political Theory* (Oxford: Clarendon Press, 1992); T R S Allan, *Law, Liberty and Justice: The Foundations of British Constitutionalism* (Oxford: Clarendon Press, 1993); P P Craig, "Public Law, Political Theory and Legal Theory" [2000] *PL* 211.

[70] See above at 49–56.

may be justified in normative terms. Approaching the issue from this perspective, T R S Allan, for instance, reaches the conclusion that, since Parliament derives its legitimacy from the democratic mandate which the electorate confers upon it, it must follow that Parliament is legally unable to do anything which would destroy the very foundations on which its legitimacy depends. If democracy justifies the exercise of legislative power by Parliament, then the democratic principle must stand above and prior to Parliament's law-making competence.[71]

Indeed Craig argues that, viewed in historical perspective, British constitutionalists traditionally evaluated Parliament's role, and the extent of its legislative power, within a framework which took account of justificatory questions:

> The traditional vision of constitutional law from the sixteenth century onwards was one in which parliamentary sovereignty was premised on the existence of justificatory arguments drawn from legal and political theory which served to legitimate the ascription of this power to Parliament.[72]

In contrast, says Craig, the work of writers such as Wade, Heuston and Jennings, considered above, constitutes a modern aberration which effects an undesirable dislocation between the conclusion that sovereign power ought to be ascribed to Parliament and the process of normative evaluation which ought to precede that, or any other, conclusion as to the extent of legislative authority.[73] In any event, irrespective of whether the recent trend towards evaluating legislative power by reference to normative considerations drawn from political theory constitutes a new approach or simply the reassertion of an earlier methodology it is, quite clearly, an important part of the impetus that is driving contemporary critiques of unlimited parliamentary competence.[74]

The third factor which lies behind modern re-evaluations of sovereignty theory relates to the practical context within which legislative power is asserted by Parliament. In its idealised form, the British constitution was viewed as a balanced constitution which possessed a self-correcting quality that militated against the abuse of power. Such notions led writers like Dicey to assert that Parliament's legislative power did not need to be subjected to legal control, because the architecture of the constitution as a whole would ensure that such power was exercised responsibly.[75] Even if this view of the constitution once

---

[71] Allan, above n. 69, at 282. So, on this view, legislation which, *e.g.*, removed the franchise from a substantial part of the electorate would be beyond Parliament's competence. See also T R S Allan, "The Limits of Parliamentary Sovereignty" [1985] *PL* 614.

[72] Craig, above n. 69, at 211.

[73] *Ibid.* at 223–4.

[74] Although Craig, above n. 69, at 230, carefully notes that an evaluative approach which takes account of normative justificatory arguments "does not necessarily lead to the conclusion that there should be constitutional review of statutes policed by the courts". Rather, "It opens the way for legal argument about whether a legally untrammelled Parliament is justified in the present day".

[75] A V Dicey, *An Introduction to the Study of the Law of the Constitution* (E C S Wade, ed.) (London: Macmillan, 1964) at 83.

accorded with reality—which, in itself, is doubtful—few would adopt such a complacent attitude today. A variety of factors combine which raise concerns, in some quarters at least, about whether the political safeguards inherent in the constitution are strong enough to render judicial control of legislation unnecessary. Prominent among those factors are the domination of the House of Commons by the executive branch, the highly disciplined nature of modern political parties (and the consequent relative inability of the legislature to hold the executive to account) and the traditional subservience of the House of Lords (in light of its lack of democratic legitimacy).[76]

Taken together, these features combine to prise open a divide between the theory and the reality of the constitution: in all practical senses, legislative power is wielded by a single political party which forms the executive, acting through the conduit of a Lower Chamber dominated by that governing party and a Parliament which is dominated by the Lower Chamber.[77] Just as the decline in the legislature's ability effectively to scrutinise the administrative work of government precipitated the modern expansion of judicial review of executive action,[78] so Parliament's increasing ineffectiveness as a scrutineer of executive-instigated legislative programmes naturally calls into question whether the courts ought to become involved in judicial review of primary legislation. Of course, this is not to suggest that Parliament is a wholly ineffective scrutineer. Political and legal mechanisms of accountability must properly be regarded as complements, not competitors. But, in an age which pays greater attention than any other to individual rights and to their vindication by litigious means, political accountability, when it is compared with constitutional review, is increasingly perceived as a rather blunt tool.[79] It is against this background that the discourse which questions the appropriateness of parliamentary sovereignty has developed in recent years.

---

[76] However, the legitimacy deficit of the House of Lords has arguably been reduced by the House of Lords Act 1999 which removed the right of hereditary peers to participate in the legislative functions of the Upper Chamber. Moreover, if further reform of the House of Lords is effected—which, if the recommendations of the Royal Commission on Reform of the House of Lords are followed, will lead to some members of the second chamber being elected—the House of Lords is likely to adopt a more confident approach to its scrutiny of governments' legislative programmes. See generally Cm 4534, *A House for the Future* (London, 2000).

[77] See *ibid.* at 24–5.

[78] See above, Ch. 1.

[79] Self-evidently, however, dissatisfaction with political modes of accountability need not inevitably lead to the adoption of constitutional review. The obvious alternative to following that route would be to strengthen Parliament's constitutional position such that it is able to effect more rigorous and independent-minded scrutiny of the government's legislative programme.

2.4.2. *Two variants of the anti-sovereignty discourse*

Within that discourse, T R S Allan,[80] Lord Cooke,[81] Sir John Laws,[82] Sir Stephen Sedley[83] and Lord Woolf[84] have been particularly influential. Although they have all expressed dissatisfaction with sovereignty theory's ascription of unlimited legislative authority to Parliament, the critiques which the leading commentators advance differ in material respects. For present purposes those points of divergence need not be considered in detail;[85] it is, however, necessary to identify a broad distinction in the literature which, it is submitted, demonstrates that there are two principal variants of the critique of parliamentary supremacy.

It is useful to begin with Trevor Allan. In some of his earlier work—particularly his article on "Legislative Supremacy and the Rule of Law"—he expounds the view that, provided the idea of parliamentary sovereignty is viewed within its proper constitutional context, it need not be regarded as a negative phenomenon.[86] In particular, he is critical of the tendency of lawyers and jurists to overlook the fact that the doctrine of legislative supremacy formed "only one of the pillars" of the constitutional order within Dicey's influential account of the British constitution.[87] "Its importance," observes Allan, "was matched by that of the second [pillar]: the rule of supremacy of law."[88] By casting the rule of law

[80] See "Parliamentary Sovereignty: Lord Denning's Dexterous Revolution" (1983) *OJLS* 22; "Legislative Supremacy and the Rule of Law: Democracy and Constitutionalism" (1985) 44 *CLJ* 111; "The Limits of Parliamentary Sovereignty" [1985] *PL* 614; *Law, Liberty, and Justice: The Legal Foundations of British Constitutionalism* (Oxford: Clarendon Press, 1993); "Parliamentary Sovereignty: Law, Politics, and Revolution" (1997) 113 *LQR* 443; "Fairness, Equality, Rationality: Constitutional Theory and Judicial Review" in C F Forsyth and I C Hare (eds.), *The Golden Metwand and the Crooked Cord* (Oxford: Clarendon Press, 1998).

[81] Both judicially and extra-curially, Lord Cooke of Thorndon has long maintained that some rights are so fundamental that it must lie beyond the competence of legislatures to interfere with them. See *L v. M* [1979] 2 NZLR 519 at 529; *Brader v. Ministry of Transport* [1981] 1 NZLR 73 at 78; *New Zealand Drivers' Association v. New Zealand Road Carriers* [1982] NZLR 374 at 390; *Fraser v. State Services Commission* [1984] 1 NZLR 116 at 121; *Taylor v. New Zealand Poultry Board* [1984] 1 NZLR 394 at 398; "Fundamentals" [1988] *New Zealand Law Journal* 158. For discussion, see P Rishworth, "Lord Cooke and the Bill of Rights" and M Kirby, "Lord Cooke and Fundamental Rights" in P Rishworth (ed.), *The Struggle for Simplicity in the Law* (Wellington: Butterworths, 1997).

[82] See "Judicial Remedies and the Constitution" (1994) 57 *MLR* 213; "Law and Democracy" [1995] *PL* 72; "The Constitution: Morals and Rights" [1996] *PL* 622.

[83] See "Human Rights: A Twenty-First Century Agenda" [1995] *PL* 386; "The Constitution in the Twenty-First Century" in Lord Nolan and Sir Stephen Sedley (eds.), *The Making and Remaking of the British Constitution* (London: Blackstone Press, 1997).

[84] See *Droit Public*—English Style" [1995] *PL* 57. However, Lord Woolf expressed contrasting views in "Judicial Review—The Tensions between the Executive and the Judiciary" (1998) 114 *LQR* 579.

[85] For useful surveys and analyses of the literature, see J Goldsworthy, *The Sovereignty of Parliament* (Oxford: Clarendon Press, 1999), ch. 10; R Mullender, "Parliamentary Sovereignty, the Constitution, and the Judiciary" (1998) 49 *NILQ* 138.

[86] T R S Allan, "Legislative Supremacy and the Rule of Law: Democracy and Constitutionalism" (1985) 44 *CLJ* 111.

[87] *Ibid.* at 112.

[88] *Ibid.*

as a juristic principle which gives rise to a particular approach to statutory interpretation, Allan argues that it is possible to move beyond the preconception that sovereignty is necessarily a threat to liberty: hence "the protection of individual liberties can coexist with recognition of the ultimate supremacy of the democratic will of Parliament".[89] Within Allan's discourse, however, this is permitted to occur by using the rule of law only as an aid to interpretation:

> None of these presumptions [founded on the rule of law] may be applied to frustrate the purposes of an Act of Parliament. The principle of the sovereignty of Parliament requires judicial obedience to the strict terms of the statute. In the process of applying a statute, however, uncertainties are bound to arise. The rule of law requires that these uncertainties be resolved, *so far as possible*, in a manner which would most conform to the reasonable understanding of the subject to whom the statute is primarily addressed.[90]

On the basis of these views alone, it may seem strange that Allan is characterised as a critic of parliamentary sovereignty. His approach is manifestly consistent with the attribution of legislative supremacy to Parliament, albeit that legislation is construed, not in a vacuum, but in a constitutional context which colours the meaning which is ascribed to Parliament's enactments. Such a model is eminently compatible with the orthodox view of parliamentary sovereignty; it is clearly evident in the case law, and is strongly supported by Lord Steyn, among others.[91]

However, "Legislative Supremacy and the Rule of Law" does not reflect the more dominant approach which is evident in Allan's work. Although he continues to be persuaded of the importance of using the rule of law as a juristic principle to guide the interpretation of legislation, he no longer views this as sufficient means by which to temper the legislative power of Parliament.[92] Instead, Allan adopts as his starting point the premise that legal principles—including those which determine the ambit of Parliament's legislative authority—must be justified in normative terms:

> . . . the fundamental rule that accords legal validity to Acts of Parliament is not itself the foundation of the legal order, beyond which the lawyer is forbidden to look. That fundamental rule derives its legal authority from the underlying moral or political theory to which it belongs.[93]

---

[89] *Ibid.*

[90] *Ibid.* at 121 (emphasis added).

[91] See Lord Steyn, "Incorporation and Devolution: A Few Reflections on the Changing Scene" [1998] *European Human Rights Law Review* 153; *R v. Secretary of State for the Home Department, ex parte Pierson* [1998] AC 539 at 587–90; *R v. Secretary of State for the Home Department, ex parte Simms* [1999] 3 WLR 328 at 340.

[92] It is unnecessary to consider whether the views which Allan has expressed can be reconciled. Arguably, they can, given that he maintains that there is no clear distinction between the interpretation of a statute based on a strong presumption and the disapplication of a statute: see T R S Allan, *Law, Liberty, and Justice: The Legal Foundations of British Constitutionalism* (Oxford: Clarendon Press, 1993) at 266–7.

[93] *Ibid.* at 265–6.

Within that framework, Allan reasons that the normative justification which underpins Parliament's legislative power is the commitment to representative democracy which lies at the core of the British polity. It follows from this that legislation which was inimical to the democratic principle would "forfeit . . . any claim to be recognised as law": the political morality which gives rise to and normatively justifies Parliament's legislative power also, on this view, traces the circumference of that power.[94]

For present purposes it is of particular significance that Allan's account of parliamentary authority is a constant one.[95] This is not to say that, within his analysis, the limits on legislative power may not alter over time: self-evidently they can, given that legislative authority is, on this view, a function of a political morality which may itself evolve with the passage of time. However, Allan's theory is "constant" in the sense that it does not propose a move from full sovereignty to a more limited conception of legislative power: rather, it holds that the perimeter of Parliament's law-making power is, and always has been, a function of that conception of political morality which furnishes the normative justification for ascribing legislative authority to Parliament in the first place.

This feature of Allan's account is evident from the way in which he evaluates the impact of EU membership on the United Kingdom's constitutional order.[96] Thus, the *Factortame* case[97]—in which the House of Lords disapplied primary legislation which was incompatible with EU law—did not involve the imposition of novel limits on parliamentary competence, but constituted "a rational attempt to explore the boundaries of legislative sovereignty within the contemporary constitution". Consequently, "membership of the Community reveals the nature of the ultimate principle in all its *existing* complexity—integral to a larger, if mainly implicit, constitutional theory".[98] The significance of this point for the argument advanced in this book *vis-à-vis* the basis of judicial review will be elaborated below.[99] For the time being it is sufficient to note that it is this aspect of Allan's work—which we may term the first variant of the anti-sovereignty discourse—that distinguishes it from the arguments of many other critics of the sovereignty principle.

It is to the second variant of that discourse which we now turn. It is relatively clear that Trevor Allan's attitude to sovereignty is coloured most heavily by the second of three catalysts (considered above) which drive the arguments against

---

[94] T R S Allan, *Law, Liberty, and Justice: The Legal Foundations of British Constitutionalism* (Oxford: Clarendon Press, 1993) at 282 ff.

[95] It also appears from Lord Cooke's judgments and extra-curial writings (above n. 81) that he views legislative power as *inherently* limited; this conceptualisation is to be contrasted with the second variant of the anti-sovereignty discourse, discussed below, which postulates the *development* of limits on legislative authority, such that a new constitutional paradigm emerges to replace the old orthodoxy of unlimited legislative power.

[96] This matter is considered in more detail below at 80–6.

[97] R v. *Secretary of State for Transport, ex parte Factortame Ltd. (No. 2)* [1991] 1 AC 603.

[98] T R S Allan, "Parliamentary Sovereignty: Law, Politics, and Revolution" (1997) 113 *LQR* 443 at 448–9 (original emphasis).

[99] At 65.

legislative supremacy: thus it is the need (or perceived need)[100] to relate the scope of Parliament's power to the normative factors which, in the first place, justify the existence of that power which predominantly underpins Allan's critique.[101] In contrast, the second variant critiques are motivated primarily by the first of the factors discussed above—namely, the view that the normative worth of human rights dictates that they must be placed beyond legislative interference. Although, in practice, this approach produces similar outcomes—in terms of legislative competence and constitutional review—to Allan's model, there exist subtle, but important, distinctions. One, in particular, needs to be outlined.

It has already been noted that the first variant supplies a constant account of Parliament's role within the polity: it postulates that legislative authority has always been justified by—and limited by—the political morality of the constitution. Wholly untrammelled legislative power is thus firmly rejected. In contrast, the second variant furnishes a dynamic, rather than a constant, account of legislative power. Shaped by the increasing concentration on human rights as legal constructs—and, in particular, by the notion that such rights can be adequately protected only by recourse to judicial review of primary legislation—it is, in essence, an argument for constitutional change. It urges abandonment of the traditional principle of parliamentary sovereignty, and advocates the adoption of a new fundamental constitutional principle which more readily captures the contemporary emphasis on human rights. In this sense, the second variant, unlike the first, concedes that Parliament once was—and, perhaps, still is—sovereign in the Diceyan sense, but that such thinking is increasingly inappropriate to modern conceptions of constitutionalism such that it is being—or ought to be—discarded.

This philosophy is evident in Sir Stephen Sedley's contribution to the debate on parliamentary sovereignty. He argues that:

> . . . we have today both in this country and in those with which it shares aspects of its political and judicial culture a *new* and *still emerging* constitutional paradigm, no longer of Dicey's supreme parliament to whose will the rule of law must finally bend, but of a bi-polar sovereignty of the Crown in Parliament and the Crown in its courts . . .[102]

That Sedley's vision is a dynamic one, based on a reordering of the constitution rather than on a description of how the constitution has always been, is apparent from his prediction that "It is possible that . . . the courts may *one day* find

---

[100] Whether the need is real or perceived is, of course, a function of whether one's starting point is positivist or non-positivist.

[101] This is not to say that Allan is unconcerned with the issues raised by the other catalysts (*viz.* the importance of human rights and the fiction of the balanced constitution). In particular, it is clear from his work that the conception of democracy which he draws upon in order to justify—and limit—Parliament's authority is sufficiently broad to encompass fundamental human rights. See T R S Allan, "Parliamentary Sovereignty: Law, Politics, and Revolution" (1997) 113 *LQR* 443 at 449.

[102] Sir Stephen Sedley, "Human Rights: A Twenty-First Century Agenda" [1995] *PL* 386 at 389 (emphasis added).

themselves emboldened or provoked to strike down primary legislation as unconstitutional".[103]

The point is perhaps even more apparent in some of Sir John Laws's work. Although, at times, he appears to assert that Parliament is, at the present time, constrained by a higher order of law which ensures respect for human rights,[104] he ultimately resiles from this position. In his judicial capacity, he unequivocally accepts that:

> The common law does not generally speak in the language of constitutional rights, for the good reason that in the absence of any sovereign text, a written constitution which is logically and legally prior to the power of legislature, executive and judiciary alike, there is on the face of it no hierarchy of rights such that any one of them is more entrenched by the law than any other . . . In the unwritten legal order of the British state, at a time when the common law continues to accord a legislative supremacy to Parliament, the notion of a constitutional right can in my judgment inhere only in this proposition, that the right in question cannot be abrogated by the state save by specific provision in an Act of Parliament, or by regulations whose vires in main legislation specifically confers the power to abrogate.[105]

Extra-curially, Laws has attempted to reconcile this orthodoxy with his views on human rights by explaining that a higher order law which limits Parliament's ability to abrogate fundamental rights is a future possibility, rather than a present reality. Hence legislative sovereignty:

> remains the plainest constitutional fundamental at the present time; a departure from it will only happen, in the tranquil development of the common law, with a gradual re-ordering of our constitutional priorities to bring alive the nascent idea that a democratic legislature cannot be above the law.[106]

Thus Laws appears readily to accept that parliamentary sovereignty is presently a feature of the British constitution, notwithstanding that he considers that the weight of the normative arguments against sovereignty will eventually prompt its replacement with a model based on higher order law.[107] The significance of this point now falls to be explained.

---

[103] Sir Stephen Sedley, "The Moral Economy of Judicial Review" in G P Wilson (ed.), *The Frontiers of Legal Scholarship: Twenty Five Years of Warwick Law School* (Chichester: Wiley, 1995) at 160 (emphasis added). It should be noted, however, that Sedley has, at times, expressed views which appear to be closer to the first than to the second variant of the anti-sovereignty discourse. See, *e.g.*, "The Common Law and the Constitution" in Lord Nolan and Sir Stephen Sedley (eds.), *The Making and Remaking of the British Constitution* (London: Blackstone Press, 1997), ch. 2, in which he appears to argue that "the sovereignties of the state" *already* reside in both Parliament and the courts.

[104] See Sir John Laws, "Law and Democracy" [1995] *PL* 72 at 84–7.

[105] *R v. Lord Chancellor, ex parte Witham* [1998] QB 575 at 581.

[106] Sir John Laws, "Illegality: The Problem of Jurisdiction" in M Supperstone and J Goudie (eds.), *Judicial Review* (London: Butterworths, 1997) at 4.17.

[107] Lord Woolf's position is rather less clear. In "*Droit Public—English Style*" [1995] *PL* 57 at 68–9 he unequivocally argues that both Parliament and the courts "derive their authority from the rule of law"; thus, "both are subject to it and can not act in manner which involves its repudiation" so that "ultimately there are . . . limits on the supremacy of Parliament which it is the courts' inalien

2.4.3. *Theoretical and empirical aspects of the anti-sovereignty discourse*

The previous sections sketch the three principal modes of thought *vis-à-vis* the legislative powers of the United Kingdom Parliament. Notwithstanding the substantial differences which divide them, the orthodox (or continuing) model, the "new view" and the second variant of the anti-sovereignty discourse share one central characteristic: they each acknowledge that, at the present time, Parliament is sovereign in the sense that it enjoys the power to legislate on any substantive issue.

This is consistent with the first strand of the argument which Christopher Forsyth deploys in order to establish that the ultra vires doctrine is imperative if judicial review is to be constitutionally legitimate. It will be recalled that a core part of his argument *vis-à-vis* the necessity of ultra vires is that it constitutes the only way in which the operation of the supervisory jurisdiction may be reconciled with the constitutional order *given that the constitution embodies the notion of parliamentary sovereignty.* Consequently, the continuing and new views, together with the arguments of those who accept that Parliament is presently—but may not in the future be—sovereign, present no challenge to the first premise on which Forsyth's argument in favour of ultra vires rests.

However, the critique of sovereignty which is espoused primarily by T R S Allan holds that Parliament is not now, and never was, sovereign, because its authority derives from, and must therefore be limited by, the political morality of the constitution. Prima facie, this directly challenges Forsyth's thesis and it appears that, if accepted, it would undermine his claim that ultra vires is a constitutional prerequisite. The implications of Allan's account therefore need to be explored further. Two principal matters require consideration. First, Allan's theory will be evaluated, relatively briefly, in empirical terms. Secondly, it will be argued in section 2.5 that, even if Allan's account of parliamentary sovereignty is accepted, this does not necessarily undermine Forsyth's assertion that the ultra vires doctrine constitutes the only means by which judicial review may be conceptualised in a manner which is constitutionally legitimate.

The account which Allan provides can be divided into two strands. In part, it is a *theoretical* account which begins from the non-positivist premise that legislative power must be justified and that, *a priori*, the conception of political morality which legitimates the exercise of legislative power cannot be eviscerated

able responsibility to identify and uphold". More recently, however, in "Judicial Review—The Tensions between the Executive and the Judiciary" (1998) 114 *LQR* 579 at 581, Lord Woolf said that "the courts accept the sovereignty of Parliament" and went on to suggest that the rule of law can be vindicated only interpretatively. This latter approach is consistent with that which T R S Allan proposed in "Legislative Supremacy and the Rule of Law: Democracy and Constitutionalism" (1985) 44 *CLJ* 111 (discussed above). The equivocal nature of Lord Woolf's writings on this point calls to mind the ambiguity in the famous dictum of Coke CJ in *Dr. Bonham's Case* (1610) 8 Co. Rep. 113; 77 ER 638: writers disagree on whether he was advocating the application of a strong rule of construction or judicial disobedience to certain statutes. Allan, however, would argue that the distinction between interpretation and non-application is, in any event, one only of degree rather than type: see "The Limits of Parliamentary Sovereignty" [1985] *PL* 614.

through an exercise of that power. Whether or not one accepts this premise depends upon the fundamental view which is adopted *vis-à-vis* the nature of power and whether its existence needs to be justified in normative terms. It is unnecessary, for present purposes, to engage in that debate.

In addition to its theoretical aspect, Allan's account of legislative power also possesses an *empirical* strand. To state (as the theoretical premise does) that the perimeter of legislative authority is traced by whatever conception of political morality justifies its existence says nothing about the content of that political morality and hence tells us nothing about the real constraints which limit the legislature's power.[108] That morality, and those limits, fall to be determined empirically, and may well vary across time. The question therefore arises whether, as matters presently stand, the prevailing conception of political morality which obtains in Britain ascribes to Parliament a limited or an unlimited competence. Self-evidently it is impossible to ascertain the content of this political morality with any precision.[109] However, it is worth mentioning two factors which provide at least some indication that, in the United Kingdom, the political morality of the constitution embraces the notion that Parliament enjoys unlimited legislative competence.

2.4.4. Judicial attitude

Within Allan's model, it is—in all practical senses—the judges who discern and articulate the content of whatever version of political morality is current. This is not to say that it is for the judges to fabricate that conception of political morality: however, given that these matters ultimately crystallise in hard cases where the courts are forced to choose whether to give effect to legislation which arguably offends that sense of morality which the constitution is said to institutionalise, it is, ultimately, the courts which have to search for and give expression to that morality. Consequently, from an empirical perspective, it is

---

[108] This is not to say that Allan does not provide such an empirical explanation—he provides precisely such empirical content through his writing on the rule of law which is a recurrent theme in his work. Rather, the point is that the empirical part of the explanation is separable from the theoretical premise which, in the first place, requires the empirical content to be articulated. Thus acceptance of the theoretical strand of Allan's argument simply opens up a debate about the precise nature of the political morality which gives rise to and limits parliamentary authority.

[109] This reveals a difficulty which is unavoidably raised by Allan's approach. If the political morality of the constitution were to supply the constraints which limit Parliament's competence—and which would be capable of vindication through constitutional review—then those limits ought to be readily identifiable. The fact that no means exist by which they can be identified with certainty creates the risk that the judiciary may (of necessity) create its own conception of political morality which enjoys no inherent legitimacy. If the normative principle which justifies and limits parliamentary power is democracy, then it would be ironic if it were left to unelected judges to manufacture a particular conception of that principle in hard cases. The position is, of course, different if society has articulated a consensus view of the political morality which ought to circumscribe legislative action by adopting an entrenched bill of rights. The difference, however, is one only of degree, given the enormous latitude which judges enjoy in interpreting bills of rights: on this point, see further Lord Irvine, "Judges and Decision-Makers: The Theory and Practice of *Wednesbury* Review" [1996] *PL* 59 and below, Ch. 6.

important to examine the attitude of British courts in an attempt to determine what limits, if any, constitutional morality imposes on the authority of Parliament. An entire book could be devoted to such an inquiry, but it is sufficient here to mention two matters which are indicative of the courts' attitude.

First, the courts' general pronouncements on the role of Parliament may be considered. It is well known that, in *Dr. Bonham's Case*, Coke CJ declared that "when an Act of Parliament is against common right or reason, or repugnant, or impossible to be performed, the common law will controul it, and adjudge such Act to be void".[110] However, it is significant that this statement was made before the sovereignty of Parliament was firmly established at the end of the seventeenth century[111] and that, in any event, Sir Edward Coke later resiled from that position, concluding that Parliament possessed a "transcendent and abundant" jurisdiction which could not be "confined . . . within any bounds".[112] Moreover, there exists substantial disagreement about whether Coke ever actually intended to assert a power to quash primary legislation.[113]

In any event, the more recent judicial attitude is unequivocal. As Irvine has observed, there exists a "superfluity of judicial statement" to the effect that the courts recognise and respect Parliament's sovereignty.[114] The modern judicial view was distilled with particular clarity by Lord Reid:

> The idea that a court is entitled to disregard a provision in an Act of Parliament on any ground must seem strange and startling to anyone with any knowledge of the history and law of our constitution . . . In earlier times many learned lawyers seem to have believed that an Act of Parliament could be disregarded in so far as it was contrary to the law of God or the law of nature or natural justice, but since the supremacy of Parliament was finally demonstrated by the Revolution of 1688 any such idea has become obsolete.[115]

Writing more recently—and, importantly, within the specific context of the human rights discourse—Lord Browne-Wilkinson asserts that:

> [T]he courts have no power to declare that legislation is void as infringing fundamental human rights; the Queen in Parliament is sovereign and what is clearly enacted by statute cannot be challenged in the courts.[116]

Lord Steyn has expressed equally orthodox views on this matter:

---

[110] *Dr. Bonham's Case* (1610) 8 Co. Rep. 113 at 118; 77 ER 638 at 652. See also *Day v. Savadge* (1615) Hob. 85 at 87; 80 ER 235 at 237, *per* Hobart CJ.

[111] See generally J Goldsworthy, *The Sovereignty of Parliament* (Oxford: Clarendon Press, 1999), chs. 6–7.

[112] Sir Edward Coke, *The Fourth Part of the Institutes of the Law of England Concerning the Jurisdiction of the Courts* (London: M Flesher, 1644) at 36.

[113] Some writers suggest that Coke was arguing merely in favour of a particular approach to *interpretation*, rather than for a judicial power to *quash* legislation. See, *e.g.*, J W Gough, *Fundamental Law in English Constitutional History* (Oxford: Clarendon Press, 1955) at 40–1.

[114] Irvine, above n. 109, at 61.

[115] *British Railways Board v. Pickin* [1974] AC 765 at 782.

[116] Lord Browne-Wilkinson, "The Infiltration of a Bill of Rights" [1992] *PL* 397 at 398.

The relationship between the judiciary and the legislature is simple and straightforward. Parliament asserts sovereign legislative power. The courts acknowledge the sovereignty of Parliament. And in countless decisions the courts have declared the unqualified supremacy of Parliament. There are no exceptions . . . Parliamentary sovereignty is the ultimate principle of our constitution. And the judiciary unreservedly respects the will of Parliament as expressed in statutes. The task of judges in a case involving a statute is simply to construe and apply the statute . . . [The courts owe] unqualified loyalty . . . to the supremacy of Parliament . . .[117]

Lord Bingham thus says that it would be "preposterous" to suggest that the judges are "in any way equivocal in their deference to parliamentary sovereignty".[118] These judicial attitudes are important, particularly when it is recalled that those judges who are characterised as critics of parliamentary sovereignty have not issued such criticism from the Bench[119] and do not call into question the fact that, *for the time being*, the principle of parliamentary sovereignty accurately captures the role of the legislature and the scope of its powers. The senior judiciary thus appears to be unaware that its constitutional task, according to Allan's view, is to discern and enforce a constitutional morality which inherently limits Parliament's power.

The second issue which may be considered—as part of an empirical inquiry into the judiciary's perception of how the constitution's political morality impacts upon Parliament's law-making authority—arises as a response to an assertion made by Sir Stephen Sedley. He has suggested that the growth of judicial review furnishes evidence of the demise of the sovereignty principle: thus the "reassertion of judicial oversight of government which has been the achievement of the 1970s and 1980s" has led to "a judicial refashioning . . . of our organic constitution" so that "we have today . . . a new and still emerging constitutional paradigm, no longer Dicey's supreme parliament to whose will the rule of law must finally bend, but of bi-polar sovereignty of the Crown in Parliament and the Crown in its courts".[120] It has already been observed that, ultimately, Sedley accepts that this new paradigm has not yet fully emerged. Nevertheless, it is useful to consider his argument in order to see whether the courts' jurisprudence on judicial review provides any indications—as Sedley suggests it does—of a judicial awareness that its task is to uncover and enforce a constitutional morality which defines the boundaries of Parliament's legislative competence.

It is undeniable that, during the latter part of the twentieth century, the courts substantially developed and refined the law of judicial review: Lord Diplock regarded this as "the greatest achievement of the English courts" in his judicial

---

[117] Lord Steyn, "The Weakest and Least Dangerous Department of Government" [1997] *PL* 84 at 84–6.

[118] "Judges 'Not Taking the Role of Ministers' ", *The Daily Telegraph*, 18 July 1996.

[119] Although Lord Cooke of Thorndon, as Sir Robin Cooke, questioned the sovereignty of the New Zealand Parliament in New Zealand's courts (see the cases cited above at n. 81).

[120] Sir Stephen Sedley, "Human Rights: A Twenty-First Century Agenda" [1995] *PL* 386 at 388–9.

lifetime.[121] It is, however, difficult to see how this reveals a judicial attitude of antipathy to the notion of legislative supremacy. Indeed it is possible to identify two principal ways in which the growth of judicial review, far from somehow eviscerating parliamentary sovereignty, has been premised on and profoundly influenced by that principle.

First, in spite of the considerable growth of review, and the numerous restrictions on jurisdiction which the courts have cast off in recent decades, it remains the case that English reviewing courts are concerned only with *executive*, not *legislative*, action.[122] As Irvine remarks:

> [A]gainst [a] . . . background of what has, at times, appeared to be the inexorable expansion of judicial supervision, the judges have—quite rightly—accepted one constant limit on their power [*viz.* the doctrine of parliamentary sovereignty] . . . It traces an immovable perimeter of judicial power by absolutely precluding the courts from interfering with that which has received the imprimatur of the elected legislature.[123]

The principle of parliamentary sovereignty has thus served to mark the outer limit of judicial review during a period of immense expansionism.

Secondly, by invoking the ultra vires doctrine as the juridical basis of administrative law, the courts have implicitly acknowledged that judicial review must be reconciled with parliamentary sovereignty. The House of Lords recently reaffirmed that ultra vires "is the essential constitutional underpinning of the statute based part of our administrative law".[124] Moreover, although Lord Woolf has, extra-curially, derided the ultra vires principle as a "fairy tale",[125] he has fully embraced it in his judicial capacity, recently explaining that, in imposing standards of fairness on decision-makers, "the court is ensuring that decisions of the executive are taken in the manner required by Parliament".[126]

Against this background it is somewhat unpersuasive to advance the growth of judicial review as evidence of the eclipse of parliamentary sovereignty. Far from robbing Parliament of its legislative supremacy, the courts' development of administrative law speaks volumes about their recognition and acceptance of that principle. Sedley is right in one sense to speak of a "refashioning of our organic constitution" in recent years. As the executive's political accountability has declined, legal control of government has commensurately grown. Indeed, it is one of the strengths of the unwritten constitution that such informal evolution is possible. However, the courts appear to have risen to these challenges in

---

[121] *Inland Revenue Commissioners* v. *National Federation of Self-Employed and Small Businesses Ltd.* [1982] AC 617 at 641.

[122] Subject, of course, to review of delegated legislation and the impact of EU law. On the latter point, see below at 80–6.

[123] Lord Irvine, "Principle and Pragmatism: The Development of English Public Law under the Separation of Powers" (lecture delivered at the High Court in Hong Kong, September 1998).

[124] *Boddington* v. *British Transport Police* [1999] 2 AC 143 at 172, *per* Lord Steyn. Lords Browne-Wilkinson and Irvine LC expressed similar views at 164 and 158 respectively. Lords Slynn and Hoffmann delivered only short concurring speeches.

[125] Lord Woolf, "*Droit Public*—English Style" [1995] *PL* 57 at 66.

[126] *R* v. *Secretary of State for the Home Department, ex parte Fayed* [1998] 1 WLR 763 at 766–7.

a way that respects, rather than replaces, the orthodoxy of parliamentary sovereignty, which, in turn, remains a "steady beacon . . . in the otherwise ever-changing firmament of British public law".[127]

2.4.5. *The Human Rights Act 1998*

One further example may be given of the manner in which the empirical evidence does not appear to support Allan's thesis that the political morality of the constitution imposes substantive limits on Parliament's legislative authority.

The Human Rights Act 1998, which entered into force in October 2000, is likely to effect a substantial reorientation, in practical terms, of the relationship between Parliament and the other two branches of government. The dual prospects of judicial declarations of incompatibility and administrative amendments to parliamentary enactments are likely to encourage the legislature to exercise self-regulation in order to ensure that, save in exceptional circumstances, legislation is consistent with the rights protected by the European Convention on Human Rights.[128] In this pragmatic sense, the Act will fetter Parliament's legislative freedom.

However, while these important *practical* implications must not be overlooked, it is the impact of incorporation on the *theoretical* notion of parliamentary sovereignty which is of central relevance to the present argument. In fact, the government's approach directly contradicted the modern tendency to question the doctrine of parliamentary sovereignty. The White Paper stated that the government would not favour granting to the courts the power to set aside primary legislation in light of "the importance which the government attaches to parliamentary sovereignty".[129] Thus the Act provides that neither the duty of consistent construction nor the issue of declarations of incompatibility will affect the "validity, continuing operation or enforcement" of primary legislation.[130]

In itself, the fact that the United Kingdom's domestic human rights regime has been constituted in a manner which explicitly assumes the sovereignty of Parliament is significant.[131] It suggests that, within the British polity, political morality does not at present require that the courts ought to have the power to strike down Acts of Parliament which are inconsistent with human rights. This conclusion is bolstered when the reaction of leading commentators to the Human Rights Act is considered. Lord Bingham, for example, has welcomed the

---

[127] Irvine, above n. 123.
[128] The mode of operation of the Human Rights Act 1998 is explained below at 200–2.
[129] Cm 3782, *Rights Brought Home: The Human Rights Bill* (London: TSO, 1997) at 10.
[130] Human Rights Act 1998, ss. 3(2)(b) and 4(6)(a).
[131] It is also worth noting that other parts of the constitutional reform scheme—most notably the devolution programme—are clearly premised on the principle of parliamentary sovereignty. See generally R Brazier, "The Constitution of the United Kingdom" (1999) 58 *CLJ* 96 at 101–15. This suggests that the weight attached to the principle of regional autonomy by the constitution's political morality is not such as to place interference with that principle beyond the reach of the Westminster Parliament.

approach adopted by the Act,[132] noting that it is "vastly preferable" that judges should not be involved in the disapplication of statutes which affront fundamental rights, because this is "not part of our constitutional tradition".[133] Similarly, Lord Lester has praised the Act, calling it "an ingenious and successful reconciliation of the principles of parliamentary sovereignty and the need for effective domestic remedies".[134] And Lord Woolf—once a critic of parliamentary sovereignty[135]—had this to say about the human rights legislation while it was still before Parliament:

> . . . I am pleased that the Bill restricts the courts' powers to declaring that an Act of Parliament is inconsistent with a provision of the Convention and does not give the courts power to strike down or otherwise to affect the validity of an Act of Parliament. In this the Bill reflects the views of the vast majority, if not possibly all, the senior judiciary. The judiciary regard what is being proposed as far more desirable than a Bill which enables the judiciary to strike down legislation. It is in accord with our constitutional traditions for legislation not to be struck down . . . I anticipate that there will be few cases where the courts will be unable to construe legislation in accordance with the Convention. But if they cannot, Parliament should decide how the situation should be rectified. A political decision of this sort is not an appropriate task for the courts.[136]

2.4.6. *Connecting the theoretical and empirical aspects of the anti-sovereignty discourse*

The foregoing is not, and does not purport to be, an exhaustive analysis of the empirical evidence *vis-à-vis* what limits, if any, the political morality of the constitution imposes on Parliament's law-making power. This is reflected in the fact that the empirical evidence, as presented, provides no definitive guidance on what the constitutional settlement prescribes so far as legislative authority is concerned. It does, however, point towards one of two principal conclusions.

First, it may be argued that the empirical evidence—drawn from decided cases, judicial attitudes, the approach to fundamental rights embodied in the Human Rights Act 1998 and the reaction of judges and others to that legislation—implies that Allan's theoretical premise is itself wrong. It was suggested above that Allan's thesis can be resolved into two components: the theoretical aspect maintains that legislative authority is legitimated by, and is therefore limited by, a normative conception of democracy; the empirical dimension then serves to furnish the specific conception of democracy which is in play, so as to permit the ascertainment of (or at least a starting point for exploring) how

---

[132] Lord Bingham, "The Way We Live Now: Human Rights in the New Millennium" [1998] 1 *Web Journal of Current Legal Issues*.
[133] "Bingham Rejects New Privacy Law", *The Daily Telegraph*, 9 October 1997.
[134] HL Debs., 18 November 1997, col. 521.
[135] See "*Droit Public*—English Style" [1995] *PL* 57.
[136] Lord Woolf, "Judicial Review—The Tensions between the Executive and the Judiciary" (1998) 114 *LQR* 579 at 592.

Parliament's law-making power is bounded. Given the consistency with which the idea of parliamentary sovereignty—which implies unlimited legislative power—is asserted and accepted, it may be argued that this empirical perspective calls Allan's theoretical premise itself into question. If, empirically, it appears that unlimited legislative power is accepted as a feature of the British constitution, this casts doubt on the prior assertion that legislative authority is bounded by the democratic principle which legitimates it. Viewed in this manner, it may be argued that the empirical data imply that the non-positivist theory which Allan develops simply does not provide an accurate map of how the British polity operates.

In many senses, however, reaching such a conclusion would be dissatisfying. The reason for this becomes apparent when the first part of Allan's argument—his theoretical premise—is unpacked. It can itself be resolved into two components. The first holds that some normative reason must be articulated if the ascription of legislative power to Parliament is to be justified. It is now broadly accepted that such a justification does exist—in the form of representative democracy—and that such justification is also necessary. It is therefore submitted that this part of Allan's theory does capture the contemporary notion of political morality. The second part of Allan's theoretical premise follows logically from the first: if it is accepted that a justification must be articulated, it must follow *a priori* that Parliament cannot destroy that which, in the first place, legitimates its authority. Thus it appears that Allan's theoretical premise both accurately captures contemporary thinking about legislative authority and is internally logically consistent. This suggests that the difficulty lies in the second—that is, the empirical—part of Allan's argument. The empirical evidence considered earlier demonstrates a clear commitment to the idea of parliamentary sovereignty. In particular, the Human Rights Act and the reaction to it imply a broad consensus which ascribes to Parliament the authority to interfere with fundamental rights and to resolve disputes about how rights should be balanced against each other and against competing claims.

The question then becomes whether, and if so how, this empirical fact can be reconciled with Allan's theoretical perspective about the nature of sovereignty. The answer, it is suggested, lies in how "democracy" is conceptualised. If democracy is cast as the principle which legitimates—and, hence, limits—Parliament's power to make law, the content of that principle becomes the live issue. The empirical evidence suggests that, in the United Kingdom at the present time, that conception of democracy which justifies and thus limits legislative power is a relatively bare one. In practical terms this means that, following Allan's theoretical perspective, it may be correct to assert that legislation which strikes at the very core of the democratic principle—by, for example, prolonging the life of Parliament indefinitely or removing the franchise from substantial parts of the population—may lie outwith Parliament's power: such legislation would be inconsistent with the core democratic principle which normatively justifies the exercise of legislative authority.

However, the consistency with which the width of Parliament's law-making authority is empirically stated suggests that the democratic principle which, within Allan's model, limits Parliament's competence is a very narrow one. Consequently, certain rights—such as freedom of expression—which, on a broad interpretation, would be inherent in the democratic principle, appear to lie outside that conception of democracy which underpins and hence limits the power of the legislature in the UK. This approach permits the empirical evidence—which exhibits antipathy towards suggestions that, for example, Parliament is unable to qualify human rights norms—to be reconciled with Allan's core theoretical perspective which maintains that the democratic principle both legitimates and limits Parliament's assertion of law-making authority.

2.5. From Theory to Reality: The Necessity of Ultra Vires within the Limited Competence Model

2.5.1 Introduction

It is necessary, at this point, to draw some conclusions from the foregoing discussion of sovereignty theory. It is worth beginning by underscoring the purpose of that discussion. It was prompted by Christopher Forsyth's claim that, so long as Parliament is sovereign, judicial review can be rendered legitimate only by the application of ultra vires theory.[137] The question therefore arises whether Parliament is "sovereign". It is clear, from the analysis above, that the orthodox model, the new view and the second variant of the anti-sovereignty discourse[138] attribute to Parliament unlimited legislative competence over substantive matters. Those conceptions of Parliament's role are therefore consistent with the view of the constitutional framework which Forsyth advances in order to argue for the necessity of ultra vires.

However, as we have seen, Allan paints a different picture of Parliament's role within the constitutional order which holds that Parliament is not "sovereign" in the Diceyan sense. The purpose of the present section is to demonstrate that, even if that view is adopted, it does not establish that Forsyth's thesis is incorrect. In other words, it will be argued that the ultra vires doctrine remains constitutionally imperative even if Allan's model of legislative authority is accepted.

---

[137] It will be recalled that the correctness of Forsyth's claim also turns on the argument that ultra vires and intra vires are mutually exclusive and collectively exhaustive concepts. The validity of that claim is assessed below at 87–95.

[138] The second variant of the anti-sovereignty discourse is that which is propounded by, *inter alios*, Sir John Laws. He maintains that Parliament is sovereign for the time being, but that the normative arguments against sovereignty will eventually prevail by prompting a shift to a new constitutional paradigm which will recognise a higher order of law which limits Parliament's freedom of action.

Forsyth's argument is founded on the idea that decision-makers must logically act either within or beyond the powers which Parliament chooses to confer. If this view is accepted,[139] and if, moreover, Parliament's will is legally unchallengeable, judicial review must be regarded as an exercise in statutory construction, as judges attempt to determine the precise location of the line which separates intra vires and ultra vires conduct. This follows because administrators' action must lie either within or beyond their conferred competence, and the sovereignty principle prohibits judicial interference with that which is intra vires.

The situation is different, however, if it is accepted that Parliament is no longer omnicompetent. Within a limited competence model, the effect and limits of a legislative scheme are not determined purely by interpretation. Since, on this view, certain matters lie beyond Parliament's legislative capacity, a court seeking to ascertain the legal impact of legislation must have regard to the limits of the legislature's authority. To adopt Allan's terminology, the political morality of the constitution directs that certain matters lie beyond Parliament's power, and legislation which purports to deal with such matters can logically be of no effect.

If such a model were adopted, would the ultra vires doctrine remain constitutionally essential? That question is best answered in two stages. First, it will be shown that the limited competence model, if adopted, has *potentially* far-reaching implications for the theoretical basis of judicial review. Secondly, however, it will be argued that acceptance of the limited competence model is merely a *necessary*, not a *sufficient*, condition precedent to the abandonment of ultra vires reasoning.[140]

2.5.2. Abandoning ultra vires: The theoretical potential of the limited competence model

The central proposition of the anti-sovereignty discourse is that certain matters lie beyond the legislative reach of Parliament. However, within its area of legislative competence, Parliament's enactments must *a priori* remain legally unchallengeable. The duty of judicial fidelity to legislation therefore remains in all cases except those in which Parliament transgresses the boundaries of its legislative province. Consequently, whether the connection between enabling legislation and judicial review can be abandoned within a limited competence model depends on the nature of the limits to which Parliament is subject.

In orthodox theory, the importance of relating review to legislation derives from the fact that a sovereign Parliament can choose whether to grant adminis-

---

[139] See further below at 87–95.

[140] To express the argument in terms consistent with the analysis, above, of Allan's theory, his theoretical premise, if accepted, establishes the possibility of moving beyond ultra vires; but the manner in which the empirical aspect of the argument is constructed is determinative of whether abandonment of ultra vires is, at any given time, a constitutional possibility. These ideas are elaborated below.

trative power subject to or free from an obligation to adhere to the principles of good administration. Assuming that Parliament is sovereign, judicial insistence on, say, a fair procedure where Parliament intended that no such requirement should apply is constitutionally improper because it involves judicial contradiction of legislative intention.[141]

However, this analysis may not apply within a limited competence model. Under this approach, it may be that Parliament's legislative capacity would be limited such that it would lack the ability to empower decision-makers to act contrary to the principles of good administration. Those principles could then be viewed as forming part of the definition of Parliament's competence: for writers such as Laws, they would constitute part of the higher order law which limits Parliament's freedom of action; to similar effect, they would, for Allan, form part of the normative political morality which both justifies and demarcates parliamentary authority.

On this view, the courts' enforcement of the principles of good administration could not then be rationalised by reliance on the intention-based methodology of ultra vires. Judicial analysis would shift from the determination and effectuation of the limits of discretionary power which Parliament had chosen or intended to grant, to the ascertainment and enforcement of those fetters on statutory power which would derive from Parliament's limited legislative capacity.

There are a number of similarities between this model and the ultra vires doctrine. According to both, donees of statutory power are required to observe the principles of good administration; furthermore, each provides that those exercising such power enjoy a derived competence and may therefore act only within a demarcated area. Hence, in both models, the obligation to adhere to the principles of good administration follows from the limited nature of the power granted to the donee.

The essential difference concerns the reasoning process which leads to the conclusion that the grant of power is limited thus. According to the ultra vires doctrine, this follows from Parliament's choosing to attenuate the competence of decision-makers. In contrast, within the limited competence model, the limits of executive competence derive from Parliament's inability to grant discretionary power free from an obligation to abide by the principles of good administration. This second approach divorces the justification of judicial review from parliamentary intention, adopting instead the perimeter of parliamentary competence as the determinant of the ambit of discretionary power and, therefore, as the source of the principles of good administration.

However, it must be emphasised that discarding the intention-based approach of ultra vires in favour of a justification founded on the limitation of Parliament's own power may be adopted only if the limited competence model

---

[141] Assuming, for the time being, that ultra vires and intra vires are mutually exclusive and collectively exhaustive concepts.

is constructed in a particular manner: it must operate so as to deprive Parliament of the legislative capacity to create arbitrary discretionary power to which no requirements of fairness and rationality attach.

Forsyth has explained that the focus of the ultra vires doctrine on legislative intention is necessitated by the fact that "what an *all powerful* Parliament does not prohibit, it must authorise either expressly or impliedly".[142] This assumes absolute legislative supremacy, so his reference to an "all powerful Parliament" describes both its *omnicompetence* and its capacity to generate *unchallengeable* law within that uncircumscribed sphere of competence. However, even if it is thought that Parliament's competence is limited, Forsyth's point is still relevant: within such a model, Parliament continues to generate unchallengeable law, albeit only within those regions of legislative competence allocated by higher constitutional norms.

Consequently if, within the limited competence model, Parliament remained able to grant or withhold the power to contravene the principles of good administration, judicial enforcement of those principles would still have to be justified by invoking the intention-based approach of ultra vires: any other approach would be as constitutionally improper in this situation as it would be within the traditional model of sovereignty since, in each case, rationalising review otherwise than by reference to legislative intention would necessarily entail judicial interference with administrative action which would be intra vires according to Parliament. The constitutional impropriety inherent in such a course follows from the legally unchallengeable status of parliamentary intention: under the traditional conception of sovereignty, this is always so; within the limited competence model, Parliament's will cannot legitimately be questioned by the courts provided that Parliament has remained within its allotted constitutional province.

2.5.3. *Abandoning ultra vires: The empirical reality of the limited competence model*

It follows that there are two conditions precedent to the legitimate abandonment of a vires-based theory of judicial review. First, the theoretical possibility of limits on Parliament's legislative competence must exist. Secondly, those limits must dictate that Parliament lacks the competence to confer on those exercising statutory power the ability to act contrary to the principles of good administration. It is submitted that, even if the first condition is satisfied, the second is not.

It is notable that those writers who propound the existence of limits on Parliament's competence consistently emphasise that those limits relate only to the most fundamental of issues. Thus the postulated attenuation of legislative

---

[142] C F Forsyth, "Of Fig Leaves and Fairy Tales: The Ultra Vires Doctrine, the Sovereignty of Parliament and Judicial Review" (1996) 55 *CLJ* 122 at 133 (emphasis added).

competence is minimal in theoretical terms and, in practical terms, virtually non-existent. For example, Woolf[143] cites Mann's suggestion that Parliament lacks the ability to introduce legislation discriminating directly on religious or racial grounds or "vesting the property of all red haired women in the State".[144] Indeed, Woolf readily admits that the "limits on the supremacy of Parliament which it is the courts' inalienable responsibility to identify and uphold . . . are limits of the most modest dimensions which I believe any democrat would accept".[145] Lord Cooke[146] and Sir John Laws[147] espouse similar views on this matter.

Allan also advocates the attenuation of sovereignty only to a very limited extent. He begins from the premise that, "The limits of sovereignty clearly cannot be stated with any precision. The scope of the legal doctrine, and its implications for constitutional change, cannot be settled except by analysis of the political morality from which it derives its authority."[148] Nevertheless, it is tolerably clear that Allan's model requires Parliament to be deprived of the legislative capacity to interfere only with the most fundamental of rights and interests. For instance, because the sovereignty principle "expresses the courts' commitment to British parliamentary democracy", legislation "whose effect would be the destruction of any recognisable form of democracy . . . could not consistently be applied as law".[149]

This analysis can usefully be related back to the discussion, above,[150] of Allan's model of limited legislative competence. It was argued that his theory possesses two elements—one theoretical, one empirical. The former holds that democracy legitimates parliamentary authority and *a priori* limits it. If this view is accepted, the focus then shifts to the empirical reality of the particular conception of democracy which the political order embodies. It was suggested above that the conception of democracy from which Parliament's authority may be said to spring, and which therefore sets the putative boundaries of legislative power, is a relatively bare one. This helps to explain why the empirical evidence furnished by court decisions and judicial opinions tends to emphasise the breadth—indeed, the unlimited nature—of Parliament's law-making power. This conclusion is supported by the attitude of the critics of parliamentary sovereignty. The limits which they propose should apply to Parliament's competence are modest in the extreme: they are built around core conceptions of democracy, and tend not to encompass the broader human rights norms which more sophisticated versions of democracy would embody.

---

[143] Lord Woolf, "*Droit Public*—English Style" [1995] *PL* 57 at 68.
[144] F A Mann, *Further Studies in International Law* (Oxford: Clarendon Press, 1990) at 104.
[145] Woolf, above n. 143, at 69.
[146] Sir Robin Cooke, "Fundamentals" [1988] *New Zealand Law Journal* 158 at 164.
[147] Sir John Laws, "Judicial Remedies and the Constitution" (1994) 57 MLR 213 at 223–4.
[148] T R S Allan, "The Limits of Parliamentary Sovereignty" [1985] *PL* 614 at 627.
[149] T R S Allan, *Law, Liberty, and Justice: The Legal Foundations of British Constitutionalism* (Oxford: Clarendon Press, 1993) at 282.
[150] At 65–6.

Critics of sovereignty therefore envisage only minimal restrictions on Parliament's competence, deriving largely from what may be termed a "bare" or "core" conception of "democracy". These modest fetters fall into a different and altogether more fundamental category from the matters which are dealt with by the principles of good administration. Indeed, Sir John Laws explicitly acknowledges that it does *not* lie outside the legislature's capacity to interfere with the grounds of review, recognising that "Parliament may at any stage legislate so as to change, curtail, or qualify" them.[151]

Thus, although it is contended by some that Parliament cannot abrogate the most basic tenets of the British democratic tradition, it is another matter entirely to argue that the rules governing administrative decision-making are so fundamental that Parliament may never, whatever the circumstances, provide for their alteration. To deprive Parliament of the ability to interfere with—and, in appropriate situations, suspend the operation of—the principles of good administration[152] would make much more significant inroads into its legislative capacity than can be supported by reference to either the critiques of sovereignty advanced by writers such as Woolf and Laws or the empirical evidence of the political morality of the constitution which delimits Parliament's authority within Allan's normative theoretical perspective.[153]

For this reason, it is necessary to distinguish between Parliament's ability to effect the wholesale *abolition* of judicial review and to provide legislative *regulation* of the supervisory jurisdiction. Woolf argues, in order to exemplify the sort of limits on parliamentary sovereignty which he envisages, that "if a party with a large majority in Parliament uses that majority to abolish the courts' entire power of judicial review in express terms", this would constitute a legislative excess which the courts would be justified in refusing to recognise as law.[154] However, even if Parliament were subject to such a limitation, this would fall far short of holding that it lies beyond its power to interfere in any way with the principles of good administration. Completely abolishing all review in every context is an entirely different enterprise from statutory modification of the intensity, nature or availability of review in a particular area. While it may be possible to categorise the former as constitutionally anathema, the same is not true of the latter, which may well constitute a legitimate choice

---

[151] Sir John Laws, "Illegality: The Problem of Jurisdiction" in M Supperstone and J Goudie (eds.), *Judicial Review* (London: Butterworths, 1997) at 4.18.

[152] It is worth recalling that the norms protected by the Human Rights Act 1998 are not placed, by that legislation, beyond parliamentary interference.

[153] In his most recent contribution to the debate, Allan suggests that the values protected by the principles of good administration *do* form part of the political morality of the constitution, such that interference with them may lie beyond Parliament's capacity: see T R S Allan, "The Rule of Law as the Foundation of Judicial Review" in C F Forsyth (ed.), *Judicial Review and the Constitution* (Oxford: Hart Publishing, 2000) at 414. However, this view is contradicted by the consistent concession of the common law theorists that Parliament is free to curtail the operation of the principles of good administration: see Laws, above n. 151 and accompanying text; P P Craig, *Administrative Law* (London: Sweet and Maxwell, 1999) at 19.

[154] Lord Woolf, "*Droit Public*—English Style" [1995] PL 57 at 67.

which is necessary, within a particular factual and policy environment, for effective government.

Indeed, the courts' willingness to give effect to statutory provisions which preclude review following the expiry of a particular time period clearly illustrates judicial recognition that Parliament is capable of modifying the application of the principles of good administration.[155] Moreover, although the courts are much more reluctant to give literal effect to provisions which appear entirely to exclude review of a particular discretion,[156] Laws J, in *Witham*,[157] accepted in terms that the courts can protect access to justice only by the application of a strong rule of construction and that, where legislation cannot be interpretatively reconciled with the right of access to justice, the legislation must be given effect.

Hence, even if Woolf's argument is embraced, with the result that the abolition of review lies beyond the competence of Parliament, it is plain from the courts' reasoning that Parliament remains capable of interfering with the grounds of review. Acceptance of Woolf's thesis, therefore, need not entail any inconsistency with recognising the continued relevance of the ultra vires principle within a limited competence model.

2.6. Conclusion

Forsyth asserts that when Parliament creates administrative power, it follows *a priori* that the limits on executive competence reflect the perimeter of the power which Parliament actually conferred; all executive action is therefore either intra vires or ultra vires. Assuming that this is the case, the following conclusions can be drawn from the foregoing discussion.

First, if Parliament is sovereign in the traditional sense, judicial review can be constitutionally legitimate only if it can be related to (implicit or explicit) legislative provision regarding the scope of discretionary power. To divorce review from the methodology of interpretation would raise the prospect of the courts imposing limits on statutory power where no such limits were intended by Parliament. The judges would therefore be involved in removing from administrators powers which the sovereign Parliament had conferred upon them.

Secondly, if the notion of unlimited parliamentary authority is rejected, it is necessary to determine the extent to which its competence is fettered. It is widely accepted that it does not lie beyond Parliament's competence to interfere with or, in appropriate cases, suspend the application of the principles of good administration. Nor does the empirical evidence suggest that the political morality of the British constitution removes such matters from Parliament's

---

[155] See *Smith v. East Elloe Rural District Council* [1956] AC 736; *R v. Secretary of State for the Environment, ex parte Ostler* [1977] QB 122. See generally H W R Wade and C F Forsyth, *Administrative Law* (Oxford: Oxford University Press, 2000) at 714–26.

[156] See, *e.g.*, *Anisminic Ltd. v. Foreign Compensation Commission* [1969] 2 AC 147.

[157] *R v. Lord Chancellor, ex parte Witham* [1998] QB 575.

reach. The principles of good administration do not, therefore, form part of the definition of Parliament's competence. Hence a non-sovereign Parliament would retain the capacity to grant administrative power either subject to or free from an obligation to respect the principles of good administration. It follows that, even within the limited competence model, it is constitutionally necessary to explain judicial enforcement of the principles of good administration in terms of the implementation of enabling legislation: any other approach would entail the proposition that the courts, on review, prevent administrators from exercising powers which lie within the competence lawfully conferred by Parliament.

Importantly, therefore, it is possible to acknowledge the constitutional necessity of ultra vires theory without adopting a purely positivist perspective.[158] Even within a normative model which justifies the ascription of legislative authority to Parliament by reference to democratic principles, the ultra vires doctrine remains essential provided that the particular political morality which is in play does not place the suspension of the principles of good administration beyond Parliament's reach. The empirical evidence strongly indicates that the conception of political morality which the British polity presently embodies does *not* locate that competence outwith Parliament's legislative province.

To abandon the connection between legislation and review is therefore improper, irrespective of whether Parliament is fully sovereign in the traditional sense. However, this conclusion is based on the assumption that Forsyth's second proposition—that ultra vires and intra vires are mutually exclusive concepts—is true. That must be tested shortly. First, though, it is necessary to explain why the argument which has been advanced thus far, concerning the legislative competence of Parliament, is not undermined by the impact on parliamentary sovereignty of the UK's membership of the European Union.

2.7. European Union Law and Parliamentary Sovereignty

2.7.1. *The impact of European Union law on parliamentary sovereignty*

It is clear that English courts are now willing to disapply primary legislation which is irreconcilable with directly effective provisions of EU law.[159] Although

---

[158] The argument here is that recognising the constitutional necessity of ultra vires methodology does not require the adoption of a positivist perspective. In Ch. 4, below, the related, but distinct, argument will be advanced that the ultra vires doctrine—understood in the modified form which is elaborated in this book—is itself not positivist in nature. Rather, it embraces precisely the sort of interpenetration between legislation and the rule of law which Allan sets out in "Legislative Supremacy and the Rule of Law: Democracy and Constitutionalism" (1985) 44 *CLJ* 111.

[159] See *R v. Secretary of State for Transport, ex parte Factortame (No. 2)* [1991] 1 AC 603; *R v. Secretary of State for Employment, ex parte Equal Opportunities Commission* [1995] 1 AC 1. For discussion see, *inter alios*, N Gravells, "Disapplying an Act of Parliament Pending a Preliminary Ruling: Constitutional Enormity or Community Law Right?" [1989] *PL* 568; P P Craig, "United Kingdom Sovereignty after *Factortame*" (1991) 11 *Yearbook of European Law* 221.

there are a number of ways in which this constitutional innovation may be explained, the rationalisations can be divided into two broad categories.

The first school of thought holds that the UK Parliament is now subject to a substantive limitation, in that it lies beyond its competence to legislate inconsistently with directly effective EU law. On this view, the Diceyan conception of unlimited law-making power no longer applies to the Westminster Parliament. There are two principal routes to this conclusion, the route which is adopted being determined by the theory of sovereignty which forms the starting point of the analysis.

Those who view sovereignty in terms of a political fact which constitutes the legal system and which cannot, therefore, be altered by legislation resort to the notion that there has been a constitutional revolution. Entry into the European Communities is thus seen as having prompted a shift in the *Grundnorm*: the primacy of EU law replaces the supremacy of Parliament as the ultimate constitutional principle.[160]

In contrast, those who locate legislative authority within a normative framework which demands that it is justified and limited by political morality argue that the primacy of EU law can be accommodated without resort to notions of revolution or legal discontinuity.[161] Rather, membership of the European Union feeds into the contemporary conception of political morality which constitutes and demarcates Parliament's power. The *Factortame* case is thus presented as "a rational attempt to explore the boundaries of legislative sovereignty within the contemporary constitution".[162]

The central features of these two conceptions of legislative authority were considered above,[163] and it is not necessary, for present purposes, to consider which furnishes the most satisfactory accommodation of the *Factortame* litigation. Rather, the important point is that both ultimately arrive at the same conclusion: that, whether or not Parliament was sovereign in the Diceyan sense before Britain joined the European Communities, it is not sovereign in that sense at the present time.

The second school of thought seeks to rationalise the impact of EU law in terms of statutory construction. It is said that membership of the Union has given rise to a rule of interpretation which leads the courts conclusively to presume that Parliament intends to legislate consistently with EU law unless it makes express contrary provision. Indeed Lord Bridge advanced this view in the first *Factortame* case.[164] Wade notes that this approach appears to be "less revolutionary" than the first, because it "does not require [the courts] to accept and

---

[160] See H W R Wade, "Sovereignty—Revolution or Evolution?" (1996) 112 *LQR* 568.

[161] See T R S Allan, "Parliamentary Sovereignty: Law, Politics, and Revolution" (1997) 113 *LQR* 443.

[162] *Ibid.* at 448.

[163] At 44–9 and 56–73.

[164] *Factortame Ltd.* v. *Secretary of State for Transport* [1990] 2 AC 85 at 140. Sir John Laws, "Law and Democracy" [1995] *PL* 72 at 89 takes a similar view.

enforce some novel limitation on Parliament's sovereignty".[165] This prompts two comments.

First, it is entirely misleading to characterise cases like *Factortame* merely as exercises in statutory interpretation. English lawyers are familiar with strong presumptions about the intention of Parliament: take, for example, the principle that a statute will not be construed to give retroactive force to criminal provisions unless it clearly does so in express words or by necessary implication.[166] It is clear that, if Parliament, through primary legislation, created a new criminal offence, the definition of which necessarily involved retroactivity, a court would be forced to accept that Parliament had chosen to derogate from the non-retrospectivity principle. Normal rules of construction therefore yield to a sufficiently clear contrary intention, and it would be nonsensical to impugn legislation on the ground of its inconsistency with a principle enshrined in a mere rule of interpretation.

In contrast, the rule of construction which was supposedly applied in *Factortame* did not yield: it prevailed over a legislative intention which was acknowledged to be inconsistent. It follows that when Parliament legislates in a manner which is wholly irreconcilable with directly effective EU law, it is not open to a court to hold that Parliament has chosen to exercise its sovereignty by derogating from the presumption that it intends to legislate consistently with EU law (unless perhaps Parliament says as much in express terms). Wade is therefore correct to say that *Factortame* involved "much more than an exercise in construction".[167]

Secondly, it may be argued that this school is best understood as an application of the "new view" of sovereignty, as articulated by commentators such as Heuston and Jennings.[168] Writers who are associated with the first model tend to hold that no amount of express language can render a statute enforceable if it is inconsistent with directly effective EU law.[169] In contrast, proponents of the second approach are willing to accept that Parliament may derogate from EU law provided that it explicitly states its intention to do so.[170] This fits readily into the "new view": Parliament is still substantively capable of legislating on all matters, but must use a particular form of words if it wishes to enact legislation which contradicts directly effective European Union law.

---

[165] Wade, above n. 160, at 568–9, paraphrasing, in part, Craig, above n. 159, at 251 ff.

[166] See *Waddington v. Miah* [1974] 1 WLR 683.

[167] H W R Wade, "Sovereignty—Revolution or Evolution?" (1996) 112 *LQR* 568 at 570.

[168] See above at 49–56.

[169] Wade, above n. 167, at 570–1.

[170] See, *e.g.*, T C Hartley, *The Foundations of European Community Law* (Oxford: Oxford University Press, 1998) at 255: "Community law will always prevail [over inconsistent primary legislation] unless Parliament clearly and expressly states in a future Act that the latter is to override Community law". This view derives support from the judgment of Lord Denning MR in *Macarthys Ltd. v. Smith* [1979] 3 All ER 325 at 329: "If the time should come when our Parliament deliberately passes an Act with the intention of . . . acting inconsistently with [EU law] . . . and says so in express terms then I should have thought that it would be the duty of our courts to follow the statute of our Parliament".

Consequently, the impact of EU law on parliamentary sovereignty may be rationalised in one of two ways. On the one hand, it is viewed as having introduced a substantive fetter which precludes Parliament from transgressing directly effective EU law (either by a revolution which gives rise to a new ultimate constitutional principle, or by an evolutionary change in the political morality which legitimates and demarcates parliamentary competence). On the other hand, the European Communities Act 1972 is seen as changing the rule which specifies the form which legislation must take if it is to be effective in spite of inconsistent EU provisions; on this view, no substantive limitation on parliamentary authority is envisaged.

2.7.2. *The justification of judicial review*

The foregoing analysis places us in a position to evaluate what impact, if any, EU membership has on the argument that the ultra vires doctrine is the only means by which to justify judicial review. Importantly, there exist a number of differences between the limitations on parliamentary competence implied by EU membership and the limitations which anti-sovereignty theorists contend for.

In the first place, the limitation entailed by EU membership is different in nature from that which the critics of sovereignty envisage. For example, it is central to Woolf's argument that it is wholly beyond Parliament's competence to abolish review: this represents an absolute and immovable perimeter of legislative power. However, for a number of reasons the same cannot be said of the limit which EU membership entails. First, it is a limit which Parliament *voluntarily* accepted;[171] in contrast, the limits which critics of sovereignty envisage are categorically imposed on Parliament involuntarily. Secondly, it may be that the limitations on Parliament's competence which membership of the Communities involves can be *circumvented*, provided that Parliament explicitly states its intention to legislate in contravention of EU law. Thirdly, the impairment of sovereignty which follows from EU membership is *reversible*: it is widely accepted that Parliament is competent to repeal the European Communities Act 1972, restoring its full sovereignty in the process. In this sense, Parliament retains its ultimate sovereignty even during British membership of the Union.[172]

However, for present purposes, the real interest lies not in the *nature* of the limitation implied by EU membership but, rather, in the *substance* of that limitation. It is suggested above that the argument concerning the necessity of ultra vires theory can hold true even if it is acknowledged that Parliament is not sovereign in the orthodox sense. Provided that it remains within Parliament's competence to confer decision-making power either subject to or free from an

---

[171] R v. *Secretary of State for Transport, ex parte Factortame (No. 2)* [1991] 1 AC 603 at 659, *per* Lord Bridge.
[172] See, *e.g.*, H W R Wade, "Sovereignty—Revolution or Evolution?" (1996) 112 *LQR* 568 at 573–4.

obligation to abide by the principles of good administration, the requirement that administrators must act consistently with those principles must be rationalised by reference to the legislative scheme (assuming, for the time being, that the concepts of intra vires and ultra vires are mutually exclusive and collectively exhaustive). The discussion, above, of contemporary critiques of parliamentary sovereignty concluded that those critiques do not envisage the limitation of legislative competence on a scale sufficient to remove from Parliament the authority to confer decision-making powers free from an obligation to act consistently with the principles of judicial review. In other words, the principles of good administration are not (or, at least, have not yet become) part of the definition of Parliament's competence.

Against this background it is clear that, for present purposes, there arises only one significant issue *vis-à-vis* EU law—*viz.* whether the modification of the sovereignty principle which membership of the EU involves impacts upon Parliament's freedom to choose, when it confers decision-making power, whether or not to attach an obligation requiring the administrator to act consistently with the principles of good administration. If EU membership leaves Parliament's freedom to make that choice fully intact, then it has no bearing on the ultra vires debate. Contrariwise, if EU law makes such inroads into Parliament's authority as to preclude it from conferring decision-making powers free from an obligation to adhere to the principles of good administration, then the contention of ultra vires theory—that those principles apply because Parliament intends (that is, chooses) that they should apply—is clearly challenged.

It is evident that, in the majority of situations, EU membership has no impact whatsoever on Parliament's freedom to choose whether the decision-making powers which it confers should be accompanied by an obligation to adhere to the principles of good administration. This follows because EU law constrains Parliament's legislative autonomy only in those fields in which, in the first place, EU law operates. Consequently, when Parliament creates decision-making powers in which EU law has no voice—and in which, therefore, Parliament's legislative authority is unconstrained by EU law—it remains free to decide whether to limit the agency's power by reference to the principles of good administration.

The more difficult question, however, concerns situations in which Parliament creates discretionary powers in areas which are governed by EU law. An example may help to clarify the issues which are at stake in this area. Assume that Parliament creates a decision-making power pursuant to an obligation imposed upon the United Kingdom by EU law. Ultra vires theory holds that in normal circumstances (that is, in areas in which EU law does *not* operate) the perimeter of that power is set by reference to Parliament's intention (as determined by the courts pursuant to the process of statutory construction). This follows because Parliament is free to create any power which it chooses and can attach as many or as few limits to that power as it wishes. However, if the decision-making power under consideration was created pursuant to EU law, then EU law enjoys primacy and the position is rather different. In this situation, the scope of the power falls to be determined by reference both to Parliament's intention and EU law: crucially, if Parliament is found to have intended to confer a power whose scope would be inconsistent with EU law, then EU law prevails.

The implications of this for ultra vires theory become apparent once the substantive content of EU law is taken into account. The European Court of Justice has articulated a number of general principles of EU law which are of particular relevance to the present discussion.[173] For instance, it has set out a doctrine of fundamental human rights, based on the constitutional traditions of Member States[174] and on the international conventions—most notably the European Convention on Human Rights—to which they are parties,[175] and has held those human rights norms to be binding not only on the Community institutions but also on the Member States when they act in areas governed by EU law.[176] The Court has similarly embraced (*inter alia*) the doctrines of proportionality[177] and legitimate expectation.[178]

Given that Member State action is constrained by these general principles when they act pursuant to EU law, it must follow that it is impossible for Parliament, when creating discretionary powers in such areas, to confer upon administrators the authority to act inconsistently with those principles.[179] Consequently, when a domestic court reviews the legality of administrative action committed pursuant to such a power, at least some of the limits which it enforces (that is, those which derive from general principles of EU law) do not apply because Parliament chose or intended that that should be so but, rather, because EU law precluded Parliament from conferring discretionary power free from an obligation, incumbent upon the donee, to respect those principles.

---

[173] See generally T Tridimas, *The General Principles of EC Law* (Oxford: Oxford University Press, 1999).

[174] See, *e.g.*, Case 4/73, *Nold KG v. Commission of the European Communities* [1974] ECR 491.

[175] See, *e.g.*, Case 36/75, *Rutili v. Minister for the Interior* [1975] ECR 1219. The special relevance of the ECHR is recognised by Art. 6(2) of the Treaty on European Union.

[176] See, *e.g.*, Case 249/86, *Commission of the European Communities v. Germany* [1989] ECR 1263, and Art. 46 of the Treaty of Amsterdam which made Art. 6(2) of the Treaty on European Union (see above, n. 175) justiciable. It follows that, in areas within the scope of EU law, the Member States are unable to derogate from the ECHR rights; to that extent, the protection conferred upon the ECHR rights by EU law is stronger than that which the Human Rights Act 1998 supplies (given that the latter permits derogation in situations where primary legislation is inconsistent with the ECHR). On the Human Rights Act, see further below at 200–2.

[177] The EU institutions are required to respect the principle of proportionality (see, *e.g.*, Case 114/76, *Bela-Mühle Josef Bergman KG v. Grows-Farm GmbH* [1977] ECR 1211), as are Member States (for a well-known example see Case 120/78, *Rewe Zentrale v. Bundesmonopolverwaltung für Branntwein* [1979] ECR 649 ("*Cassis de Dijon*")).

[178] See, *e.g.*, Case 120/86, *Mulder v. Minister van Landbouw en Visserij* [1988] ECR 2321.

[179] Note, however, that the general principles of EU law do not bite on Member States' legislative or administrative competence in all situations when their action impacts upon EU affairs. Rather, the general principles constrain the Member States only when they act *pursuant to* EU law (*e.g.* when national measures are adopted in order to implement a directive). See *R v. Ministry of Agriculture, Fisheries and Food, ex parte First City Trading Ltd.* [1997] 1 CMLR 250.

Thus, in those areas in which Parliament's competence is constrained by EU law, the ambit of the administrative discretions which it confers is a function not simply of parliamentary intention, but also of parliamentary competence. In conceptual terms, the position is precisely the same as it is under ultra vires theory, so that the central principle in play is that the administrator may not validly act beyond the powers conferred upon it.[180] Crucially, however, when it acts pursuant to EU law, Parliament is, in the first place, incapable of conferring discretionary power free from an obligation to adhere to the general principles of EU law. Nothing prevents the imposition of intention-based limits which provide for more rigorous requirements of fairness and so on upon the administrator; but the general principles of EU law demarcate a minimum level of administrative justice from which no amount of parliamentary intention can justify administrative derogation.

Two points can be made in conclusion. First, this analysis provides the common law theory of judicial review with no support. The limitations to which administrators are subject as a result of the impact of EU law take effect as automatic constraints on the power which is legislatively conferred upon them: there is therefore no scope for arguing that such limits are supplied by the common law.

Secondly, and most significantly for present purposes, the foregoing analysis concerning EU law does not bear upon the argument advanced in this book concerning the general importance of ultra vires theory. The supremacy of EU law simply means that, when Parliament creates discretionary powers in areas where its legislative freedom is attenuated by operation of EU law, some of the limits to which administrators are subject are rationalised by recourse to the scope of Parliament's competence, rather than to its intention. However, this does nothing to displace the argument, advanced in the rest of this chapter, that the ultra vires doctrine is needed to justify judicial review of discretionary powers created by Parliament in fields where it remains free to choose whether to require decision-makers to adhere to the principles of good administration.[181] Consequently, the implications of EU membership, properly understood, are entirely of a piece with the argument advanced in this book—that ultra vires theory is necessary, as the juridical foundation of judicial review, so long as, and in those contexts in which, Parliament's law-making authority is free from relevant limitations.

---

[180] The fact that the illegality of the administrative action depends, at a conceptual level, on the administrator having exceeded the scope of its conferred power is of potentially substantial practical importance. The reasons for this are explored below at 145–61.

[181] Parliament remains free to do so (that is, it is unconstrained by the general principles of EU law) in all situations in which it does not act *pursuant to* EU law: see above at 85, n. 179.

3. LEGISLATION AND THE SCOPE OF DISCRETIONARY POWER

3.1. Introduction

It was explained above that the argument concerning the constitutional necessity of ultra vires theory turns on the correctness of *two* propositions: that
Parliament is sovereign (or that it is not sovereign but that its competence is
not so fettered as to render it unable to interfere with the operation of the principles of good administration) and that the notions of ultra vires and intra vires
are collectively exhaustive and mutually exclusive concepts. Provided that both
of these conditions are satisfied, it follows that the courts' endeavour in judicial review cases must be confined to the identification of administrative action
which is ultra vires; interference with any other action (which, according to the
second proposition, *must* be intra vires) would contravene the legislative
scheme (which, according to the first proposition, would be constitutionally
anathema).

It has already been argued that the first proposition is correct—that either the
British constitution ascribes to Parliament a full sovereignty in the traditional
Diceyan sense or that, even if Parliament's power is constrained by a higher
political morality, the conception of democracy which forms that morality is
sufficiently bare to leave Parliament's competence to interfere with the supervisory jurisdiction[182] intact.

It is the correctness of the second proposition—that administrative action
must be either ultra vires or intra vires—which now falls to be considered. In
doing so, it is logical to begin with the work of Sir John Laws. He is alone among
the critics of ultra vires directly to address this central issue. The essence of
Laws's critique is apparent from the following excerpt from one of his many
illuminating contributions to the debate concerning the role and foundations of
modern public law:

> I think . . . [Forsyth's] reasoning as to the "analytical consequences" of the abandon-
> ment of ultra vires is faulty. I do not accept that "what an all powerful Parliament does
> not prohibit, it must authorise expressly or impliedly" . . . The absence of a legislative
> prohibition does not entail a legislative permission . . . Forsyth's argument is vitiated
> by an implicit mistake: the mistake of assuming that because Parliament can authorise
> or prohibit anything, all authorities and prohibitions must come from Parliament. It
> is a *non sequitur*. It neglects what the logicians call the "undistributed middle"—an
> obscure, but useful, academic expression, meaning that although X and Y may be
> opposites, like praise and blame, they do not cover the whole field; there might be Z,
> which involves neither. Thus Forsyth mistakes the nature of legislative supremacy,
> which is trumps not all four suits; specific, not wall-to-wall. How could it be other-
> wise? A legislature makes and unmakes laws when it thinks it needs to; the fact that in

---

[182] And, for that matter, broader human rights norms.

England the common law allows it to make or unmake any law it likes confers upon it no metaphysic of universality.[183]

It is important, at the outset, to understand the implications of this argument. If it were accepted, then four highly significant consequences would follow.

First, the foregoing discussion of sovereignty would become irrelevant. The thrust of the argument in favour of ultra vires is that, if a decision-maker can act only ultra vires or intra vires, and if it is constitutionally impossible for the courts to challenge that which lies intra vires, ultra vires methodology is demonstrably crucial. However, Laws's argument suggests that administrative action need not be ultra vires or intra vires: it may occupy an innominate middle ground which Parliament has not covered. It would follow from this that the question, considered above, whether it is constitutionally possible for the courts to act incompatibly with the will of Parliament would be beside the point, for in respect of judicial review there would exist no relevant legislative provision capable of either effectuation or contradiction by the judges.

Secondly, this would clear the way for a radical approach to the justification of review.[184] Laws's "undistributed middle" would open up a vacuum which the common law could legitimately fill by supplying a set of principles of good administration wholly unrelated to legislative intention. An autonomous theory of review could thus be articulated without any need to explain it by reference to the will of Parliament.

Thirdly, it would be imperative, not merely possible, to adopt a radical solution to the justification of review: if it is assumed that there exists an "undistributed middle", then the limits of administrative competence cannot be conceptualised as reflections of the perimeter of the power conferred by Parliament quite simply because, in the first place, Parliament is taken not to have—explicitly or implicitly—erected any such perimeter.

Fourthly, Laws's approach appears to give the courts considerable freedom in determining how administrative power should be limited. It was seen above that, even if the principles of good administration were part of the definition of Parliament's competence, this would not give the courts a free hand: rather, it would shift the focus of judicial analysis from Parliament's intention to the limits of its competence. Contrariwise, on Laws's view, the courts acquire an apparently unfettered discretion to determine what limits should be imposed on the administrative process. Thus, whereas challenging parliamentary sovereignty merely shifts the basis of review from the limits prescribed by legislative intention to those which are ordained by legislative incapacity, an approach based on the absence of parliamentary intention clears the way for a wholly autonomous set of common law principles of review, in favour of which the crit-

---

[183] Sir John Laws, "Illegality: The Problem of Jurisdiction" in M Supperstone and J Goudie (eds.), *Judicial Review* (London: Butterworths, 1997) at 4.17–4.18.

[184] It will be recalled that a "radical" approach is one which divorces the justification for review from the notion of judicial enforcement of legislation. See above Ch. 2.

ics of ultra vires have long agitated. This explodes the myth[185] that the common law approach is *inherently* more determinate than the ultra vires doctrine. Saying that the common law is the basis of judicial review tells us nothing *in itself* about the normative values which are thereby vindicated.[186]

It therefore becomes apparent that attacking this second element of the argument in favour of ultra vires has profound consequences. The nature of that challenge must therefore be carefully evaluated.

3.2. The Nature and Consequences of Parliamentary Sovereignty

For Forsyth, the proposition that "what an all powerful Parliament does not prohibit, it must permit either expressly or impliedly" dictates the logical necessity of relating judicial review to the enabling legislation.[187] The first ground on which Laws challenges this argument is founded on the suggestion that Forsyth misconceives the nature and consequences of parliamentary sovereignty. It is said that his statement can be reduced to the bald proposition that "because Parliament can authorise or prohibit anything, all authorities and prohibitions must come from Parliament".[188] Thus, says Laws, Forsyth presents a wholly inaccurate, "wall-to-wall" view of sovereignty.

If this were a faithful representation of Forsyth's view, Laws would be right to condemn it. If all prohibitions really had to come from Parliament, then it would not even be constitutionally possible for the courts to impose such classic common law requirements as the duty to take care to avoid harming one's neighbour: the legitimacy of the common law itself would thus be undermined within any model which postulated Parliament as the sole source of law within the constitutional order. Such a view of sovereignty would therefore manifestly fail to accord with the reality of the British legal system.

However, in truth, the consequences of sovereignty which Forsyth identifies are much more modest. It is no part of his argument that all authorities and prohibitions must derive from legislation. By stating that "what an all powerful Parliament does not prohibit, it must authorise expressly or impliedly", he simply asserts that, once *Parliament* has created a power, the limits which the *courts* impose on that power must logically either coincide with or cut across the scope of the power which Parliament, as a matter of empirical fact, conferred. That

---

[185] See, *e.g.*, P P Craig, "Ultra Vires and the Foundations and Judicial Review" (1998) 57 *CLJ* 63 at 66–7.

[186] The same is, of course, true of the contrary proposition that ultra vires is the foundation of judicial review. For precisely that reason it is argued, in Ch. 4 below, that it is necessary to look to the constitutional setting within which the ultra vires doctrine subsists in order to determine the substantive content of the judicial controls whose conceptual foundation the ultra vires principle supplies. But this does not displace the argument being made here that to expound the "common law" as the basis of review is, in itself, a statement which is normatively barren.

[187] C F Forsyth, "Of Fig Leaves and Fairy Tales: The Ultra Vires Doctrine, the Sovereignty of Parliament and Judicial Review" (1996) 55 *CLJ* 122 at 133.

[188] Laws, above n. 183, at 4.17–4.18.

Forsyth's assertion is thus limited is clear from his explanation that "if Parliament grants a power to a minister, that minister either acts within those powers or outside those powers. There is no grey area between authorisation and prohibition or between empowerment and the denial of power."[189]

An analogy, drawn from the law of the European Union, may help to illustrate the point. It is a central principle of EU law that, once the EU has adopted a regulation in relation to a particular matter, it is no longer open to Member States to legislate on the same topic. Professor Weatherill explains the principle in the following terms:

> Under the "classic" preemption doctrine, once the Community legislates in a field, it occupies that field, thereby precluding Member State action. The Community has assumed exclusive competence in the field.[190]

Thus the European Court of Justice has held that:

> there can be no question . . . that the States may . . . take measures the purpose of which is to amend [a regulation's] scope or to add to its provisions. In so far as the Member States have conferred on the Community legislative powers . . . they no longer have the power to issue independent provisions in [the relevant] field.[191]

Hence, once the EU has validly enacted legislation in the form of a regulation (which is, of course, a supreme form of law in all Member States), national legislatures cannot interfere in the sphere which the regulation concerns. No-one would suggest that this means that the Community legislature enjoys "wall-to-wall" competence in the sense that "all authorities and prohibitions" must come from it. On the contrary, it is usually open to Member States to enact their own legislation until such time as the EU "occupies the field". However, once the European Union has enacted a regulation, it is no longer open to national legislatures to enact laws in the same area.

This is precisely the approach which Forsyth envisages as regards the sovereignty of the United Kingdom Parliament. Thus—as Chapter 5 explains—in the absence of a statutory framework, it is for the courts, by imposing common law requirements of rationality and fairness, to regulate the use of *de facto* governmental power. However, once *de facto* power is replaced with statutory power, regulated by a statutory framework, any limits which the courts subsequently impose on the use of such power through judicial review must relate to the scope of the power which Parliament granted. Once Parliament has "occupied the field", it is improper for the courts to use the common law to impose limits on the power concerned which differ from those which inhere in the grant of power itself, just as the constitutional order of the EU prevents national legislatures

[189] Forsyth, above n. 187, at 133.
[190] S Weatherill, "Beyond Preemption? Shared Competence and Constitutional Change in the European Community" in D O'Keeffe and P M Twomey (eds.), *Legal Issues of the Maastricht Treaty* (London: Chancery Law, 1994) at 16.
[191] Case 74/69, *Hauptzollamt Bremen-Freihafen* v. *Waren-Import-Gesellschaft Krohn and Co.* [1970] ECR 451 at 459.

from invoking domestic law to modify the scope of regulations adopted by the Union.

Neither of these propositions ascribes a "wall-to-wall" sovereignty to the legislature concerned, in the sense that "all authorities and prohibitions must come from" that legislature. The position is more subtle. Properly understood, Forsyth's approach holds that, once Parliament has occupied the field by creating an administrative competence, no legitimate opportunity exists for the common law to impose independent limits on that power since, logically, the limits of such a power must consist in the perimeter of the competence which Parliament actually conferred.

3.3. The "Undistributed Middle"

3.3.1. The nature of the argument

Laws's first criticism of the argument in favour of ultra vires, considered above, incorrectly asserts that it is externally unworkable—that it fails to fit with the way in which we think about the constitutional order. His second criticism relates to the internal operation of the ultra vires doctrine. Laws contends that those who argue in favour of the necessity of ultra vires overlook a crucial point: their argument "neglects what the logicians call the 'undistributed middle'—an obscure, but useful, academic expression, meaning that although X and Y may be opposites, like praise and blame, they do not cover the whole field; there might be Z, which involves neither".[192]

For Laws, the principles of good administration fall into this neutral middle ground: they are a matter about which Parliament is agnostic. Hence, when Parliament grants administrative power, the grant itself is not exhaustive of the conditions which regulate its exercise. While some limits may be related to the legislation (such as those appearing expressly in the enabling provision), it is assumed that, as regards other limitations (*viz.* the principles of good administration), Parliament possesses no intention whatsoever. It is this vacuum—or "undistributed middle"—which creates the opportunity for the common law to intervene and supply duties of good administration. This, it is said, occurs without constitutional impropriety because the common law is not being set up against legislative provision; rather, it is filling a gap where no provision exists.

It is interesting to note that Laws has espoused views which directly contradict this contention:

Any but the crudest society will be ordered, will have, in whatever form, a government. Its citizens will make judgments about the government. The government can no more deny their right to do so, without also denying their nature as free and rational

---

[192] Sir John Laws, "Illegality: The Problem of Jurisdiction" in M Supperstone and J Goudie (eds.), *Judicial Review* (London: Butterworths, 1997) at 4.18.

beings, than it can deny their right to make judgments upon each other. But more than this, the government cannot be *neutral* about free speech. If it is not to be denied, it must be permitted; there is no room for what the logicians would call an undistributed middle . . .[193]

This statement can be reconciled with Laws's later work only if he is understood as arguing that while it is impossible for governments to be neutral about substantive rights such as free speech, it is impossible for legislatures to be anything but neutral about the procedural rights which are enshrined in the principles of good administration. It is hard to see how this follows.

Nevertheless, Laws's argument concerning the "undistributed middle" is important and must be addressed on its own terms. Indeed, it is the only contribution to the debate which has sought to tackle this core part of the ultra vires argument. Before examining Laws's approach to this issue in any detail, however, it is worth noting that two other leading critics of ultra vires theory have, in fact, accepted the core of the ultra vires argument, albeit without acknowledging its implications.

First, Professor David Dyzenhaus concedes that:

In . . . a legal order [which embraced legislative supremacy], it would follow that the only legitimate basis for judicial review of administrative action is something like the ultra vires doctrine, which says that the judges must only enforce those legal limits on administrative action which the legislature intended them to enforce. That is, since the legislature delegated authority to public officials, the limits on their authority are exactly the limits intended in that delegation. For judges to conclude otherwise, for example, by finding limits in common law principles, would amount to an illegitimate arrogation of authority.[194]

This illuminating statement contains two central strands. First, Dyzenhaus clearly accepts that, if Parliament is regarded as sovereign, ultra vires theory must be deployed in order to render judicial review constitutionally workable: any other approach would involve the courts holding unlawful administrative action which was intra vires which, given the sovereignty of the legislature, would amount to "an illegitimate arrogation of authority" by the courts. Secondly, however, Dyzenhaus argues that the logic of this argument need not detain us because, in the United Kingdom, Parliament is not in any event sovereign.

This prompts two remarks. First, Dyzenhaus's conclusion—that Parliament is not sovereign—is an essentially empirical one which, as discussed earlier, conflicts directly with the weight of evidence *vis-à-vis* the United Kingdom Parliament and, in any event, overlooks the argument that ultra vires remains essential even if modest limits on legislative authority are embraced.[195]

[193] Sir John Laws, "Law and Democracy" [1995] *PL* 72 at 84 (original emphasis).
[194] D Dyzenhaus, "Form and Substance in the Rule of Law: A Democratic Justification for Judicial Review" in C F Forsyth (ed.), *Judicial Review and the Constitution* (Oxford: Hart Publishing, 2000) at 153–4.
[195] Dyzenhaus readily acknowledges that his analysis is "relentlessly abstract" (*ibid.*, at 142). However, as C F Forsyth, "Heat and Light: A Plea for Reconciliation" in C F Forsyth (ed.), *Judicial*

Secondly—and, for present purposes, more significantly—Dyzenhaus clearly concedes that, in legal systems which embrace the notion of legislative supremacy, ultra vires theory is constitutionally essential; hence he appears to accept the conceptual argument that ultra vires and intra vires are mutually exclusive and collectively exhaustive notions.

Professor Paul Craig's remarks on this subject are also worth noting. He deals with Forsyth's argument of logic by suggesting that a common law model of review could be legitimated by deploying

> a common law presumption that the common law proscription against the making of vague or unreasonable regulations could be operative, and hence such regulations would be prohibited, unless there was some very clear indication from Parliament to the contrary.[196]

It is important to note that, in this passage, Craig accepts that intention is relevant in two distinct ways.

In the first place, he accepts that parliamentary intention certainly possesses what may be termed *negative relevance*. This means that if Parliament makes sufficiently clear provision—by means, for example, of an adequate preclusive clause—then the operation of the principles of good administration can be excluded within a specific statutory context. That Craig ascribes such a role to intention is unremarkable; other critics of ultra vires theory adopt the same view.

However, it is implicit that, in the foregoing excerpt, Craig also attributes a second, *positive relevance* to legislative intention. He argues that, by deploying a "common law presumption", it is possible to conclude that Parliament permits the principles of good administration to operate. The use of the words *common law* must not be allowed to obscure the fact that it is, self-evidently, a presumption about what *Parliament* intends. This reasoning clearly ascribes to legislative intention a positive relevance, by conceding that the operation of judge-made (or "common law") principles of good administration is legitimate only if Parliament is taken to permit this.

Consequently, Craig clearly attaches both positive and negative relevance to parliamentary intention: the courts are justified in enforcing limits on statutory power because Parliament is presumed to permit the enforcement of such limits (positive relevance), unless this presumption is displaced by sufficiently clear contrary provision (negative relevance). Professor Craig therefore appears to accept that there must exist some form of connection between legislative intention and the law of judicial review, such that intention serves an active, legitimating function, not merely a residual, prohibitive function. Thus Craig seems to acknowledge the logic which underpins the argument in favour of ultra vires,

Review and the Constitution (Oxford: Hart Publishing, 2000) at 404–5 comments, the real challenge is to fashion a justification for judicial review given the constraints of the British constitutional order, rather than to develop an abstract theory which ignores the realities of that framework.

[196] P P Craig, "Ultra Vires and the Foundations of Judicial Review" (1998) 57 *CLJ* 63 at 74.

and his rejection of the language of ultra vires therefore appears to be a largely semantic objection. It is true that, in his most recent contribution to the ultra vires debate, Craig departs from this view and asserts that legislative intention is relevant only in a negative, prohibiting sense, rather than a positive, legitimating sense.[197] However, that assertion is unaccompanied by any explanation of the reasons underlying his change of position.

We thus reach the position that two leading critics of ultra vires theory have accepted—Professor Dyzenhaus in clear terms, and Professor Craig rather more equivocally, given the inconsistency between his two main contributions on this point—the logical argument in favour of retaining that principle so long as Parliament is regarded as sovereign. Sir John Laws, in contrast, has not accepted the force of that argument, and it is to his critique that we now return.

At a superficial level, Laws's approach to the ultra vires question is attractive. For the reasons set out above,[198] it permits the implication-based ultra vires principle to be replaced by a straightforward set of common law rules of good administration, and allows open acknowledgment of the judiciary's enormous contribution to the development of those rules. However, the common law model is not without problems. They can be separated into two categories.

3.3.2. Considerations of abstract logic

It is not at all clear that Laws is correct, as a matter of logic, to assert that there can exist an "undistributed middle" in the present context. His conclusion that such a phenomenon exists appears to follow from his belief that the opposite conclusion would have to be founded on a misconceived "wall-to-wall" view of sovereignty. It has already been explained that this is not so.

The argument is not that "all authorities and prohibitions" must come from Parliament. Rather, the contention is simply that *once Parliament has created a power*, it must either include or omit the competence, for example, to adopt an unfair decision-making procedure. This follows as a matter of logic. A statutory provision which confers administrative competence or discretion is, in effect, conferring on an official the *power* to do something. By definition, therefore, the statute is empowering the official to make a decision which he would not otherwise be legally able to make, or to procure an outcome which he would not otherwise be legally capable of securing. If the position were otherwise, the grant of "power" would be otiose. Given that the legislation is conferring upon the administrator the power to do that which he would not otherwise be able to do, it must follow *a priori* that the things which he is newly empowered to do must be determined by reference to the statute: the legislative provision creates the competence and therefore must, conceptually, mark the limits of that competence.

---

[197] P P Craig, "Competing Models of Judicial Review" in C F Forsyth (ed.), *Judicial Review and the Constitution* (Oxford: Hart Publishing, 2000) at 381–4.

[198] At 88–9.

Consequently, any decision-maker exercising (or purporting to exercise) a statutory discretion must act either within or beyond the scope of the power created by the legislation. It follows from this that the notions of ultra vires and intra vires are mutually exclusive and collectively exhaustive: it is impossible to be *both* within the power granted by Parliament and outside it, yet one must be *either* inside or beyond the power which was actually conferred. "It is like pregnancy, you either are pregnant or you are not, or like a light switch which is either on or off."[199]

This is not to deny that it is for the courts, through the forensic process, to determine precisely where the dividing line lies between intra vires and ultra vires executive action. The argument is simply that, for reasons already given, when the courts undertake this task, they must be viewed in conceptual terms as determining the perimeter of the power conferred, rather than imposing autonomous common law limits which bear no relation to the scope of the power which Parliament created.

There is thus a strong case for concluding that the conceptual argument which lies at the heart of the defence of ultra vires theory is correct, such that administrative action taken under statutory power must logically fall either within or outside the scope of the competence actually conferred. It follows from this, given the constitutional status of legislation, that an explanation must be provided which connects judicial review with legislative intention. In light of the patent shortcomings of the traditional ultra vires doctrine, it therefore becomes necessary to articulate a more realistic relationship between intention and review; this task is undertaken in Chapter 4.

3.3.3. *Considerations of constitutional logic and pragmatism*

Even if the foregoing analysis is disputed, such that it is felt that an "undistributed middle" *may* exist in the manner which Laws suggests, this does not advance the common law theorists' argument very far. Accepting this contention merely means that it is theoretically *possible* that there may exist an "undistributed middle" in the present context. It does not determine that Parliament *must* be deemed to be agnostic about the operation of the principles of administrative law. Rather, it gives rise to a *choice*: either Parliament is presumed to be neutral, in which case the common law can legitimately regulate decision-making, or it is presumed that there is some connection between the legislative framework and the principles of good administration. It will be argued in the following chapter that there exists—quite independently of the argument of pure logic considered in this chapter—a rich set of reasons, founded in constitutional pragmatism and constitutional logic, which militates in favour of the latter approach.

---

[199] C F Forsyth, "Heat and Light: A Plea for Reconciliation" in C F Forsyth (ed.), *Judicial Review and the Constitution* (Oxford: Hart Publishing, 2000) at 402.

4. CONCLUSION

The purpose of this chapter has been to begin exploring the question whether the juridical basis of the supervisory jurisdiction should embrace a connection between intention and review.

The better view, it is suggested, is that, so long as Parliament remains capable of choosing whether the principles of judicial review should be operative, the necessity of connecting review with enabling legislation and the intention which underlies it arises as a matter of pure logic. The decision-maker necessarily acts either within or beyond his conferred powers, so that constitutional propriety precludes the courts, on review, from doing anything other than determining whether executive action is intra vires or ultra vires. This is a strong argument, and it is one which has not been satisfactorily rebutted by the critics of ultra vires.

Alternatively, it may be thought that Laws makes a valid point, such that a common law approach to review can be legitimated by invoking the idea of an "undistributed middle". It then becomes necessary to determine whether such an approach should be preferred over one which embraces a connection between legislation and review. This requires recourse to arguments which engage broader matters than abstract logic. These issues will be addressed in Chapter 4, where it will be argued that even if the necessity of a vires-based approach is not accepted on *a priori* grounds wider considerations of constitutional logic and pragmatism point towards the adoption of such a model.

4

The Modified Ultra Vires Principle

1. INTRODUCTION

IT WAS ARGUED in the previous chapter that, in order to build a satisfactory basis for judicial review of statutory power, some connection must be retained between the principles of good administration which courts of public law jurisdiction enforce and the express and implied provisions of the legislation which creates discretionary power. For this reason it was contended that the common law model of review, according to which the principles of good administration are autonomous constructs which take effect independently of the legislative scheme, is constitutionally unworkable. However, as Chapter 2 explained, the traditional ultra vires doctrine—which postulates a direct connection between judicial review and legislative intention, thereby characterising the former as nothing more than curial implementation of the latter—is in many respects unconvincing and unsatisfactory.

The challenge, therefore, is to articulate a model of judicial review which is both convincing, in the sense that it provides a satisfactory account of the derivation and operation of the principles of review, and constitutionally workable, in that it supplies a conceptual basis for administrative law which is consistent with the constitutional order generally and the principle of legislative supremacy in particular. Thus, to adopt the terminology adopted in Chapter 2, it is necessary to develop a juridical basis for judicial review which at once enjoys both internal and structural coherence.[1]

This task is undertaken in three principal stages. First, in sections 2 and 3 of this chapter, the *modified ultra vires principle* is developed. This constitutes an attempt to articulate a theory of review which postulates a realistic connection between enabling legislation and the principles of good administration, and which therefore satisfies the dual imperatives of internal and structural coherence. Secondly, it is argued in section 4 that the modified ultra vires principle avoids the shortcomings of the traditional ultra vires model—that, in other words, it succeeds where the traditional model fails by securing an internally coherent account of the basis of judicial review. Finally, in section 5, it is contended that, for a series of theoretical and pragmatic reasons, the modified ultra

---

[1] The meaning of these terms is set out in greater detail above at 23–7.

vires principle is to be preferred over the common law theory as the juridical basis of review of statutory power.[2]

2. JUDICIAL REVIEW AND THE RULE OF LAW

2.1. Introduction

Christopher Forsyth's rationalisation of the constitutional basis of judicial review was considered at length in Chapter 3.[3] The relationship which he envisages between legislative intention and judicial review is certainly a good deal less artificial than the direct connection which the traditional ultra vires doctrine postulates. Specifically, he argues that the development of the principles of modern administrative law "took place against the background of a sovereign legislature that could have intervened at any moment" but which generally chose not to.[4] Parliament must therefore be taken tacitly to have approved the fashioning of broad grounds of review. Hence legislative intention is relevant not because it can be divined and turned into specific principles of review, but because "the legislature is taken to have granted an imprimatur to the judges to develop the law" themselves.[5]

This analysis is to be welcomed to the extent that it provides an alternative to the unconvincing dogma of the traditional ultra vires doctrine, which postulates a more simplistic framework within which the courts merely identify and enforce those unwritten limits on discretionary power which Parliament is taken to have intended. Nevertheless, Forsyth's account does not provide a complete explanation. In particular, acknowledging that the detailed grounds of review are judge-made against a background of legislative acquiescence does not illuminate *why* the courts have developed the principles of good administration in the particular manner which they have adopted.

It is helpful to approach this matter by reference to the shortcomings of the orthodox ultra vires doctrine identified in Chapter 2. In advancing his theory of tacit legislative acquiescence, Forsyth seeks to circumvent the fiction—perpetuated by the orthodox ultra vires account—that the complex law of judicial

---

[2] It will be recalled that in Ch. 3 it was suggested that there exists a compelling reason for preferring an approach based on ultra vires methodology over the common law model. This concerned the argument that the latter, unlike the former, cannot be reconciled with the constitutional framework given that ultra vires and intra vires are collectively exhaustive and mutually exclusive concepts and that, at the present stage of the evolution of the British constitution, it is improper for the courts to hold unlawful that which is intra vires. This argument in favour of a vires-based approach, and against an autonomous common law basis of judicial review, rests on considerations of abstract logic and constitutional theory. In contrast, the factors advanced in section 5, below, are more pragmatic in nature, and complement the conceptual argument set out in Ch. 3.

[3] For an overview of Forsyth's thesis see above at 37–42.

[4] C F Forsyth, "Of Fig Leaves and Fairy Tales: The Ultra Vires Doctrine, the Sovereignty of Parliament and Judicial Review" (1996) 55 *CLJ* 122 at 135.

[5] *Ibid.*

review can be related directly to parliamentary intention. In Chapter 2, this difficulty was termed the problem of *passive artificiality*, and arguably represents the most substantial shortcoming of the traditional ultra vires doctrine. By replacing judicial enforcement of unwritten legislative intention with judicial creativity against a backdrop of legislative acquiescence, Forsyth succeeds in avoiding the passive artificiality of the orthodox principle. The difficulty, however, is that the problem of *emptiness*—also discussed in Chapter 2—remains: in other words, some explanation is still required of the normative considerations which motivate the courts in developing the law of judicial review given the imprimatur to do so which, within Forsyth's account, they are accorded by Parliament.

It can be argued that a solution to these difficulties lies ready to hand in the form of the rule of law doctrine. As section 2.2 explains, there appears to exist a natural relationship between, on the one hand, the specific legal principles which the courts vindicate by way of judicial review and, on the other hand, the ethos of the rule of law. It is argued below that, by acknowledging this relationship, it is possible to begin to deal with the difficulties which prevent the traditional ultra vires principle from furnishing an adequate juridical account of judicial review. These claims are substantiated in detail below, but it is helpful to set them out briefly at the outset.

First, by acknowledging that the rule of law principle underlies the courts' supervisory endeavour, the *passive artificiality* of ultra vires is circumvented. While it is difficult to perceive the connection postulated by the orthodox ultra vires theory between what is essentially legislative silence and the principles of good administration, the link between the grounds of review and the norms embodied in the rule of law is significantly clearer.[6] Secondly, it was observed in Chapter 2 that the orthodox ultra vires doctrine suffers from the problem of *active artificiality*, given that it seeks to justify judicial review *in terms of* legislative intent while the courts appear to effect review *in spite of* the statutory scheme in cases which involve strong ouster clauses. It is argued below that this problem can be avoided if it is acknowledged that review is about vindicating the rule of law rather than mechanically implementing Parliament's will.[7] Thirdly, by founding judicial review on the rule of law, the *emptiness* of ultra vires can be avoided: open acknowledgment of the role played by the rule of law facilitates appreciation and frank discussion of the normative foundations upon which the judiciary is relying as it fashions the specific legal controls which are applied to decision-makers. These ideas are developed in greater detail below. First, however, it is necessary to consider how, in general terms, it may be possible to relate the law of judicial review to the principle of the rule of law.

---

[6] See below at 100–4.
[7] See below at 121–5.

2.2. Relating Judicial Review to the Rule of Law

The precise content of the rule of law is notoriously controversial. At one extreme it may represent a barren principle of legality which requires nothing more than the adoption of proper procedures in creating legal rules and powers.[8] Conversely, it may be so broad that it constitutes "a complete social philosophy".[9] There is particular disagreement concerning the extent to which the rule of law transcends procedural values by embodying substantive norms.[10] It is beyond the scope of this work to engage in the debate concerning the theoretical nature of the rule of law. The present contention is simply that the principles of good administration which are vindicated through judicial review are based firmly on the rule of law doctrine as it is presently understood within the context of the British constitution.[11] This proposition is uncontroversial because it relies only on a modest view of the rule of law.

The kernel of any conception of the principle is that all claims of governmental power must be justified in law. It is this philosophy which very clearly underpins jurisdictional review in its narrow sense.[12] The importance of ensuring that government cannot arrogate to itself powers which it does not in law possess—action which is fundamentally repugnant to the principle of legality—thus supplies the normative basis on which the courts police the straightforward boundaries of governmental power which are set by enabling legislation.

Few writers, however, countenance a conception of the rule of law which goes no further than this. The British constitution certainly embodies a rule of law doctrine which is substantially broader than the bare principle of legality. In particular, the rule of law not only demands that governmental action should be formally justified by reference to enabling legislation; it also directs that the powers so conferred should not be exercised abusively. More specifically, this means that public power must be exercised in a manner which is fair and reasonable in order that citizens are protected from capricious and arbitrary governmental action. It is clear that, in developing modern administrative law,

---

[8] Few writers, however, envisage such a narrow conception of the rule of law. J Raz, *The Authority of Law* (Oxford: Clarendon Press, 1979), for instance, advocates a modest view of the rule of law, but still conceives of it more broadly than this.

[9] Raz, above n. 8, at 213, criticising this approach. See, *e.g.*, the final resolution of the Delhi Congress of the International Commission of Jurists: the rule of law "should be employed not only to safeguard and advance the civil and political rights of the individual in a free society, but also to establish social, economic, educational and cultural conditions under which his legitimate aspirations and dignity may be realised" (quoted by T R S Allan, *Law, Liberty, and Justice: The Legal Foundations of British Constitutionalism* (Oxford: Clarendon Press, 1993) at 20, n. 3).

[10] For overviews of this debate, see P P Craig, "Formal and Substantive Conceptions of the Rule of Law: An Analytical Framework" [1997] *PL* 467; Sir John Laws, "Illegality: The Problem of Jurisdiction" in M Supperstone and J Goudie (eds.), *Judicial Review* (London: Butterworths, 1997) at 4.30–4.35.

[11] See J Jowell, "The Rule of Law Today" in J Jowell and D Oliver (eds.), *The Changing Constitution* (Oxford: Oxford University Press, 2000) at 17–20.

[12] This form of review is discussed above at 28–9.

British judges have largely drawn upon a conception of the rule of law which is directed more towards the *procedure* by which executive decisions are made than the *substance* of such decisions, although the division between procedural and substantive review is far from clear. The reasons underlying this are discussed in Chapter 6; however, the contention presently being advanced is simply that the procedural norms which the courts currently vindicate on review are clearly based on a modest conception of the rule of law which is an integral element of the British constitutional order.

For example, it is widely accepted that, by requiring administrators to adopt fair procedures, the courts are giving effect to the rule of law. As Allan explains, "The principles of natural justice find a place even within a formal doctrine of the rule of law: the requirements of a fair and open hearing and the absence of bias are recognized as essential for the correct application of the law".[13] Thus Dicey's observation that "wide, arbitrary" powers are anathema to the rule of law indicates that rules are needed which ensure fairness in public decision-making.[14] Similarly, in spite of his narrow view of the doctrine, Raz accepts that the rule of law embodies notions of natural justice and fairness.[15]

Those grounds of review which are directed towards the reasoning process adopted by administrators—such as the prohibitions on taking account of irrelevant considerations[16] and acting for improper purposes[17]—are essentially elaborations of the basic principle that administrators should use the power entrusted to them in a reasonable, as opposed to an arbitrary or capricious, manner. Once again, this reflects a modest conception of the rule of law. It inheres in Dicey's axiom that "arbitrary" power is anathema, and it is also supported by Raz (in spite of his narrow approach) who has argued that the doctrine embodies "the basic idea that the law should be capable of providing effective guidance".[18] Since unpredictability and uncertainty are inevitable products of arbitrary decision-making, curial regulation of the reasoning process is clearly justified by reference even to a modest notion of the rule of law.

Review on the ground of irrationality—or "*Wednesbury* unreasonableness"[19]—also fits comfortably into this approach. Since this form of intervention is concerned with the outcome of the decision-making process, it must rest on a rather broader conception of the rule of law than those grounds which focus on procedure. However, by ensuring that irrationality review lies only in very limited circumstances—and by largely resisting, prior to the activation of the Human Rights Act 1998, the temptation to replace it with a more rigorous

---

[13] T R S Allan, *Law, Liberty, and Justice: The Legal Foundations of British Constitutionalism* (Oxford: Clarendon Press, 1993) at 28.

[14] A V Dicey, *An Introduction to the Study of the Law of the Constitution* (E C S Wade, ed.) (London: Macmillan, 1964) at 188.

[15] J Raz, *The Authority of Law* (Oxford: Clarendon Press, 1979) at 218.

[16] See, *e.g.*, *Roberts* v. *Hopwood* [1925] AC 578.

[17] See, *e.g.*, *Wheeler* v. *Leicester City Council* [1985] AC 1054.

[18] Raz, above n. 15, at 218.

[19] See *Associated Provincial Picture Houses Ltd.* v. *Wednesbury Corporation* [1948] 1 KB 223.

form of substantive review founded on the doctrine of proportionality[20]—the courts have ensured that this head of review can clearly be justified by reference to a conception of the rule of law which is still relatively modest.[21] Thus Professor Jeffrey Jowell comments that the reasonableness doctrine is underpinned by the rule of law because it "is a principle that promotes the virtues of regularity, rationality, and integrity on the part of officials".[22] In this manner, the conception of the rule of law which underlies rationality review is of a piece with that which underpins those grounds that are directed towards fairness and reasonableness in the decision-making process. All of these heads of review rest on the foundational values of the constitution which demand that government should occur in a fair and reasonable, rather than an arbitrary and capricious, way.

Thus it is primarily a concern to give effect to the rule of law and to ensure that government respects the principles which it embodies that provides the inspiration for the exercise of the courts' judicial review jurisdiction. As T R S Allan remarks, "[u]nderstood as a constitutional ideal . . . the rule of law provides the true foundation of judicial review".[23] This proposition has an excellent historical pedigree;[24] and, although Allan remarks that, "[i]n striking contrast to the doctrine of parliamentary sovereignty, it has been the fate of the rule of law to operate *sub silentio*",[25] this position is rapidly changing. Contemporary judicial decisions in the public law sphere clearly demonstrate that the rule of law principle is regarded as central to the existence and development of the judicial review jurisdiction, as modern judges have taken to heart Allan's contention that the rule of law is a "constitutional principle" which "carries the force of law" and which "operates to direct the reasoning and functions of the courts".[26] There are numerous examples in the case law which substantiate this claim. For instance,[27] the rule of law has explicitly influenced the courts in their application of the principle of legal certainty;[28] the adoption of a

---

[20] The relationship between and the constitutional implications of judicial review on irrationality and proportionality grounds is discussed below, ch.6.

[21] See Lord Irvine, "Response to Sir John Laws 1996" [1996] *PL* 636; "Constitutional Change in the United Kingdom: British Solutions to Universal Problems" (the 1998 National Heritage Lecture, delivered at the Supreme Court in Washington DC, USA, March 1998); "Principle and Pragmatism: The Development of English Public Law under the Separation of Powers" (lecture delivered at the High Court in Hong Kong, September 1998).

[22] J Jowell, "The Rule of Law Today" in J Jowell and D Oliver (eds.), *The Changing Constitution* (Oxford: Oxford University Press, 2000) at 20.

[23] T R S Allan, "The Rule of Law as the Foundation of Judicial Review" in C F Forsyth (ed.), *Judicial Review and the Constitution* (Oxford: Hart Publishing, 2000) at 419.

[24] See L L Jaffe and E G Henderson, "Judicial Review and the Rule of Law: Historical Origins" (1956) 72 *LQR* 345.

[25] T R S Allan, "Legislative Supremacy and the Rule of Law: Democracy and Constitutionalism" (1985) 44 *CLJ* 111 at 114.

[26] *Ibid.*

[27] The following examples are highly selective, and could easily be multiplied. They are merely intended to convey a flavour of the manner in which the courts deploy the rule of law as a juristic principle which shapes their decisions and their interpretation of legislation.

[28] See, *e.g.*, *Black-Clawson International Ltd.* v. *Papierwerke Waldhof-Aschaffenburg AG* [1975] AC 591 at 638, *per* Lord Diplock.

robust judicial attitude to the interpretation of preclusive provisions[29] and other measures which appear to inhibit access to the courts;[30] holding ministers liable in contempt[31]; developing the abuse of process doctrine[32]; considering what constitutes "sufficient interest" in order to launch judicial review proceedings;[33] evaluating the legality of the regime for sentencing prisoners,[34] and determining the circumstances in which administrative acts and decisions should be amenable to collateral challenge.[35]

Importantly, it is clear that these are not to be regarded as *ad hoc* examples of judicial invocation of the rule of law in public law cases. Rather, as Lord Steyn has explained, the rule of law is properly to be regarded as an overarching ethos which is fundamental to the broad scheme of English administrative law:

> By the rule of law we primarily mean the principle of legality, *viz.* that every exercise of governmental power must be justified in law. But the rule of law also comprehends in a broad sense a system of principles developed by the courts to ensure that the exercise of executive power is not abused . . . The rule of law has played a vital part in the development of public law [in Britain].[36]

To similar effect, Jowell writes that:

> The Rule of Law . . . disables government from abusing its power . . . Administrative Law is the implementation of the constitutional principle of the Rule of Law . . . The implementation of each of [the various grounds of review] . . . involves the courts in applying different aspects of the Rule of Law.[37]

This ascription to the rule of law of the status of organising principle within the public law domain is echoed by Sir John Laws. He observes that, although the three heads of review—illegality, irrationality and procedural impropriety—

---

[29] See, *e.g., Anisminic Ltd.* v. *Foreign Compensation Commission* [1969] 2 AC 147 (judicial application of "[t]he well established rule that a provision ousting the jurisdiction of the court must be strictly construed . . . [which] derives directly from the rule of law": see Allan, above n. 25, at 126).

[30] See, *e.g., R* v. *Lord Chancellor, ex parte Witham* [1998] QB 575.

[31] See, *e.g., In re M* [1994] 1 AC 377 at 425–6, *per* Lord Woolf: "the object of the exercise [of holding a minister liable for contempt] is not so much to punish an individual as to vindicate the rule of law".

[32] See, *e.g., R* v. *Horseferry Road Magistrates' Court, ex parte Bennett* [1994] 1 AC 42 at 62, *per* Lord Griffiths, and 67, *per* Lord Bridge.

[33] See, *e.g., Inland Revenue Commissioners* v. *National Federation of Self-Employed and Small Businesses Ltd.* [1982] AC 617 at 644, *per* Lord Diplock; *R* v. *Secretary of State for Foreign and Commonwealth Affairs, ex parte World Development Movement Ltd.* [1995] 1 WLR 386 at 395, *per* Rose LJ.

[34] See, *e.g., R* v. *Secretary of State for the Home Department, ex parte Pierson* [1998] AC 539 at 587, *per* Lord Steyn.

[35] See, *e.g., Boddington* v. *British Transport Police* [1999] 2 AC 143. It is particularly clear from the speeches of Lord Irvine LC and Lord Steyn that the rule of law was the driving force behind the decision which the House of Lords reached in this case.

[36] Lord Steyn, "The Weakest and Least Dangerous Department of Government" [1997] *PL* 84 at 86.

[37] J Jowell, "The Rule of Law Today" in J Jowell and D Oliver (eds.), *The Changing Constitution* (Oxford: Clarendon Press, 1994) at 72–3. A similar passage appears in the 4th edn of Jowell and Oliver at 17–18.

classically set out by Lord Diplock in the *GCHQ* case[38] are "the central characteristics of judicial review in action", it is imperative to recognise that "what binds them together is a free-standing principle, which is logically prior to all of them . . . The free-standing principle may be described as the rule of law".[39]

2.3.   Judicial Review, the Rule of Law and Judicial Creativity

Thus there exists a broad consensus that the rule of law is the driving force behind—and the normative basis of—modern administrative law. In light of this—and, in particular, given the way in which the rule of law appears to offer a solution to the shortcomings of the intention-based rationale offered by the traditional ultra vires doctrine—it is clearly necessary to consider how the rule of law may operate as part of a juridical account of the constitutional basis of the supervisory jurisdiction. That task is undertaken in section 3, below, where a modified version of the ultra vires model is developed in order to take account of the central importance of the rule of law. However, before turning to the modified ultra vires principle, it is necessary to enter two caveats concerning the role which the rule of law principle can play in this area.

The first caveat stems from Craig's observation that the rule of law is not sufficiently exact to allow it to determine the precise content of the administrative law principles which the courts enforce.[40] This prompts two responses. On the one hand, the vagueness of the rule of law doctrine, while undeniable, is a somewhat variable phenomenon. The scope for argument over its content is at its greatest when it is considered in abstract, theoretical terms. When it is viewed from the perspective of a particular legal culture, it is possible to ascribe more—although certainly not wholly—precise content to it. In this sense, when it is applied to a particular legal system, the "rule of law" is simply convenient label which describes the fundamental values on which that system is based, albeit that, in order to qualify in the first place for the "rule of law" epithet, those values must be broadly rooted in the normative heritage which the rule of law ethos represents.[41] The argument which the present work advances is that, in effecting judicial review, the courts are seeking to give effect to a body of norms which

---

[38] *Council of Civil Service Unions* v. *Minister for the Civil Service* [1985] AC 374 at 410.

[39] Sir John Laws, "Illegality: The Problem of Jurisdiction" in M Supperstone and J Goudie (eds.), *Judicial Review* (London: Butterworths, 1997) at 4.31.

[40] P P Craig, *Administrative Law* (London: Sweet and Maxwell, 1999) at 25–8.

[41] The same point can be made in relation to the separation of powers principle, which "has been subjected to a multitude of interpretations. No two legal systems which claim adherence to the doctrine have identical institutional arrangements. This is unsurprising. While the separation of powers is based upon certain shared values, the manner in which those values are given practical expression is naturally coloured by the individual traditions of national legal orders". See Lord Irvine, "Principle and Pragmatism: The Development of English Public Law under the Separation of Powers" (lecture delivered at the High Court in Hong Kong, September 1998).

lies at the core of the British legal culture. It is, therefore, that set of norms—and not any abstract notion of the rule of law—which is of central concern.[42]

On the other hand, however, even when the rule of law is located within a particular legal system, it is undeniable that its content remains somewhat uncertain. Therefore, while appreciating the relevance of the rule of law to judicial review, it is also necessary to be clear about what it does *not* achieve. One of the most significant shortcomings of the traditional ultra vires doctrine is its inability to acknowledge that the creative endeavour of the judiciary has contributed fundamentally to the development of modern administrative law. It would be misguided to attempt to replace a strained explanation of review based on mechanical judicial effectuation of legislative will with an equally unconvincing account based on the mechanical implementation of the rule of law, given that the latter clearly does not possess a legal texture which renders it susceptible to such use.

Acknowledging the relevance of the rule of law does not, therefore, require or permit the creativity of the judges to be overlooked or ignored. Indeed, the reverse is true. It is for the judges to turn the general principles embodied in the rule of law into specific legal principles which can be deployed to control governmental action. It is for the judges to determine precisely how the principles of review should apply within the context of specific cases. And it is for the judges to develop administrative law as the unwritten constitution, and the rule of law ethos which it embodies, evolve in response to changes in the broader social and political environments.

The rule of law thus *guides* the courts' exercise and development of the supervisory jurisdiction, in contrast to the ultra vires doctrine which, Craig correctly observes, is incapable of providing any *"ex ante* guidance" on the content of the grounds of review.[43] The rule of law directs the courts' attention to the underlying values on which the polity is based and which have long been reflected in the common law; in this manner, an explanation of review which embraces the relevance of the rule of law is able to furnish the courts with a principled *starting point* in their determination of precisely how governmental power should be controlled. It cannot, for the reasons discussed above, dictate the precise *conclusions* at which the courts should arrive, but it would be misguided to suppose that anything, save the forensic process itself, could be capable of establishing the exact content of the controls which apply to discretionary powers. This view is echoed by Jowell:

> [C]onstitutional principles [such as the rule of law] are not rules. They lack that element of specificity. They are prescriptive in character but indeterminate in content. Their content crystallises over time when concrete problems throw up the need to settle competing claims of power and authority and rights. Judging these claims requires

---

[42] That is not to say, however, that debate concerning the ideal of the rule of law is not important: such discussion serves as a crucial force for pushing forward and refining the conception of the doctrine which obtains in specific legal systems at any given time.

[43] P P Craig, "Ultra Vires and the Foundations of Judicial Review" (1998) 57 *CLJ* 63 at 67.

a strong empirical sense that allows an evaluation, within the bounds of democracy's inherent requirements, of changes in practice and expectations. New principles emerge by a process of accretion reflecting a constitution's changing imperatives and shifting settlements. These are based upon altering notions of the proper scope of governmental power as well as upon other fundamental social values which become endorsed over time.[44]

Thus the rule of law operates, in the present context, as a guide rather than as a precise prescription. It is, however, no less important for that.

A second caveat must also be entered. The purpose of this book is to develop a justification for judicial review which both provides a convincing account of its operation in practice and reconciles it with the constitutional framework.[45] In order to supply such an account, it is necessary to articulate a conceptual structure which permits acknowledgment of the fact that, in developing administrative law, the judges have built upon a rich set of normative constitutional foundations rooted in the rule of law. However, the detailed content—actual or ideal—of those normative values and the specific principles of judicial review to which they give rise are not addressed in the present work. Thus the objective here is not to conduct the debate concerning the content of the norms upon which the courts rely—or ought to rely—in public law adjudication but, rather, to construct a theoretical framework which, in the first place, permits that debate to take place openly.[46] It is with the articulation of such a framework that the following section is concerned.

3. ULTRA VIRES METHODOLOGY IN A CONSTITUTIONAL SETTING

3.1. Introduction

At this point it is worth restating some of the conclusions which have been reached thus far. On the one hand it is self-evident that the traditional ultra vires doctrine's rationalisation of judicial review in terms of the straightforward

---

[44] J Jowell, "Of Vires and Vacuums: The Constitutional Context of Judicial Review" in C F Forsyth (ed.), *Judicial Review and the Constitution* (Oxford: Hart Publishing, 2000) at 335 (footnotes omitted).

[45] In this book, these imperatives are termed *internal coherence* and *structural coherence*. See above at 23–7.

[46] N Bamforth, "Ultra Vires and Institutional Interdependence" in C F Forsyth (ed.), *Judicial Review and the Constitution* (Oxford: Hart Publishing, 2000) at 124 criticises the modified ultra vires principle because it is unaccompanied by a detailed account of any specific version of the rule of law doctrine. This criticism is, however, misplaced and is based on a misapprehension of the purpose of the modified ultra vires theory. Its objective is not to supply the substantive account of the rule of law doctrine which gives rise to judicial review but, rather, to provide a conceptual framework within which the evident contribution of the rule of law principle can be acknowledged in a manner which is consistent with the constitutional order. Once this is appreciated, it becomes clear that to criticise the modified ultra vires principle for not furnishing a detailed account of a specific conception of the rule of law is to criticise it for failing to do that which it does not, in the first place, purport to do.

implementation of legislative intention is wholly unconvincing.[47] On the other hand it is equally clear that a much more natural relationship exists between the legal controls which the courts apply to administrators via the supervisory jurisdiction and the normative constitutional principles which make up the rule of law. In this way it becomes apparent that the courts' endeavour, in judicial review cases, can most readily be explained in terms of the implementation of the rule of law rather than the effectuation of unwritten parliamentary intention.

At first glance this appears to create a substantial difficulty. It was argued in Chapter 2 that judicial review must be legitimated by reference to a justificatory model which possesses two central characteristics: it must be internally coherent, by furnishing a convincing account of the derivation of the grounds of review and the operation of judicial review, but it must also be structurally coherent, in that it must be compatible with the constitutional order generally and the principle of legislative sovereignty in particular. On the basis of the foregoing analysis these dual imperatives appear to pull in opposite directions. The requirement of internal coherence points towards a model of judicial review that is based on the rule of law and which thereby supplies a convincing and open account of the normative principles from which administrative law is derived. However, considerations of structural coherence point towards a different approach in light of the conclusion reached in Chapter 3 that judicial review can be reconciled with the constitutional order only if it is conceptualised in a vires-based, construction-oriented manner.

This analysis reveals the shape which a fully satisfactory justificatory model must take. If both structural and internal coherence are to be secured, it becomes necessary to find a way of characterising the courts' supervisory endeavour in terms which are interpretative, but which also fully acknowledge the normative imperatives, rooted in the constitutional principle of the rule of law, which self-evidently underpin the substance of the modern law of judicial review. The modified ultra vires principle characterises judicial review in precisely those terms. It is centrally concerned with the constitutional setting within which the process of statutory construction occurs, and it is therefore with the notion of interpretation that we begin.

3.2. Statutory Interpretation in Constitutional Context

It is trite, but nevertheless worth stating, that it is impossible to make sense of any text without interpreting it. Individual words acquire real meaning only when they are viewed and interpreted within context. Myriad factors may combine to constitute that context: the other words within the sentence; the other sentences within the paragraph; the purpose of the text as a whole; the identity

---

[47] See above, Ch. 2.

of the author and the expectations which we have of him; the identity of the reader; the social, cultural or political perspective from which he approaches the text, and so on. Thus it is naïve to suppose that any text may have a fixed and settled meaning. Any given meaning which is ascribed to a text is, at least in large measure, a product of the external factors which influence its interpretation: the inherent meaning of the words which combine to form the text merely demarcate the parameters within which a range of specific meanings can be ascribed to that text.

These observations are self-evident, and they apply to legal materials as forcefully as they do to any other type of text. The context within which legal documents—such as legislation—are construed is, accordingly, a composite of many different factors: the purpose of the legislation; the need to make different parts of a statutory scheme fit together coherently; the perspectives of individual judges; the way in which the court as a whole perceives its function, and the social background against which the interpretative process takes place are among the many influences which affect the precise meaning which a court attaches to legislation at any given time.

There can be no clearer illustration of this than the jurisprudence of the Supreme Court of the United States on the constitutionality of racial segregation. As is well known, at one time the Court held that the so-called "separate but equal" policy did not violate the guarantee of equality enshrined in the Fourteenth Amendment to the Constitution.[48] Half a century later, however, in the celebrated case of *Brown* v. *Board of Education of Topeka*,[49] the Supreme Court, under Warren CJ, reached a very different conclusion, holding that racial segregation was indeed unconstitutional. Plainly the text of the Fourteenth Amendment did not change in the years which passed between those two decisions; its meaning, however, altered radically as a result of changes in the broader social context within which constitutional interpretation inevitably occurs.

Although the context within which statutory construction takes place is a complex construct made up of many factors, one of those factors is of particular importance within the field of public law adjudication. The collection of values which are regarded as constitutionally central—and which together compose the rule of law—influences the interpretative process in a fundamental way. Such values constitute the normative bedrock upon which the interpretative process is founded: they supply the starting point—or default perspective—which pervasively colours the meaning which is ascribed to legislation. The importance, at a *conceptual* level, of the rule of law in the public law sphere was considered above; the present point, however, is that the interpretative process is a core mechanism by which the constitutional principle of the rule of law is accorded *practical* expression as a legal—rather than a purely aspirational—construct.

[48] *Plessy v. Ferguson* (1896) 153 US 537.
[49] (1953) 347 US 483.

This approach to interpretation is commonplace, but its basis has been articulated with particular clarity by Lord Steyn:

> Parliament does not legislate in a vacuum. Parliament legislates for a European liberal democracy founded on the principles and traditions of the common law. And the courts may approach legislation on this initial assumption.[50]

Much has traditionally been made of this methodology in relation, for example, to statutory provisions which appear to impact upon personal freedom or proprietary rights. In such areas, the courts habitually—and openly—interpret legislation from the starting point that those values are fundamental, such that legislation must, wherever possible, be interpreted in a manner which is consistent with them. This is not properly to be regarded as a conflict between Parliament and the courts; rather, it reflects a judicial endeavour to give meaning to legislation within a constitutional context which is founded on certain core values. Those norms should not, therefore, be considered as peculiarly judicial constructs which are deployed *against* parliamentary legislation; the better view is that they are pervasive constitutional values which shape the environment within which Parliament enacts legislation and which therefore properly colours the context within which the courts give meaning to statutory texts.

However, although the courts—and commentators—are evidently (and rightly) comfortable with this approach in relation to such matters as the protection of personal liberty and proprietary interests, it receives rather less attention in the sphere of judicial review. Just as the courts' construction of legislation dealing with, say, personal liberty is rationalised in terms of a legislative endeavour that is fundamentally shaped by constitutional principle, so the courts' approach to legislation which creates discretionary powers may be conceptualised as an interpretative process which is normatively premised on those values which make up the rule of law.

Consequently, when Parliament enacts legislation which (typically) confers wide discretionary power and which makes no explicit reference to the controls which should regulate the exercise of the power, the courts are constitutionally entitled—and constitutionally right—to assume that it was Parliament's intention to legislate in conformity with the rule of law principle. This means that Parliament is properly to be regarded as having conferred upon the decision-maker only such power as is consistent with that principle. It follows from this that, in the absence of very clear contrary provision, Parliament must be taken to withhold from decision-makers the power to treat individuals in a manner which offends the rule of law: for this reason, the competence to act unfairly and unreasonably should be assumed to be absent from any parliamentary grant. However, the task of transforming this general intention—that the executive

---

[50] R v. *Secretary of State for the Home Department, ex parte Pierson* [1998] AC 539 at 587. See also *ibid.* at 573–4, *per* Lord Browne-Wilkinson; Lord Steyn, "Incorporation and Devolution: A Few Reflections on the Changing Scene" [1998] *European Human Rights Law Review* 153 at 154–5.

should respect the rule of law—into detailed, legally enforceable rules of fairness and rationality is clearly a matter for the courts, through the incremental methodology of the forensic process. Parliament thus leaves it to the judges to set the precise limits of administrative competence. It is, therefore, the simple and plausible assumption—which is widely made in other contexts—that Parliament intends to legislate in conformity with the rule of law which bridges the apparent gulf between legislative silence and the developed body of administrative law which today regulates the use of executive discretion.

Hence, on this view, there is a relationship between parliamentary legislation and the grounds of review. However, whereas the traditional ultra vires principle conceptualises the relationship as *direct* in nature, the present approach maintains that the relationship exists in *indirect* form. While the details of the principles of review are not attributed to parliamentary intention, the judicially-created principles of good administration are applied consistently with Parliament's general intention that the discretionary power which it confers should be limited in accordance with the requirements of the rule of law. Thus it is possible to acknowledge the role of judicial creativity while ensuring that the limits which the judges impose on administrators can be reconciled with the intention of Parliament.

It is worth emphasising that the proposition lying at the heart of the modified ultra vires doctrine—that Parliament possesses a general intention concerning the limitation of discretionary power by reference to the rule of law, while leaving it to the courts to translate that general intention into specific legal principles—involves no conceptual novelty. Occasionally legislation explicitly indicates that the courts have the task of elaborating a particular principle which is relevant to the operation of a statutory scheme. For instance, the Occupiers' Liability Act 1957 requires an "occupier" of premises to take reasonable care for the safety of his visitors.[51] The legislation states that the term "occupier"—the meaning of which is central to the Act's scope and practical effect—is to be accorded the same definition as that which it bears at common law.[52] Thus Parliament, recognising that the notion of occupation is complex, leaves to the courts the task of determining its precise meaning.

It is more common, however, for Parliament implicitly to leave such a task to the judiciary. For example, a great deal of protective legislation extends only to individuals who are parties to a particular class of legal relationship. Hence tenants acquire many more statutory rights than mere licensees,[53] and employees benefit from a much more generous regime of employment protection than independent contractors.[54] Yet the protective legislation which confers such

[51] S. 2(1).
[52] S. 1(2).
[53] See, *e.g.*, Landlord and Tenant Act 1954; Rent Act 1977; Housing Act 1988.
[54] See, *e.g.*, Employment Rights Act 1996.

benefits on tenants and employees, while withholding them from licensees and independent contractors, does not define those types of relationship. As with "occupation", so with "tenancy" and "employment": Parliament, recognising the complexity of such concepts, realises that it is desirable to leave to the courts the task of determining their exact content. No-one would question the existence of a relationship between the legislation and the courts' jurisprudence on the meaning of terms such as "occupier", "tenant" and "employee". The courts are, quite clearly, determining the reach of the protective legislation pursuant to an explicit or implicit legislative warrant.

There is a clear analogy between the courts' activities in these private law fields and their public law jurisprudence on the ambit of discretionary power created by Parliament. The relationship between legislative intention and the grounds of review is similar, in many respects, to the relationship between parliamentary intention and the meaning attributed to terms such as "employee". No-one would maintain that Parliament intends the nuances of the complex definition of that term which the courts have, in the best traditions of the common law, developed incrementally over many years; nor would they deny the existence of a relationship between legislative intention and the courts' jurisprudence on the point, since it is clear that the courts' interpretative endeavour is undertaken pursuant to parliamentary direction. By the same token it cannot realistically be maintained that Parliament intends the precise details of the limits which the courts impose on discretionary power. However, as the private law analogies demonstrate, this does not mean that there is no relationship between the legislature's intention and the courts' jurisprudence. In each case the relationship exists, but in indirect form.

Thus, once legislation which creates discretionary power is located within its proper constitutional context, it becomes clear that the rule of law must operate to limit and control the exercise of that power. Since the rule of law is a pervasive constitutional principle which shapes both the environment within which Parliament legislates and the context within which statutes are interpreted, the courts rightly impute to Parliament an intention that the rule of law should be upheld. In this manner the courts' vindication of the rule of law is of a piece with Parliament's will, and judicial review comes to rest on a secure constitutional foundation which acknowledges both its normative roots and its relationship with legislative intention. The benefits of the modified ultra vires model are explored in more detail below. First, however, it is useful to point out that the interpretative methodology which it harnesses is widely supported by other writers. Two, in particular, should be mentioned.

First, the view on which modified ultra vires theory is based—that statutory construction is a function of context, and that the rule of law forms a fundamental part of that context—derives support from the work of T R S Allan, who has written extensively on the relationship between interpretation and the rule of law. In particular, Allan emphasises the manner in which constitutional principle shapes the meaning of legislation:

The rule of law authorises, and requires, a manner of interpreting the statutory text: it is that text, as interpreted, which constitutes the law. The incorporation of common law notions of justice and fairness is not therefore to be viewed as a curb on parliamentary intention, but as an integral part of the process of ascertaining that intention.[55]

Such norms as justice and fairness are thus characterised as interpretative constructs which shape the internal meaning of legislative provisions. Conceptualised thus, their application to provisions which create discretionary powers entails the identification of the contours and reach of those powers. Hence the rule of law is treated as a determinant of the extent of the vires which Parliament is taken to grant to decision-makers, rather than as an external common law principle which takes effect independently of and in isolation from the legislative scheme. This exactly mirrors the approach of the modified ultra vires theory.[56]

Support for the methodology which lies at the heart of that model can also be found in the recent work of Jeffrey Jowell:

> . . . the very general statement that ultra vires is the foundation of judicial review massively begs the question of what we mean by vires. In its strict sense, vires refers to the powers conferred by statute. The accepted ground of review of legality then permits the courts quite properly to ensure that discretionary powers have been exercised within the circumference of those powers. But there is a broader sense of vires, which it is open to the courts to recognise . . . The courts now engage directly with constitutional principle and do not summon the medium in the statute to thump the table on behalf of that principle. Vires becomes power in context; it respects identifiable legislative intent, but draws the very practical inference that our legislature is legislating in and for a society governed by a framework of democracy . . .[57]

---

[55] T R S Allan, "Legislative Supremacy and the Rule of Law: Democracy and Constitutionalism" (1985) 44 *CLJ* 111 at 139.

[56] See also the following excerpt from Lord Hoffmann's speech in *R v. Secretary of State for the Home Department, ex parte Simms* [1999] 3 WLR 328 at 341: "Parliamentary sovereignty means that Parliament can, if it chooses, legislate contrary to fundamental principles of human rights . . . But the principle of legality means that Parliament must squarely confront what it is doing and accept the political cost. Fundamental rights cannot be overridden by general or ambiguous words. This is because there is too great a risk that the full implications of their unqualified meaning may have passed unnoticed in the democratic process. In the absence of express language or necessary implication to the contrary, the courts therefore presume that even the most general words were intended to be subject to the basic rights of the individual." This is wholly consistent with the modified ultra vires concept, which holds that Parliament can properly be taken to intend that the discretionary powers which it creates, although expressed in general words, should be subject to the rule of law and to the due process rights which the courts derive from it.

[57] J Jowell, "Of Vires and Vacuums: The Constitutional Context of Judicial Review" in C F Forsyth (ed.), *Judicial Review and the Constitution* (Oxford: Hart Publishing, 2000) at 337. P P Craig, "Competing Models of Judicial Review" in C F Forsyth (ed.), *Judicial Review and the Constitution* (Oxford: Hart Publishing, 2000) at 391 acknowledges that Jowell's work epitomises "modern mainstream thinking about the rule of law". However, Craig also suggests that the modified ultra vires doctrine is fundamentally inconsistent with leading academic opinion on the relationship between legislation and the rule of law. There therefore arises something of a paradox, given that Jowell's most recent work ascribes to the rule of law a role which is strikingly similar to that which it occupies within the modified ultra vires framework.

In spite of the fact that this approach echoes that which is adopted by the modified ultra vires theory, Jowell criticises that theory.[58] His dissatisfaction appears to rest on a perception that the modified ultra vires doctrine *does* "summon the medium in the statute to thump the table on behalf of [constitutional] . . . principle".[59] However, it is submitted that this rather misrepresents the modified ultra vires theory. Two main points arise.

First, it is correct to say that parliamentary intention forms an important part of the juridical foundation which the modified theory constructs for judicial review. The necessity of making legislative intention part of the equation derives, in part, from the argument of constitutional logic, analysed in Chapter 3, which indicates that any model which failed to adopt a construction-oriented approach would be unable to reconcile the operation of the supervisory jurisdiction with the theory of parliamentary supremacy. It is for this reason that, within the modified ultra vires framework, the rule of law is vindicated interpretatively, by means of deploying the well-established presumption that Parliament is taken to legislate with the intention that its enactments should be consistent with constitutional principle.

Secondly, however, there is nothing in this approach which denies that those constitutional principles to which judicial review gives effect possess an inherent normative value which exists independently of legislative intention. Indeed, one of the purposes of the modified theory is to permit open acknowledgement of the intrinsic worth of the principles on which administrative law is founded. Holding that Parliament's intention is consistent with respect for those constitutional principles does not, therefore, rob them of their autonomous normative resonance. Rather, it simply recognises that the constitutional order itself locates the legislature and the legislation which it passes within a framework which is founded on the rule of law, and which therefore attributes to the legislature an intention to act consistently with that principle. Far from denying the inherent normative worth of constitutional principles, such an approach recognises the pervasiveness of the values on which the constitution is founded, such that judicial vindication of the rule of law through judicial review is seen to fulfil, rather than conflict with, the endeavours of the legislature.

3.3. The Implications of the Modified Ultra Vires Principle

It is appropriate at this point to consider some broader implications of the modified ultra vires principle. The need to do so arises principally as a result of suggestions made by Professor Paul Craig that the logical consequences of the principle are such as to render it unworkable. His specific arguments are considered in detail below. First, however, it is necessary to make a more general point.

[58] Jowell, above n. 57, at 337 (especially n. 36).
[59] *Ibid.*

This relates to the way in which Craig presents the modified ultra vires theory. His critique of it is littered with assertions that the theory postulates "legislative intent" as the "central principle" of administrative law.[60] This is incorrect. The repeated use of the epithet "central principle" in Craig's critique is an implicit reference to the title of the article—"The Ultra Vires Doctrine in a Constitutional Setting: Still the Central Principle of Administrative Law"[61]—in which, building upon Christopher Forsyth's work, the modified ultra vires principle was first fully articulated. In turn, the use of the epithet "central principle" in that paper echoes the statement of Sir William Wade that, "The simple proposition that a public authority may not act outside its powers (ultra vires) might fitly be called the central principle of administrative law".[62]

It is perfectly clear, both from the title of the paper on modified ultra vires theory and from Professor Wade's statement, that the contention of that theory is that it is the *interpretative methodology of ultra vires*, and *not* the notion of *legislative intention*, which is central. Indeed the driving force behind the modified theory is that an explanation of judicial review based simply on judicial enforcement of legislative intention is wholly inadequate.[63] This misreading of the modified ultra vires theory fundamentally undermines Craig's critique at a general level and, at least in part, underlies the error into which he falls in making more specific criticisms of the modified ultra vires doctrine.[64] This becomes apparent upon consideration of Craig's arguments to the effect that the doctrine is seriously flawed because it produces absurd consequences. He perceives two such consequences, which need to be considered in turn.

The first consequence which Craig ascribes to the modified ultra vires principle concerns the *application of private law to statutory agencies*. The modified theory of ultra vires (as presented above) holds that, at a conceptual level, statutory agencies are required to respect public law principles because, when parliamentary legislation confers authority upon them, the grant is inherently limited by reference to the general presumption that Parliament grants only such power as is consistent with the rule of law. Consequently Parliament is taken not to confer upon statutory agencies the power to contravene the principles of public law, although it is left to the courts to determine the precise legal content of those principles. Craig suggests that, if this argument is accepted, then it logically follows that the application to public bodies of private law principles must

---

[60] P P Craig, "Competing Models of Judicial Review" in C F Forsyth (ed.), *Judicial Review and the Constitution* (Oxford: Hart Publishing, 2000). This error, which is apparent in the two excerpts from Craig's critique set out below, is in fact pervasive throughout his paper.

[61] M C Elliott, "The Ultra Vires Doctrine in a Constitutional Setting: Still the Central Principle of Administrative Law" (1999) 58 *CLJ* 129.

[62] H W R Wade and C F Forsyth, *Administrative Law* (Oxford: Oxford University Press, 2000) at 35.

[63] See above at 27–35.

[64] This fundamental flaw in Craig's critique of the modified ultra vires theory is also noted by C F Forsyth, "Heat and Light: A Plea for Reconciliation" in C F Forsyth (ed.), *Judicial Review and the Constitution* (Oxford: Hart Publishing, 2000) at 403.

be explained symmetrically. Thus, says Craig, it would be necessary to reason that:

> . . . Parliament in a constitutional democracy intends a just system of civil liability, and that it then delegates the detailed implementation of this task to the courts to be decided in accordance with the normative principles which should govern such a system. If no such intent can be found then the existence and application of such principles cannot be justified. If we are satisfied that the requisite intent can be found then we can and must say that the "central principle" of this area of the law is legislative intent. We must, moreover, say this notwithstanding the fact that the principles of civil liability which are thus applied to public bodies have a normative force of their own which warrants their application to public bodies and to private bodies where there is no relevant background statute.[65]

Craig is correct to say that "this reasoning does not accord with how we think of the application of the rules of civil liability to public bodies".[66] However, he falls into error when he concludes that this is an accurate description of the implications of the modified ultra vires theory. This point can best be substantiated by reconsidering what that theory says about the application of *public law* principles to statutory agencies, before addressing Craig's point concerning the relationship between *private law* and public bodies.

It is central to the modified ultra vires principle that the constitutional order embodies a number of key values which, collectively, may be termed the rule of law. These principles are entirely autonomous. Their *existence* is self-justified by their normative worth and is in no way dependent upon any exercise of parliamentary intention, actual or imputed. However, the modified ultra vires principle goes on to hold that it is necessary carefully to construct the framework which supplies the conceptual basis for rationalising the *application* of those principles to statutory agencies. That framework invokes interpretative methodology in order to ensure that the application of constitutional principles to public bodies is conceptualised as fulfilling, rather than cutting across, the contours of the statutory scheme created by Parliament. In this manner, the operation of judicial review is rendered consistent with the established constitutional order and Parliament's place within it. However, the fact that the *application* of public law principles is justified in this way is not in any sense inconsistent with the view that the *existence* of such principles is to be justified by recourse to their inherent normative worth.

It is this distinction between the existence of legal principles and the mechanisms by which their application is effected which reveals the error into which Professor Craig falls. It is, self-evidently, counter-intuitive and unconvincing to suggest that the principles of private law (or, for that matter, public law) have been developed by the courts at the tacit behest of Parliament. It is perfectly

---

[65] P P Craig, "Competing Models of Judicial Review" in C F Forsyth (ed.), *Judicial Review and the Constitution* (Oxford: Hart Publishing, 2000) at 379.
[66] *Ibid.*

obvious to all concerned that those principles owe their existence to the judiciary's creativity and the incremental method of the common law. Such principles are therefore self-evidently—and explicitly—developed by reference to a process of normative evaluation and evolution.

Crucially, however, no part of the modified ultra vires principle runs counter to this mode of thinking. The impact of that principle on how we think about private law and public authorities relates not to the *existence* of the principles of private law; instead, it is confined to the way in which the *application* of private law principles to statutory agencies is conceptualised. It therefore merely requires acknowledgment of the fact that, when Parliament creates a statutory discretionary power, it cannot sensibly be taken to intend anything other than that it should be exercised according to law. It follows from this that, within the modified ultra vires framework, legislative intention does not purport to underlie the existence or development of the legal rules—public or private—which are applied to statutory agencies; rather, intention is relevant only to the application of public and private law principles to such agencies, in the sense that Parliament is plausibly taken to intend that the bodies which it creates should be subject to law.

Within this model, therefore, legislative intention and judicial creativity serve distinct but complementary functions. The courts, acting within their proper constitutional sphere, develop principles of private and public law liability, while Parliament, acting within its legislative province, ordains that the agencies which it creates should be subject to the values which underpin public and private law and to the specific legal rules which the courts develop in order to give practical effect to those values. The fact that statutory agencies are regulated by private law thus presents no obstacle to the modified ultra vires theory. That theory does not necessitate recourse to the fiction that private law has been developed pursuant to parliamentary will, nor does it require the normative values which underpin private law to be denied or disguised. In truth, modified ultra vires theory merely requires recognition of the fact that Parliament legislates in a legal environment which embodies public and private law principles and must surely be taken to intend that the bodies which it creates should be subject to, rather than above, the law.

As with public law, so with private law: the imputation to Parliament of this modest intention ensures that the application of legal rules to statutory bodies fulfils rather than cuts across legislative schemes and, in this manner, judicial regulation of public agencies is rendered consistent with, rather than a challenge to, the legislative supremacy of Parliament. Crucially, however, this is achieved without producing the absurd consequences which Craig ascribes to the modified ultra vires theory. That this is so becomes self-evident once the existence of legal principles is differentiated from the mechanisms which effect their application to statutory agencies.

The second argument which Craig deploys in order to contend that the modified ultra vires principle produces absurd consequences concerns *legislation which regulates matters in the private sphere.* He writes:

Much legislation is enacted on topics relating to commercial law, banking, trusts, employment law, land law and the like . . . If we adhere to the strictures of Forsyth and Elliott then we must say that legislative intent is the "central principle" of the relevant area of the law. We must therefore construct some species of general legislative intent. It might be argued that Parliament in a constitutional democracy intends there to be a just relationship between, for example, banks and their customers, and that Parliament intends to delegate the working out of this relationship to the courts. When the courts fashion the relevant rules they will doubtless draw on pre-existing concepts from the law of contract, trusts, restitution, etc., which have a normative force of their own, and are often applied in circumstances where there is no statutory background. Notwithstanding this, supporters of the modified ultra vires doctrine would insist that if no such intent can be found then no limits are warranted, and that if such general intent can be found then this justifies the conclusion that legislative intent is the 'central principle' in the relevant area. If this is true then writers in areas as diverse as labour law, company law, commercial law and tax will have a good deal of re-writing to do in their subjects.[67]

It appears that this argument relates to situations (which are commonplace) in which private activities are regulated by a mixture of common law and statutory intervention. The employment context—and, specifically, the relationship between employers and employees—is a good example. That relationship is founded on the law of contract, which is, at root, a creation of the common law. However, for various reasons (most notably the substantial inequality of bargaining power which characterises relationships of this type) legislation operates so as to regulate how employers and employees relate to one another, thus modifying the principle of freedom of contract which is the common law's starting point. Consequently the relationship between employers and employees is governed by both the common law and legislation.

It is Craig's contention that, if the modified ultra vires principle is embraced, it necessarily follows that in areas such as employment law, where Parliament has intervened to regulate certain aspects of the employer–employee relationship, the *entire* body of law in that area—including the common law—must be related to legislative intention. If this analysis was correct, then the modified ultra vires theory would indeed be an absurdity. The analysis is, however, flawed. It is founded on two fundamental misconceptions.

The first misconception springs from a misunderstanding of the purpose of the modified ultra vires principle. It is clear from the foregoing description of the principle that its objective is to supply a mechanism through which the norms of public law can be applied to statutory agencies in a manner which is consistent with the theory of parliamentary sovereignty. It is therefore self-apparent that the principle is directed only towards situations in which the courts apply controls to discretionary powers conferred by legislation. For this reason it is crucial to distinguish between the legal regulation of exercises of, on the one hand, *statutory power* and, on the other hand, *residual liberty*.

---

[67] Craig, above n. 65, at 379–80.

Whenever an agency exercises statutory power it logically follows that it must act either within or beyond the scope of its derived competence. Thus it is argued at length in Chapter 3 that judicial regulation of the exercise of statutory power must be rationalised in terms of the delineation and enforcement of the scope of the conferred power; any other approach would involve judicial contradiction of the statutory scheme which, it has been argued,[68] is constitutionally anathema (irrespective of whether sovereignty theory is embraced in its purely orthodox form): hence the need for the modified ultra vires doctrine as the mechanism by which public law principles are enforced *vis-à-vis* statutory agencies.

However, the same position does not obtain in relation to the regulation of private matters. Take, for example, the employer–employee relationship. When a private person decides to employ a worker, he does not act pursuant to any power which has been conferred upon him by Parliament; rather, he exercises the liberty—which every British citizen possesses—to do as he pleases, save to the extent that the law confines his freedom. Any law—whether it derives from the common law or from legislation—which regulates such private matters therefore has the effect of restricting the residual liberty of the citizen. Since, in this situation, the law attenuates a residual liberty rather than a statutory power, it is neither necessary nor possible to relate the restrictions imposed by law to the perimeter of any conferred statutory competence. The motivation for doing so in the context of judicial control of statutory agencies is to ensure that the limits which are applied trace, rather than cut across, the contours of the grant of power, thereby avoiding conflict with the statutory scheme. No such imperative arises, however, in private contexts, given that no relevant statutory power exists. Thus, once the purpose of modified ultra vires theory is properly appreciated, it becomes apparent that it has no implications whatsoever for the way in which we think about legal regulation in the private sphere. Returning to the example of the employment context, the relationship between employers and employees is, self-evidently, governed by a mixture of common law and statutory intervention—and nothing in the modified ultra vires principle requires the common law, as it applies to the employment relationship, to be regarded as having been developed pursuant to any form of legislative intention.

Craig's analysis of this matter is also based on a second misconception. He represents that the modified ultra vires principle logically implies that, once Parliament intervenes in a given area to any extent, it follows that all of the law which applies in that area (whether it exists as a result of legislative intervention or the development of the common law) must henceforth be regarded as existing as a result of legislative intention. According to this view, once Parliament intervenes, any pre-existing principles of the common law must be regarded as acquiring their legitimacy from Parliament's supposed general intention that they should exist.

---

[68] See above at 73–80.

The error which undermines this argument is substantially similar to the mistake which Sir John Laws makes in his characterisation of the conception of sovereignty which underlies Christopher Forsyth's defence of ultra vires.[69] Laws argues that Forsyth's thesis rests on a "wall-to-wall" view of sovereignty, such that "all authorities and prohibitions must come from Parliament".[70] Chapter 3 explains that this conclusion is incorrect. The contention of ultra vires theory is simply that, once Parliament has created a statutory discretionary power, the limits of the power which the decision-maker thereby acquires must, in conceptual terms, be determined by the scope of the original grant. Once it is appreciated that the claim underlying ultra vires theory is limited in this manner, it becomes clear that both Laws and Craig misrepresent the implications of the theory. Contrary to Laws's argument, it does not imply that "all authorities and prohibitions must come from Parliament". By the same token, Craig is wrong when he asserts that it is implicit in ultra vires theory that, once Parliament intervenes in a private law field, all laws in that area must be legitimated by reference to parliamentary intention. The logic which underpins the modified ultra vires doctrine concerns the implications which ensue once Parliament creates a statutory discretionary power. Craig's conclusion that the doctrine requires private law principles developed at common law to be related to legislative intention is therefore based upon a misunderstanding of the purpose of the modified ultra vires theory and the logic upon which it rests.

In conclusion, Professor Craig's critique of the modified ultra vires theory is seriously flawed. It is incorrect to assert that the theory postulates "legislative intent" as the "central principle" of judicial review. It is wrong to conclude that the modified ultra vires doctrine requires the principles of private law, as they are applied to public bodies, to be characterised as having been created pursuant to parliamentary intention. And it is incorrect to say that the modified ultra vires principle logically requires all law to be related to parliamentary intention whenever Parliament has intervened to change the law in a given sphere to any extent. These mistakes are based upon fundamental misunderstandings of the nature and purpose of the modified ultra vires theory, and of the logic which underpins it. In reality, the theory is confined to justifying the application of public law principles to statutory bodies, and it produces none of the absurd consequences which Professor Craig ascribes to it.

3.4. Structural Coherence and Internal Coherence

Having set out the modified ultra vires principle, it is necessary to consider in detail why it is contended that it offers a justification for judicial review which is more convincing that those which are offered by other models. The first point

---

[69] See above at 89–91.

[70] Sir John Laws, "Illegality: The Problem of Jurisdiction" in M Supperstone and J Goudie (eds.), *Judicial Review* (London: Butterworths, 1997) at 4.18.

which must be made in this regard relates to the prerequisites, considered in Chapter 2, of any satisfactory justificatory model. It was argued that a justification for judicial review must enjoy both internal and structural coherence: that is, it must provide an account which convincingly explains the operation of review and the derivation of the principles applied on review, and which also places the supervisory jurisdiction on a strong constitutional foundation which is consistent with the theory of parliamentary sovereignty. The principal strength of the modified theory of ultra vires is that it is coherent in *both* of these senses.

Internal coherence is secured by avoiding the passive artificiality and emptiness of the ultra vires doctrine.[71] The central role which normative constitutional principle occupies within the modified ultra vires framework addresses both of those difficulties simultaneously: it avoids the problem of passive artificiality by dispensing with the fiction that judicial review is about nothing more than the effectuation of legislative intention; and, far from providing an empty account of administrative law, it supplies an account which is normatively rich, drawing as it does upon the constitutional principle of the rule of law as the substantive foundation of the law of judicial review.

Crucially, however, such internal coherence is not purchased at the expense of its structural counterpart. By holding that the courts' endeavour is consistent with parliamentary intention—in light of the fact that the rule of law is postulated as a pervasive constitutional principle which colours the contexts within which Parliament legislates and the courts interpret—it is possible to ensure that the principles of good administration reflect the contours of the discretionary powers which legislation confers. In this manner, the norms of administrative law fulfil rather than cut across the legislative will of Parliament, and judicial review is rendered constitutionally secure.

In contradistinction to the modified ultra vires theory, neither of the other models possesses both internal and structural coherence. Chapter 2 explains that, although the traditional ultra vires doctrine is formally consistent with the constitutional order at a structural level, it provides an account of judicial review which is unconvincing and artificial, and which thereby robs it of internal coherence. Equally, Chapter 3 establishes that, while the common law model is superficially attractive—given that it furnishes a more open account of judicial review which appears to be internally coherent—it is, nevertheless, unsatisfactory: by divorcing administrative law from legislative intention it renders the exercise of the supervisory jurisdiction conceptually inconsistent with the theory of legislative supremacy.

The remainder of this chapter explores the contrasts between the modified ultra vires theory and the competing models in greater detail. Section 4 compares the traditional and modified ultra vires theories; in particular, it argues that the deficiencies which beset the former model are not present in the latter.

---

[71] The problem of active artificiality is considered below at 121–5.

Then, in section 5, the modified ultra vires principle is compared with the common law model of review. It has already been argued in Chapter 3 that the former should be preferred over the latter for reasons of structural coherence; however, section 5 below elaborates a number of additional advantages which the modified theory of ultra vires enjoys over the common law model, and which complement the argument of logic set out in chapter three.

4. THE MODIFIED ULTRA VIRES PRINCIPLE: OVERCOMING THE DEFICIENCIES
OF THE TRADITIONAL MODEL

4.1. Avoiding the Problem of Active Artificiality

It will be recalled from Chapter 2 that the ultra vires doctrine encounters particular problems when the courts effect judicial review in the face of ouster provisions which appear to preclude supervision of the discretionary power in question. The problem arises because the orthodox version of ultra vires holds that review is about nothing more than the straightforward implementation of legislative intention: if this is so, it is difficult to see why the courts refuse to give effect to the plain and natural meaning of such provisions. The ultra vires principle was, for this reason, said to be not only passively but also actively artificial.[72] Viewed from a broader perspective, the problem of active artificiality springs from the one-dimensional view of the constitutional order which the traditional theory of ultra vires reflects: its emphasis on the legislative command of the sovereign Parliament leads to a blinkered approach which tends to overlook the richness of the constitutional framework within which judicial review is effected.

The same difficulties do not beset the modified ultra vires doctrine. It recognises that, through the process of statutory construction, courts can quite legitimately ascribe to legislation a meaning which differs from that which it may at first appear to bear. This approach follows from the constitutional vision which lies at the heart of modified ultra vires theory—of a Parliament that legislates not in a vacuum but within a particular constitutional context which embodies a commitment to certain fundamental norms. For present purposes it is significant that—as a long line of authority attests—one of the most fundamental values which enjoys constitutional status in Britain is the citizen's right of access to courts of general jurisdiction.[73] As Denning LJ rightly observed, "If tribunals

---

[72] See above at 30–4.

[73] See, *inter alia, Chester v. Bateson* [1920] 1 KB 829; *Pyx Granite Co. Ltd. v. Minister of Housing and Local Government* [1960] AC 260; *Commissioners of Customs and Excise v. Cure and Deeley Ltd.* [1962] 1 QB 340; *Anisminic Ltd. v. Foreign Compensation Commission* [1969] 2 AC 147; *Raymond v. Honey* [1983] 1 AC 1; *R v. Secretary of State for the Home Department, ex parte Anderson* [1984] QB 778; *R v. Secretary of State for the Home Department, ex parte Leech* [1994] QB 198; *R v. Lord Chancellor, ex parte Witham* [1998] QB 575.

were to be at liberty to exceed their jurisdiction without any check by the courts, the rule of law would be at an end".[74]

Ouster provisions thus present the courts with a tension which they must seek to resolve. On the one hand their literal meaning appears to preclude access to justice; on the other hand, however, there is the deeply embedded constitutional principle that citizens should have access to the courts for the resolution of legal disputes. Two countervailing forces are thus at work, which the courts must seek to balance by attempting to attribute to ouster clauses a meaning which does not frustrate the rule of law. Acceptance of the modified ultra vires doctrine allows this task to be undertaken in a manner which openly acknowledges the nature of the interpretative process which is involved and the values on which it is based.

This methodology—by which the meaning attributed to legislation differs from the meaning which it appears to bear—is certainly not peculiar to the construction of ouster provisions. For instance, British courts have long been required to look beyond the plain meaning of national legislation in order to construe it compatibly with European Union law, whenever possible.[75] Similarly the Human Rights Act 1998 creates a comparable interpretative obligation, requiring legislation to be read and given effect to in a way which is compatible with fundamental rights, so far as this is possible.[76] In each instance, the interpretative function of the judiciary transcends the mechanical implementation of the words which Parliament employs. The demands of EU membership and the Human Rights Act each contribute to the rich tapestry which forms the constitutional backdrop against which British courts discharge their interpretative duties. This is equally true of the rule of law, which favours access to the courts and the fair and rational exercise of discretionary power.

To the extent that the traditional ultra vires doctrine denies the courts any interpretative role beyond the literal implementation of Parliament's enactments, it is indeed incapable of accommodating the creative approach to ouster clauses which is evident in such cases as *Anisminic*.[77] This has led some writers to argue that, in their decisions concerning preclusive clauses, the courts may be enforcing some deeper constitutional logic which is prior even to Parliament's

---

[74] R v. *Medical Appeal Tribunal, ex parte Gilmore* [1957] 1 QB 574 at 586.

[75] See Case 14/83, *Von Colson* v. *Land Nordrhein-Westfalen* [1984] ECR 1891; Case C–106/89, *Marleasing SA* v. *La Comercial Internacional de Alimentatión SA* [1990] ECR I–4135.

[76] Human Rights Act 1998, s. 3(1). Writers have suggested that one of the consequences of the Human Rights Act is that the search for parliamentary intention is no longer the touchstone of the interpretative process, given that the courts now strive to construe legislation compatibly with the Convention. However, it must be recalled that the courts' adoption of this interpretative technique is, in the first place, attributable to Parliament's intention as expressed in the 1998 Act. The same point arises in relation to judicial attempts to construe legislation compatibly with the rule of law: since Parliament is presumed to intend to uphold the rule of law, the courts' interpretative endeavour in this area seeks to fulfil, not circumvent, Parliament's intention.

[77] In which the House of Lords held a discretionary power amenable to judicial review notwithstanding that the enabling legislation provided that no determinations of the tribunal could be "called in question in any court of law". See *Anisminic Ltd.* v. *Foreign Compensation Commission* [1969] 2 AC 147.

sovereignty.[78] However, this rationalisation of the courts' jurisprudence is fundamentally inconsistent with the British constitutional framework, given that it fails to accord with the principle of legislative supremacy which continues to command wide support and which holds that there exists no higher order law that constrains Parliament's legislative freedom. Moreover, as Chapter 3 explains,[79] even if it is accepted that Parliament's authority to legislate is ultimately limited, the suggestion that it cannot preclude judicial review of specific discretionary powers makes inroads into Parliament's competence which are much more substantial than those which the leading critiques of sovereignty theory support.

In contrast, placing the ultra vires doctrine within its proper constitutional setting makes it possible to explain the courts' treatment of preclusive clauses in a way which accommodates both the theory of parliamentary sovereignty and the constitutional duty of the judges to uphold the rule of law. This approach, according to which the vindication of the citizen's right of access to justice is effected by recourse to interpretative means, is captured well by Lord Irvine LC:

> . . . in approaching the issue of statutory construction the courts proceed from a strong appreciation that ours is a country subject to the rule of law. This means that it is well recognised to be important for the maintenance of the rule of law and the preservation of liberty that individuals . . . should have a fair opportunity . . . to vindicate their rights in court proceedings. There is a strong presumption that Parliament will not legislate to prevent them from doing so.[80]

Of course, this interpretive approach does not always make it possible for the courts to construe ouster provisions so as to preserve some role for review. Indeed the courts accept that they must, for instance, enforce clauses which preclude vindication of public law rights after the expiry of a certain time limit.[81] The field of collateral challenge also illustrates judicial acceptance that Parliament can reduce the scope for vindication of public law values in the courts. Thus, in *R v. Wicks*,[82] the House of Lords recognised that, although the rule of law generally requires defendants in criminal proceedings to be able to raise as a defence the invalidity of the secondary legislation under which they are charged, this will not be permitted when it would be inconsistent with the relevant statutory scheme. Lord Nicholls thus accepted that "the general principles [which favour the availability of collateral challenge] . . . must always take effect

---

[78] See H W R Wade and C F Forsyth, *Administrative Law* (Oxford: Oxford University Press, 2000) at 706–9; T R S Allan, "Parliamentary Sovereignty: Law, Politics, and Revolution" (1997) 113 *LQR* 443 at 448.

[79] See above at 76–9.

[80] *Boddington v. British Transport Police* [1999] 2 AC 143 at 161. See also Lord Woolf, "Judicial Review—The Tensions between the Executive and the Judiciary" (1998) 114 *LQR* 579 at 581.

[81] See, *e.g.*, *Smith v. East Elloe Rural District Council* [1956] AC 736; *R v. Secretary of State for the Environment, ex parte Ostler* [1977] QB 122. Note that, in relation to ouster clauses of this type, the tension between the plain meaning of Parliament's words and the rule of law is not so great since, even on a literal interpretation, some role is preserved for judicial review.

[82] [1998] AC 92.

subject to any contrary indication in the relevant legislation".[83] However, courts are more likely to conclude that Parliament truly intended to prevent collateral challenge, thereby precluding recourse to public law norms, when the defendant had ample opportunity to question the validity of the delegated legislation by administrative means since, in this situation, the threat to the rule of law is not so serious.[84]

Nevertheless, so long as the British constitution continues to accord legislative supremacy to Parliament, any *irreconcilable* conflict between the intention of Parliament and the rule of law must ultimately be resolved in favour of the former, and judicial decisions which fail to respect this axiom must be rejected as lacking constitutional legitimacy. Indeed it is precisely this relationship between legislation and constitutional principle which the Human Rights Act 1998 reflects, according to which the courts must strive to interpret enactments consistently with fundamental norms but must, ultimately, enforce primary legislation if consistent construction proves impossible.[85]

Thus, as Slade LJ has explained, the presumption in favour of access to justice is precisely that: a presumption. Hence there exists "no . . . absolute and unqualified rule" that the courts can always intervene when administrative agencies act ultra vires: "the presumption is that, where a decision-making power is conferred on a tribunal or authority . . . Parliament did not intend to confer . . . [the] power [to act in excess of jurisdiction]. Nevertheless, the presumption is not irrebuttable."[86] Indeed, some ouster clauses enacted since the *Anisminic* decision seek to circumvent the reasoning employed in that case by, for example, providing that even "purported determinations"[87] or decisions "as to jurisdiction"[88] are not reviewable. It may be that such clauses would, if put to the test, be held to evince a legislative intention which is sufficiently clear to preclude review. It would then be the courts' duty to enforce those provisions. Thus, as Irvine explains, "constitutional logic dictates that some form of words must exist which would be sufficiently clear to insulate a given discretionary power from judicial review. If this was not the case, Parliament would not be truly sovereign."[89]

However, it is the function of the judiciary to ensure that, so far as possible, legislation is interpreted in a manner which is consistent with the rule of law. The values which underlie the British constitution dictate that Parliament cannot be assumed—in the absence of very clear countervailing evidence—to intend anything else. Understood thus, the judicial attitude to ouster clauses and the modified ultra vires doctrine are of a piece with one another: in each case,

---

[83] [1998] AC 92 at 109.

[84] See *Boddington v. British Transport Police* [1999] 2 AC 143 at 160, *per* Irvine LC.

[85] Human Rights Act 1998, ss. 3 and 4.

[86] *R v. Registrar of Companies, ex parte Central Bank of India* [1986] QB 1114 at 1176.

[87] Foreign Compensation Act 1969, s. 3(3) and (9).

[88] Interception of Communications Act 1985, s. 7(8); Security Service Act 1989, s. 5(4).

[89] Lord Irvine, "Principle and Pragmatism: The Development of English Public Law under the Separation of Powers" (lecture delivered at the High Court in Hong Kong, September 1998).

the courts' jurisprudence springs from the interpretation of legislation within a framework based firmly on the rule of law.[90]

4.2. The Development of Administrative Law Across Time

As well as the problems which it encounters in relation to preclusive provisions, the orthodox version of ultra vires also struggles to deal with the manner in which administrative law evolves over time. Judicial review has developed considerably over recent decades.[91] For instance, the courts have substantially expanded the notion of jurisdictional error of law;[92] they have recognised a doctrine of legitimate expectation[93] and, more recently, have demonstrated their willingness to protect such expectations substantively;[94] they apply the principles of procedural fairness to a much broader range of discretionary powers than once they did,[95] and the idea of irrationality is now deployed in a much more rigorous fashion—in some contexts—than it formerly was.[96] These examples of how the controls applied by the courts have, over time, evolved confront the orthodox ultra vires doctrine with a significant problem. If judicial review is simply about the enforcement of legislative intention, then every change in the controls enforced by the judiciary through the supervisory jurisdiction must be related back to corresponding changes in legislative intention; yet, as critics of

[90] I C Hare, "The Separation of Powers and Judicial Review for Error of Law" in C F Forsyth and I C Hare (eds.), *The Golden Metwand and the Crooked Cord* (Oxford: Clarendon Press, 1998) is correct to argue that the separation of powers is also relevant to the courts' treatment of ouster provisions: the idea that courts of law should ultimately have jurisdiction to determine questions of law buttresses the courts' policy of seeking to preserve judicial review of the legality of executive action in the face of a preclusive provision. However, Hare argues that, when a court is confronted with an ouster provision, the separation of powers justifies judicial review even if this is, on any interpretation, inconsistent with Parliament's intention. Such an approach is clearly incompatible with the established constitutional order; it must, therefore, be accepted that while the separation of powers—like the rule of law—is a constitutional principle which influences the courts' interpretation of ouster provisions, it cannot, at the present stage of our constitutional evolution, legitimate disapplication of such clauses.

[91] See above at 1–3.

[92] See *Anisminic Ltd.* v. *Foreign Compensation Commission* [1969] 2 AC 147; *R* v. *Lord President of the Privy Council, ex parte Page* [1993] AC 682.

[93] The doctrine of legitimate expectation was first recognised by an English court in *Schmidt* v. *Secretary of State for Home Affairs* [1969] 2 Ch. 149. See generally C F Forsyth, "The Provenance and Protection of Legitimate Expectations" (1988) 47 *CLJ* 238.

[94] The clearest example of substantive protection of substantive legitimate expectations is found in the Court of Appeal's decision in *R* v. *North and East Devon Health Authority, ex parte Coughlan* [2000] 2 WLR 622. Prior to *Coughlan*, the case law was, at best, ambiguous about whether substantive protection was possible. See generally M C Elliott, "*Coughlan*: Substantive Protection of Legitimate Expectations Revisited" [2000] *Judicial Review* 27.

[95] See pre-eminently *Ridge* v. *Baldwin* [1964] AC 40.

[96] See, *e.g.*, *R* v. *Secretary of State for the Home Department, ex parte Brind* [1991] 1 AC 696; *R* v. *Ministry of Defence, ex parte Smith* [1996] QB 517; *R* v. *Secretary of State for the Home Department, ex parte Simms* [1999] 3 WLR 328. For further discussion see below at 209–12.

ultra vires rightly observe, such reasoning is highly unsatisfactory and implausible.[97]

The inability of the orthodox version of ultra vires to deal with the manner in which administrative law evidently evolves is not, however, shared by the modified version of that doctrine. Once the notion of ultra vires is understood within its constitutional setting, the development of administrative law over time is readily comprehensible. Within the modified ultra vires model the task of the courts is not to ascertain and effectuate a crystallised legislative intention regarding the limits which apply to discretionary power. Rather, the creativity of the judicial function can be openly acknowledged. It is for the courts to decide how discretionary power should be limited in order to ensure that its exercise complies with the requirements of the rule of law.

Consequently, instead of relating the development of administrative law to putative changes in legislative intention, the modified ultra vires model holds that such developments relate to the evolution, across time, of the content of the constitutional principle of the rule of law. Thus, as the fluid and dynamic British constitution develops, so the courts rightly draw on changing constitutional norms in order to fashion new principles of judicial review and reformulate old ones. The manner in which, prior to the activation of the Human Rights Act 1998, the courts approached judicial review in cases concerning human rights is a good illustration of this point: the increasing intensity with which the principles of review have been applied in such cases clearly reflects the heightened status which human rights are in the process of acquiring within the constitutional order of the United Kingdom.[98]

This approach to statutory interpretation, according to which legislative provisions are construed in light of prevailing conditions, is widely recognised, as Professor Jack Beatson has explained:

> The vitality of the common law is preserved by the presumption that Parliament intends the court to apply to an ongoing statute . . . a construction that continually updates its meaning to allow for changes since it was initially framed. This means that in its application on any date the language of the Act, though necessarily embedded in its own time, is nevertheless to be construed in accordance with the need to treat it as current law . . . [For example,] at the time the Land Registration Act 1925 was passed giving a person "in actual occupation" of property an overriding interest, the balance of authority suggested that a wife residing with her husband where the husband alone was the legal owner of the property was not "in actual occupation". But by the beginning of the 1980s the social and legal status of husband and wife had changed and it was held that the wife was "in actual occupation" and entitled to the statutory protection. The solution was derived from a consideration of the statute in light of current social conditions.[99]

---

[97] See, *e.g.*, P P Craig, "Ultra Vires and the Foundations of Judicial Review" (1998) 57 *CLJ* 63 at 68.

[98] See further above at 56–7 and below, Ch. 6.

[99] J Beatson, "Has the Common Law a Future?" (1997) 56 *CLJ* 291 at 302–3.

Just as the courts' interpretation of legislation changes according to social conditions, so their view of what limits on discretionary power are required by the rule of law alters as the constitution develops over time. Thus, as Jowell remarks, the precise content of the rule of law "requires elaboration in the light of the practical reason of each generation".[100] It is for this reason that, as Lord Mustill observed, "The standards of fairness are not immutable. They may change with the passage of time, both in general and in their application to decisions of a particular type."[101] The same point applies with equal force to the other principles of judicial review.

The dynamism of administrative law can thus be rationalised by placing it within an analytical model which ascribes a relevance to legislative intention, but which does not resort to the strained proposition that changes in judicial control correspond directly to alterations in the will of Parliament. The perimeter of administrative autonomy is a fluid phenomenon which responds to changes in the broader constitutional context; yet, ultimately, it is also consistent with Parliament's constant intention that public officials should respect the rule of law.

4.3. The Scope of Judicial Review

One of criticisms which is most frequently levelled at the traditional ultra vires principle is its inability to justify the entirety of judicial review.[102] As Chapter 1 explained, the fact that courts are now willing to supervise the use of not only statutory power, but also prerogative and *de facto* power, raises important problems for proponents of ultra vires. This is because review of non-statutory power "cannot be rationalised through the idea [embodied in the traditional ultra vires principle] that the courts are delineating the boundaries of Parliament's intent".[103] This prompts Sir William Wade to remark that, "The dynamism of judicial review is such that it has burst through its logical boundaries".[104]

If the boundaries of review were taken to be wholly delimited by the ultra vires rule, then review of prerogative and other non-statutory power would indeed be unjustifiable. However, the constitution would be highly defective if it were incapable of legitimising review of non-statutory forms of governmental power. Indeed, in light of its capacity to adapt to changing circumstances—which derives from its unwritten and flexible character—the British constitution should be well placed to rise to new challenges such as the need to regulate the exercise of different forms of governmental power.

---

[100] J Jowell, "The Rule of Law Today" in J Jowell and D Oliver (eds.), *The Changing Constitution* (Oxford: Oxford University Press, 2000) at 20.
[101] *R v. Secretary of State for the Home Department, ex parte Doody* [1994] 1 AC 531 at 560.
[102] See generally below, Ch. 5.
[103] P P Craig, "Ultra Vires and the Foundations of Judicial Review" (1998) 57 *CLJ* 63 at 70.
[104] H W R Wade, "Judicial Review of Ministerial Guidance" (1986) 102 *LQR* 173 at 175.

In light of this proponents of ultra vires may argue that, while that principle can explain review of statutory discretions, a different justification needs to be articulated in relation to review of other types of power. This view, however, raises a paradox. On the one hand it holds that the justifications for review of statutory and non-statutory powers are entirely distinct. On the other hand, however, the courts apply the same grounds of review to all forms of governmental power which have been held amenable to judicial supervision,[105] subject, of course, to considerations of justiciability.[106] It is very difficult to see why entirely distinct juridical foundations should yield identical supervisory regimes.[107]

These problems are avoided by the modified ultra vires principle. It does not seek to explain review of statutory power purely in terms of legislative delegation, nor does it require the justifications for judicial review of different types of power to be separated into watertight compartments. Rather, it holds that administrative law constitutes the legal expression of foundational constitutional principles. It was explained above that the methodology of ultra vires is concerned merely with the provision of a mechanism by which the *application* of those principles to statutory power may be effected in a manner which is consistent with the theory of parliamentary supremacy.[108] Within this framework, the *existence* of those principles is attributed not to legislative intention but to the normative foundations from which they self-evidently spring.

Once this distinction is appreciated, together with the limited scope of the purpose of the modified ultra vires principle which the distinction reflects, it

---

[105] E.g., in *Council of Civil Service Unions* v. *Minister for the Civil Service* [1985] AC 374 at 411, Lord Diplock explained that the grounds of review based on "illegality" and "procedural impropriety" apply both to statutory and prerogative power; he also said that there is "no a priori reason to rule out 'irrationality' as a ground for judicial review of ministerial decisions taken in exercise of 'prerogative' powers", although he explained that the fields which are still governed by prerogative power are such that judicial review will lie less frequently on this ground because "[s]uch decisions will generally involve the application of government policy". See further F Wheeler, "Judicial Review of Prerogative Power in Australia: Issues and Prospects" (1992) 14 *Sydney Law Review* 432 at 466–72; D Pollard, "Judicial Review of Prerogative Power in the United Kingdom and France" in P Leyland and T Woods (eds.), *Administrative Law Facing the Future: Old Constraints and New Horizons* (London: Blackstone Press, 1997) at 307–9.

[106] On which see Wheeler, above n. 105, at 449–61; Pollard, above n. 105, at 301–7.

[107] Of course, the precise content of the grounds of review and the intensity with which they are applied, varies according to the context. As regards review of statutory power, the legislative framework may well indicate, *e.g.*, what fairness requires and which considerations are relevant and irrelevant (see further below at 138–40). Such guidance may still exist in relation to non-statutory power, albeit in a more diffuse form. For instance, in *R* v. *Panel on Take-overs and Mergers, ex parte Datafin plc* [1987] QB 815 at 841, Lord Donaldson MR said that the court could intervene if (*inter alia*) the Panel misconstrued its Code, thereby leading it to commit what would be an "error of law" but for the non-legal character of the Code. However, the Panel had to be given a generous margin of appreciation in discharging this interpretive function because it could choose to change the rules at any time, and because of their open-textured nature. Nevertheless, in spite of this context-sensitivity in judicial application of the grounds of review, it remains the case that, at root, the courts apply the same broad requirements of fairness and rationality irrespective of the source of the power concerned.

[108] See above at 115.

becomes clear that the modified theory of ultra vires encounters no difficulty in the face of judicial review of non-statutory power. The fact that the courts apply the same principles of review irrespective of whether they are dealing with statutory or non-statutory power is unremarkable. In each situation the law of judicial review provides for control of discretionary power by reference to the underlying constitutional principles which form the rule of law. In this sense, the substantive, or normative, foundations of judicial review of statutory and non-statutory power are identical. The question then becomes how those substantive principles are to be legally effectuated.

It is at this point that it is necessary to distinguish between statutory and non-statutory power. So far as the former is concerned, the modified ultra vires principle is deployed in order that the controls enforced by the courts may be conceptualised in a manner which is consistent with the theory of legislative sovereignty. In contrast, the issue of achieving consistency with the sovereignty principle does not arise in relation to non-statutory power for the simple reason that there exists no relevant manifestation of legislative intention with which judicial review needs to be reconciled in order to satisfy the requirements of constitutional orthodoxy. Thus, in relation to review of statutory power, the sovereignty principle raises special considerations which require the rule of law to be vindicated *interpretatively* in order to ensure that review can be reconciled with constitutional principle.[109] Outside the realm of statutory power the rule of law can be effectuated *directly*, since the constraints which the sovereignty principle imposes on review of statutory power are of no application in non-statutory contexts.

These arguments are set out in greater detail in Chapter 5. For the time being it is sufficient to observe that the ultra vires doctrine, within its proper constitutional setting, is consistent with a supervisory regime which transcends the control of statutory discretions and which applies identical principles of good administration, based on the rule of law, to all types of governmental power. The fact that interpretative methodology is applicable only in the statutory sphere should not be perceived as a criticism of the modified ultra vires model but, rather, as an important strength. It is this feature of the model which allows requirements of legality to be applied to powers created by Parliament in a way which is compatible with the doctrine of legislative supremacy, yet within a coherent framework which embraces judicial review of all forms of governmental power.

---

[109] A series of additional factors also militates in favour of conceptualising controls on statutory discretions as implicit limits on the scope of the power: see below at 145–61.

5. THE ADVANTAGES OF THE MODIFIED ULTRA VIRES PRINCIPLE OVER THE COMMON LAW THEORY OF REVIEW

5.1. Introduction

As the foregoing section demonstrates, the modified ultra vires theory supplies a juridical foundation for judicial review which is free from the shortcomings which beset the orthodox version of ultra vires. It ascribes a role to legislative intention which is realistic and which avoids the artificiality of the orthodox theory, while preserving the structural coherence which is the traditional doctrine's principal strength. It provides a more open account of the courts' approach to ouster clauses, by articulating the values-based interpretive approach which characterises public law adjudication; and the modified theory is much better placed to accommodate the way in which, as time progresses, judicial review develops in terms both of the content of the controls applied by the courts and the range of decision-making functions to which the supervisory jurisdiction extends. All of these considerations point towards the conclusion that the modified ultra vires principle provides a much stronger and more workable constitutional foundation for judicial review than the traditional conception of the doctrine.

However, it is also necessary to compare the modified ultra vires principle with the common law model, which is the other principal putative justification for judicial review and which commands the support of a number of influential writers. In part, this task has already been undertaken. In Chapter 3, the claim made by Christopher Forsyth—that adoption of the common law model in preference to an interpretive, vires-based approach would be fundamentally inconsistent with the constitutional order—was subjected to detailed evaluation. The conclusion was reached that Forsyth's argument is correct, and that it holds true even if the orthodox conception of wholly unlimited parliamentary competence is rejected in favour of an account which embraces the idea of limited legislative authority.[110] Thus the ability of the modified ultra vires doctrine to reconcile judicial review with the constitutional framework is the principal ground on which it can be distinguished from the common law model, which constructs a foundation for judicial review which is fundamentally inconsistent with the structure of the constitutional order.

The purpose of the remainder of this chapter is to identify a number of additional factors which differentiate the modified ultra vires and common law theories. Many of those factors are relatively pragmatic in nature, in that they indicate that adoption of the common law theory would substantially undermine the practical coherence of administrative law by introducing unnecessary

---

[110] Provided that Parliament remains free to suspend the operation of the principles of good administration in specific contexts. The leading critics of ultra vires theory concede that Parliament is able to do this.

distinctions and technicalities and by reducing judicial review's ability to safeguard the due process rights of the citizen. However, it is necessary to begin by considering how one of the leading common law theorists seeks to challenge the conclusion reached in Chapter 3 that, at a conceptual level, the common law model is inconsistent with the constitutional framework.

5.2. Purchasing Structural Coherence for the Common Law Model

Sir John Laws's work provides the most thoughtful and elaborate conceptual argument to the effect that a common law theory of judicial review can be reconciled with the constitutional structure.[111] His argument was described in detail in Chapter 3,[112] and need therefore be restated only in outline here.

The conceptual defence of ultra vires methodology which was evaluated in Chapter 3 relies on the dual precepts that the courts may not contradict statutory schemes created by primary legislation and that a decision-maker acting pursuant to such a scheme necessarily acts either intra vires or ultra vires. If these premises are accepted, then it follows *a priori* that the courts' role on judicial review must be confined to the identification and condemnation of executive action which is committed ultra vires. Chapter 3 concluded that the first proposition is an accurate empirical description of how Parliament's role within the constitutional order is perceived,[113] and that the second proposition is correct as a matter of abstract logic.[114]

Laws, however, questions the latter conclusion. He argues that administrative action may be neither ultra vires nor intra vires but may, instead, fall into an innominate third category. This third category is said to arise because Parliament may have no intention, one way or the other, about the manner in which the discretionary power which it creates should be exercised: thus there exists what Laws calls an "undistributed middle". The purpose of this rationalisation is to create a legislative vacuum which generates a space within which a common law set of principles of administrative law may legitimately operate: if the statutory scheme simply does not (explicitly or implicitly) have anything to say about whether discretionary power may be used in a given way, then the principles of good administration—which regulate how administrative power is used—may be supplied by the common law without any risk of illegitimately contradicting Parliament's scheme.

Self-evidently this argument is advanced in order to secure structural coherence for the common law model by establishing that it is not inconsistent with

---

[111] See Sir John Laws, "Illegality: The Problem of Jurisdiction" in M Supperstone and J Goudie (eds.), *Judicial Review* (London: Butterworths, 1997).

[112] See above at 87–95.

[113] Or that it is sufficiently correct to leave the argument concerning ultra vires undisturbed: provided that Parliament is capable of choosing whether to confer administrative power free from or subject to the principles of good administration, the argument holds true. See above at 73–80.

[114] See above at 87–95.

the theory of legislative sovereignty. However, the attempt is ultimately unsuccessful for two reasons. On the one hand, there are compelling logical reasons which suggest that Laws is wrong to conclude that there can exist an "undistributed middle"; those reasons were considered in Chapter 3. On the other hand, even if it is accepted that there *may*, as a matter of abstract logic, be an "undistributed middle" in this context, considerations of pragmatism and constitutional logic suggest that no such phenomenon exists *in fact*. This conclusion is reached because, if Laws's approach is adopted, in an attempt to purchase structural coherence for the common law theory, a very high price is paid which ultimately robs that theory of internal coherence.

The "undistributed middle" can exist in the present context only if Parliament is taken to be wholly neutral about the extent of the administrative power which it grants and the manner in which such power is exercised. Parliament must be taken neither to prescribe nor to proscribe limits to the executive power which it creates. This presumption, whose sole purpose is to purchase structural coherence for the common law model, renders it as internally incoherent as the traditional ultra vires doctrine. Saying that Parliament is agnostic about whether public power should be abused is just as artificial as the contention that every detail of the principles of good administration can be divined from the unwritten will of Parliament. To presume that Parliament is entirely neutral about whether discretionary power is used abusively; for improper purposes; in bad faith; irrationally, or in a manner which is procedurally unfair, is to attribute to Parliament an intention which is unreasonable and absurd. It is precisely because the orthodox ultra vires doctrine ascribes an unsustainable intention to Parliament that the common law theorists criticise it; yet the device of the "undistributed middle" which must, of necessity, be deployed at common law in order to render it structurally coherent, involves the ascription of an equally artificial intention to Parliament. Forsyth thus remarks that the assumption of neutrality underlying the "undistributed middle" is "self-evidently unrealistic—even the most dim-witted legislator, or officious back-bencher, will, if asked, say that in legislating they intend that the powers granted should be fairly exercised".[115]

Ironically, Sir John Laws has, elsewhere, accepted that an approach which assumes such neutrality is wholly implausible:

> In an age when respect for human rights has received the imprimatur of civilized society, which regards it not as a political option but as a moral necessity, the reasonable decision-maker is bound to entertain a bias against any infraction of such rights . . . A public authority cannot be *neutral* about the demands of individual freedom without building a wall between itself and current public morality. So, in the name of reasonableness, the law insists that the decision-maker is not neutral.[116]

---

[115] C F Forsyth, "Heat and Light: A Plea for Reconciliation" in C F Forsyth (ed.), *Judicial Review and the Constitution* (Oxford: Hart Publishing, 2000) at 401.

[116] Sir John Laws, "*Wednesbury*" in C F Forsyth and I C Hare (eds.), *The Golden Metwand and the Crooked Cord* (Oxford: Clarendon Press, 1998) at 195 (original emphasis).

If it is unreasonable to be neutral about the substantive freedoms with which this excerpt is concerned, then neutrality *vis-à-vis* the procedural rights which are vindicated by way of judicial review must be equally unreasonable. Furthermore, if—as Laws contends—neutrality on this matter is unreasonable on the part of administrative authorities, then it must be just as unreasonable on the part of the legislature.

Laws argues that "in the name of reasonableness" the law (by which he means the judiciary) precludes such neutrality. However, in relation to the scope of discretionary power created by Parliament the courts do not need to *insist* that Parliament favours, rather than is neutral about, respect for individuals' procedural rights. If Parliament is not to be taken as neutral—and therefore, on Laws's own argument, unreasonable—then it must be presumed that Parliament itself possesses such a bias when it legislates to create discretionary power. It is precisely such a bias which is attributed to Parliament within the modified ultra vires framework. Indeed, as will be discussed below, the common law model's presumption that Parliament entertains no such bias is fundamentally inconsistent with the deeply embedded canon of construction according to which courts approach legislation on the presumption that the legislature intends to respect the rule of law.

The choice between the common law and modified ultra vires theories is therefore stark. The latter attributes to Parliament a reasonable, plausible and straightforward intention—that it should be taken to legislate in a manner which is consistent with constitutional principle—while leaving it to the good sense and experience of the courts to determine precisely how this should be secured in practical terms. In sharp contrast, the common law approach must, if it is to be constitutionally legitimate, impute to Parliament an intention which is implausible, necessitating the assumption that Parliament is entirely unconcerned about the use and misuse of the governmental power which it creates.

More generally, the common law model, and the notion of the "undistributed middle" which it encompasses, presents a skewed picture of the constitutional order. It postulates that constitutional principle is something which is created by the judges and with which the judges are exclusively concerned; thus the courts are viewed as *imposing* the rule of law on the other parts of government. Meanwhile, the modified ultra vires principle treats the rule of law as a pervasive constitutional principle which influences the contexts within which legislation is both enacted by Parliament and interpreted by the courts. This captures much more accurately the way in which we think about the values on which the constitutional order is founded given that, by definition, constitutional values (such as those to which judicial review gives expression) are shared values which possess an overarching resonance. To regard them as uniquely *judicial* constructs is ultimately to deny their *constitutional* status.

It follows that attempting to purchase structural coherence for the common law model ultimately deprives it of internal coherence. Although (on Laws's argument) formal consistency with the constitutional framework can be achieved by recourse to the idea of the "undistributed middle", this necessarily attributes to Parliament an intention which is untenable. Understood thus, the common law theory does not constitute any advance on the traditional ultra vires doctrine. Both claim compatibility with the sovereignty principle, but neither provides a satisfactory explanation for judicial review: the orthodox ultra vires model fails because it implausibly assumes that parliamentary intention does everything, and the common law model falters because it rests on the equally implausible assumption that there exists no relevant intention whatsoever. As the following sections seek to demonstrate, this approach is unsustainable both in practical terms and as a matter of constitutional logic.

5.3.   An Unwelcome Distinction in Administrative Law

5.3.1. Introduction

Even the most emphatic critics of ultra vires do not advocate its wholesale abandonment. It is broadly accepted that the doctrine provides a good explanation of some instances of review. For example, when administrative action is set aside because it is committed in breach of explicit statutory provisions concerning the jurisdictional limits or due process conditions which attach to the exercise of a discretionary power, the courts are self-evidently enforcing those limits on vires which Parliament intended should be effective.[117] In such situations the common law model is simply not engaged—its concern is with those situations in which judicial review goes beyond straightforward judicial enforcement of evident statutory requirements.

It follows that the common law model does not—and logically cannot—explain the whole of judicial review. Although it is often presented by its proponents as a panacea which supplies an overarching justification for the operation of the supervisory jurisdiction, it is self-evidently impossible to assert that, in enforcing requirements which very clearly derive from the statutory scheme, the courts are utilising common law principles. Consequently the common law model can rationalise only some of the controls which the courts apply on judicial review. While it may be argued that the common law is the basis of the principles of good administration (such as the general duty of fairness), it is very clear that legislation—not the common law—is the source of at least some of the limits which the judiciary enforces on discretionary powers.

Thus it transpires that the common law model of review, if it were adopted, would have to co-exist with a vires-based, interpretative justification for the enforcement of some grounds of review. It therefore becomes necessary to ask precisely where the dividing line would be drawn between those grounds of review which would be attributed to the creativity of the common law and those

---

[117] See above at 28–9.

which would be explained by reference to legislative intention. This raises very significant difficulties for the common law model.

Two particular points fall to be considered. First, it is very difficult, in practical terms, to force the grounds of review into two such watertight compartments. These problems are addressed in section 5.3.2. Secondly, section 5.3.3 considers the reasons which underpin this difficulty; it concludes that the distinction which the common law model necessarily postulates—between grounds of review which, on the one hand, derive from and, on the other hand, have nothing to do with legislative intention—is unduly simplistic and rests on a flawed view of the way in which constitutional values are legally vindicated in English law.

5.3.2. The problem

The central problem which arises in the present context is that of separating the grounds of judicial review into two clearly distinct categories.[118] The decision of the Divisional Court in *Bugg* v. *Director of Public Prosecutions*[119]—and the problems which it generated—usefully illustrates how difficult this undertaking is. The case concerned the circumstances in which litigants could collaterally raise defects in executive action.[120] Giving the judgment of the court, Woolf LJ held that whether such a defect could be raised collaterally depended on which of two distinct categories it fell into. First, "substantive invalidity" would arise when:

> the byelaw is on its face invalid because either it is outwith the power pursuant to which it was made because, for example, it seeks to deal with matters outside the scope of the enabling legislation, or it is patently unreasonable.[121]

Secondly, a byelaw would suffer from "procedural invalidity" where:

> there has been non-compliance with a procedural requirement with regard to the making of that byelaw. This can be due to the manner in which the byelaw was made; for example, if there was a failure to consult.[122]

It was held in *Bugg* that substantive defects could render executive action collaterally impeachable, but that procedural defects could be challenged only directly in judicial review proceedings. The correctness of this conclusion was doubted by the House of Lords in *R* v. *Wicks*[123] and, ultimately, the Appellate Committee overruled *Bugg* in the case of *Boddington* v. *British Transport*

---

[118] It is imperative that the distinction can be drawn very clearly because the categorisation of a ground of review as either vires-based or common law may have substantial practical consequences. See below at 145–61.

[119] [1993] QB 473.

[120] *Bugg* was concerned with collateral challenges to byelaws, but the reasoning is applicable to administrative decisions of all types.

[121] [1993] QB 473 at 494.

[122] *Ibid.*

[123] [1998] AC 92.

Police,[124] holding that the legality of administrative action may be questioned collaterally on any ground. Although a number of reasons underpinned the decision in *Boddington*, one of the main factors which led the House of Lords to overrule *Bugg* was the difficulty which inhered in any attempt to separate the grounds of review into the two categories enunciated by Woolf LJ in that case. As Irvine LC explained in *Boddington*:

> ... the distinction between orders which are "substantively" invalid and orders which are 'procedurally' invalid is not a practical distinction which is capable of being maintained in a principled way across the broad range of administrative action ... Many different types of challenge, which shade into each other, may be made to the legality of byelaws or administrative acts. The decision in *Anisminic* freed the law from a dependency on technical distinctions between different types of illegality. The law should not now be developed to create a new, and unstable, technical distinction between "substantive" and "procedural" invalidity.[125]

Lord Steyn took this point, too:

> There is ... a formidable difficulty of categorisation created by *Bugg*'s case ... A distinction between substantive and procedural invalidity will often be impossible or difficult to draw. Woolf LJ recognised [in *Bugg*] that there may be cases in a grey area, *e.g.* cases of bad faith ... I fear that in reality the grey area covers a far greater terrain.[126]

Consequently, in *Boddington*, their Lordships concluded that it was necessary to abandon any attempt to delineate a class of defects which rendered administrative action merely voidable and, therefore, collaterally unimpeachable.

Although *Bugg* and *Boddington* were concerned specifically with the division of the grounds of review into "substantive" and "procedural" categories, they point towards a broader conclusion. Just as Woolf LJ's attempt to divide the grounds of review into those which could and those which could not found collateral challenges was beset with practical difficulties, so any attempt to demarcate a boundary between those grounds of review which are attributable to legislative intention and those which rest on common law foundations would also, to use Lord Steyn's words, raise "formidable difficulties of categorisation".

This point is underscored by the experience of those jurisdictions—notably South Africa and Australia—which have embraced common law grounds of review. It is now received wisdom in Australia that the rules of natural justice are creations of the common law, having nothing to do with implicit statutory provision.[127] Thus the Chief Justice of New South Wales has explained that the standards of fairness "are not merely propositions of statutory construction. Rather they are imposed on the exercise of public power by the common

---

[124] See below at 157–61 for more detailed discussion of this case.
[125] [1999] 2 AC 143 at 159.
[126] *Ibid.* at 170.
[127] *Kioa v. West* (1985) 159 CLR 550.

law."[128] However, once the rules of natural justice are regarded as autonomous common law grounds of challenge, it becomes necessary to ask which other broad principles of review should be regarded as resting on similar foundations. The difficulty lies in deciding where to draw the line. An Australian commentator has thus remarked that, "The distinction may seem so problematic that it should be avoided."[129]

The South African courts faced similar problems in the 1980s. In *Staatspresident* v. *United Democratic Front*,[130] the Appellate Division held that, when the courts struck down secondary legislation on the ground that it was too vague, they were enforcing a common law principle. Thus the traditional view—which had previously obtained in South Africa—that all of the heads of judicial review were species of the ultra vires doctrine was departed from. However, once it was held that vagueness was a common law, rather than a vires-based, ground of challenge, the courts were forced to determine which other principles of administrative law were to be similarly conceptualised. Thus, in *Natal Indian Congress* v. *State President*,[131] Friedman J felt obliged to hold that the doctrine of unreasonableness also fell outside the ambit of ultra vires. Similarly the requirements of fairness were held, in *Administrator, Transvaal* v. *Traub*,[132] to constitute a common law ground of challenge, unrelated to the scope of the power which the legislature initially granted.

Nevertheless, a large grey area must remain. Particular problems arise in relation to such principles of review as the obligations to take all relevant, but no irrelevant, factors into account, and to use statutory power only to further, never to frustrate, the purpose for which it was created. It is very difficult to work out on which side of the line these matters fall, since they can be understood only within the context of the legislative framework which gives rise to the discretion in the first place.[133]

However, the difficulties which arise in this context do not end once it is decided which grounds of review are vires-based and which are rooted in the common law. For instance, even if (as in Australia) it is firmly settled that procedural fairness is a common law principle, problems must logically arise in circumstances where legislation makes certain—but incomplete—provision regarding the procedural requirements which attach to the exercise of a

---

[128] J J Spigelman, "The Foundations of Administrative Law" (the 1998 Spann Oration, Sydney, Australia, 7 September 1998).

[129] P Bayne, "The Common Law Basis of Judicial Review" (1993) 67 *Australian Law Journal* 781 at 782.

[130] 1988 (4) SA 830.

[131] 1989 (3) SA 588.

[132] 1989 (4) SA 731.

[133] F Wheeler, "Judicial Review of Prerogative Power in Australia: Issues and Prospects" (1992) 14 *Sydney Law Review* 432 at 468–71 argues that grounds of challenge such as relevance of considerations and propriety of purposes may be applicable to prerogative powers notwithstanding the absence of a statutory framework; nevertheless, she concedes that this framework is highly relevant when statutory powers are reviewed on these grounds, and that the scope for deploying these heads of review when no such framework exists is severely limited.

statutory power. In this situation are the additional requirements supplied by the courts to be characterised as implied statutory provisions which are elaborations of the basic explicit statutory statement concerning procedural fairness, or are they to be placed on a common law basis such that the constituent parts of the operative duty of fairness are viewed as deriving from the explicit statutory provision and the common law respectively?

Both solutions bristle with problems. The first adopts the very methodology of statutory implication which is rejected by the ethos of the common law model of review. However, the alternative solution postulates that the various composite parts of the duty of fairness which operates in the given case rest on different legal bases: this is highly problematic in light of the arguments advanced below,[134] according to which those parts of the applicable duty of fairness which are to be regarded as common law creations would be less secure (in the face of ouster clauses and in situations in which litigants wish to raise their breach collaterally) than the vires-based parts of the duty. Neither solution is therefore satisfactory.

5.3.3. The underlying causes of the problem

It is clear, therefore, that attempting to separate the grounds of review into distinct categories is highly problematic. One reason for this is that, as Lord Greene MR remarked in the *Wednesbury* case, the principles of public law do tend to "overlap to a very great extent".[135] This is a generic reason which underlies any endeavour to categorise the heads of challenge, irrespective of the nature of the categorisation or the purpose underlying it. To this extent, it is clearly a partial explanation of the problems which beset attempts to divide the principles of judicial review into those which derive from the legislative framework giving rise to the power and those which are treated as independent creations of the common law. However, it is also possible to identify three specific factors which demonstrate that the particular distinction—which necessarily inheres in the common law model—between judicial creativity and parliamentary intention as the respective sources of different grounds of review is fundamentally ill-conceived.

The first factor concerns *the extent to which the various grounds of review are related to legislative intention*. It is evident that some of those grounds are more transparently and closely related to the legislative framework than others. For instance, the connection between review for breach of an explicit jurisdictional requirement and the legislative scheme is particularly clear. Contrariwise, the complex rules of natural justice derive less straightforwardly from enabling legislation. However, to deduce from this that there exist two quite separate cat-

---

[134] At 145–61.
[135] *Associated Provincial Picture Houses Ltd.* v. *Wednesbury Corporation* [1948] 1 KB 223 at 229, *per* Lord Greene MR. See further M Fordham, *Judicial Review Handbook* (Chichester: John Wiley, 1997) at 514–21.

egories of grounds of review, one of which is a simple product of legislative intention, the other having absolutely nothing to do with it, is unduly simplistic.

This is because, in truth, all of the principles of good administration are, in some manner, context-sensitive in their application. As noted above, this is particularly apparent in relation to factors such as propriety of purposes and relevance of considerations: the determination of these matters can be undertaken only by reference to, *inter alia*, the framework established by enabling legislation. The important point, however, is that this is—to some extent—true of most grounds of review. For instance, Friedman J noted, in a South African case, that:

> where one is dealing with questions of unreasonableness, any argument based on unreasonableness must of necessity be directed towards the empowering provision.[136]

The same point can be made with regard to procedural fairness, as Mason J observed:

> Where the decision in question is one for which provision is made by statute, the application and content of the rules of natural justice or the duty to act fairly depends to a large extent on the construction of the statute.[137]

Thus the principles of good administration are flexible requirements, the precise content of which cannot be determined without reference to the relevant statutory scheme. It follows from this that it makes no sense to argue in favour of a category of grounds of review to which legislative intention is deemed to be wholly irrelevant. To posit a watertight division between heads of challenge to which intention is respectively relevant and irrelevant is implausible, and is a significant shortcoming of the common law model of review.

The better approach is to acknowledge that there is, in relation to the principles of good administration, a spectrum of relevance of legislative intention. At one end of this continuum, where grounds of review such as narrow jurisdictional error are found, the relevance of intention is highly conspicuous. At the other end, intention is still relevant, but less obviously and less directly: such principles as natural justice and reasonableness fall into this category. Grounds of challenge such as propriety and relevance are likely to be found towards the mid-point of the continuum. Such an approach recognises that the precise content and impact of the principles of good administration must always ultimately be determined by reference to, *inter alia*, the legislation which gives rise to the administrative discretion in question. In this manner it is possible to avoid the

---

[136] *Natal Indian Congress v. State President* 1989 (3) SA 588 at 594. Friedman J's conclusion that unreasonableness was nevertheless a common law ground of challenge was reached reluctantly, on the basis that the Appellate Division's decision in *Staatspresident* v. *United Democratic Front* 1988 (4) SA 830 dictated this outcome.

[137] *Kioa* v. *West* (1985) 159 CLR 550 at 584. See also *Re HK (An Infant)* [1967] 2 QB 617 at 630, *per* Lord Parker CJ.

artificiality which inheres in the common law theory's attempt to establish a set of grounds of review which is wholly unrelated to legislative intention.

The second factor which helps to explain why it is unsatisfactory to attempt to distinguish between common law and vires-based grounds of review has been touched upon already,[138] but is worth re-emphasising here. The assertion of common law theorists that the principles of good administration are judge-made constructs which have nothing to do with the intention of Parliament appears, at least at first glance, appealingly simple. In truth, however, *to argue in favour of a category of grounds of review to which legislative intention is wholly irrelevant is to embrace the manifestly absurd.*

Take, for example, the decision of the South African Appellate Division in *Staatspresident* v. *United Democratic Front*.[139] It will be recalled that the court reached the conclusion that, when an administrative body enacts vague regulations, it breaches a provision of the common law but does not exceed the power conferred by the enabling legislation. This assumption—that the administrator does not act ultra vires—*necessarily* implies that Parliament is taken to confer rule-making powers which are unlimited by any requirement to avoid making vague regulations.

It is worth unpacking the implications which follow from the ascription of such an intention to Parliament. It is uncontroversial that a regulation which is so vague as to be reviewable is one which is so unclear and imprecise as to be incapable of being reasonably complied with and which therefore serves no useful purpose. It must follow that a vague regulation is made outwith the purposes for which Parliament, in the first place, created the rule-making power: as Grogan commented, in a strong critique of the *United Democratic Front* case, "Delegated legislation which [is so vague that it] serves no purpose, or purposes which cannot be ascertained, falls as far short of the purposes stipulated in an enabling provision as that which serves some ulterior or improper purpose".[140]

Two problems for the common law model thus arise. First, there is a connection between the ideas of vagueness and purpose, and, as noted above, purpose is a matter which cannot be determined without recourse to the statutory framework. Secondly, unless an absurd intention is attributed to the legislature, it *must* be presumed that it did not intend the rule-making power which it conferred to be used to create regulations which are impossible to comply with or which run counter to the purpose for which the power was in the first place created. To suggest—as common law theorists do—that parliamentary intention is irrelevant to the prohibition on vague regulations is therefore untenable; as Haysom and Plasket observe, it means that "the legislature in conferring power on an official to make regulations allows him, in the absence of an express pro-

---

[138] See above at 131–4.
[139] 1988 (4) 830.
[140] J Grogan, "The Appellate Division and the Emergency: Another Step Backward" (1989) 106 *South African Law Journal* 14 at 22–3.

hibition, to make meaningless regulations".[141] Even if we accept Sir John Laws's contention that Parliament may be deemed to be agnostic about such matters,[142] this does not advance the common law argument very far: it simply means that Parliament is (equally implausibly) assumed to be indifferent whether regulations which are meaningless, or which contradict the purpose of the statutory scheme, are made.

This point applies with equal force to other grounds of review. Any suggestion that the doctrine of irrationality is not part of the ultra vires rule means that Parliament is taken to grant discretionary power without attaching any limit to prevent a decision from being made which is "outrageous in its defiance of logic or of accepted moral standards".[143] Similarly, if the rules of natural justice are no part of the ultra vires doctrine, it must follow that Parliament grants discretionary powers which are not limited by any requirement to act fairly. On this view, Parliament's will would not be frustrated or contradicted by the official who sits as judge in his own cause or by the minister who makes a decision which is so flagrantly discriminatory or contrary to common sense that it must, on any view, be regarded as irrational. Nevertheless, the attribution of such absurd intentions to the legislature is an inevitable function of the common law model.

More fundamentally, the common law's ascription of such intentions to the legislature inherently postulates that Parliament legislates in a moral vacuum. It is viewed as being disinterested in how the executive power which it creates is exercised, and the judiciary is cast as the only branch of government which is concerned about such matters. To render the conditions which attach to the exercise of administrative power the exclusive concern of the courts is to deny the pervasive, constitutional quality that the values underpinning judicial review evidently possess. Ironically, therefore, the common law model's professed objective of exposing the normative constitutional foundation on which judicial review rests is ultimately frustrated by the dogma which it conceals, according to which the judiciary is unique in its concern with administrative justice. The heads of review are, in this sense, demoted from the status of overarching constitutional principles to that of judicial constructs.

It is certainly true that the traditional ultra vires doctrine, which proposes a direct relationship between intention and the grounds of review, is highly artificial. However, to suggest that legislative intention is of no relevance at all to the principles of review is equally implausible. While this is a serious shortcoming of the common law theory, it is one from which the modified ultra vires principle does not suffer. By embracing the idea that the relationships between

---

[141] N Haysom and C Plasket, "The War and Against Law: Judicial Activism and the Appellate Division" (1988) 4 *South African Journal on Human Rights* 303 at 329.

[142] This argument, it will be recalled, is based on the concept of the "undistributed middle", which is invoked in an attempt to show that common law principles of review do not run counter to parliamentary intention. For criticism of this approach, see above at 131–4.

[143] *Council of Civil Service Unions v. Minister for the Civil Service* [1985] AC 374 at 410, *per* Lord Diplock.

legislative intention and the different grounds of review vary in their directness, it is able to furnish a realistic alternative to the traditional and common law models which respectively exaggerate and ignore the self-evident relevance of legislative intention to judicial review of statutory discretions.

The third factor which assists in explaining why it is unsatisfactory to postulate a clear distinction between vires-based and common law grounds of review relates to *the way in which the interpretative process is perceived*. It is a cardinal principle of statutory construction in English law that the courts approach legislation on the initial presumption that Parliament intends that the rule of law should be upheld. This approach to statutory construction was considered earlier in this chapter,[144] and it was noted in Chapter 3 that it is a major theme within the work of T R S Allan.[145] The interpretive vindication of the rule of law is a methodology of broad application, and extends far beyond the administrative law sphere. Take, for instance, the strong presumption that Parliament does not intend to create criminal offences which have retroactive effect: as Lord Reid explained in *Waddington v. Miah*, the courts approach penal statutes on the basis that "it is hardly credible that any government department would promote or that Parliament would pass retrospective criminal legislation".[146]

The breadth of the presumption regarding Parliament's intention to legislate consistently with the rule of law was made plain by Lord Steyn in *R v. Secretary of State for the Home Department, ex parte Pierson*, in a dictum cited above.[147] It is precisely this presumption which forms the basis of the modified ultra vires doctrine. However, it is the obverse assumption which necessarily inheres in the common law theory of review: it holds that legislative intention has nothing at all to do with the principles of good administration which, as we saw earlier in this chapter, are clearly related to the rule of law doctrine.

In this manner, the common law model is fundamentally inconsistent with the English courts' long-established approach to statutory construction. While the courts generally presume that Parliament intends to uphold the rule of law, common law theorists direct that the judges must, when approaching legislation which creates discretionary power, suspend that presumption. Instead, the courts must hold that, at worst, Parliament grants powers which are so ample that they encompass the competence to disregard the rule of law or, at best, Parliament is agnostic whether decision-makers should be accorded the compe-

---

[144] At 107–13.

[145] See generally T R S Allan, "Legislative Supremacy and the Rule of Law: Democracy and Constitutionalism" (1985) 44 *CLJ* 111 and above at 60–1.

[146] [1974] 1 WLR 683 at 694. In this passage Lord Reid rightly indicates that constitutional principle is to be regarded as pervasive: thus he characterises it as a factor which is present within the environment within which Parliament legislates and the context within which the administration operates. This is consistent with the view adopted in this work, and reflected in the modified ultra vires theory, that the rule of law is to be regarded as an overarching ethos with which all three branches of government are to be taken to be concerned, rather than as a purely judicial construct which is imposed unilaterally by the judiciary upon the other institutions of the state.

[147] At 109, text to n. 50.

tence to abrogate the principles of fairness and reasonableness to which the rule
of law doctrine gives rise.

Consideration of the principle of access to justice reveals, in particularly stark
terms, this flaw in the common law model of review. The constitutional right of
recourse to the courts finds practical expression in two particular circumstances.

First, the judges vindicate it by approaching preclusive provisions in primary
legislation on the initial presumption that Parliament does not intend to abrogate the rule of law by interfering with citizens' access to the courts.[148] It is
argued below that only by adopting an *interpretative* approach to ouster
clauses, based on this *presumption*, is it possible to justify departure from their
prima facie meaning; an approach not based on interpretation and presumption
would necessarily entail judicial disobedience to Parliament.[149] It is sufficient
here to note that an interpretive attempt to attribute to preclusive provisions a
meaning which is compatible with the rule of law is of a piece with the courts'
long-standing approach to the construction of legislation within a framework
based on that constitutional principle.

Secondly, access to justice finds expression as a ground of judicial review. The
courts regularly hold that the executive should not use its decision- and rule-
making powers to impede access to the courts.[150] However, the common law
theory of review maintains that the limits which the courts apply to the administration's discretionary powers are, "categorically, judicial creations . . . They
have nothing to do with the intention of Parliament."[151] On this approach,
Parliament must taken either to grant to officials the power to impede access to
justice or, at best, to be agnostic about the matter.

A contradiction thus arises. The courts generally approach primary legislation on the presumption that Parliament does not intend to inhibit access to justice (which is one facet of the broader presumption that Parliament legislates
consistently with the rule of law); it is on the strength of this presumption that
the courts limit the impact of provisions in primary legislation which, at least on
their face, appear to curtail the jurisdiction of the courts. However, the common
law theory of review maintains that the principles of good administration—one
of which is that officials should not make decisions or regulations which impede
access to justice—rest on common law foundations and have nothing to do with
the intention of Parliament. This necessarily entails that Parliament does not
entertain any bias in favour of access to justice, and is therefore wholly incompatible with the well-established presumption that Parliament does not intend
to fetter citizens' access to the courts. Once again it is apparent that the common

---

[148] See, *e.g.*, *Pyx Granite Co. Ltd. v. Minister of Housing and Local Government* [1960] AC 260
at 286, *per* Viscount Simonds: "It is a principle not by any means to be whittled down that the subject's recourse to Her Majesty's courts for the determination of his rights is not to be excluded
except by clear words".

[149] This argument is developed below at 147–54.

[150] See, *inter alia*, *Raymond v. Honey* [1983] 1 AC 1; *R v. Secretary of State for the Home
Department, ex parte Leech* [1994] QB 198; *R v. Lord Chancellor, ex parte Witham* [1998] QB 575.

[151] Sir John Laws, "Law and Democracy" [1995] *PL* 72 at 79.

law model of review entails a high degree of artificiality. It accords with neither the reality of judicial practice nor the logic of constitutional theory.

The true position is that the constitutional principle which favours access to the courts rests on the same foundations whether it is applied, on the one hand, to primary legislation or, on the other hand, to administrative action and secondary legislation. It is, categorically, an interpretive rule based on the presumption that Parliament does not intend to abrogate access to justice. The courts approach *all* legislation on this basis. Just as it is presumed that Parliament itself does not intend to inhibit recourse to the courts (via ouster clauses, for example), so it is also presumed that Parliament does not intend to confer on officials the competence to attenuate access to justice. Thus, whenever the courts uphold the citizen's right of access to the courts, they do so on the basis that, once the relevant legislation is properly construed, it becomes apparent that it was never meant to sanction interference with access to justice. This is of a piece with the modified ultra vires doctrine, which is based on the proposition that the courts approach all legislation, including provisions which create discretionary powers, on the presumption that Parliament intends to legislate consistently with the norms on which the legal system is founded.

5.3.4. Conclusion

The foregoing discussion underlines a number of important and unsatisfactory implications which would attend acceptance of the common law theory of judicial review. Although proponents of that model have not adverted to the problem, it is self-apparent that the common law theory, if adopted, would have to co-exist with an intention-based explanation of those instances of judicial review which are clearly related to the enabling legislation. This, in turn, would require a distinction to be drawn between vires-based and common law grounds of review.

It has been argued that it would be extremely difficult to do this, largely because the impetus which underlies the distinction rests on premises which are fundamentally flawed. It wrongly presupposes that legislative intention is either relevant or irrelevant to any given ground of review, overlooking the more subtle approach which holds that enabling legislation inevitably forms the backdrop to review of statutory discretions, but that the proximity of the relationship between intention and review varies according to the specific head of challenge under consideration. Moreover, the putative distinction between vires-based and common law grounds of review involves the ascription of absurd intentions to Parliament which are inconsistent with the characterisation of judicial review as the legal expression of pervasive constitutional principles (as opposed to purely judicial constructs) and which fundamentally contradict the way in which we think about how the rule of law relates to the interpretive process.

Thus the distinction between intention-based and common law grounds of review is unsatisfactory in principle and difficult to sustain in practice. It is now necessary to consider how, additionally, the introduction of such a distinction into administrative law would seriously damage its capacity to protect individual citizens against maladministration.

5.4. The Courts' Response to Preclusive Provisions

It has already been argued that the modified ultra vires doctrine is better able than the traditional ultra vires principle to accommodate the courts' approach to ouster clauses. The present section argues that the same conclusion is reached when the modified ultra vires doctrine is compared to the common law theory of review.

5.4.1. *Preclusive provisions and the logical implications of ultra vires*

Before assessing the implications of the modified ultra vires and common law theories in relation to hard cases involving preclusive provisions, it is useful to compare how the two models deal with straightforward ouster clauses.[152] The South African Appellate Division's decision in *Staatspresident* v. *United Democratic Front* forms a useful starting point.[153] In that case the validity of certain regulations, said to have been made under section 3 of the Public Safety Act 1953, was contested on the ground that they were vague. However, section 5B provided that "no court shall be competent to enquire into or give judgment on the validity of any proclamation [made] under section 3 [of the Act]".

Had the court accepted ultra vires as the theoretical foundation of review, it would have begun by reminding itself that Parliament confers only limited powers on administrators. For the reasons explored above, it would be absurd for Parliament to grant a competence which extended to the making of vague regulations.[154] Consequently the assumption would have been made that the power to create such regulations was, *ab initio*, withheld. The creation of vague regulations would therefore have constituted an excess of jurisdiction and would not have amounted to a proclamation "made under" section 3 of the Act since, properly interpreted, the Act would never, in the first place, have conferred the power to make such regulations. The ouster clause would thus not have operated to prevent review for vagueness.

However, the Appellate Division held that vagueness was a common law, not a vires-based, principle of review. Therefore, by definition, the power conferred *by the Act* was not limited by a requirement to desist from making vague

[152] See further C F Forsyth, "Of Fig Leaves and Fairy Tales: The Ultra Vires Doctrine, the Sovereignty of Parliament and Judicial Review" (1996) 55 *CLJ* 122 at 129–33 and "Heat and Light: A Plea for Reconciliation" in C F Forsyth (ed.), *Judicial Review and the Constitution* (Oxford: Hart Publishing, 2000) at 405–7.
[153] 1988 (4) SA 830.
[154] See 140.

regulations because, on the court's analysis, it was the common law, not the Act, which prohibited vague regulations. The regulations therefore constituted a proclamation made under the Act but in breach of a common law rule. It followed straightforwardly that the ouster provision operated to preclude review.

Such reasoning would apply with equal force if English courts moved away from ultra vires theory. For example, section 25 of the Acquisition of Land Act 1981 provides that compulsory purchase orders "shall not . . . be questioned in any legal proceedings whatsoever". However, section 23 creates an exception to this general prohibition: any person wishing to question the validity of a relevant order may apply to the High Court within six weeks of the publication of the notice confirming the order, and may question the validity of the order on the ground that it "is not empowered to be granted under this Act" or that "any requirement of this Act" has not been complied with.

Given that this statutory remedy is the only way in which compulsory purchase orders can be challenged, it becomes necessary to determine precisely what an aggrieved person may complain of. It is clear that, so long as ultra vires theory is adhered to, any breach of the principles of good administration, as well as any excess of jurisdiction in the narrow sense, will take the administrator outwith his powers under the Act and will cause him to breach a requirement which is imposed, explicitly or implicitly, by the Act.[155] Under this approach statutory provisions of this nature operate only to limit the time period within which public law rights may be vindicated: within that time period applicants can invoke any of the principles of good administration because they are all regarded as species of ultra vires.

However, breach of principles of good administration which constitute common law constructs would not cause the official to trespass beyond the powers delegated *by the Act* or to breach a requirement imposed *by the Act*. If all the broad principles of review were conceptualised as common law rules, they would cease to be enforceable even *within* the six-week period and citizens would be able to raise only narrow jurisdictional errors (which, on any view, are vires-based grounds of complaint). Since ousters of this type are relatively commonplace, this reasoning would have a very substantial impact on the courts' ability to provide protection against executive abuse. This would clearly run fundamentally counter to the courts' long-standing approach to ouster clauses which reflects a policy which is rooted firmly in the rule of law and, specifically, the citizen's right of access to justice.

Crucially, however, the normative force of those policy arguments on their own are insufficient. The courts must also have available to them the conceptual

---

[155] In *Smith* v. *East Elloe Rural District Council* [1956] AC 736, there was some confusion about exactly which heads of challenge could be brought under the statutory remedy. However, the better view is that of Lord Radcliffe in that case and of Lord Denning MR in *Webb* v. *Minister of Housing and Local Government* [1965] 1 WLR 755, according to which any narrow or broad ground of review can be raised under the statutory remedy. As H W R Wade and C F Forsyth, *Administrative Law* (Oxford: Oxford University Press, 2000) at 723 explain, "'Not within the powers of this Act' is simply a draftsman's translation of 'ultra vires', comprising all its varieties . . .".

means by which to effectuate that policy. The South African jurisprudence vividly illustrates that those means, which are supplied by the ultra vires doctrine, are lost once the common law is embraced as the basis of judicial review. Moreover, the fact that the *United Democratic Front* case was decided in a radically different context from that which obtains in the United Kingdom today is beside the point: the argument is a conceptual one, and its applicability is not, therefore, a function of the political context within which judicial review occurs.

5.4.2. Preclusive provisions and statutory construction

The relatively straightforward types of ouster clause considered above demonstrate that, as a matter of logic, ultra vires theory is better placed than the common law to provide the courts with the necessary conceptual tools to preserve some role for judicial review. However, the ultra vires principle also draws strength in this context from a range of other factors which transcend the argument of logic advanced above.

The central difficulty which preclusive provisions inevitably raise relates to the tension which they cause between the dual imperatives of judicial loyalty to parliamentary enactment and judicial vindication of the rule of law. The present section argues that the only way in which these competing objectives may be reconciled is by recourse to the methodology of statutory interpretation, and that only the modified ultra vires doctrine is compatible with an approach to ouster clauses founded on that methodology. This argument is best substantiated by considering the various ways in which the courts' response to ouster clauses may be characterised. Four principal methods require discussion.

The first possibility is that the judges' treatment of preclusive clauses constitutes nothing more than the *implementation of the plain and natural meaning of the words which Parliament uses.* This is consistent with the traditional ultra vires doctrine, which holds that review itself is simply about the vindication of legislative intention. However, it has already been noted that this explanation is untenable: quite clearly, the courts' treatment of ouster clauses—like their general approach to provisions conferring discretionary power—is about much more than the mechanical implementation of legislative intention.[156]

Secondly, it may be that, as Sir William Wade argues, ouster clauses, properly construed, preclude review, but that *the courts effect review in spite of Parliament's intention.*[157] This rationalisation possesses many attractive features, not least its openness and simplicity. However, it is clearly inconsistent with the doctrine of parliamentary sovereignty which still commands widespread, albeit

---

[156] See above at 30–4.

[157] H W R Wade, "Constitutional and Administrative Aspects of the *Anisminic* Case" (1969) 85 LQR 198; Wade and Forsyth, above n. 155, at 706–10. Similar views are expressed by Sir Robin Cooke, "The Struggle for Simplicity in Administrative Law" in M Taggart (ed.), *Judicial Review of Administrative Action in the 1980s* (Auckland: Oxford University Press, 1986) at 10.

not universal, support.[158] Moreover, it was noted in Chapter 3 that even those writers who question the idea of unbounded legislative competence advocate only very modest limits on Parliament's power. Importantly, for present purposes, there is widespread agreement that Parliament remains capable of precluding judicial review of specific statutory discretions.[159] In light of this, the suggestion that review in the face of ouster clauses amounts to judicial disobedience to Parliament is highly unsatisfactory.

The third approach to ouster clauses which falls to be discussed is that which Sir John Laws articulates. Like the second model, it seeks to provide an open account of the courts' reaction to preclusive provisions, but it attempts to do so in a manner which avoids the charge of constitutional impropriety which the second approach attracts. Laws suggests that the courts' response to ouster provisions rests on the axiom that *Parliament can abrogate the rule of law only by an express measure to that effect*.[160] Judicial treatment of ouster clauses is therefore characterised as the vindication of "constitutional principle" rather than as an exercise in interpretation.[161] In this manner Laws seeks to avoid the complexities of an approach based on statutory construction by invoking a simple constitutional rule to the effect that review obtains unless Parliament expressly excludes it. This raises two points.

First, there arises the difficult practical problem of ascertaining what constitutes an "express" ouster clause. This must, in itself, raise questions of construction. It must therefore be concluded that presenting the courts' approach to ouster clauses as the application of a straightforward constitutional principle, which permits the exclusion of review only by the use of express language, does not circumvent the difficulties of statutory interpretation which have long beset this area of public law.

Secondly, if Laws's approach is to be legitimate, it must be based upon the *presumption* that Parliament intends the rule of law to be upheld, so that only very clear—indeed, on Laws's view, express—language is capable of rebutting that presumption. It is necessary to emphasise this point. If a presumptive model is embraced in the present context, it is possible to reconcile Laws's approach to ouster provisions with the theory of parliamentary sovereignty: it is assumed that any such provision which does not expressly exclude review was not, in truth, intended to have that effect. This permits theoretical reconciliation of a robust approach to ouster provisions with the doctrine of legislative sovereignty: the courts do not *refuse* to apply non-express preclusive clauses; rather, they *interpret* them such that they do not, properly understood, preclude review. Disobedience to Parliament is thus avoided, at least at a formal level.

---

[158] See generally above, Ch.3.

[159] See, *inter alios*, Sir John Laws, "Illegality: The Problem of Jurisdiction" in M Supperstone and J Goudie (eds.), *Judicial Review* (London: Butterworths, 1997) at 4.18; P P Craig, *Administrative Law* (London: Sweet and Maxwell, 1999) at 19.

[160] Laws, above n. 159, at 4.26.

[161] Laws, above n. 159, at 4.20–4.26.

However, if the idea of presumption is jettisoned, the situation must arise in which the courts simply refuse to apply non-express ouster provisions *without* justifying such action by reference to the assumption that Parliament could not have intended to abrogate review other than via express language. Unless the effect of the non-express ouster clause is neutralised by such a presumption, the courts' failure to give effect to it amounts to outright disobedience to Parliament.

Thus the position is reached that, so long as Parliament remains competent to suspend and modify the application of the principles of good administration, the courts' approach to ouster clauses can be founded on nothing other than statutory construction. A "rule" to the effect that Parliament must use express language to preclude review is quite beside the point. The real—and only—question is whether, properly interpreted, Parliament legislated to preclude review. At a pragmatic level it is certainly true that Parliament must use very clear language in order to displace the principles of judicial review. This, however, does not follow from any constitutional rule which allows the courts to *disregard* purported ouster provisions which are not "express". Rather, it follows from the application of a rule of *construction* which is based on the presumption that Parliament would not wish to abrogate citizens' basic rights. There can, therefore, be no question of the courts' *ignoring* Parliament's intention: they may only *interpret* legislative provisions from a particular starting-point, *viz.* a presumption that the rule of law should be upheld.

This approach derives support from views expressed in the House of Lords. In his judgment in the Divisional Court in *R v. Lord Chancellor, ex parte Witham*,[162] Laws J, consistently with his extra-judicial comments, sought to establish a straightforward rule to the effect that citizens' access to the courts may be abrogated only by express provision in primary legislation.[163] However, in *R v. Secretary of State for the Home Department, ex parte Pierson*,[164] Lord Browne-Wilkinson questioned the correctness of this proposition. While he agreed that the courts should certainly seek to uphold the rule of law by attempting to preserve access to justice, he made it very clear that this task can be undertaken only interpretatively. Thus very clear legislative language is required in order to abrogate access to justice, not because the courts are entitled to *ignore* purported ouster provisions which are not "express" but, rather, because the courts *presume* that Parliament does not intend to abrogate fundamental rights:

> Such basic rights [as access to justice] are not to be overridden by the general words of a statute since the *presumption* is against the impairment of such basic rights.[165]

---

[162] [1998] QB 575.
[163] Or by secondary legislation made pursuant to primary legislation which expressly confers the power to abrogate the right.
[164] [1998] AC 539.
[165] *Ibid.* at 575, *per* Lord Browne-Wilkinson (emphasis added).

Lord Hoffmann proposed a similar approach in *Simms*, commenting that

> Fundamental rights cannot be overridden by general or ambiguous words. This is because there is too great a risk that the full implications of their unqualified meaning may have passed unnoticed in the democratic process. In the absence of express language *or necessary implication* to the contrary, the courts therefore presume that even the most general words were intended to be subject to the basic rights of the individual.[166]

Clearly this is the correct approach. Only by adopting an interpretative methodology, based on presumption, is it possible to reconcile a sceptical approach to ouster provisions—or to any other provisions which appear to compromise fundamental rights—with the sovereignty of Parliament. Indeed this technique of *statutory construction within a framework based on the rule of law* is precisely the approach which is advocated in this work[167] and is the fourth of the four possible approaches to ouster provisions which falls to be considered. The crucial point for present purposes is that, while this approach is eminently consistent with the modified ultra vires doctrine, it logically cannot be adopted by those who propound a common law basis of review, as the following paragraphs explain.

According to the modified theory of ultra vires, the law of judicial review is based on the simple proposition that the constitutional principle of the rule of law colours the contexts within which legislation is both enacted and interpreted. This supplies a conceptual basis for both the limits which the courts apply to discretionary powers[168] and their endeavours to interpret ouster provisions in a manner which preserves the operation of those limits.[169] The basic premise of the modified ultra vires principle thus accommodates an interpretive, and therefore legitimate, explanation of the courts' approach to ouster clauses. The same is not true, however, of the rival common law theory of review. Indeed, a contradiction exists at the heart of that theory.

In the first place it is clear, as the foregoing discussion demonstrates, that the courts' treatment of ouster clauses can be rendered constitutionally proper only if a presumption is applied to the effect that Parliament, in the absence of clear contrary provision, is taken to intend that the principles of good administration should be operative and enforceable, in order that individuals may have recourse to courts of general jurisdiction. Only by making such a presumption about what Parliament meant is it possible to explain substantial departure from the plain and natural meaning of the ouster provision without recourse to notions of judicial disobedience.

In the second place, however, Sir John Laws—one of the leading common law theorists—concedes that, in order for the common law model of review to oper-

---

[166] R v. *Secretary of State for the Home Department, ex parte Simms* [1999] 3 WLR 328 at 341 (emphasis added).
[167] See above at 121–5.
[168] See above at 107–13.
[169] See above at 121–5.

ate legitimately, it must be assumed that Parliament is agnostic about the limitation of discretionary power. Thus he postulates the existence of an "undistributed middle"—a legislative vacuum which reflects Parliament's supposed neutrality about the operation of the principles of good administration. The problem with this approach is that, if Parliament is taken to be neutral about the vindication of the values underlying judicial review, this necessarily precludes the adoption of an approach to ouster clauses based on presumption. It is logically impossible to argue that the courts are justified in narrowly interpreting ouster clauses because Parliament is taken to intend that the principles of good administration should be operative, while also contending that the common law model of review is constitutionally legitimate because Parliament is neutral about the controls which apply to the exercise of discretionary power.

In the context of ouster clauses, therefore, the common law and modified ultra vires theories differ markedly. The latter embraces the idea that the entire administrative law enterprise constitutes an endeavour shared by courts and Parliament to secure government under the rule of law. The same idea—of judicial interpretation of legislation against the background presumption that Parliament intends to uphold the rule of law—explains both the conceptual basis of the principles of review and the courts' enthusiasm to apply those principles to all discretionary powers unless there is very clear contrary provision. The common law model falters, however, because it seeks to make judicial review an exclusively judicial endeavour. The artificial neutrality which is thus ascribed to Parliament *vis-à-vis* the limitation of discretionary power (which, as Laws acknowledges, is necessary to legitimate a common law system of review) simultaneously deprives the courts of any adequate interpretative machinery which can be employed in relation to ouster provisions. It is therefore clear that the modified ultra vires principle, unlike the common law model, is able to accommodate an interpretive approach to ouster clauses which permits them to be read narrowly, thus preserving the citizen's right of access to justice wherever possible.

However, it is necessary, at this point, to emphasise that there are certainly limits to what this methodology is able to achieve. The whole purpose of an approach based on interpretation is to reconcile the courts' treatment of preclusive provisions with the principle that parliamentary enactments may not be disregarded by the judiciary. It is therefore crucial that the strong construction-based approach to ouster clauses which the modified ultra theory facilitates does not ultimately amount to *de facto* disapplication of such clauses. Since, as Trevor Allan correctly observes, there is no absolutely clear dividing line between bold interpretation and outright disregard of legislation,[170] it is all the more important that the courts' jurisprudence in this field should be subjected to close scrutiny.

---

[170] T R S Allan, *Law, Liberty, and Justice: The Legal Foundations of British Constitutionalism* (Oxford: Clarendon Press, 1993) at 65.

It was noted above[171] that some commentators believe that the courts have already gone beyond bold interpretation and have *de facto* disapplied ouster clauses.[172] They point, in particular, to the case of *Anisminic Ltd. v. Foreign Compensation Commission*,[173] arguing that the words of the ouster clause in that case were simply incapable of bearing the construction which the House of Lords sought to place upon them and that, rather than interpreting the provision, the court actually rendered it meaningless.[174] Until relatively recently it was possible to maintain that *Anisminic* did not altogether deprive preclusive clauses of any effect: as Sir William Wade noted, writing shortly after the *Anisminic* decision was handed down, "a limited meaning can still be given to ouster clauses by allowing them to bar applications for certiorari to quash for error on the face of the record".[175] However, following *R v. Lord President of the Privy Council, ex parte Page*,[176] in which it was held that such errors are simply a species of ultra vires, *Anisminic* logic directs that ouster provisions fail to immunise them against review. Wade thus concludes that, in the light of this decision, the courts' "interpretation" of ouster clauses actually renders them wholly devoid of meaning, and must therefore amount to *de facto* disapplication:

> According to the logic of the House of Lords, "shall not be questioned" clauses must now be *totally ineffective*. Every error of law is jurisdictional; and error of fact, if not jurisdictional, is unreviewable anyway. So there is no situation in which these clauses can have any effect. The policy of the courts thus becomes one of total disobedience to Parliament.[177]

There are various attempts which may be made to counter this argument.

First, it may be noted that appeal tends to be concerned with the *questioning* of *determinations* (or *decisions*), whereas the supervisory jurisdiction is oriented more towards the *review* of the *legality* of the decision-making *process*. On this basis it could be contended that, where a statutory right of appeal would otherwise exist, the effect of a "shall not be questioned clause" is to preclude appeal,

---

[171] At 31–2.

[172] See, *e.g.*, H W R Wade, "Constitutional and Administrative Aspects of the *Anisminic* Case" (1969) 85 *LQR* 198; B Schwartz, "*Anisminic* and Activism—Preclusion Provisions in English Administrative Law" (1986) 38 *Administrative Law Review* 33; J Beatson, "The Scope of Judicial Review for Error of Law" (1984) 4 *OJLS* 22; H W R Wade and C F Forsyth, *Administrative Law* (Oxford: Oxford University Press, 2000) at 706–9; I C Hare, "The Separation of Powers and Judicial Review for Error of Law" in C F Forsyth and I C Hare (eds.), *The Golden Metwand and the Crooked Cord* (Oxford: Clarendon Press, 1998). *Cf* T R S Allan, "Parliamentary Sovereignty: Law, Politics, and Revolution" (1997) 113 *LQR* 443, who takes a more equivocal view.

[173] [1969] 2 AC 147.

[174] S. 4(4) of the Foreign Compensation Act 1950 provided that, "The determination by the Commission of any application made to them under this Act shall not be called in question in any court of law".

[175] H W R Wade, "Constitutional and Administrative Aspects of the *Anisminic* Case" (1969) 85 *LQR* 198 at 204.

[176] [1993] AC 682.

[177] H W R Wade and C F Forsyth, *Administrative Law* (Oxford: Oxford University Press, 2000) at 707 (footnote omitted) (emphasis added).

not review.[178] However, this approach achieves little in situations where there is not, in the first place, a statutory right of appeal which is capable of being excluded.

A second, related approach would be to draw an analogy with subjective language clauses. At one time the courts held that statutory provisions which phrased discretionary powers subjectively—through the use of such phrases as "if the minister is satisfied"—largely inhibited judicial review.[179] The modern tendency, however, is to hold that, in spite of such provisions, the agency must nevertheless satisfy the court that its decision was reached in accordance with the central principles of administrative law.[180] The effect of subjective language clauses is therefore simply to emphasise that the agency possesses a kernel of autonomy into which the court should not enquire. It might be argued that similar effect should be accorded to "shall not be questioned clauses" by holding that, in light of their orientation towards the questioning of the decision itself, they underscore the existence of a core of agency autonomy with which the court must not interfere. The practical effect of this may be to modify the intensity of review, especially in relation to the rationality doctrine (which carries a particular risk of undue judicial interference with the merits of a decision).

Thirdly, it has been held that private law actions can be precluded when they relate to the exercise of discretionary powers which are protected by a finality clause.[181] There is no reason why a "shall not be questioned" clause could not be given similar effect in appropriate cases.

Thus it is at least arguable that, following *Anisminic* and *Page*, "shall not be questioned" clauses are not wholly devoid of effect. Nevertheless, there exists an alternative response to this problem. The contention of the present section is simply that the modified ultra vires doctrine places judges in a *strong*, not an *unassailable*, position in relation to ouster provisions. When *Anisminic* was decided, the construction accorded to the preclusive provision did not entirely deprive it of meaning. If, however, it is felt that, in light of the *Page* decision, "shall not be questioned" provisions are now denied any meaning if they are held not to prohibit judicial review, then it must be accepted that the only possible way to interpret them is to hold that they do preclude judicial review. In such a situation it would be the judges' constitutional duty to acknowledge Parliament's supremacy by construing the ouster clause thus. Unless (or until) the time comes when it is openly and explicitly acknowledged that the constitutional order prevents Parliament from conferring unreviewable discretionary powers, interpretative endeavour must ultimately yield to parliamentary

---

[178] This meaning was attributed to a finality clause in *R v. Medical Appeal Tribunal, ex parte Gilmore* [1957] 1 QB 574.

[179] See, *e.g.*, *Robinson v. Minister of Town and Country Planning* [1947] KB 702 at 713, *per* Lord Greene MR.

[180] See, *e.g.*, *Commissions of Customs and Excise v. Cure and Deeley Ltd.* [1962] 1 QB 340 at 366–7, *per* Sachs J; *Secretary of State for Education and Science v. Tameside Metropolitan Borough Council* [1977] AC 1014 at 1047, *per* Lord Wilberforce.

[181] See *Jones v. Department of Employment* [1989] QB 1.

sovereignty in this context. Nevertheless, as they engage in that interpretative process, the judges' position is significantly strengthened if ultra vires theory is retained.

5.4.3. The dual foundations of an interpretative approach to preclusive provisions

Thus far, two principal arguments have been advanced concerning preclusive provisions. In section 5.4.1 it was argued that the ultra vires doctrine places the courts in a conceptually strong position *vis-à-vis* ouster clauses because it postulates that, *ab initio*, legislation withholds from decision-makers the power to contravene the principles of good administration. Section 5.4.2 then argued that ultra vires also puts the courts in a more secure position given, first, that the only legitimate approach open to the courts is an interpretative one and, secondly, that the common law model of review (unlike the modified ultra vires principle) logically precludes the adoption of a methodology founded on presumption and construction. It is now necessary to consider the connections between these two arguments. By doing so it will become apparent that the ability of the courts to read ouster provisions narrowly rests on two distinct but mutually complementary foundations. This argument is best substantiated by example.

Assume that primary legislation establishes a commission to disburse compensation payments to a statutorily defined category of persons. Payments to persons outwith the stated class will be unlawful on the ground that they constitute an excess of jurisdiction in the narrow sense. Furthermore, payments which are, *inter alia*, irrational or made pursuant to an unfair decision-making process will be vulnerable to review because they contravene the principles of good administration which, depending on one's point of view, are either deemed terms of any grant of statutory power or autonomous requirements imposed by the common law. Assume, further, that the legislation establishing the commission provides that "no determination of the commission shall be called in question in any court of law". This factual matrix raises two specific issues.

The first question which arises is whether, in spite of the "shall not be questioned" clause, review nevertheless lies on the narrow ground which is explicit in the statute (*viz.* that the commission should pay compensation only to persons within the stated class). There is a strong argument that review should be available on this ground. As Lord Wilberforce asked in *Anisminic*, "What would be the purpose of defining by statute the limit of a tribunal's powers if, by means of a clause inserted in the instrument of definition, those limits could safely be passed?"[182] On this view a "shall not be questioned" clause does nothing to displace the *existence* of the stated jurisdictional limit; it merely appears, on one reading, to prevent its *enforcement*. Since it would be perverse for

---

[182] *Anisminic Ltd. v. Foreign Compensation Commission* [1969] 2 AC 147 at 208.

Parliament to state jurisdictional limits, only to render such limits wholly ineffective, the courts are right to strive to attribute to the legislation a meaning which avoids such a result.

The second question concerns the broader limits on power represented by the principles of good administration. It is at this point that the dual foundations of the courts' approach to ouster provisions become particularly important. According to the modified ultra vires doctrine, Parliament is (in the absence of very clear countervailing evidence) taken to intend that the discretionary powers which it creates are, *ab initio*, limited by reference to the principles of good administration,[183] and it is further presumed (by recourse to the interpretative approach set out above)[184] that Parliament intends those limits to be legally effective such that citizens should be able to vindicate them by seeking judicial review. The two foundations underlying the courts' approach to ouster clauses thus relate respectively to the *existence* of the limits which apply to the decision-making power and the *enforceability* of those limits by recourse to judicial review.

It is quite clearly arguable that a clause which says that a decision "shall not be called in question in any court" seeks to preclude a court from adjudicating on—or "questioning"—the validity of the decision. On this reading, the ouster clause is directed only towards preventing the *enforcement* of broad limits on power, but does not say anything which displaces the *existence* of those limits. As with the narrow ground of review, so with the broader grounds: it would be absurd to understand the legislation as preventing the enforcement of those limits on power which Parliament is taken to intend should exist. It is therefore right that the courts should seek to ascribe a meaning to the preclusive provision which avoids such a perverse outcome, by reading the clause narrowly and vouchsafing the enforceability of those intended limits on power whose existence the preclusive provision arguably does nothing to displace.

The position is very different if the common law is adopted as the basis of some grounds of review. Within that model the principles of good administration are entirely unrelated to the inherent scope of statutory power, taking effect, instead, as autonomous, extrinsic rules which decision-makers are required to obey. This means that an ouster provision presents courts operating within a common law model of review with no paradox. Since the grounds of review do not take effect as intended jurisdictional limits, there is no absurdity in concluding that Parliament, via the preclusive provision, intended to exclude their operation: it is not preventing the enforcement of limits whose existence it is taken to intend; rather, it is simply excluding the operation of principles about whose existence it was, at best, entirely neutral.

It therefore becomes clear that the modified ultra vires doctrine places the courts in a much stronger position than the common law theory to ascribe a narrow meaning to preclusive provisions. Within the former model, narrow

---

[183] See above at 107–13.
[184] See above at 121–5.

construction is justified by reference both to the need to obviate absurdity (by interpretatively avoiding a situation in which Parliament is understood as preventing the enforcement of jurisdictional limits whose existence was explicitly or implicitly intended) and to effectuate Parliament's deemed intention that the rule of law should be upheld (by seeking to attribute to the legislation a meaning which preserves the individual's access to justice). The common law model precludes reliance on both of these strategies: since there exists neither a presumption that Parliament intends the rule of law to be upheld nor a paradox to resolve, the courts are denuded of any justification for departing from the literal meaning of the ouster provision.

5.4.4. A common law basis of review and the differential impact of preclusive provisions

It is necessary to point out one further drawback which would attend acceptance of the common law theory of review *vis-à-vis* the courts' approach to ouster clauses. The foregoing analysis demonstrates that the impact of many ouster clauses depends fundamentally upon the distinction between intra vires and ultra vires executive action. Provided that breach of any of the principles of good administration renders a decision ultra vires, standard preclusive clauses do not hinder review on any ground.[185] However, adherence to the common law theory demands recognition of two sets of grounds of review, one based on vires and the other on the common law. As seen above, standard ousters would tend to bite on the latter but not the former. On this approach the impact of preclusive clauses varies according to whether the particular ground of review in question is characterised as an inherent limit on the scope of the conferred power or an external control imposed by the common law. This raises two particular difficulties.

First, assume that two individuals have both suffered an abuse of power by a particular administrative agency the decisions of which are protected by, say, an ouster clause of the type found in the Acquisition of Land Act 1981, considered above.[186] Assume further that the illegality in the first case consists in the breach of a narrow jurisdictional limit on the agency's competence, while the second applicant's complaint relates to the transgression of a broader common law rule of good administration. The ouster provision would operate to preclude review in the second, but not the first, case. Two victims of unlawful administrative action would therefore have their cases treated in very different ways because of a technical distinction between the juridical bases of different forms of admin-

---

[185] Although the possibility remains of the adoption of a formula strong enough to prevent review on *every* ground.

[186] See above at 146–7. The type of ouster clause under consideration provides that orders "shall not . . . be questioned in any legal proceedings whatsoever" but that, within a stated period, the validity of an order may be challenged on the ground that it "is not empowered to be granted under this Act" or that "any requirement of this Act" has not been complied with.

istrative defect. Perhaps even more perversely, a single victim of a variety of abuses of power would be able to complain about some forms of illegality, but not others.

Secondly, the distinction between those administrative defects which are protected by ousters and those which are not would be extremely difficult to draw in practice. It has already been observed that any attempt to distinguish between ultra vires and common law grounds of review would be plagued by practical difficulties. Therefore, not only would victims of unlawful executive action have their cases treated differently; it would also be extremely difficult, in light of the nebulous nature of the distinction between ultra vires and common law grounds, to predict which unlawful acts would be protected by an ouster clause.

This differential treatment and unpredictability is fundamentally inconsistent with the existence of a developed and coherent system of administrative law which aims to provide citizens with effective protection against executive abuse. More generally it is clear from the foregoing discussion that acceptance of the common law model of judicial review would raise very substantial problems in relation to preclusive clauses. The manner in which the juridical foundation of the supervisory jurisdiction is constructed thus has important practical, as well as conceptual, implications. It is not, therefore, a purely abstract issue of constitutional theory—a point which the following section underscores.

5.5. Voidness and Collateral Challenge

5.5.1. *The logical connection between ultra vires and voidness*

It is a logical consequence of the ultra vires doctrine that administrative action which is committed in excess of jurisdiction is void, as Lord Diplock explained:

> It would . . . be inconsistent with the doctrine of ultra vires as it has been developed in English law . . . if the judgment of a court . . . that a statutory instrument was ultra vires were to have any lesser consequence in law than to render the instrument incapable of ever having had any legal effect upon the rights and duties of the parties to the proceedings.[187]

This conclusion follows from the simple fact that executive action which is ultra vires lacks any basis in law. Although there remains a certain amount of confusion regarding the practical effects of action which is ultra vires and void,[188] the

---

[187] *Hoffman-La Roche and Co. AG v. Secretary of State for Trade and Industry* [1975] AC 295 at 365.

[188] The better view is that which is advanced by C F Forsyth, "'The Metaphysic of Nullity': Invalidity, Conceptual Reasoning and the Rule of Law" in C F Forsyth and I C Hare (eds.), *The Golden Metwand and the Crooked Cord* (Oxford: Clarendon Press, 1998). On this approach ultra vires action is void as a matter of law, but may nevertheless exist as a matter of fact. This distinction was recognised by Schiemann LJ in *Percy v. Hall* [1997] Q.B. 924 at 951, who commented that, "Manifestly in daily life the [ultra vires and void] enactment will have an effect in the sense that people have regulated their conduct in the light of it". As Forsyth, above, at 159, explains, if further

important point for present purposes is that the voidness of administrative action is a matter which can be raised not only directly in judicial review proceedings, but also collaterally in any other proceedings in which it is relevant.[189] There is therefore an *a priori* relationship between ultra vires theory, voidness and collateral challenge, as Forsyth has observed:

> Where a matter is properly raised by collateral challenge, then, once the unlawfulness of the act has been established, the court has no discretion, and rightly so, but to uphold the law. Indeed, this underlies the necessity that the unlawful act should be void. When the matter is raised collaterally, the unlawful act is denied effect without its having been quashed by the court; how can this be unless the unlawful act is void? Collateral challenge and the voidness of unlawful acts stand or fall together.[190]

Thus if an administrative act is ultra vires it must, logically, be void; and, if it is void, then it can be challenged in private or criminal law proceedings without its first having to be quashed in public law proceedings. However, while there is an inevitable connection between ultra vires action, voidness and collateral challenge, the same position does not obtain within a common law model of review.

Ultra vires action is necessarily void and collaterally impeachable because it constitutes action committed without any legal justification: the condemnation of ultra vires entails that the administrator has acted outwith the scope of his legal powers, so that his action is void as a matter of law. The common law model, in contrast, maintains that the principles of good administration are autonomous rules which are unrelated to the perimeter of the power conferred by enabling legislation. The analysis is not, according to this approach, directed towards the question whether the action was within or outwith the conferred authority; in result, holding that executive action is in breach of a common law rule of good administration does not necessarily entail that it is outside the scope of the conferred power. There is, therefore, no ineluctable connection between administrative action which is unlawful at common law and the ideas of voidness and collateral impeachability.

This argument is illuminated by the Divisional Court's decision in *Bugg* v. *Director of Public Prosecutions*.[191] It was explained above that, in this case, Woolf LJ distinguished between procedurally and substantively defective administrative action: the former was voidable, meaning that it had to be treated as valid until and unless a court of public law jurisdiction quashed it, whereas the latter was void, and therefore amenable to collateral challenge.

---

legal decisions are taken in reliance on an earlier ultra vires act, the legality of those decisions depends on whether the "second actor has legal power to act validly notwithstanding the invalidity of the first act". In *Boddington* v. *British Transport Police* [1999] 2 AC 143 at 172, Lord Steyn adopted this analysis and accepted that, although ultra vires action may thus produce practical consequences, this does not detract from its voidness as a matter of law.

[189] Provided that Parliament does not provide otherwise: *R* v. *Wicks* [1998] AC 92.

[190] Forsyth, above n. 188, at 157.

[191] [1993] QB 473.

It is important to note that Woolf LJ's attack on the traditional view—that defective administrative action is void and hence collaterally impeachable—was intimately connected with a departure from ultra vires theory. His Lordship tacitly signalled his desire to discard ultra vires as the foundation of some parts of the law of judicial review when he stated that he would "not categorise procedural invalidity as being properly a question of excess . . . of power".[192] The *Bugg* decision thus clearly demonstrates the connection between ultra vires and the voidness of unlawful administrative action, and indicates that abandonment of the ultra vires doctrine would be likely to herald a departure from the voidness—and amenability to collateral challenge—of such action.[193]

The lapse represented by *Bugg* was corrected by the decision of the House of Lords in *Boddington* v. *British Transport Police*. Irvine LC explained that:

> The *Anisminic* decision established . . . that there was a single category of errors of law, all of which rendered a decision ultra vires. No distinction is to be drawn between a patent (or substantive) error of law or a latent (or procedural) error of law. An ultra vires act or subordinate legislation is unlawful simpliciter and, if the presumption in favour of its legality is overcome by a litigant before a court of competent jurisdiction [which includes a criminal court], is of no legal effect whatsoever.[194]

This dictum clearly demonstrates the logical connection between ultra vires, voidness and collateral impeachability, and the *Boddington* decision is to be welcomed as a significant reassertion of the constitutional logic which lies at the heart of English administrative law.[195]

5.5.2. *Abandoning ultra vires: The consequences for voidness and collateral challenge*

It is apparent from the foregoing that if the views of the critics of ultra vires were adopted, such that some grounds of review were regarded as common law constructs, important implications would arise *vis-à-vis* voidness and collateral challenge. This conclusion follows from the fact that, while voidness is an inevitable consequence of ultra vires administrative action, it is not—as *Bugg* so vividly illustrates—a necessary concomitant of executive action which merely breaches common law principles of good administration. Two particular points must be made.

---

[192] *Ibid.* at 500. However, Lord Woolf has now resiled from this position and has stated that the rules of natural justice *are* based on presumed legislative intention. See *R* v. *Secretary of State for the Home Department, ex parte Fayed* [1998] 1 WLR 763 at 766–7.

[193] This conclusion is confirmed by the courts' jurisprudence on error on the face of the record. At one time, that was considered to be an exceptional, non-jurisdictional ground of review. Being unconnected to the ultra vires doctrine, such errors rendered executive action merely voidable, with the consequence that no collateral challenge was possible. However, now that such errors are regarded as species of ultra vires (see *R* v. *Lord President of the Privy Council, ex parte Page* [1993] AC 682), voidness and collateral impeachability must logically follow.

[194] [1999] 2 AC 143 at 158.

[195] See further M C Elliott, "*Boddington*: Rediscovering the Constitutional Logic of Administrative Law" [1998] *Judicial Review* 144.

First, it would be thoroughly objectionable were a category of administrative action to exist which was inconsistent with the principles of public law but collaterally unimpeachable. As Lord Steyn observed in his speech in *Boddington*, such a situation would be "unacceptable . . . in a democracy based on the rule of law" since the consequences—particularly for defendants in criminal proceedings—"are too austere and indeed too authoritarian to be compatible with the traditions of the common law".[196] Moreover, "[t]he possibility of judicial review will . . . in no way compensate [a defendant] for the loss of *the right* to defend himself by a defensive challenge to the byelaw".[197] His Lordship noted that a number of factors—including the inconvenience and cost of launching judicial review proceedings while also mounting a defence in criminal proceedings; the problems associated with obtaining legal aid for judicial review; the need to apply for leave, and the discretionary nature of remedies following judicial review—make it highly unsatisfactory for defendants to have to institute separate proceedings in order to challenge the legality of the secondary legislation under which they are charged. Thus the rule of law requires unlawful administrative action to be susceptible to collateral challenge, and the ultra vires doctrine—together with voidness, which is its logical product—vouchsafes this position.

Secondly, for the reasons advanced above,[198] the dividing line between those defects which could and could not be questioned collaterally would be lamentably unclear. Defendants in criminal proceedings—and others—would be faced with very considerable uncertainty about the possibility of raising faults in the decision-making process which foreshadowed the relevant subordinate legislation or administrative decision. This point demonstrates, perhaps more powerfully than most, that the way in which the theoretical foundation of administrative law is constructed can produce practical—and potentially very serious—implications for individuals. This did not escape Lord Nicholls in *R v. Wicks*:

> There is . . . an imperative need for the boundary line [between defects which can and cannot be challenged collaterally] to be fixed and crystal clear. There can be no room for an ambiguous grey area . . . [T]he boundary is not merely concerned with identifying the proceedings in which, as a matter of procedure, the unlawfulness issue can be raised. Rather, the boundary can represent the difference between committing a criminal offence and not committing a criminal offence.[199]

Although his Lordship was speaking in the context of the putative distinction between substantively and procedurally defective executive action which Woolf LJ sought to introduce in *Bugg v. Director of Public Prosecutions*, his remarks apply with precisely the same force to the distinction between ultra vires and

---

[196] [1999] 2 AC 143 at 173.
[197] *Ibid.* (original emphasis).
[198] At 138–44.
[199] [1998] AC 92 at 108.

common law species of unlawful administrative action which must necessarily be drawn if the common law model of review is embraced.

Irvine LC has noted that:

> The decision in *Anisminic* freed the law from a dependency on technical distinctions between different types of illegality. The law should not now be developed to create a new, and unstable, technical distinction between "substantive" and "procedural" invalidity.[200]

Any attempted distinction between administrative action which is unlawful at common law on the one hand, and under the ultra vires doctrine on the other, would be equally unstable. It would undermine the theoretical foundation on which English administrative law rests and would produce practical consequences for individuals that would be inimical to the rule of law.

6. CONCLUSION

The common law model of legality has emerged largely as a reaction to the evident inability of traditional ultra vires theory to furnish a satisfactory justification for judicial review. However, although the common law approach is superficially attractive, detailed analysis reveals that it creates more problems than it solves.

Properly understood, it purports to purchase internal coherence, but does so at the expense of structural incoherence.[201] This argument was advanced at length in Chapter 3, where it was concluded that to abandon vires-based review in favour of autonomous common law rules of good administration is to challenge the sovereignty of Parliament. This conclusion was based on the fact that the notions of ultra vires and intra vires are mutually exclusive: it follows that judicial review is legitimate only to the extent that it involves identifying and impugning executive action which transgresses the boundaries of the power conferred by enabling legislation. Moreover, there exists a series of more tangible arguments, rooted in constitutional logic and pragmatism, which underlines the undesirability of abandoning ultra vires theory in favour of the common law. Those matters have been set out at length in this chapter.

Although the impetus which underpins the desire of many critics to articulate an autonomous justification for review is complex, it undoubtedly stems in substantial part from a wish to acknowledge and give credit to the fundamental role which the judiciary has played in fashioning the modern corpus of administrative law, and to allow open and honest recognition of the constitutional norms which the courts have relied upon in doing so. This is certainly true for Laws:

---

[200] *Boddington* v. *British Transport Police* [1999] 2 AC 143 at 159.

[201] The common law approach merely *purports* to secure internal coherence: it has been argued (above at 131–4) that it actually fails in this endeavour, given that it attributes to Parliament an intention which is as absurd as that which the traditional ultra vires principle imputes to the legislature.

The judges' duty is to uphold constitutional rights: to secure order, certainly, but to temper the rule of the state by freedom and justice. In our unwritten legal system the substance of such rights is to be found in the public law principles which the courts have developed, and continue to develop. Parliament may (in the present stage of our constitutional evolution) override them, but can only do so by express, focused provision. Since ultra vires consigns everything to the intention of the legislature, it may obscure and undermine the judges' duty . . . More deeply, ultra vires must logically reduce the constitutional norms of public law to the same condition of moral neutrality as in principle applies to legislation, because by virtue of it the decisions of the courts are only a function of Parliament's absolute power. It means that the goodness of the common law is as short or as long as the legislature's wisdom. But the common law does not lie on any such Procrustean bed.[202]

It is the contention of the present work that these concerns can be fully addressed without abandoning vires-based theory, with all the constitutional and practical disadvantages which would attend such a course of action. The courts' development of administrative law undeniably amounts to the creation of a substantive body of public law which has its basis in judicial creativity. Located within its constitutional setting, the ultra vires doctrine does not consign this judicial achievement to the intention of the legislature; nor does it reduce the emerging and developing norms of public law to a position of moral neutrality. In truth, the courts' public law jurisprudence is based on the vindication and elaboration of the rule of law, which forms part of the bedrock of the British constitution. Neither constitutional propriety nor the ultra vires doctrine, understood within its proper constitutional setting, requires the courts to conceal the true nature of their enterprise in this regard.

Nevertheless, so long as the common law accords a legislative supremacy to Parliament, it must be possible to reconcile the courts' public law jurisprudence with this constitutional principle. It is the interpretive methodology of ultra vires which is capable of securing this reconciliation. It does so not through any sleight of hand or trick of logic, but simply by recognising the good sense in the dual propositions that the courts are concerned to vindicate the rule of law, and that, in thus requiring administrators to respect that principle, the courts are fulfilling the intention of a Parliament which legislates for a constitutional order in which the rule of law is fundamental. Understood thus, the modified ultra vires principle renders judicial review constitutionally secure by openly recognising that its substantive basis subsists in the normative principles which form the very bedrock of the constitution, while acknowledging that, at least for the time being, the constitutional order also embraces the sovereignty of Parliament.

One of the most puzzling features of the debate regarding the foundations of judicial review is the unwillingness of writers belonging to the common law school to recognise that the modified ultra vires theory is largely in accordance with their views concerning how review ought to be justified. It openly acknow-

---

[202] Sir John Laws, "Illegality: The Problem of Jurisdiction" in M Supperstone and J Goudie (eds.), *Judicial Review* (London: Butterworths, 1997) at 4.18–4.19.

ledges the substantive foundations on which administrative law rests; it locates judicial review within a normative framework which fully embraces the constitutional ideal of the rule of law; it eschews the positivistic conception of public law adjudication which inheres in the orthodox view of ultra vires; it precisely captures the way in which we think about the interpenetration of legislation and constitutional principle; it produces none of the absurd consequences which have been ascribed to it by its critics; it vouchsafes administrative law's capacity to protect citizens against executive abuse; it avoids the introduction of an unstable and technical distinction (between grounds of review resting on diverse juridical bases) into administrative law; and the argument concerning its necessity, far from depending upon acceptance of the orthodox model of unlimited parliamentary authority, is consistent with a normative account of legislative competence rooted in the primacy of democracy. In short, the modified ultra vires principle answers the well-founded criticisms which have long been levelled at the orthodox model while safeguarding both the internal coherence of administrative law and its compatibility with the constitutional framework.

Trevor Allan writes that "the [British] constitution possesses its own harmony, in which the protection of individual liberties can coexist with recognition of the ultimate supremacy of the democratic will of Parliament".[203] It is precisely this view of the constitutional order which is captured by the ultra vires principle, once it is located within its proper constitutional setting.

---

[203] T R S Allan, "Legislative Supremacy and the Rule of Law: Democracy and Constitutionalism" (1985) 44 *CLJ* 111 at 112.

5

Beyond the Logical Boundary? Judicial Review of Non-Statutory Power

1. INTRODUCTION

THE MODIFIED ultra vires principle, which was set out and whose implications were explored in the previous chapter, seeks to provide a juridical basis for review of statutory powers. However, in light of its reliance on interpretative methodology, it logically cannot—and does not purport to—supply a justification for judicial review of other types of power. The purpose of this chapter is therefore to examine the constitutional foundations which underpin curial supervision of the exercise of non-statutory forms of governmental power.

The case of *Gillick v. West Norfolk and Wisbech Area Health Authority*[1]— in which the House of Lords, on one view at least, reviewed the exercise of a non-statutory governmental function—prompted Sir William Wade to remark that, "The dynamism of judicial review is such that it has burst through its logical boundaries".[2] If judicial review could be legitimated only through parliamentary intention—as the traditional ultra vires doctrine appears to suggest—then Wade would be right to reach this conclusion. In the absence of a Judicial Review Act providing for supervision of non-statutory powers, an immovable obstacle would block the application of the principles of good administration to powers which do not owe their existence to the will of Parliament, however significant those powers and however desirable judicial oversight of them may be.

One of the central themes of the modified ultra vires theory, though, is that curial scrutiny of the use of statutory power does not rest on the one-dimensional foundation of judicial implementation of legislative intention. Although the will of Parliament is constitutionally important in relation to the review of statutory power, it represents only part of the picture. In truth a much richer set of constitutional principles underlies the courts' supervision of those discretionary powers which Parliament entrusts to the executive. And this wider constitutional setting, within which the ultra vires doctrine operates, forms the starting point for any attempt to articulate the constitutional basis of judicial review of other forms of power.

---

[1] [1986] AC 112. For discussion of this case see above at 8–9.
[2] H W R Wade, "Judicial Review of Ministerial Guidance" (1986) 102 *LQR* 173 at 175.

2. THE SOURCES OF GOVERNMENTAL POWER

2.1. The Importance of Sources of Power

As the reach of the supervisory jurisdiction has expanded to cover prerogative and *de facto* powers,[3] the amenability of discretions to judicial review has come to depend axiomatically upon substantive questions of justiciability rather than on technical questions concerning the type of power which is in issue. The perception has thus arisen that sources of power are no longer important.[4] This perception is only partly accurate. It is true that the question of sources is now largely irrelevant to the question *whether* a particular governmental activity may be reviewed. However, the same is not true of the prior question *why*, in constitutional terms, a certain decision-making function is susceptible to judicial supervision. The nature of the power in question thus remains central to the juridical foundation upon which its amenability to review depends.

For instance, it is clear from the discussion in Chapters 3 and 4 that the doctrine of parliamentary sovereignty—the relevance of which is specific to review of *statutory* power—raises important issues which fundamentally shape the way in which judicial review of such power is justified in constitutional terms. In particular, the sovereignty principle requires review of statutory discretions to be conceptualised as an interpretive endeavour. It is equally clear, however, that sovereignty theory and the construction-oriented methodology to which it requires recourse are of no relevance in relation to *non-statutory* power; therefore, judicial review of such power can—and, given the absence of any statute to interpret, must—be justified by other means. Thus the distinction between statutory and non-statutory decision-making powers has important implications for the way in which review of those different forms of power is theoretically justified.

Moreover, even *within* the category of non-statutory power, variations between the different forms of such power necessitate distinct, context-appropriate theoretical explanations of the operation of review. In particular, as section 2.2 shows, there are important conceptual differences between the government's prerogative and *de facto* powers which, in turn, impact upon how review of those powers can be justified at a juridical level. Thus, in light of the fact that—at least as far as the rationalisation of judicial review in terms of constitutional theory is concerned—sources of power *are* still relevant, it is necessary to begin by trying to demarcate the respective provinces of statutory, prerogative and *de facto* power.

---

[3] In the expression "*de facto* power" the word "power" does not connote legal power; rather, it is used more broadly to describe factual "control or influence over individual legal persons or a section of the community". See B V Harris, "The 'Third Source' of Authority for Governmental Action" (1992) 108 *LQR* 626 at 629.

[4] See further above at 9–10.

2.2. Legal Power and Residual Liberty

This task is best approached from a pragmatic perspective by considering the utility to government of different forms of power. When the legality of governmental action is challenged in the courts, the way in which the government argues its case is determined, *inter alia*, by the type of power which it claims to have used. Broadly speaking, the government has two choices: it can assert that it was relying on a legal (that is, statutory or prerogative) power or it can submit that it was exercising a residual liberty (that is, a *de facto*, not a legal, power). It is necessary to consider each of these alternatives in turn.

Most judicial review cases self-evidently concern the exercise of *legal power* given that, in any situation where the government attempts to do that which would otherwise be unlawful, or purports to alter the legal rights, status or obligations of citizens, its action is lawful and able to produce its intended legal effects only if it can establish that it possesses legal authority to commit the act in question. The point was expressed well by Lord Roskill:

> [T]he right of the executive to do a lawful act affecting the rights of the citizen . . . is founded upon the giving to the executive of a power enabling it to do that act . . . In most cases that power is derived from statute though in some cases . . . it may still be derived from the prerogative.[5]

Wade thus remarks that such governmental action must "be shown to have a strictly legal pedigree".[6] If the position were otherwise, the government would possess unlimited and arbitrary power which, in turn, would be a fundamental affront to the rule of law. Consequently cases of this type involve, first, a determination that legal power is needed to support the relevant action and, secondly, examination of whether the government remained within or trespassed beyond the limits of the power, properly defined. Indeed, it is this mode of enquiry which epitomises judicial review proceedings, and—given that the legal powers upon which the respondent usually relies are statutory in nature—the ultra vires principle accurately captures the idea that the court's role is to ensure that the state has remained within the bounds of the legal authority upon which the legality and effectiveness of its action depends.

However, some instances of judicial review do not fit into this conceptual framework. Rather than accepting that it requires legal power to commit the action in question and arguing that it acted within the scope of such power, it is sometimes open to the government to contend that it does not, in the first place, need to demonstrate any legal authority in support of the decision under review. This follows from the fact that the Crown, as a natural person, may do all that

---

[5] *Council of Civil Service Unions v. Minister for the Civil Service* [1985] AC 374 at 417.
[6] H W R Wade and C F Forsyth, *Administrative Law* (Oxford: Oxford University Press, 2000) at 20.

other natural persons may do; and the government may, in the Crown's name, do those things too.

The case of *Malone v. Metropolitan Police Commissioner* usefully illustrates this point.[7] The claimant contended that his privacy had been unlawfully invaded by the defendant's tapping of his telephone. Rather than seeking to establish that it had acted under—and remained within the bounds of—any legal power, the defendant simply argued that it was free to commit the action in question because no law prevented it from doing so. Since the claimant could not establish a legal right to privacy under English law,[8] the defendant did not need to invoke legal authorisation to justify the commission of what would otherwise have been an unlawful act; nor was the defendant seeking to commit an act which produced legal effects in terms of changing the claimant's (or any-one else's) legal rights, obligations or status. It was therefore unnecessary for the defendant to justify its action by reference to any legal power, as Sir Robert Megarry VC explained:

> England is not a country where everything is forbidden except what is expressly per-mitted . . . Neither in principle nor in authority can I see any justification for this view, and I reject it. If the tapping of telephones by the Post Office at the request of the police can be carried out without any breach of the law, *it does not require any statutory or common law power to justify it: it can be done simply because there is nothing to make it unlawful.*[9]

Hence, in appropriate cases, the government does not need to identify any "power" in order to justify its conduct. Rather, it can argue that its action is law-ful because nothing makes it unlawful. Cases of this type thus involve the exer-cise not of legal power but of *residual liberty*—the state is exercising the right, which it enjoys in common with citizens, to do those things which the law does not prohibit.

While, as will be seen below, judicial review can lie in relation to exercises of both, the distinction between legal power and residual liberty is conceptually important. When courts review the use of legal power, they are concerned to identify the limits of that power: any governmental action beyond those limits is unlawful because the necessary legal authority is absent. Logically, however, this approach cannot apply to review of the exercise, by government or anyone else, of residual liberties. Since—as *Malone* demonstrates—there is not, in the first place, any need to establish a legal basis for such action, the courts cannot exercise a review jurisdiction based on policing the scope of such non-existent power. A different explanation of this type of review must therefore be articu-lated. The implications of this conceptual distinction between exercises of legal

---

[7] [1979] Ch. 344.

[8] Subsequently, however, the European Court of Human Rights held in *Malone v. United Kingdom* (1984) 7 EHRR 14 that the litigant's right of privacy under Art. 8 of the European Convention on Human Rights had been infringed. British law was therefore amended by the Interception of Communications Act 1985.

[9] [1979] Ch.344 at 366–7 (emphasis added).

power and residual liberty are considered in more detail below. Before doing so, however, it is necessary to consider a case which calls into question whether, in the first place, the government may actually possess any residual liberties.

In R v. *Somerset County Council, ex parte Fewings* the respondent council, which had permitted deer hunting to take place on certain land which it had acquired, later resolved to prohibit this practice on the ground that it involved unacceptable cruelty.[10] The applicant contended that this was not, in law, a valid reason on which the council could base its decision and, therefore, that the ban was unlawful. The respondent, however, considered that it had an unfettered discretion in this area, arguing that "it is for every landholder to decide . . . what activities he or she wishes to allow on his land".[11] Thus the applicant argued that the respondent's decision was unlawful because that decision ought to have been, but was not, supported by legal authority; in contrast, the respondent's contention was that it was exercising its residual liberty, in common with other landowners, to decide how its land should be used and therefore needed to show no authorisation for its decision. Consequently the courts had to decide which of these modes of analysis applied to the case.

Both the High Court and the Court of Appeal accepted the applicant's argument, holding that the council had to show that it was acting pursuant to, and within the scope of, statutory power. That this conclusion was reached is entirely unsurprising. It is a well-established principle that local authorities, being statutory corporations, possess only those powers which are expressly or impliedly given to them by Act of Parliament,[12] as Professor Stephen Bailey explains:

> Unlike a natural person who can in general do whatever he pleases so long as what he does is not forbidden by law or contrary to law, a statutory corporation can do only those things which it is authorised to do by statute . . . If such a corporation acts otherwise than in this way its acts are ultra vires.[13]

However, although the *conclusion* in *Fewings* was sound, the same is not true of the *reasoning* process which preceded it. The courts held that the respondent had to show positive legal justification for its decision, not because its status as a statutory corporation required this but, rather, because *all* public authorities have to demonstrate legal authorisation for *everything* which they do. Hence the approach of Sir Robert Megarry VC in *Malone*—which, surprisingly, was not referred to in any of the judgments in *Fewings*—was implicitly rejected. Laws J opined that:

[10] [1995] 1 All ER 513 (QBD); [1995] 1 WLR 1037 (CA).

[11] [1995] 1 WLR 1037 at 1042.

[12] *Baroness Wenlock* v. *River Dee Co.* (1885) 10 App. Cas. 354 at 362–3, *per* Lord Watson. Local authorities can also do that which is "calculated to facilitate, or is conducive or incidental to, the discharge of any of their functions": Local Government Act 1972, s. 111(1), affirming the common law rule set out by Lord Selbourne LC in *Attorney-General* v. *The Directors of the Great Eastern Railway Co.* (1880) 5 App. Cas. 473 at 478.

[13] S H Bailey (ed.), *Cross on Principles of Local Government Law* (London: Sweet and Maxwell, 1997) at 10.

> For private persons, the rule is that you may do anything you choose which the law does not prohibit . . . But for public bodies the rule is opposite, and so of another character altogether. It is that any action to be taken must be justified by positive law.[14]

Sir Thomas Bingham MR expressed the same view in the Court of Appeal:

> To the famous question asked by the owner of the vineyard: "Is it not lawful for me to do what I will with mine own?"[15] . . . the modern answer would be clear: "Yes, subject to such regulatory and other constraints as the law imposes." But if the same question were posed by a local authority the answer would be different. It would be: "No, it is not lawful for you to do anything save what the law expressly or impliedly authorises. You enjoy no unfettered discretions. There are legal limits to every power you have."[16]

The broad implication of these passages—that governmental authorities have no residual liberty—conflicts starkly with both government practice and established legal principle. It is perfectly clear that there are many things which the government can do without any positive legal authorisation, as Daintith observes:

> Plenty of attention is devoted in the textbooks to the peculiar legal powers of government—those common-law and statutory powers which go beyond the legal capacities of ordinary persons and enable government to fulfil its specific mission . . . [But] it is important to remember that alongside these special powers government also possesses the legal capacities of an ordinary person of full age, not subject to any legal disabilities. For purposes of policy implementation, these "ordinary" capacities of government are of major significance. In their exercise the government . . . may make promises, conclude contracts, acquire and dispose of property, acquire and disseminate information, make and receive gifts, form companies, set up committees and agencies, and perform a wide variety of other functions within the policy process.[17]

The courts recognise that this is so.[18] Thus it is too simplistic to say that every act of government must be justified by reference to positive law. Subject to the special rule concerning statutory corporations, whether governmental action must be legally authorised depends on its nature. Action which aims to produce legal consequences—by, for example, affecting the legal rights or status of others—must be justified by reference to positive law. Similarly legal authorisation is necessary to justify the commission of that which would otherwise be unlawful.[19] In contrast, where the government seeks merely to do something which is

---

[14] [1995] 1 All ER 513 at 524.

[15] St. Matthew's Gospel, ch. 20, v. 15.

[16] [1995] 1 WLR 1037 at 1042.

[17] T C Daintith, "The Techniques of Government" in J Jowell and D Oliver, *The Changing Constitution* (Oxford: Clarendon Press, 1994) at 211. See also B V Harris, "The 'Third Source' of Authority for Governmental Action" (1992) 108 *LQR* 626.

[18] See, *e.g.*, *Malone v. Metropolitan Police Commissioner* [1979] Ch. 344 (telephone tapping); *Gillick v. West Norfolk and Wisbech Area Health Authority* [1986] AC 112 (disseminating information).

[19] *Entick v. Carrington* (1765) 19 St. Tr. 1030; 95 ER 807.

not intended to provoke legal changes and which is not unlawful, it can rely on its residual liberty.

However, this proposition must be qualified in one important respect. If the state initially enjoys freedom to pursue a particular activity, then no legal authority need be marshalled when it acts in that field because its conduct is not unlawful and does not seek to produce legal consequences. However, if Parliament later enacts legislation which sets out a statutory framework which regulates how and for what purposes the government may act in the relevant field, the position changes. In such a situation it would make a nonsense of Parliament's legislative efforts if government could circumvent the system of statutory regulation by relying on its pre-existing (unregulated) residual liberty to pursue the activity in question. Indeed this would threaten the rule of law by placing the government beyond effective legal control. It seems that a desire to avoid this outcome formed, at least in part, the motivation behind the judgments in *Fewings*. Crucially, however, it is possible to address this issue *without* resort to the reasoning—according to which all governmental activity must be supported by positive legal justification—adopted in that case.

The solution to this problem lies ready to hand in the familiar case of *Attorney-General* v. *De Keyser's Royal Hotel Ltd.*[20] That case concerned the question whether the Crown was required to pay compensation when it took possession of property for purposes connected with the defence of the realm. The Crown argued that no such requirement attached to its prerogative power to commit such acts. However, the Defence Act 1842 set out a statutory framework in this field and directed that compensation did have to be paid. The question, therefore, was whether the Crown could rely on its (putative) broad, unregulated prerogative power, or was forced to use the statutory power, remaining within its limits and abiding by the conditions which it prescribed. So far as Lord Atkinson was concerned, the answer was clear:

> It is quite obvious that it would be useless and meaningless for the Legislature to impose restrictions and limitations upon, and to attach conditions to, the exercise by the Crown of the powers conferred by a statute, if the Crown were free at its pleasure to disregard these provisions, and by virtue of its prerogative to do the very thing the statutes empowered it to do.[21]

It was therefore held that a statutory framework displaces pre-existing prerogative power:

> [W]hen a statute is passed empowering the Crown to do a certain thing which it might theretofore have done by virtue of its prerogative, . . . it abridges the Royal Prerogative while it is in force to this extent: that the Crown can only do the particular thing under and in accordance with the statutory provisions, and that its prerogative power to do that thing is in abeyance . . . [A]fter the statute has been passed, and while it is in force, *the thing it empowers the Crown to do can thenceforth only be done by and under the*

---

[20] [1920] AC 508.
[21] *Ibid.* at 539.

statute, and subject to all the limitations, restrictions and conditions by it imposed, however unrestricted the Royal Prerogative may theretofore have been.[22]

Although the *De Keyser* case concerned the relationship between statutory and prerogative power, the logic which underpins the decision is equally applicable to the relationship between statutory power and residual liberty. Thus, although the motivation underlying the broadly framed judgments in *Fewings* was a desire to ensure that government could not rely on residual liberty in order to avoid the requirements of a statutory scheme, it is possible to secure this position without denying the possibility of the government's possessing any residual liberties. As *De Keyser* implies, this can be achieved by recognising that such liberties exist only so long as Parliament desists from enacting a statutory framework governing the relevant area. Once Parliament takes such a step, it cannot plausibly be maintained that the relevant residual liberty continues to exist; rather, the legislative framework supplants it, just as a statutory scheme replaces pre-existing prerogative power. In such a situation, judicial review is quite properly directed not towards the regulation of liberty, but to the determination of the express and implied limits of the relevant body's statutory powers. As will be seen, this distinction has significant implications for the theoretical basis of review.

2.3. Conclusions

It is clear from the foregoing discussion that the government possesses two principal forms of non-statutory power. First, it is uncontroversial that government can exercise prerogative power, which is a legal form of non-statutory power. Secondly, notwithstanding the dicta in *Fewings*, it is equally clear that the government is free to act without legal authority in circumstances where no legal power is needed; in using its residual liberty in this way, the government may therefore be said to be exercising *de facto*, rather than legal, power. Non-governmental bodies may also exercise such power. Thus it is necessary to consider the juridical basis of judicial review of governmental action—and action which is governmental in nature, notwithstanding that it takes place outwith the formal structure of government—committed pursuant to both of these forms of non-statutory power. That task is undertaken in sections 3 and 4, below. Before doing so, however, it is necessary to address two further preliminary issues.

2.3.1. Prerogative power and de facto power

Thus far the discussion has focussed on the difference between governmental exercises of legal and non-legal power. It is necessary, at this point, to refer more specifically to the related distinction between prerogative and *de facto* power.

---

[22] [1920] AC 508 at 539–40, *per* Lord Atkinson (emphasis added).

The precise definition of prerogative power has long been a cause of disagreement among constitutional lawyers. A V Dicey argued that, "Every act which the executive government can lawfully do without the authority of an Act of Parliament is done in virtue of . . . [the] prerogative".[23] Sir William Blackstone, however, suggested that the prerogative must be "singular and eccentrical", comprising only "those rights and capacities which the King enjoys alone, in contradistinction to others, and not . . . those which he enjoys in common with any of his subjects".[24]

It becomes clear, in light of the foregoing discussion, that the locus of prerogative power should trace the distinction between legal power and residual liberty. It makes no sense to refer to the government's possessing a prerogative power to do something which it could do anyway. If "prerogative power" means anything, it must refer to an ability to do that which otherwise could not be done. It is therefore submitted that prerogative power should be understood as describing the government's competence to commit acts which it could not otherwise commit, either because those acts would constitute legal wrongs or because such acts would not be able to produce their intended legal consequences. Those things which the government is able to do in common with other persons it does in reliance on neither statutory nor prerogative power. Such acts involve the exercise of *de facto* power or residual liberty, not legal power (unless, of course, such liberty has been supplanted by a statutory framework).

This argument—that the division between prerogative and *de facto* power should reflect the distinction between legal power and residual liberty—is strongly supported by Professor Wade:

> the prerogative consists of *legal* power—that is to say, the ability to alter people's rights, duties or status under the laws of this country which the courts of this country enforce. Thus when Parliament is dissolved under the prerogative it can no longer validly do business. When a man is made a peer, he may no longer vote in a parliamentary election. When a university is incorporated by royal charter, a new legal person enters the world. All these legal transformations are effected in terms of rights, duties, disabilities, etc., which the courts will acknowledge and enforce. The power to bring them about is vested in the Crown by the common law, so it clearly falls within the definition of the royal prerogative as 'the common law powers of the Crown"[25]

In contrast:

> There is nothing whatever "prerogative" about the making of a government contract or an *ex gratia* payment by a government department. The Crown can do such things because any one and every one can do them, and it has no need of 'singular and eccentrical' power for the purpose.[26]

---

[23] A V Dicey, *An Introduction to the Study of the Law of the Constitution* (E C S Wade, ed.) (London: Macmillan, 1964) at 425.

[24] Sir William Blackstone, *Commentaries on the Laws of England* (Oxford: Clarendon Press, 1765), vol. 1 at 239.

[25] H W R Wade, *Constitutional Fundamentals* (London: Stevens, 1980) at 46–7 (emphasis added).

[26] H W R Wade, "Procedure and Prerogative in Public Law" (1985) 101 *LQR* 180 at 191.

The force of these arguments received a judicial seal of approval from Lloyd LJ in the *Datafin* case: he concluded that, "Strictly the term 'prerogative' should be confined to those powers which are unique to the Crown".[27]

2.3.2. *The conceptual basis of judicial review*

Given that the dividing line between prerogative and *de facto* powers mirrors the distinction between legal powers and residual liberties, it is necessary to consider how this impacts upon the foundations of judicial review.

It has already been noted that the courts' jurisprudence in recent decades has meant that these distinctions are of limited practical importance. Since the courts now claim supervisory jurisdiction over both the government's legal powers (whether statutory or prerogative) and its *de facto* powers (provided that they are truly "governmental" in nature), sources are of limited pragmatic relevance to an intending applicant for judicial review. However, this homogeneity at the stage of practical outcomes should not be permitted to obscure the considerable theoretical importance of the distinction between legal power and residual discretion.

In particular, we have seen that this distinction determines whether the government's starting point in relation to a given activity is a specific power (the limits of which it must be careful not to transgress) or a broad freedom. This, in turn, has important implications for the way in which the underpinnings of judicial review of prerogative power on the one hand and *de facto* power on the other are explained. When supervising the prerogative, the courts are concerned with the question whether or not the government's claim of power can be substantiated in law; the judges' attention is therefore directed towards the scope and contours of the relevant power. The same cannot be true, however, of action taken under *de facto* powers: since it is not necessary to establish any legal basis for such action, review must be concerned with something other than the determination and enforcement of the scope of any power.

It is against the background of these fundamental conceptual differences between prerogative and *de facto* power that the constitutional and legal bases of judicial review in these areas fall to be addressed.

---

[27] R v. *Panel on Take-overs and Mergers, ex parte Datafin plc* [1987] QB 815 at 848. For this "first glimmering judicial recognition that the prerogative consists [only] of powers which are unique to the Crown", Sir William Wade conferred upon Lloyd LJ a "special merit award": see H W R Wade, "New Vistas of Judicial Review" (1987) 103 *LQR* 323 at 325. However, this more rigorous definition of "prerogative" is not yet pervasive within the courts: see, *e.g.*, R v. *Secretary of State for the Home Department, ex parte Fire Brigades Union* [1995] 2 AC 513, in which it was assumed that the establishment of a scheme to compensate victims of crime had been established pursuant to prerogative power.

In considering the foundations of judicial supervision of prerogative power, it is useful to distinguish the three principal categories into which review in this area falls, and which reflect the cautious, incremental approach which the courts have adopted in their assertion of supervisory jurisdiction over the prerogative.[28] Section 3.1 addresses the basis of courts' long-established jurisdiction to review the *existence and extent* of prerogative power. Then, in section 3.2, the more recent willingness of the courts to control the *manner of exercise* of the prerogative is considered. Finally, section 3.3 examines the justificatory issues which are raised by judicial review of *delegated prerogative power*.

3.1. Judicial Review of the Existence and Extent of Prerogative Power

It is universally accepted that, whatever the position may once have been, the Crown does not now enjoy unfettered prerogative power. As early as 1611, Sir Edward Coke stated that, "The King hath no prerogative, but that which the law of the land allows him".[29] This position was affirmed by the constitutional settlement of 1689, which "established that the powers of the Crown were subject to law and that there were no powers of the Crown which could not be taken away or controlled by statute".[30] The prerogative power of the sovereign acting alone therefore differs fundamentally from the legislative power enjoyed by the sovereign in Parliament. Whereas the former is unbounded, the latter exists only in isolated—and, given the capacity of statute to erode the prerogative,[31] ever-diminishing—pockets.

In light of this the courts have long been willing to adjudicate upon claims of prerogative power by determining whether asserted powers exist and, if so, how broad they are. Consideration of the constitutional foundations of this long-standing jurisdiction to review the existence and extent of prerogative power is a necessary precursor to any investigation of the juridical basis of the more extensive powers of review which the courts now exercise in relation to the royal prerogative.

---

[28] For an overview, see C R Munro, *Studies in Constitutional Law* (London: Butterworths, 1999) at 278–87. For broader perspectives see F Wheeler, "Judicial Review of Prerogative Power in Australia: Issues and Prospects" (1992) 14 *Sydney Law Review* 432; D Pollard, "Judicial Review of Prerogative Power in the United Kingdom and France" in P Leyland and T Woods (eds.), *Administrative Law Facing the Future: Old Constraints and New Horizons* (London: Blackstone Press, 1997).

[29] *Case of Proclamations* (1611) 12 Co. Rep. 74 at 76; 77 ER 1352 at 1354.

[30] A W Bradley and K D Ewing, *Constitutional and Administrative Law* (London: Longman, 1997) at 271.

[31] This follows from the principle set out in *Attorney-General* v. *De Keyser's Royal Hotel Ltd.* [1920] AC 508.

It was suggested in Chapter 1 that examination of the constitutional legitimacy of judicial review in any area implicitly requires consideration of two key matters. First, it is necessary enquire into the impetus—or *constitutional warrant*—which underpins review of the given form of power. In relation to statutory power, it was argued in Chapter 4 that the constitutional impetus for review lies in the rule of law principle which gives rise to the various heads of judicial review. Secondly, the enquiry must address the more technical question of the *legal basis*—or location—of the principles which the courts apply on judicial review. It was seen in Chapters 3 and 4 that, so far as statutory power is concerned, the legal basis of review has to be conceptualised carefully, so as to ensure that the supervisory jurisdiction is rendered compatible with the principle of legislative sovereignty. For this reason the principles of good administration, as they are applied to statutory discretions, were characterised as interpretative constructs; logically, however, the legal basis of review of non-statutory power must lie elsewhere.

These analytical tools direct attention towards the fundamental issues which arise as part of any investigation into the constitutional legitimacy of judicial review, and they can therefore usefully be deployed as part of the present examination of the basis of review of non-statutory power. So far as review of the existence and extent of the prerogative is concerned, the fact that—as discussed above—prerogative power is inherently limited in its scope is fundamental to both the legal basis of this form of review and its overarching constitutional rationale. Each of these aspects of constitutional legitimacy falls to be considered in turn, beginning with the former.

In relation to statutory power, a distinction was drawn between "narrow" and "broad" review.[32] The former concerns judicial enforcement of jurisdictional limits which plainly derive from the enabling legislation, while the latter relates to the broader principles of good administration which are less clearly based on straightforward implementation of the statute. These two species of review have clear analogues in the context of the prerogative. The courts have (relatively recently) asserted jurisdiction to review the prerogative on broad grounds, by invoking the principles of good administration in order to regulate the manner in which prerogative power is exercised; this is considered in section 3.2, below. However, of present concern is the jurisdiction which the courts' have long asserted to review the prerogative on narrow grounds; this mirrors narrow jurisdictional review in the statutory context, according to which the courts ensure that statutory decision-makers remain within the four corners of the power conferred upon them by Parliament.

In relation to narrow review of both statutory and prerogative power, the courts' purpose is to determine the extent of the relevant power: in other words, to identify where there is power and where there is not. Narrow review of the prerogative is therefore premised on the fact that, like statutory discretionary

---

[32] See above at 28–9.

power, it is not infinite but, instead, exists only within defined areas. This impacts fundamentally upon how we conceptualise the legal basis of this form of review of prerogative power. It would be over-complicated to refer to the courts' enforcing a set of "rules" whose location must be identified. Quite simply, the legal basis of such review subsists in the limited nature of the relevant power. Just as the legal basis of narrow review of statutory power inheres in the fact that such power is finite, so the legal basis of "existence and extent" review of the prerogative is to be found in the limited character of prerogative power. It is therefore both unnecessary and inappropriate to invoke any theory of common law principles of review in this context, given that the courts' endeavour is simply to identify the limits of the legal powers which arise under the prerogative.[33] In this sense, narrow review of the prerogative is of a piece with narrow review of statutory power: in each case, the courts' role is best described in terms of policing the boundaries of the decision-maker's vires.

The other issue which falls for consideration is the constitutional warrant, or rationale, which underlies this judicial endeavour. To state that, in effecting this form of review of the prerogative, the courts are merely policing the boundary of prerogative power is to tell only half of the story, since it begs the question why, in the first place, the courts are concerned to make the limits of the prerogative legally effective. The answer lies in the constitutional principle of the rule of law. As discussed above, the government asserts the existence of prerogative power when it seeks to commit acts which it otherwise could not commit (either because they would constitute legal wrongs or because they are intended to produce legal consequences for others beyond those which could be produced by individuals). The constitutional order dictates that such legal authorisation must be shown: to hold otherwise would be to permit unlimited and arbitrary governmental action. It follows that it is constitutionally imperative that governmental claims of legal power must be open to judicial scrutiny.[34] This principle of legality lies at the very heart of any conception of the rule of law, as Allan explains:

> The idea of the rule of law, in contradistinction to rule by men, is an ancient one. At its core is the conviction that law provides the most secure means of protecting each citizen from the arbitrary will of every other . . . The doctrine's most obvious application to constitutional theory is the requirement that the actions of the executive, and those of every other civil authority or government official, should be justified in law. No one is entitled, by virtue of his office, to disregard the law.[35]

---

[33] This conclusion contradicts the tendency of some writers to assert that autonomous common law principles must necessarily be in play whenever the courts review anything other than statutory power. Narrow review of the prerogative can be about nothing other than the identification of the limits of the relevant power, in which context common law principles of review are quite beside the point. As we shall see in section 3.2 below, a similar conceptual analysis is to be preferred so far as broad review of the prerogative is concerned.

[34] See, pre-eminently, *Entick* v. *Carrington* (1765) 19 St. Tr. 1030; 95 ER 807.

[35] T R S Allan, "Legislative Supremacy and the Rule of Law: Democracy and Constitutionalism" (1985) 44 *CLJ* 111 at 112–13 (footnote omitted).

It may well be thought that legal authorisation for governmental action should have to derive from a statutory source in order to ensure that a representative legislature has had the opportunity to delimit the government's powers and attach appropriate conditions to their exercise.[36] Thus it might be argued that the continued existence of the prerogative as a source of legal authority for the British government is highly anomalous.[37] However, these issues are beyond the scope of the present work. It is sufficient to reiterate that, so long as the prerogative continues to be a source of legal power for the British government, the rule of law demands that the courts must be able to scrutinise claims of prerogative power. It is therefore the simple principle of legality, which lies at the centre of the rule of law ideal, which both justifies and requires judicial examination of the existence and extent of the government's prerogatives.

Thus it is clear that there is a high degree of symmetry between the juridical foundations of narrow jurisdictional review of statutory and prerogative power. In each case, the legal basis of review subsists in the inherently limited nature of those forms of power, while the constitutional rationale which explains why those limits need to be enforced by the courts is self-evidently supplied by the principle of legality which occupies a central place in the rule of law theory. In turn, these conclusions impact upon how the foundations of broad review of the prerogative are conceptualised. It is to that question which we now turn.

3.2. Judicial Review of the Manner of Exercise of Prerogative Power

For a long time, the courts were unwilling to examine anything other than the existence and extent of prerogative power. In the *GCHQ* case, Lord Fraser stated the traditional approach in the following terms:

> [T]he courts will inquire into whether a particular prerogative power exists or not, and, if it does exist, into its extent. But once the existence and extent of a power are established to the satisfaction of the court, the courts cannot [according to the traditional view] inquire into the propriety of its exercise.[38]

However, over the course of the twentieth century the judges grew increasing dissatisfied with this state of affairs; as a result, their attitude underwent a gradual process of liberalisation. For instance, Lord Devlin remarked in *Chandler* v. *Director of Public Prosecutions* that "inquiry is not altogether excluded [into the manner of exercise of the prerogative]. The courts will not review the proper

---

[36] This view was adopted by the Institute of Public Policy Research which, in a draft constitution for the United Kingdom, proposed that prerogative power should be abolished and that any governmental action would have to be justified by reference to powers conferred by the constitution. See *The Constitution of the United Kingdom* (London: Institute for Public Policy Research, 1991).

[37] The problem is, though, ameliorated to some extent by the fact that it is always open to Parliament to attenuate the prerogative or replace it with a statutory framework. See above at 171–2.

[38] *Council of Civil Service Unions* v. *Minister for the Civil Service* [1985] AC 374 at 398.

exercise of discretionary power but they will intervene to correct excess or abuse." He noted that this was already "a familiar doctrine in connection with statutory powers".[39] Thus in *R v. Criminal Injuries Compensation Board, ex parte Lain* it was held that the courts had jurisdiction to review the acts of a body established under prerogative powers.[40] Such thinking was strongly endorsed by Lord Denning MR who, in *Laker Airways Ltd. v. Department of Trade*, remarked:

> Seeing that the prerogative is a discretionary power to be exercised for the public good, it follows that its exercise can be examined by the courts just as any other discretionary power which is vested in the executive.[41]

The evolution in judicial attitude was completed by the House of Lords in the *GCHQ* case.[42] Lords Scarman, Diplock and Roskill were clearly of the opinion that standards of legality could be applied to the prerogative in order to regulate its mode of use.[43] Although national security considerations precluded review from occurring in that case, the courts have since held themselves competent to consider the manner of exercise of prerogative powers[44] covering such matters as mercy,[45] the issuing of passports[46] and the establishment of a criminal injuries compensation scheme.[47] It is therefore necessary to address the constitutional basis of this significant extension of the supervisory jurisdiction, which facilitates the application of the broad principles of good administration to prerogative power, beginning with the constitutional rationale which operates in this area.

Section 3.1 explains that the principle of legality, which lies at the heart of any conception of the rule of law, supplies the constitutional impetus for the narrow "existence and extent" review jurisdiction which the courts have long exercised in relation to the prerogative. Once it is recognised that the rule of law thus underpins this narrow form of review, the question becomes how broad is the conception of the rule of law which is in play.

---

[39] [1964] AC 763 at 810.

[40] [1967] 2 QB 864. As observed above at 7, n. 33, this case cannot be said to have concerned prerogative power if the narrow (and, it is submitted, correct) definition propounded by Blackstone and Wade is preferred to that of Dicey. Nevertheless, *Lain* disclosed an important change of judicial attitude in this field.

[41] [1977] QB 643 at 705.

[42] For comment, see C F Forsyth, "Judicial Review, the Royal Prerogative and National Security" (1985) 36 *NILQ* 25.

[43] *Council of Civil Service Unions v. Minister for the Civil Service* [1985] AC 374 at 407, 410–11 and 417, respectively. Lord Brandon, at 424, preferred to leave the question open. Lord Fraser, at 398, thought that the courts could only examine the manner of exercise of delegated prerogative power: see below at 182–5.

[44] Or, at least, powers which the courts considered to be prerogative in nature.

[45] See *R v. Secretary of State for the Home Department, ex parte Bentley* [1994] QB 349.

[46] See *R v. Secretary of State for Foreign and Commonwealth Affairs, ex parte Everett* [1989] QB 811.

[47] See *R v. Secretary of State for the Home Department, ex parte Fire Brigades Union* [1995] 2 AC 513.

The doctrine of legality—which requires that decision-makers must be able to marshal legal authority whenever they wish to commit action which produces legal effects, and which therefore requires them to be prevented from exceeding the four corners of that authority—is but one aspect of the rule of law. Given that the prerogative has—at least for the last 300 years—been subject to, rather than above, the rule of law, it must follow that the scope of prerogative power is a function of the contemporary rule of law doctrine. Self-evidently, therefore, that conception of the rule of law, discussed in Chapter 4,[48] which supports the application of broad limits to statutory powers also underpins the enforcement of the principles of good administration in relation to prerogative powers. There is, therefore, a clear symmetry between the constitutional rationale for review of statutory and prerogative power; in each case, the courts ensure that executive authority is used only in a manner which is consistent with the prevailing conception of the rule of law principle. It is therefore wholly unsurprising that exercises of both statutory and prerogative power are constrained by the same principles of good administration, given that those principles rest on a single normative foundation.

However, the fact that the substantive principles of judicial review which apply to statutory and prerogative power spring from the same constitutional source does not mean that the mechanism by which those principles are applied in relation to the two forms of power need necessarily be the same. In other words, the existence of a common underlying constitutional rationale does not imply that the legal basis on which the implementation of the principles of good administration depends is similarly shared. Indeed, given that those principles take effect as interpretive constructs in the statutory context, and that, in relation to the prerogative, there exists no relevant legislation onto which the grounds of review can be grafted, it follows *a priori* that the legal bases of broad review in these two fields must be distinct.

It will be recalled that, in relation to statutory power, there are two conflicting schools of thought *vis-à-vis* the legal basis of the principles of good administration. Ultra vires theorists hold that those principles reflect the contours and scope of the power conferred by Parliament: they therefore represent inherent limits on power which are present from the very point of its creation. In contrast, the common law school holds that the principles of good administration are autonomous constructs: they externally constrain the exercise of the power, rather than internally shaping its contours *ab initio*.

These competing views of the basis of the broad review of *statutory* power have analogues in the context of *prerogative* power. Translated into the sphere of the prerogative, the vires-based conceptualisation would view the rule of law (and the public law principles to which it gives rise) as determining the perimeter of prerogative power. Thus the rule of law would operate to set the limits of

---

[48] At 100–4.

the prerogative *ab initio*.[49] The other school would hold that the rule of law gives rise to common law principles of good administration which regulate how the prerogative is used: on this view, those principles would take effect as an external set of rules which those exercising prerogative power would have to obey, but they would not be cast as determinants of the internal scope of the power. There are three strong reasons for preferring the former approach.

First, it has already been noted that, within the British constitutional order, the government's prerogative powers are subject to the rule of law. It therefore makes little sense to say that the prerogative is sufficiently wide to encompass breaches of the rule of law doctrine, but that the common law renders such action unlawful. It is more logical to conceptualise the rule of law as determining the scope of prerogative power from the outset. This accurately reflects the idea that, within the contemporary constitution, the rule of law stands prior to, and therefore limits, the Crown's prerogative powers.

Secondly, this approach is consistent with the analysis, set out above,[50] of the nature of prerogative power. The reason why, in the first place, respondents seek to invoke the prerogative derives from their need to establish that they possess the legal power necessary to do that which they have done. This, in turn, reflects the underlying principle of legality which requires the government to marshal legal authority whenever it seeks to commit action which aims to produce legal effects. In light of this, the court's analysis is directed towards the question whether or not the requisite power exists. Any illegality which attaches to uses of the prerogative derives from an excess of power which renders the government's action a nullity given the absence of any valid legal basis. It would not be consistent with this analysis to conceptualise the principles of good administration as free-standing common law rules which regulate the use of prerogative power. In analytical and constitutional terms, judicial review of the prerogative is not about the application of a regulatory framework of rules to an otherwise unfettered power. Instead, the courts are engaged in policing the boundaries of a power which, according to constitutional principle, is limited by the rule of law from the outset. The vires-based model captures this idea much more accurately than the common law approach based on autonomous principles of review.

Thirdly, the vires-based model is consistent with the explanation, set out above, of the constitutional basis of narrow, "existence and extent" review of the prerogative. Narrow review and broad review are both examples of judicial vindication of (different aspects of) the rule of law. It is therefore appropriate

---

[49] It is important to note, however, that while this approach is similar, it is not identical, to the operation of ultra vires theory *vis-à-vis* statutory power: although in both contexts the rule of law is characterised as determining the scope of the power (rather than precluding the power from being used in certain ways), the application of the rule of law in the statutory sphere is rationalised in a way which renders the imposition of the limits which it implies consistent with the intention of Parliament; however, no such rationalisation is necessary or appropriate in relation to the prerogative. On this point, see further below at 185–6.

[50] At 172–4.

that the legal basis on which review of the prerogative rests should reflect this, by providing a single conceptual foundation which is able to accommodate review on both narrow and broad grounds. The vires-based model supplies precisely such a foundation by conceptualising all review of the prerogative in terms of judicial identification of the limits of prerogative power, and condemnation of executive action committed outwith those limits. In contrast, adopting common law principles as the legal basis of broad review would introduce a conceptual distinction that would postulate distinct juridical bases for narrow and broad review and which, as discussed in Chapter 4, would be inherently unstable.[51]

For these reasons, the application of the principles of good administration to prerogative powers is best conceptualised in terms of the identification of the perimeter of the prerogative, as it is determined by the rule of law. In this manner, narrow and broad review of prerogative power are rendered conceptually consistent with one another, and received constitutional wisdom concerning the relationship between the rule of law and the prerogative is accurately reflected. More general conclusions are drawn in section 3.4, below. First, however, it is necessary to consider a further context in which review of the prerogative occurs.

3.3. Judicial Review of Exercises of Delegated Prerogative Power

Direct exercises of the prerogative are, theoretically, committed by the sovereign. In contrast, when the sovereign delegates prerogative power to a minister, exercises of such power are formally committed by the latter. In practice little turns on this distinction since convention directs that prerogative power is almost always exercised on the initiative or advice of the government. Nevertheless, it was suggested in one of the speeches in *GCHQ*[52] that the difference between direct and delegated uses of the prerogative is highly significant as regards the extent of the courts' powers of review.

The salient facts of that case are straightforward. The sovereign had, by Order in Council, delegated to the Minister for the Civil Service prerogative power for the purposes of (*inter alia*) "controlling the conduct of the service, and providing for the classification of all persons employed therein and . . . the conditions of service of all such persons".[53] In purported reliance on this delegated power, the Minister issued an instruction directing that those employed at Government Communications Headquarters would no longer be permitted to

[51] See above at 134–8.

[52] *Council of Civil Service Unions* v. *Minister for the Civil Service* [1985] AC 374. H W R Wade, "Procedure and Prerogative in Public Law" (1985) 101 *LQR* 180 at 190–4 argues that no prerogative power was actually in issue in this case. However, this does not detract from the issue of principle, which is presently under discussion, concerning the distinction between direct and delegated uses of the prerogative.

[53] Civil Service Order in Council 1982, Art. 4.

be members of trades unions. The unions challenged this decision on the principal ground that it should not have been reached without prior consultation. The question therefore arose whether the principles of good administration could be applied to the Minister's exercise of delegated prerogative power. As noted above, Lords Roskill, Diplock and Scarman felt that prerogative power (whether delegated or direct) could, in principle, be challenged in this way.

In contrast, Lord Fraser placed substantial emphasis on the distinction between direct and delegated exercises of the prerogative. In light of "the great weight of authority", he assumed—albeit "without deciding"—that "all powers exercised directly under the prerogative are immune from challenge in the courts".[54] He took a different view, though, of delegated prerogative power:

> The Order in Council of 1982 was described . . . as primary legislation; that is, in my opinion, a correct description, subject to the qualification that the Order in Council, being made under the prerogative, derives its authority from the sovereign acting alone and not, as is more commonly the case with legislation, from the sovereign in Parliament. Legislation frequently delegates power from the legislating authority— the sovereign alone in one case, the sovereign in Parliament in the other—to some other person or body and, when that is done, the delegated powers are defined more or less closely by the legislation, in this case by article 4 [of the Order in Council]. But whatever their source, powers which are defined, either by reference to their object or by reference to procedure for their exercise, or in some other way, and whether the definition is expressed or implied, are in my opinion normally subject to judicial control to ensure that they are not exceeded.[55]

It is clear that Lord Fraser's thinking was heavily influenced by the implication-based methodology which is traditionally used to rationalise judicial review of statutory power. His suggestion that the principles of good administration should be conceptualised as implicit conditions attached by the sovereign to the delegated power mirrors the idea that, as regards supervision of statutory power, the grounds of review reflect those limits on decision-making power which Parliament intends should apply (albeit implicitly and generally, rather than explicitly or specifically).

Thus Lord Fraser's approach is superficially attractive because it draws upon the familiar intention-oriented approach of ultra vires. It also appears—at least at first glance—to be highly plausible. It was argued in Chapter 4 that review of statutory power is rendered constitutionally legitimate by reference to Parliament's deemed intention that power should not be conferred upon ministers to contravene the rule of law. It might be thought that review of delegated prerogative power is similarly explicable, by reliance upon the sovereign's presumed intention that no competence to breach the rule of law ought to be devolved to ministers.

On reflection, however, it becomes apparent that to adopt such an approach would be to purchase symmetry at the expense of coherence, since it overlooks

---

[54] [1985] AC 374 at 398.
[55] *Ibid.* at 399.

a crucial difference between the powers of the sovereign in Parliament and the sovereign acting alone. It is clear that the sovereign, in exercising prerogative powers, is constrained by the rule of law: this position was established by the constitutional settlement at the end of the seventeenth century, and it is this conception of the relationship between the rule of law and the royal prerogative which forms the juridical foundation of the courts' long-standing jurisdiction to control the existence and extent of such power, as discussed in section 3.1. Moreover, it was argued in section 3.2 that, as well as confining prerogative power within its four corners, the rule of law doctrine entails further limits which ensure that such power cannot be used in a manner which conflicts with the broader norms of administrative law to which the rule of law has itself given rise.

In light of this it is meaningless to ascribe the duty to respect the principles of good administration, which is incumbent upon those exercising delegated prerogative power, to the will of the sovereign. Since the sovereign does not possess the legal power to use the prerogative in a manner which contravenes the rules of good administration, no such power can, in logic, be granted to a delegate. Thus, in delegating prerogative power, the sovereign has no choice whether public law principles should constrain the scope of that power: the sovereign's power itself is limited by those principles, and so no greater power, unfettered by them, can be delegated. It follows that the legal basis of judicial review of delegated prerogative power is of a piece with the legal basis of review of direct exercises of the prerogative: just as the prerogative itself is finite in its scope, given the constraints which the rule of law prescribes, so any delegation of prerogative power must be subject to the same limits.

It is necessary to make two further points regarding the role of intention in this sphere. First, in Chapter 4 it was noted that, if significant inroads were made into parliamentary sovereignty such that the legislature was rendered incapable of granting administrative discretion free from an obligation to adhere to the principles of good administration, the intention-based explanation of review of statutory power which is offered by ultra vires would give way to a justification based on the limited competence of Parliament. This model was ultimately rejected because it is widely accepted that Parliament's capacity is not limited thus. However, it can be seen that the same is not true of the power of the sovereign acting alone. It is precisely the approach that was rejected *vis-à-vis* statutory power which must apply to delegated prerogative power. This divergence is attributable to the crucial point that the legislative powers of the sovereign in Parliament are legally unlimited, whereas the sovereign's prerogative powers are constrained by the rule of law.

Secondly, although it is clear that review of delegated prerogative power must generally be rationalised by reference to the limited capacity—rather than the will—of the sovereign acting alone, there is no constitutional (or other) reason why the sovereign should not *further* confine the scope of delegated prerogative power. In other words, while certain bedrock limitations exist by virtue of the sovereign's own limited power, it must be open to the sovereign to add further constraints to the use of the prerogative by, for instance, stipulating that a delegated power may only be used for a stated purpose. The existence of such additional constraints must logically be explained by reference to intention.

3.4. Conclusions

The foregoing analysis points towards three principal conclusions. First, there exists a high degree of symmetry between the juridical bases of review of statutory and prerogative power. In each case, the rule of law is properly treated as the overarching constitutional justification for judicial review: in this way, the subjection of both forms of power to the same principles of good administration is readily comprehensible, because those principles are seen to rest on the same normative foundation. Moreover, the legal bases of review of statutory and prerogative power are, in one respect, substantially similar. This is because, in each case, the public law principles which those exercising both forms of power are required to respect are viewed as determinants of the scope of the power: the rule of law does not, therefore, give rise to a set of external rules which regulate the use of discretionary power; rather, it operates internally so as to delimit the scope of statutory and prerogative powers *ab initio*. For these reasons, review of both forms of power may be said to be vires-based, given that the courts' task is conceptualised in terms of identifying, and keeping the decision-maker within, the scope of the power pursuant to which it acts.

However, the second point which emerges is that, in spite of these similarities, there are also important differences. In particular, the construction-oriented methodology which explains how the rule of law takes effect so as to limit the scope of statutory powers is of no application in relation to prerogative power. This is because the imperative underlying the use of that methodology in the statutory sphere—*viz.* the principle of legislative sovereignty—does not arise in relation to prerogative power. Unlike the sovereign in Parliament, the sovereign acting alone, through the prerogative, is ultimately constrained by the rule of law. The rule of law can therefore be conceptualised as a direct limit on prerogative power and intention-based reasoning need form no part of the legal basis of review in this area.

This leads to a third, more general point. In seeking to expose the juridical foundations of judicial review in the various contexts in which it now operates, two matters are of paramount importance. On the one hand it is clearly necessary to fashion a coherent account which recognises that, ultimately, the rule of law is the common normative foundation on which all instances of judicial review rest; only in this way is it possible to accommodate the fact that the same principles of good administration are applied to all types of decision-making power. On the other hand, however, overall symmetry must not be purchased at the expense of context-sensitivity. Notwithstanding that judicial review is uniformly concerned with the subjection of decision-making processes to the values embodied in the rule of law, cognizance must be taken of the conceptual[56] and constitutional[57] differences between different forms of governmental power. Consequently, while the rule of law forms the overarching constitutional rationale for judicial review, it is necessary to articulate different mechanisms by which the effectuation of that principle is secured in legal terms. Only thus may the application of the principles of good administration to different forms of decision-making power be conceptualised in appropriate and convincing terms. It is with these dual imperatives in mind that we turn to consider review of *de facto* governmental power.

4. JUDICIAL REVIEW OF DE FACTO GOVERNMENTAL POWER

4.1. The Growth of De Facto Power and the Response of the Courts

As explained above,[58] a respondent in judicial review proceedings must be able to point to an empowering statute or prerogative in order to justify actions which would otherwise be legal wrongs or which purport to affect legal rights. A substantial amount of the business of government, however, does not fall into this category and does not, therefore, raise questions concerning the scope of legal powers.[59] Similarly many activities are carried on outside the formal structure of government which do not require statutory or prerogative authorisation, but which nevertheless produce practical consequences which are of public significance. Such acts are said to entail the use of *de facto* power. This term captures the idea that the identity of the agency or the importance of the function for which it has assumed responsibility means that it exercises substantial power in fact, albeit not in law.[60] Judges clearly recognise that these powers are just as capable of being abused as statutory and prerogative powers. For instance, some years ago, Lord Woolf remarked that:

> The interests of the public are as capable of being adversely affected by the decisions of large corporations and large associations [as by decisions of the executive] . . .

---

[56] The conceptual distinction between legal and non-legal powers is particularly obvious and important in the present context: it is for this reason that, in section 4 below, it is argued that, while a vires-based model of review is appropriate in relation to statutory and prerogative powers, a different approach must logically be adopted in relation to the government's non-legal, *de facto* powers.

[57] The importance of constitutional differences between various forms of power is illustrated by the fact that statutory discretionary power is granted by a sovereign Parliament, so that some recourse to intention-based reasoning is needed in order to rationalise the limitation of that power via judicial review. In contrast, the application of public law principles to prerogative power can be rationalised otherwise, given that the powers of the sovereign acting alone (as opposed to in Parliament) are themselves limited by the rule of law principle.

[58] At 167.

[59] See above at 170, text to n. 17.

[60] See above at 166, n. 3.

[S]hould they not be subject to challenge on *Wednesbury* grounds if their decision relates to activities which can damage the public interest?[61]

This idea that monopoly power should be subject to supervision by the courts has been supported by a number of commentators.[62] They point to eighteenth- and nineteenth-century decisions which provided that monopolists could charge only reasonable fees for their services; for instance, in *De Portibus Maris*, Lord Hale CJ said that, if only one wharf existed in a certain port, it would be "affected with a public interest, and . . . [would] cease to be *jus privati* only".[63] In light of this Forsyth asks:

[W]hy should the common law not impose on those who exercise monopoly power, whether that power derives from the ownership of property or otherwise, a more general duty to act reasonably, for instance, to heed the rules of natural justice, not to act irrationally and not to abuse their powers?[64]

More recently, the courts indicated their willingness to adapt private law doctrine in order to require non-statutory bodies to adhere to principles, such as natural justice and rationality, which are familiar in the public law field.[65] In particular, ideas such as restraint of trade and implied contractual terms have been relied upon by judges in order to inject a degree of fairness into decision-making processes which are carried out under neither statutory nor prerogative authority.[66] However, while these approaches secured a measure of judicial supervision, they achieved this by deploying private law concepts in order to furnish private law causes of action and, as such, represented a somewhat strained and awkward response to the need to control non-statutory power. The more recent approach of the courts has been to focus on the extension of the supervisory jurisdiction *per se* to the exercise of non-statutory non-prerogative

[61] Sir Harry Woolf, "Public Law—Private Law: Why the Divide? A Personal View" [1986] *PL* 220 at 224. Sir Gordon Borrie, "The Regulation of Public and Private Power" [1989] *PL* 552 expresses similar views.

[62] See, *inter alios*, P P Craig, "Constitutions, Property and Regulation" [1991] *PL* 538 and "Ultra Vires and the Foundations of Judicial Review" (1998) 57 *CLJ* 63 at 77–8; C F Forsyth, "Of Fig Leaves and Fairy Tales: The Ultra Vires Doctrine, the Sovereignty of Parliament and Judicial Review" (1996) 55 *CLJ* 122 at 124–7; Sir John Laws, "Public Law and Employment Law: Abuse of Power" [1997] *PL* 455 at 460–4; M J Beloff, "Judicial Review—2001: A Prophetic Odyssey" (1995) 58 *MLR* 143 at 146–7; D Pannick, "Who is Subject to Judicial Review and In Respect of What?" [1992] *PL* 1 at 4–5; J Alder, "Obsolescence and Renewal: Judicial Review in the Private Sector" in P Leyland and T Woods (eds.), *Administrative Law Facing the Future: Old Constraints and New Horizons* (London: Blackstone Press, 1997). See also D Oliver, "Common Values in Public and Private Law and the Public/Private Divide" [1997] *PL* 630 at 640–3, who argues in favour of broader judicial supervision of non-statutory powers, but on rather different grounds.

[63] *De Portibus Maris* (1787) 1 Harg L. Tr. 78. See also *Alnutt v. Inglis* (1810) 12 East 527; 104 ER 206.

[64] Forsyth, above n. 62, at 125.

[65] See generally Alder, above n. 62, at 171–8.

[66] See, *e.g.*, *Enderby Town Football Club v. Football Association* [1971] Ch. 591, although *cf* cases such as *Nagle v. Fielden* [1966] 2 QB 633 and *McInnes v. Onslow-Fane* [1978] 1 WLR 1520 which imposed principles of reasonableness and fairness without seeking to found this in any sort of contractual analysis.

powers. It is this development—and, specifically, its constitutional and legal underpinnings—with which we are concerned here.

The starting point of this modern approach is generally regarded as the *Lain* case, in which Lord Parker CJ viewed the reach of the courts' public law jurisdiction in very wide terms:

> We have . . . reached the position when the ambit of certiorari can be said to cover every case in which a body of persons of a public as opposed to a purely private or domestic character has to determine matters affecting subjects provided always that it has a duty to act judicially.[67]

A similarly broad approach was proposed by Sir John Donaldson MR in the *Datafin* case:

> Possibly the only essential elements [of amenability to review] are what can be described as a public element, which can take many different forms, and the exclusion from the jurisdiction of bodies whose sole source of power is a consensual submission to its jurisdiction.[68]

However, while these statements of principle clearly evidence an expansionist ethos, they leave open the most difficult—yet most important—issue concerning precisely what constitutes a sufficient "public element". Michael Beloff was right when be observed that "the problems of definition and classification" which thus arise make "the outer boundary [of judicial review] a perplexing perimeter".[69] The courts' response to this problem has led them to refine the test of amenability so as to require some form of governmental interest; in doing so, however, they have considerably restricted the availability of review of *de facto* power.[70]

Notwithstanding the expansionist language which characterises the judgments in the landmark *Datafin* case, it is possible to identify within them at least some indications of the more refined—and restrictive—model of reviewability which was to come. For instance, Sir John Donaldson MR qualified his very broad statement, cited above, by basing his conclusion—that the Take-over Panel was amenable to review—on the fact that it exercised *de facto* power which was *governmental* in nature. Thus he remarked that:

---

[67] R v. *Criminal Injuries Compensation Board, ex parte Lain* [1967] 2 QB 864 at 882.

[68] R v. *Panel on Take-overs and Mergers, ex parte Datafin plc* [1987] QB 815 at 838.

[69] M J Beloff, "The Boundaries of Judicial Review" in J Jowell and D Oliver (eds.), *New Directions in Judicial Review* (London: Stevens, 1988) at 9.

[70] *Cf* D Oliver, "Common Values in Public and Private Law and the Public/Private Divide" [1997] *PL* 630 who argues that, alongside this somewhat restrictive approach to the scope of judicial review, there is an emerging private law supervisory jurisdiction which allows judicial control of private powers which fail to satisfy the criteria for amenability to the public law jurisdiction. This contention is based on the argument that there exist certain key values which are worthy of protection in both private and public law contexts. See further D Oliver, "The Underlying Values of Public and Private Law" in M Taggart (ed.), *The Province of Administrative Law* (Oxford: Hart Publishing, 1997) and "Review of (Non-Statutory) Discretions" in C F Forsyth (ed.), *Judicial Review and the Constitution* (Oxford: Hart Publishing, 2000).

As *an act of government* it was decided that, in relation to take-overs, there should be a central self-regulatory body which would be supported and sustained by a periphery of statutory powers and penalties . . . I should be very disappointed if the courts could not recognise *the realities of executive power* and allowed their vision to be clouded by the subtlety and sometimes complexity of the way in which it can be exerted.[71]

This narrower test—based on the idea of governmental, as opposed to simply public, functions—was followed in the *Wachmann* case, leading Simon Brown J to hold that a decision of the Chief Rabbi could not be reviewed:

To say of decisions of a given body that they are public law decisions with public law consequences means something more than that they are decisions which may be of great interest or concern to the public or, indeed, which may have consequences for the public. To attract the court's supervisory jurisdiction *there must not merely be a public but a potentially governmental interest* in the decision-making power in question . . . [Reviewable non-statutory bodies operate] as an integral part of a regulatory system which, although itself non-statutory, is nevertheless supported by statutory powers and penalties clearly indicative of government concern.[72]

The same approach induced the court in *Aga Khan* to hold that a decision of the Jockey Club's Disciplinary Committee was not reviewable because, *inter alia*, such decisions did not involve a sufficient governmental element:

[T]he absence of a formal public source of power, such as statute or prerogative, is not conclusive [of reviewability]. Governmental power may be exercised de facto as well as de jure. But the power needs to be identified as governmental in nature.[73]

Although the broad principles which the courts apply in cases of this type now appear to be relatively settled, their practical application raises very difficult problems.[74] The decisions of sporting and religious bodies seem generally to be

---

[71] R v. *Panel on Take-overs and Mergers, ex parte Datafin plc* [1987] QB 815 at 835–9 (emphasis added).

[72] R v. *Chief Rabbi of the United Hebrew Congregation of Great Britain and the Commonwealth, ex parte Wachmann* [1992] 1 WLR 1036 at 1041 (emphasis added).

[73] R v. *Disciplinary Committee of the Jockey Club, ex parte Aga Khan* [1993] 1 WLR 909 at 931. At times, Sir Thomas Bingham MR (at 923) seems to indicate that *actual*, as opposed to merely *potential*, governmental involvement is needed. For comment, see N Bamforth, "The Scope of Judicial Review: Still Uncertain" [1993] *PL* 239.

[74] See, for instance, the divergent judicial opinions on the amenability of the Jockey Club to judicial review expressed in R v. *Disciplinary Committee of the Jockey Club, ex parte Massingberd-Mundy* [1993] 2 All ER 207; R v. *Jockey Club, ex parte RAM Racecourses Ltd.* [1993] 2 All ER 225; R v. *Disciplinary Committee of the Jockey Club, ex parte Aga Khan* [1993] 1 WLR 909. Although none of the challenges to the Jockey Club's decisions in those cases were upheld by any of the judges, Neill LJ and Roch J said in *Massingberd-Mundy* (at 219 and 222, respectively) that they would have held certain of the Club's functions to be amenable to review but for the fact that they felt an earlier decision of the Court of Appeal (*Law v. National Greyhound Racing Club Ltd.* [1983] 1 WLR 1302) prevented such a conclusion. Simon Brown J went further in *RAM Racecourses*, at 248, by saying (obiter) that the *Datafin* decision marked the beginning of a new approach so that the question was open; he concluded that some functions of the Jockey Club, like the "quasi-licensing function" involved in *RAM Racecourses*, were amenable to review.

beyond the reach of judicial review,[75] whereas the activities of bodies regulating financial and commercial affairs are more likely to be susceptible to supervision by the courts.[76] Although these distinctions have been rationalised[77] by reference to the "governmental element" test, it is undeniable that they are wafer-thin.[78] Indeed, many commentators argue that this test places artificial and unduly restrictive conditions on the availability of review.[79] This has led Lord Woolf to reiterate that the touchstone should be *monopolistic* rather than *governmental* power, so that the "controlling bodies of a sport and religious authorities" would be amenable to review.[80] More fundamentally, as Nicholas Bamforth has pointed out, the confusion which obtains in this area will not be resolved until the courts reach a "principled decision . . . concerning the function of judicial review".[81]

A further drawback of the present approach is that determination of what constitutes a governmental function cannot be made in a political vacuum: the more *laissez-faire* one's conception of government, the less likely it is that a given function will be considered to be "governmental" in nature. This raises the question whether the scope of judicial review may, or should, vary in light of the political colour of the government of the day and the corresponding conception of the governmental function which is current.

Clearly there exist a number of unresolved issues surrounding review of *de facto* power due largely, no doubt, to the fact that this form of review has only recently become prominent. Many of those issues essentially represent policy choices which must—and will—be made as the law in this area matures. However, a proper understanding of the juridical underpinning of this branch of judicial review—and its relationship with the courts' better established super-

---

[75] See, *inter alia*, the Jockey Club cases, above n. 74; *R v. Football Association Ltd., ex parte Football League Ltd.* [1993] 2 All ER 833; *R v. Chief Rabbi of the United Hebrew Congregation of Great Britain and the Commonwealth, ex parte Wachmann* [1992] 1 WLR 1036.

[76] See, *inter alia, R v. Panel on Take-overs and Mergers, ex parte Datafin plc* [1987] QB 815; *Bank of Scotland v. Investment Management Regulatory Organisation Ltd.* 1989 SLT 432; *R v. Advertising Standards Authority Ltd., ex parte The Insurance Service plc* (1990) 9 Tr. LR 169.

[77] See, *e.g., R v. Disciplinary Committee of the Jockey Club, ex parte Aga Khan* [1993] 1 WLR 909 at 931–2, *per* Hoffmann LJ.

[78] On other possible approaches to determining the ambit of the supervisory jurisdiction, see J Beatson, " 'Public' and 'Private' in English Administrative Law" (1987) 103 *LQR* 34; P P Craig, "Public Law and Control over Private Power" in M Taggart (ed.), *The Province of Administrative Law* (Oxford: Hart Publishing, 1997); J Alder, "Obsolescence and Renewal: Judicial Review in the Private Sector" in P Leyland and T Woods (eds.), *Administrative Law Facing the Future: Old Constraints and New Horizons* (London: Blackstone Press, 1997). On the more flexible approach which obtains in Scotland, see *West v. Secretary of State for Scotland* 1992 SLT 636; W J Wolffe, "The Scope of Judicial Review in Scots Law" [1992] *PL* 625; Lord Clyde, "The Nature of the Supervisory Jurisdiction and the Public/Private Distinction in Scots Administrative Law" in W Finnie, C M G Himsworth and N Walker (eds.), *Edinburgh Essays in Public Law* (Edinburgh: Edinburgh University Press, 1991).

[79] See, *e.g.,* C F Forsyth, "Of Fig Leaves and Fairy Tales: The Ultra Vires Doctrine, the Sovereignty of Parliament and Judicial Review" (1996) 55 *CLJ* 122 at 126.

[80] Lord Woolf, "*Droit Public*—English Style" [1995] *PL* 57 at 64. Similar views are expressed by M J Beloff, "Judicial Review—2001: A Prophetic Odyssey" (1995) 58 *MLR* 143 at 146–7.

[81] N Bamforth, "The Scope of Judicial Review: Still Uncertain" [1993] *PL* 239 at 247–8.

visory jurisdiction over statutory and prerogative powers—may help to bring at least a measure of clarity in this area. As with prerogative power, this question is best approached by considering the underlying constitutional warrant, or rationale, for review, as well as the legal mechanism by which the principles of review are applied.

4.2. Why Review?

The extension of the supervisory jurisdiction in the manner described above has been prompted largely by the rise of corporatist[82] methods of governance and the attendant growth of regulatory bodies which exist outwith the formal structures of government. In one sense, this can be viewed as a pragmatic judicial response to changing constitutional circumstances which is consistent with the traditionally *ad hoc* nature of the growth of English administrative law.[83] Nevertheless, underlying these developments there exists a firm constitutional foundation, albeit one which the courts have been reluctant to articulate.

It is elementary that the rule of law, as it is conceived within the British constitutional order, comprises a requirement of "government according to law". As discussed above, this requires, at its narrowest, that governmental action which is intended to have legal effects or which interferes with the rights and liberties of others must be based on legal (that is, statutory or prerogative) powers if it is to be lawful and produce its intended consequences. However, this principle of legality is self-evidently of no relevance in the present context, given that the defining feature of that context is that the activities under consideration are committed without—and without any need of—legal authorisation.[84]

The fact that the principle of legality is thus irrelevant does not, however, mean that the rule of law, as a whole, is irrelevant. The ethos of "government according to the law" which it embodies carries a broad meaning which transcends the core principle of legality. In particular, as explained in Chapter 4, it requires governmental power to be exercised in a manner which is consistent with the basic principles of fairness, certainty and so on. Notwithstanding the inapplicability of the narrow principle of legality to *de facto* powers, there is no reason why this broader sense of the rule of law should not impact upon their exercise.

The rationale underlying the application of a set of principles of good administration to statutory and prerogative powers is that it is constitutionally

[82] There are various conceptions of "corporatism"; however, a useful general definition is provided by P Cane, *An Introduction to Administrative Law* (Oxford: Clarendon Press, 1996) at 21–2, who describes corporatism as "cooperative arrangements between government and non-governmental groups or institutions under which the latter . . . agree to act in a way which will further government policy".

[83] See Lord Irvine, "Principle and Pragmatism: The Development of English Public Law under the Separation of Powers" (lecture delivered at the High Court in Hong Kong, September 1998).

[84] See above at 167–72.

repugnant for government to be permitted to abuse its power to the prejudice of individuals. It would, however, be inappropriate to hold that the rule of law should constrain only the government's formal legal powers, since *de facto* powers of government are equally susceptible to misuse, and individuals are just as likely to suffer as a consequence. The rule of law, which holds arbitrary treatment to be repugnant and favours access to the courts in order that such abuse may be corrected, must therefore be viewed as requiring the subjection of governmental power to judicial supervision irrespective of whether such power exists *de jure* or *de facto*. The very ethos of the rule of law calls for a substantive, rather than a formalistic, approach to public power. In this manner, it gives rise to a judicial review jurisdiction which embraces "the realities of executive power"[85] in all its forms.

It is therefore crucial that, in determining the scope of their jurisdiction over *de facto* powers, the judges should have regard to the constitutional foundations of that jurisdiction. There are some indications in the courts' jurisprudence that they have sometimes failed to do so. In particular, they have tended to hold that *de facto* powers are reviewable only if, in the absence of a non-statutory body, Parliament would have created a statutory agency to exercise the functions in question. One commentator has suggested that the courts have adopted this criterion because they think that, "to be legitimate, everything [they] . . . do in public law must be justifiable by reference to parliamentary intent".[86] If this is so, the courts are clearly labouring under a constitutional misconception. The judicial review jurisdiction does not rest on a single foundation of legislative intention: other constitutional principles also play a crucial role in this area. Better recognition of this may assist the courts to determine the scope of their supervisory jurisdiction in a more principled manner. In any event, it would ensure that the scope of judicial review was determined openly, by reference to the policy choices which are clearly at stake in this area, rather than on the basis of a constitutional misapprehension.

Of course, the courts retain a substantial degree of flexibility, since it is for the judges to decide the details of what the rule of law requires.[87] For instance, over time it may well be that, as circumstances change, the appropriate scope of judicial review of non-statutory power will evolve. Thus, to recognise that the basis of the courts' jurisdiction in this area subsists in the vindication of foundational constitutional values cannot be a panacea. Important decisions regarding the proper scope of review must still be taken by the courts. Nevertheless, it is crucial that the courts appreciate that their supervisory endeavour—in this as in every other field—is rooted in a series of values which possess a normative resonance of their own, and whose articulation and vindication are paradig-

---

[85] *R v. Panel on Take-overs and Mergers, ex parte Datafin plc* [1987] QB 815 at 838, *per* Sir John Donaldson MR.

[86] M Hunt, "Constitutionalism and Contractualisation of Government in the United Kingdom" in M Taggart (ed.), *The Province of Administrative Law* (Oxford: Hart Publishing, 1997) at 32.

[87] See above at 104–6.

matically a constitutional function of the courts. That this set of values is not static and that it is for the courts to determine their precise content should not be allowed to obscure the fact that judicial review in this field rests on rich constitutional foundations, and not on the constitutional solecism that the will of Parliament must underlie every innovation in English public law.

4.3. The Legal Basis of Review

It is evident, therefore, that the rule of law doctrine (albeit not the principle of legality) forms the constitutional rationale for judicial review of *de facto* power just as for review of statutory and prerogative power. In this sense, the principles of good administration, as they are applied to all of those types of power, share one common normative foundation. Importantly, however, the vires-based model of review by which the application of those principles to statutory and prerogative powers is effected is inappropriate so far as *de facto* power is concerned. This follows from the conceptual distinction between legal and non-legal power which was discussed above,[88] and to which we now return.

4.3.1. *Legal power and de facto power*

It was argued, in relation to statutory and prerogative power, that the principles of good administration take effect as internal limits which, *ab initio*, determine the scope of the relevant power. Within that model, when an administrator breaches the broad principles of good administration, this is analytically exactly the same as a straightforward excess of jurisdiction in the narrow sense. In each case, the decision-maker's action is either unlawful (because it interferes, without legal justification, with the rights and liberties of others) or ineffective (because, without a valid legal basis, it cannot produce its intended legal effects). This mode of analysis is appropriate in relation to statutory and prerogative power because such forms of power exist as defined islands of legal capacity within an ocean of governmental incompetence to affect others' legal rights or commit unlawful acts; and it is the courts' task to confine decision-makers to those islands of legal capacity.

Judicial review of *de facto* power is not, however, amenable to such analysis. When an act does not purport to have legal consequences or impact upon the legal rights and liberties of others, no legal power need be shown as justification for that act. Any regulation of the commission of such acts cannot, therefore, be rationalised in terms of identifying the scope of the actor's legal powers and confining the actor to the powers thus identified. It simply makes no sense to impugn the legality of an act for want of legal power when such power is not in the first place a condition precedent to the act's legality. It follows that the legal

---

[88] At 167–72.

basis of judicial review of *de facto* governmental powers cannot consist in the limited nature of those "powers".

Instead, the principles of good administration must be conceptualised as a set of positive legal obligations which regulates the behaviour of those who exercise *de facto* governmental powers. Failure to adhere to one of the principles of good administration leads to a breach of the corresponding common law rule. Hence when a *de facto* governmental power is abused the unlawfulness inherent in such conduct derives not from an absence of legal power (since such power is not, in the first place, needed), but from the breach of a common law rule which makes it unlawful to act in such a manner.[89] *De facto* powers, far from existing as isolated islands of competence, continue to form an enormous land mass made up of residual liberty; and it is for the courts to erect "no trespassing" notices, through the medium of the common law, in order to ensure that fundamental public law norms are upheld. It follows that this is one area in which a common law model of review is both appropriate and necessary.

4.3.2. Vires-based and rule-based review

A clear distinction can thus be perceived between the legal bases of review of statutory and prerogative power on the one hand, and *de facto* governmental power on the other. The former may be said to be *vires-based*, since it concerns the identification of the scope of the actor's legal power; an excess of power renders the act invalid or unlawful. In contrast, review of *de facto* power is *rule-based*. The courts are concerned not with the limits of any legal power but, rather, with the application of a set of common law rules to the exercise of an otherwise unfettered discretion. Those executing *de facto* governmental functions must abide by those rules if their action is not to be condemned as unlawful on the ground of its inconsistency with the principles of good administration which, in this context, take effect as common law constructs. Two points should be made regarding this distinction between vires-based and rule-based review.

First, although its importance is theoretical, it should certainly not be overlooked. Only by recognising the distinction is it possible to explain the bases of judicial review of various types of power in a manner which fully accommodates the differences between them. The division between vires- and rule-based review therefore reflects the fact that supervision of legal and non-legal powers is, in one sense, about different things, *viz.* the enforcement of the limits of the former and the application of a set of rules which regulates the exercise of the latter.

---

[89] There is a clear parallel here with the way in which private law rules regulate the conduct of individuals. This is unsurprising. Individuals are free to do as they please, subject to those restrictions which are imposed by law. Consequently, individuals enjoy a residual liberty which is constrained by common law and statute. Those exercising *de facto* public functions which require no legal authorisation find themselves in precisely the same position: they are acting pursuant to that residual liberty which they enjoy in common with citizens, and the regulation of that liberty is, symmetrically, effected by means of common law principles of good administration.

Secondly, however, the significance of this distinction should not be over-estimated. In particular, it should not obscure the fact that the core principle which underlies review of both *de jure* and *de facto* powers of government is the rule of law. The distinction between vires-based and rule-based review simply reflects different ways in which that constitutional principle is given practical effect in legal terms.

5. CONCLUSION

Contrary to the view which Sir William Wade expressed,[90] the ultra vires doctrine does not mark the "logical boundary" of judicial review. In truth the supervisory jurisdiction rests on much richer constitutional foundations than the intention of Parliament. To understand the basis and limits of judicial review it is necessary to have recourse to those broader constitutional principles and to approach the issue in a context-sensitive way. It is not therefore possible to articulate a single theory which embraces the courts' supervision of all forms of public power: different types of power raise different constitutional and legal issues.[91]

As has already been seen, any explanation of review of statutory power must grapple with the special considerations which the principle of legislative supremacy raises and its implications for the relationship between the three branches of government. However, just as it was necessary, in that sphere, to make legislative intention part of the justification for review, so it is equally important to eschew attachment to intention-based methodology where it is inappropriate. Hence it was pointed out earlier in this chapter that Lord Fraser's approach to review of prerogative power based on the sovereign's will is inappropriate, as is the apparent attachment of the courts to notions of tacit parliamentary intention as the justification for review of *de facto* power. Similarly, the argument of some writers[92] that the whole of judicial review should be seen to rest on common law foundations must be rejected because that view takes insufficient account of the constitutional order and of the distinction between legal and *de facto* power. Instead, it has to be accepted that judicial review is vires-based in relation to some powers and rule-based in relation to others. Thus, in endeavouring to expose the constitutional foundations of judicial review, it is crucial that constitutional doctrine is used in an appropriate manner, and that

---

[90] See above at 165, text to n. 2.

[91] This point is taken by, *inter alios*, S H Bailey, "Judicial Review in a Modern Context" and Sir Robert Carnwath, "No Need for a Single Foundation" in C F Forsyth (ed.), *Judicial Review and the Constitution* (Oxford: Hart Publishing, 2000) at 421–2 and 423 respectively.

[92] See, *e.g.*, D Oliver, "Is the Ultra Vires Rule the Basis of Judicial Review?" [1987] *PL* 543; Sir John Laws, "Illegality: The Problem of Jurisdiction" in M Supperstone and J Goudie (eds.), *Judicial Review* (London: Butterworths, 1997); P P Craig, "Ultra Vires and the Foundations of Judicial Review" (1998) 57 *CLJ* 63.

the effects and importance of particular principles (like legislative sovereignty and ultra vires) are neither exaggerated nor underestimated.

However, the importance of justifying judicial review in a manner which accommodates the differences between types of power should not be allowed to obscure the pervasive values which ultimately underpin the supervisory jurisdiction. The British constitution is firmly based on the rule of law, and the judicial review jurisdiction is perhaps the clearest manifestation of this. Thus the impetus which underlies the whole of judicial review is, essentially, a desire to ensure that governmental power is controlled by reference to those norms which are regarded as constitutionally fundamental.

Paul Craig has remarked that, if the ultra vires doctrine is postulated as the basis of review of statutory power, while review of non-statutory power is viewed as resting on distinct foundations, this leads to the strange conclusion that "the heads of review which could apply to bodies which do and do not derive their power from statute would be generally the same, but that the conceptual basis for such review powers would be strictly distinguished".[93] The analysis adopted in this book demonstrates that this is not so. Once it is recognised that the constitutional impetus which underlies judicial review is a separate matter from the legal mechanisms by which that impetus is given practical force, it becomes apparent that the application of a uniform body of public law by means which are distinct and which are appropriate to different forms of governmental power raises no contradiction. Thus context-sensitive solutions need not be adopted at the expense of a globally coherent understanding of judicial review. While appropriate principles must, of constitutional necessity, be employed in justifying review of different types of power, a desire to subject government to the rule of law is the common thread which connects review in all of the areas in which it now operates.

[93] Craig, above n. 92, at 77.

6

Judicial Review and Human Rights

THE FOCUS, thus far, has been on the basis of the established law of judicial review. However, administrative law is in the process of being fundamentally altered as a result of the activation, in October 2000, of the Human Rights Act 1998. In particular, the traditional preoccupation of English courts with the process by which governmental decisions are made is set to give way to a mode of judicial control which is concerned more with the substance of such decisions than has hitherto been the case.[1] The purpose of this chapter is to address the legal and constitutional foundations on which this new, rights-oriented mode of judicial review rests. That task is undertaken below, in sections 2 and 3. However, by way of introduction, it is appropriate to provide a brief description of the new legislative scheme and of the discourse on fundamental rights which preceded its adoption.

1. HUMAN RIGHTS IN THE UNITED KINGDOM

1.1. The Background to the Human Rights Act 1998

It was observed in Chapter 1 that, as the role of government has steadily expanded, so the ability of legislators and parliamentarians to call the executive to account has commensurately declined; thus it has increasingly fallen to the judicial branch to speak up for citizens as they interact with the institutions of government.[2] It is within this context that human rights, and, specifically, their judicial enforcement, have assumed heightened prominence in many developed legal systems in recent years. For instance, Canada, New Zealand, Israel, Hong Kong and South Africa have all adopted written catalogues of fundamental rights over the last two decades,[3] while the High Court of Australia has begun to expose a set of implied constitutional rights.[4] Closer to home the case load

---

[1] At the time of writing the Human Rights Act has only just entered into force, so it is not possible to refer to case law under it.

[2] See further above at 1–3.

[3] See, respectively, Canadian Charter of Rights and Freedoms (1982); New Zealand Bill of Rights Act 1990; Israeli Basic Law: Human Dignity and Freedom (1990); Hong Kong Bill of Rights Ordinance (1991) and Basic Law (1997); Constitution of the Republic of South Africa (1996).

[4] See *Nationwide News Pty Ltd. v. Wills* (1992) 177 CLR 1; *Australian Capital Television Pty. Ltd. v. The Commonwealth of Australia* (1992) 177 CLR 106.

and influence of the European Court of Human Rights has grown dramatically[5] as it has "gradually assumed the role of a constitutional court that lays down common standards . . . for the entire legal community of the contracting parties".[6] Similarly, the European Court of Justice has announced its enthusiasm for human rights, which have been held to form part of the general principles of European Union law.[7] Thus a broad trend towards the legalisation of human rights can be perceived, as aspirational rhetoric has been translated into enforceable legal principle.

In some senses Britain has been in the vanguard of the growing international emphasis on civil and political rights. Many of the norms enshrined in human rights documents represent values with which the common law has long been associated, and British lawyers played a central role in the drafting of the European Convention on Human Rights (ECHR).[8] Moreover, as Lester observes, "The Parliament of Westminster has . . . exported the fundamental rights and freedoms of the Convention to the new Commonwealth on a scale without parallel in the rest of the world".[9]

It is therefore ironic that, for so long, English law lacked an enforceable catalogue of basic rights. The limited protection of rights which, until recently, obtained in the UK was a somewhat *ad hoc* affair. Some fundamental rights— such as freedom from discrimination on the grounds of race and gender—have for some time benefited from specific statutory regimes of protection.[10] EU law also confers important rights on British citizens both legislatively and through the doctrine of fundamental rights which the ECJ has articulated.[11] Moreover, the domestic judiciary has played a significant role in promoting human rights in the UK. In certain limited fields the judges have identified common law rights which they have sought to safeguard against legislative and administrative encroachment;[12] and the law of judicial review ensures that, in their dealings with government, individuals are treated fairly and reasonably. In this way, citizens have acquired a set of important, though largely process-oriented, rights which are enforceable against the institutions of the state.

However, in spite of these developments, English courts did not, prior to the activation of the Human Rights Act, possess a comprehensive human rights

---

[5] See C Gearty, "The European Court of Human Rights and the Protection of Civil Liberties: An Overview" (1993) 52 *CLJ* 89 at 93.

[6] S K Martens, "Incorporating the European Convention: The Role of the Judiciary" [1998] *European Human Rights Law Review* 5 at 9.

[7] See especially Case 29/69, *Stauder* v. *City of Ulm* [1969] ECR 419; Case 11/70, *Internationale Handelsgesellschaft mbH* v. *Einfuhr- und Vorratsstelle für Getreide und Futtermittel* [1970] ECR 1125; Case 4/73, *Nold KG* v. *Commission of the European Communities* [1974] ECR 491. See also Art. 6(2) of the Treaty on European Union which provides, *inter alia*, that the European Union must respect the values set out in the European Convention on Human Rights.

[8] See A Lester, "Fundamental Rights: The United Kingdom Isolated?" [1984] *PL* 46 at 49.

[9] *Ibid.* at 56.

[10] See Sex Discrimination Act 1975; Race Relations Act 1976.

[11] See above, n. 7.

[12] See below at 212–8.

review jurisdiction: as Lord Bingham put it, the development of the law in this field was "piecemeal and incomplete".[13] Substantive human rights—such as those enshrined in the ECHR—limited neither the legislative capacity of Parliament nor the administrative competence of executive decision-makers as a matter of domestic law. Instead, British citizens who wished to vindicate such rights were usually forced to resort to international law by instituting proceedings against the UK before the European Court of Human Rights.

This traditionally limited status of fundamental rights in English law can be explained, at least in part, by reference to two tenets of the influential work of A V Dicey. First, he argued in favour of the absolute supremacy of Parliament, such that it is free to make or unmake any law which it chooses.[14] This precludes any body of higher-order rights which confines Parliament's competence, thereby preventing a system of constitutional review which, for many, represents human rights protection in its paradigm form.

Secondly, Dicey contended that written human rights instruments are unnecessary because the common law's flexibility and emphasis on remedies facilitate superior protection of individuals' rights.[15] Within this model liberty is residual, existing only to the extent that Parliament—or the executive, acting under statutory or other powers—has not provided otherwise. However, as Lord Irvine noted, this "offers little protection against a creeping erosion of freedom by a legislature willing to countenance the infringement of liberty or simply blind to the effect of an otherwise well intentioned piece of law".[16] The law on freedom of assembly epitomises this incremental erosion of basic rights. The generous liberties in this sphere which were evident in the celebrated case of *Beatty* v. *Gillbanks*[17] have been steadily encroached upon by a series of legislative provisions conferring broad powers on the police. It may be that the limits on freedom of assembly which Parliament has created are "necessary in a democratic society",[18] but the essential point is that, hitherto, such considerations have been neither at the forefront of legislators' minds nor readily justiciable in the courts.

By the 1990s an acute awareness had developed in the legal community and beyond that English law was seriously deficient in this area, as the number of Strasbourg judgments against the UK indicates.[19] Indeed numerous attempts were made to legislate for the protection of human rights, usually by means of

---

[13] Lord Bingham, "The Way We Live Now: Human Rights in the New Millennium" [1998] 1 *Web Journal of Current Legal Issues.*

[14] A V Dicey, *An Introduction to the Study of the Law of the Constitution* (E C S Wade, ed.) (London: Macmillan, 1964), ch. 1.

[15] *Ibid.* at 195–202.

[16] Lord Irvine, "The Development of Human Rights in Britain under an Incorporated Convention on Human Rights" [1998] *PL* 221 at 224.

[17] (1882) 9 QBD 308.

[18] This formula is used in (*inter alia*) Art. 11(2) of the ECHR to define those limits on freedom of assembly which are permissible.

[19] For a summary, see A W Bradley and K D Ewing, *Constitutional and Administrative Law* (London: Longman, 1997) at 470–3.

incorporating the ECHR,[20] and some writers went so far as to urge the subjugation of Parliament's legislative capacity to a set of higher-order norms based on civil and political rights.[21] Although there was, and still is, no consensus on the latter point, the proposition that substantive human rights should at least be enforceable against the administration enjoys broader support since, as Lord Browne-Wilkinson pointed out, "The main threat to our individual freedom comes not from intentional interference by Parliament, but from the creation of statutory powers expressed in general terms".[22]

1.2. The Human Rights Act 1998

This is the context within which Parliament enacted the Human Rights Act 1998.[23] Its mode of operation is, by now, widely understood, and need therefore be described here only briefly. The Act's stated purpose is to give greater effect in domestic law to the human rights set out in the ECHR. Like the New Zealand Bill of Rights Act 1990,[24] the British legislation is essentially an interpretive instrument. Fundamental rights are afforded some protection against legislative and executive encroachment by requiring the courts to interpret legislation— and, therefore, the ambit of the discretionary power of decision-makers—consistently with human rights, so far as this is possible.[25] In addition, public authorities now find themselves under an explicit obligation to respect the Convention rights.[26]

However, in contradistinction to entrenched bills of rights, nothing in the Act constrains Parliament's legal competence: as Lord Steyn observed, "It is crystal

---

[20] See M Zander, *A Bill of Rights?* (London: Sweet and Maxwell, 1997), ch. 1; Lord Lester, "The Mouse that Roared: The Human Rights Bill 1995" [1995] *PL* 198.

[21] For recent examples, see Sir Robin Cooke, "Fundamentals" [1988] *New Zealand Law Journal* 158; D Beyleveld, "The Concept of a Human Right and the Incorporation of the European Convention on Human Rights" [1995] *PL* 577; Sir John Laws, "Law and Democracy" [1995] *PL* 72; Lord Woolf, "*Droit Public*—English Style" [1995] *PL* 57; R Dworkin, *Freedom's Law* (Oxford: Oxford University Press, 1996); G Marshall, "Patriating Rights—With Reservations: The Human Rights Bill 1998" in Cambridge Centre for Public Law, *Constitutional Reform in the United Kingdom: Practice and Principles* (Oxford: Hart Publishing, 1998).

[22] Lord Browne-Wilkinson, "The Infiltration of a Bill of Rights" [1992] *PL* 397 at 409.

[23] See generally Cm 3782, *Rights Brought Home: The Human Rights Bill* (London: TSO, 1997).

[24] For an overview, see D M Paciocco, "The New Zealand Bill of Rights Act 1990: Curial Cures for a Debilitated Bill" [1990] *New Zealand Recent Law Review* 353; P T Rishworth, "Affirming the Fundamental Values of the Nation: How the Bill of Rights and the Human Rights Act affect New Zealand Law" in G Huscroft and P T Rishworth (eds.), *Rights and Freedoms* (Wellington: Brooker's, 1995); M Taggart, "Tugging on Superman's Cape: Lessons from Experience with the New Zealand Bill of Rights Act 1990" in Cambridge Centre for Public Law, *Constitutional Reform in the United Kingdom: Practice and Principles* (Oxford: Hart Publishing, 1998).

[25] Human Rights Act 1998, s. 3(1). For discussion, see Lord Irvine, "The Development of Human Rights in Britain under an Incorporated Convention on Human Rights" [1998] *PL* 221 at 228–229; G Marshall, "Interpreting Interpretation in the Human Rights Bill" [1998] *PL* 167; D Pannick, "Principles of Interpretation of Convention Rights under the Human Rights Act and the Discretionary Area of Judgment" [1998] *PL* 545 at 545–8.

[26] Human Rights Act 1998, s. 6(1).

clear that the carefully and subtly drafted Human Rights Act 1998 preserves the principle of parliamentary sovereignty".[27] Consequently it is not possible for British courts to impugn legislation which conflicts with human rights.[28] Instead, in instances when it proves impossible to interpret UK legislation consistently with the Convention, certain courts may issue a declaration to that effect.[29] This has no impact upon the validity, continuing operation or enforcement of the offending legislation,[30] although it does activate a generous administrative competence to amend UK law in order to render it consistent with the ECHR.[31] This technique has been welcomed by a number of writers because it permits adjudication on and amendment of legislative infringements of the Convention without compromising the sovereignty principle[32] (although some writers have criticised this solution because it makes the correction of national law contingent upon the exercise of administrative discretion[33]). Finally, the Act requires ministers introducing legislation into Parliament to make a statement saying whether, in their view, the legislation is compatible with the Convention.[34]

Unsurprisingly, opinions vary widely on the extent to which the Act is likely to succeed in engendering a new human rights culture in the United Kingdom. A number of writers[35] argued in favour of a stronger method of incorporation such as that which obtains in Canada, according to which legislation that is

[27] R v. *Director of Public Prosecutions, ex parte Kebilene* [1999] 3 WLR 972 at 981.

[28] However, since the ECJ has accepted that Convention rights form part of EU law, it may be that English courts are able—or even required—to disapply municipal legislation which conflicts with fundamental rights in areas governed by Community law. See N Grief, "The Domestic Impact of the European Convention on Human Rights as Mediated through Community Law" [1991] *PL* 555; Lord Browne-Wilkinson, "The Infiltration of a Bill of Rights" [1992] *PL* 397 at 399–402.

[29] Human Rights Act 1998, s. 4.

[30] *Ibid.*, s. 4(6)(a).

[31] *Ibid.*, s. 10.

[32] See, *e.g.*, Lord Bingham, "The Way We Live Now: Human Rights in the New Millennium" [1998] 1 *Web Journal of Current Legal Issues* and the contributions of Lord Lester, P Duffy and S Kentridge to Cambridge Centre for Public Law, *Constitutional Reform in the United Kingdom: Practice and Principles* (Oxford: Hart Publishing, 1998) at 106–7, 103 and 69 respectively. H Lauterpacht, *An International Bill of the Rights of Man* (New York: Columbia University Press, 1945) at 193 suggested the use of a declaration of incompatibility as a potential compromise between the sovereignty of the UK Parliament and the effective protection of human rights.

[33] See H W R Wade, "The United Kingdom's Bill of Rights" in Cambridge Centre for Public Law, *Constitutional Reform in the United Kingdom: Practice and Principles* (Oxford: Hart Publishing, 1998) at 66–7; G Marshall, "Patriating Rights—With Reservations: The Human Rights Bill 1998", *ibid.* at 83–4.

[34] Human Rights Act 1998, s. 19.

[35] See, *inter alios*, Wade, above n. 33; A Lester, "Fundamental Rights: The United Kingdom Isolated?" [1984] *PL* 46; S Kentridge, "Parliamentary Supremacy and the Judiciary under a Bill of Rights: Some Lessons from the Commonwealth" [1997] *PL* 96; R Singh, *The Future of Human Rights in the United Kingdom* (Oxford: Hart Publishing, 1997) at 28–30; M Zander, *A Bill of Rights?* (London: Sweet and Maxwell, 1997) at 120. Lord Irvine, "The Legal System and Law Reform under Labour" in D Bean (ed.), *Law Reform for All* (London: Blackstone Press, 1996) at 18–19, appeared to favour the Canadian model, but his views have now changed: see, *e.g.*, Lord Irvine, "Constitutional Change in the United Kingdom: British Solutions to Universal Problems" (the 1998 National Heritage Lecture, delivered at the Supreme Court in Washington DC, USA, March 1998).

inconsistent with the Charter of Rights and Freedoms is invalid[36] unless it explicitly takes effect notwithstanding such incompatibility.[37] On the other hand, New Zealand's Bill of Rights Act has enjoyed considerable success in spite of its non-entrenched status. It has "constitutionalised" the area of criminal justice and procedure,[38] and is beginning to influence the controls on public decision-makers mediated through administrative law.[39]

The success of the Human Rights Act will fall to be judged some years hence. At present, a different issue concerning incorporation[40] must be considered, *viz.* the constitutional basis of the new, rights-based mode of judicial review which the Act is certain to generate. This task is undertaken in two stages. In section 2, the constitutional warrant for human rights review is addressed, by examining the underlying constitutional justification for such review and, specifically, by asking why the courts generally refused to undertake human rights review prior to the activation of the Human Rights Act. Section 3 then considers the more technical question of the legal basis of human rights review; in particular, it asks whether there is any role for ultra vires methodology in relation to judicial review under the Human Rights Act.[41]

2. THE CONSTITUTIONAL FOUNDATIONS OF HUMAN RIGHTS REVIEW

2.1. Introduction

The following discussion is centrally concerned with the question why English courts generally refused to engage in human rights review prior to the activation of the Human Rights Act 1998. In light of this, it is necessary to begin by explaining what is meant here by the term *human rights review*.

---

[36] Canadian Constitution Act 1982, s. 52(1).

[37] Canadian Charter of Rights and Freedoms, s. 33(1).

[38] M Taggart, "Tugging on Superman's Cape: Lessons from Experience with the New Zealand Bill of Rights Act 1990" in Cambridge Centre for Public Law, *Constitutional Reform in the United Kingdom: Practice and Principles* (Oxford: Hart Publishing, 1998) at 90–1.

[39] New Zealand commentators predicted that the Bill of Rights would have a considerable impact on administrative law: see P T Rishworth, "The Potential of the New Zealand Bill of Rights" [1990] *New Zealand Law Journal* 68 at 71–2; J McLean, P T Rishworth and M Taggart, "The Impact of the New Zealand Bill of Rights on Administrative Law" in *The New Zealand Bill of Rights Act 1990* (Auckland: The Foundation, 1992). More recently, Taggart, above n. 38, at 93, has written that, although the Bill "has yet to set administrative law alight in New Zealand", its impact is now beginning to be felt, particularly in the area of social policy.

[40] Although, strictly speaking, the Convention rights are not "incorporated" (see 583 HL Debs., col. 522 (Lord Irvine); G Marshall, "Patriating Rights—With Reservations: The Human Rights Bill 1998" in Cambridge Centre for Public Law, *Constitutional Reform in the United Kingdom: Practice and Principles* (Oxford: Hart Publishing, 1998) at 75), the present work will use that term as convenient shorthand for the Human Rights Act's giving of greater effect to Convention rights in national law.

[41] The use of the notions of constitutional warrant and legal basis as tools by which to enquire into the foundations of different aspects of judicial review is explained in more detail above at 10–12.

It is clear that the traditional law of judicial review—that is, the supervisory regime which existed before the activation of the Human Rights Act—is concerned principally with the regulation of how executive decisions are made. The classical principles of review are thus oriented largely towards ensuring fairness and sound reasoning in the decision-making process.

Human rights review possesses three principal characteristics which distinguish it from that traditional approach. In the first place, it tends to be concerned with the protection of substantive values,[42] not just procedural norms. Secondly, in order to uphold such values, the court examines not only the process by which the relevant decision was reached, but also the content and effect of the decision. Thirdly, the court, in its evaluation of the decision and its effect, forms a primary judgment on the extent to which the infringement of the right is justifiable, necessary and proportionate to the policy being pursued, not merely a secondary judgment on (for example) the reasonableness of the decision. The jurisdiction asserted on human rights review is therefore relatively intrusive, bearing in mind the substantive nature of the values which are in play; the rigorous manner in which they are upheld, and the fact that the court's attention is directed towards the content and effect of the decision, not merely the reasoning process which preceded it.

Of course, the foregoing characterisation of human rights review is something of a caricature. In reality, there does not exist any watertight division between process and substance,[43] and any analysis based on such a putative distinction would be unsatisfactory. Few grounds of review can neatly be labelled as either purely procedural or wholly substantive.[44] For instance, although review for propriety of purpose is directed towards the process by which decisions are made (in the sense that it concerns the preconditions for valid decision-making, rather than the decision itself), the courts' determination of the question of propriety of purpose impacts substantively on the scope of the agency's competence.[45] T R S Allan is therefore right to say that, "The distinction between procedure and substance, like that between appeal and review, is essentially one of degree".[46] Similarly, to distinguish human rights review and traditional review on the grounds that the former is concerned with the content of decisions rather than how they are made, and that the former adopts an intensive standard of review while the latter does not, is again an over-simplification, since it is clear that, prior to the Human Rights Act, the traditional principles of

---

[42] *E.g.* those set out in Arts. 8–11 of the ECHR.

[43] See J Beatson, "The Scope of Judicial Review for Error of Law" (1984) 4 *OJLS* 22 at 26–9; J Jowell, "Of Vires and Vacuums: The Constitutional Context of Judicial Review" in C F Forsyth (ed.), *Judicial Review and the Constitution* (Oxford: Hart Publishing, 2000).

[44] See above at 135–6.

[45] See, *e.g.*, *R v. Secretary of State for Foreign and Commonwealth Affairs, ex parte World Development Movement Ltd.* [1995] 1 WLR 386.

[46] T R S Allan, "Fairness, Equality, Rationality: Constitutional Theory and Judicial Review" in C F Forsyth and I C Hare (eds.), *The Golden Metwand and the Crooked Cord* (Oxford: Clarendon Press, 1998) at 34.

judicial review provided, in some contexts, for scrutiny of the content of decisions, and that such scrutiny could take a relatively intensive form.[47]

There is, therefore, no absolute or rigid dividing line which separates traditional review and human rights review.[48] Rather, they represent different parts of a single continuum within which many different levels of judicial intervention ultimately shade into one another.[49] However, just because the distinction is one of degree rather than type does not mean that it is unimportant. Even though we are dealing with a continuum of different levels of review, rather than with two wholly distinct categories, it is significant that, prior to the activation of the Human Rights Act, English administrative law occupied a part of the continuum which represented a relatively low level of intervention, and which certainly fell short of paradigm human rights review (according to which a broad range of substantive rights are used in order to subject the content and impact of administrative decisions to a high level of scrutiny via devices such as proportionality and objective justification). The reasons for this are addressed below, where it is argued that the reticence of the courts to engage in full human rights review was based on sound constitutional reasoning, and that it was constitutionally proper for the courts to await legislative intervention before exercising a full human rights jurisdiction; in this sense, it will be suggested, the Human Rights Act was necessary as a constitutional warrant to establish the legitimacy of human rights review. However, before examining those matters, it is necessary to consider in more detail the role which human rights occupied in English administrative law prior to the Human Rights Act's entry into force.

2.2. Human Rights Protection Without Incorporation?

Although, due to its age, the ECHR is regarded as suffering from a number of defects, it was widely accepted that it formed at least a useful starting point for domestic protection of fundamental rights. Lord Bingham, for instance, remarked that, "In the European Convention an instrument lies ready to hand which, if not providing an ideal solution, nonetheless offers a clear improvement on the present position".[50] However, successive British governments refused to incorporate the Convention, and the attempts of individuals to introduce legislation to this effect consistently failed. As a consequence, much ink

---

[47] See below at 209–18.

[48] This perspective derives some support from the judgment of Laws LJ in *R v. Secretary of State for Education and Employment, ex parte Begbie* [2000] 1 WLR 1115, in which he emphasises that judicial review operates on a sliding scale such that the intensity of review in any given case is a function of its context. For comment, see M C Elliott, "Legitimate Expectation: The Substantive Dimension" (2000) 59 *CLJ* 421 at 424–5.

[49] To the extent that the present work refers to the existing law of judicial review as "process-oriented" and to the grounds of review which the Human Rights Act introduces as "substantive", it does so for the purpose of concision.

[50] Sir Thomas Bingham, "The European Convention on Human Rights: Time to Incorporate" (1993) 109 *LQR* 390 at 393.

was spilled on developing theories which provided for the enforcement of human rights by British judges in the absence of legislative incorporation. It is worth noting three particular strands within that discourse.

First, some writers argued that incorporation was largely unnecessary because English law embodies an indigenous doctrine of fundamental rights. Lord Browne-Wilkinson, for example, suggested that the common law's traditional preoccupation with rights relating to property and personal liberty obscures its embodiment of a broader set of fundamental rights. Hence "for most practical purposes the common law would provide protection to the individual at least equal to that provided by the ECHR".[51] This idea found some approval in the courts. For example, in *R v. Secretary of State for the Home Department, ex parte Brind*, Lord Donaldson MR commented that "you have to look long and hard before you can detect any difference between the English common law and the principles set out in the Convention".[52] Similarly, in *Derbyshire County Council v. Times Newspapers Ltd.*, the Court of Appeal held, relying explicitly on Article 10 of the ECHR, that local authorities cannot institute defamation proceedings;[53] the House of Lords, however, felt able to affirm this decision *without* recourse to the Convention, because English common law was said to be consistent with it so far as freedom of expression was concerned.[54]

Secondly, Sir John Laws argued that, while it was not for the judges to incorporate the ECHR, given the dualist tradition of English law, it could nevertheless be used as a text to inform the development of the common law. According to this argument English courts, when developing domestic law, could have looked at the Convention and its case law just as they examine the law of foreign legal systems. Laws felt that this would have prompted a change in the nature of judicial review, leading the courts to "hold that a decision which overrides a fundamental right without sufficient objective justification will, as a matter of law, necessarily be disproportionate [and therefore unlawful]".[55]

Murray Hunt advanced a further theory which would have yielded similar results.[56] He suggested that, quite independently of any legislative enjoinder (such as that which is now contained in the Human Rights Act), English judges should consider themselves to be bound by an "interpretive obligation" requiring them to enforce, in national law, the international human rights instruments to which the UK is a party. Thus English courts would give effect, by interpretative means, to international fundamental rights norms even in the absence of

---

[51] Lord Browne-Wilkinson, "The Infiltration of a Bill of Rights" [1992] *PL* 397 at 408.

[52] [1991] 1 AC 696 at 717. See also *R v. Secretary of State for the Home Department, ex parte McQuillan* [1995] 4 All ER 400 at 423, *per* Sedley J: "the standards articulated in the convention are standards which . . . march with those of the common law".

[53] [1992] QB 770.

[54] [1993] AC 534.

[55] Sir John Laws, "Is the High Court the Guardian of Fundamental Constitutional Rights?" [1993] *PL* 59 at 74.

[56] M Hunt, *Using Human Rights Law in English Courts* (Oxford: Hart Publishing, 1997), especially ch. 1.

ambiguity in the municipal law under consideration and irrespective of whether such national law was enacted in order to give effect to the relevant international obligation. As with the theories described above, one of the intended consequences of Hunt's approach is that decision-makers would be required to act in accordance with the rights enumerated in international human rights instruments, and to demonstrate adequate justification for any interference with those rights.[57]

These ideas were articulated within a broader framework of judicial enthusiasm for the promotion of fundamental rights and the adoption of a more substantive conception of the rule of law. Thus Lords Woolf[58] and Cooke[59] argued that legislative competence should be subject to certain limits based on democratic values; Lord Bingham called for[60]—and later welcomed the Government's proposals for[61]—the incorporation of the ECHR, and Sir John Laws, in a series of lectures and papers, propounded the importance of judicial enforcement of human rights.[62]

Against this background it might be expected that one of the models described above would have taken root. However, as is explained below, although a number of judicial initiatives significantly enhanced the protection afforded to human rights by judicial review, no comprehensive system of human rights review emerged prior to the activation of the Human Rights Act. This state of affairs gave rise to a striking paradox: the judges' evident enthusiasm for human rights protection formed a curious juxtaposition with their general reluctance to conceptualise them as limits on discretionary power. It will be argued later that this paradox ultimately demonstrates that the Human Rights Act was required as the constitutional warrant for human rights review. First,

---

[57] M Hunt, *Using Human Rights Law in English Courts* (Oxford: Hart Publishing, 1997), at 319–23. It was also argued, prior to incorporation, that ratification of international human rights treaties could give rise to a legitimate expectation that governmental powers would be exercised consistently with the rights set out therein. This argument was accepted by the High Court of Australia in *Minister of State for Immigration and Ethnic Affairs* v. *Teoh* (1995) 183 CLR 273 and was endorsed (*obiter*) by Lord Woolf MR in *R.* v. *Secretary of State for the Home Department, ex parte Ahmed* [1999] COD 69. However, the Divisional Court, in *R* v. *Director of Public Prosecutions, ex parte Kebilene* [1999] 3 WLR 175, refused to countenance the possibility of ratification of the ECHR giving rise to a legitimate expectation. On appeal, the House of Lords agreed that no legitimate expectation arose (see [1999] 3 WLR 972).

[58] Lord Woolf, "*Droit Public*—English Style" [1995] PL 57.

[59] Sir Robin Cooke, "Fundamentals" [1988] *New Zealand Law Journal* 158.

[60] Sir Thomas Bingham, "The European Convention on Human Rights: Time to Incorporate" (1993) 109 *LQR* 390.

[61] Lord Bingham, "The Way We Live Now: Human Rights in the New Millennium" [1998] 1 *Web Journal of Current Legal Issues*.

[62] See principally "Is the High Court the Guardian of Fundamental Constitutional Rights?" [1993] PL 59; "Judicial Remedies and the Constitution" (1994) 57 MLR 213; "Law and Democracy" [1995] PL 72; "The Constitution: Morals and Rights" [1996] PL 622; "Illegality: The Problem of Jurisdiction" in M Supperstone and J Goudie (eds.), *Judicial Review* (London: Butterworths, 1997); "*Wednesbury*" in C F Forsyth and I C Hare (eds.), *The Golden Metwand and the Crooked Cord* (Oxford: Clarendon Press, 1998); "The Limitations of Human Rights" [1998] PL 254. For a critical review of Laws's writings on human rights and the judicial function, see J A G Griffith, "The Brave New World of Sir John Laws" (2000) 63 *MLR* 159.

though, it is necessary to consider in more detail the extent to which, prior to the Human Rights Act, English courts desisted from engaging in human rights review.

2.3. Human Rights in English Administrative Law[63]

2.3.1. *The ECHR and discretionary power*

Even before the status of the ECHR in English law was enhanced by means of the Human Rights Act, English courts were willing, in a number of contexts, to take account of the Convention.[64] It could aid the construction of ambiguous legislation[65] as well as influencing the development of the common law when it was "not firmly settled".[66] It was also used to guide judicial decision-making in relation, for example, to the provision of discretionary relief[67] and the exclusion of evidence in criminal proceedings.[68]

Moreover, notwithstanding its unincorporated status, the Convention acquired some effect in the UK by operation of EU law. The European Court of Justice has stated that human rights—both those which are part of the "constitutional traditions common to the Member States"[69] and the rights enumerated in international treaties "on which the Member States have collaborated, or of which they are signatories"[70]—form part of the EU legal order. Furthermore Article 6(2) of the Treaty on European Union specifically affirms the EU's commitment to upholding the values found in the ECHR. Consequently, even prior to its incorporation via the Human Rights Act, English courts were required to take account of the Convention in cases concerning EU law. This prompted Lord Browne-Wilkinson to observe, long before the advent of the Human

---

[63] The purpose of this section is not to attempt a comprehensive survey of the case law in this area. Rather, it is to identify the major themes which emerge from the leading cases.

[64] See further M Hunt, *Using Human Rights Law in English Courts* (Oxford: Hart Publishing, 1997), ch. 6; Lord Bingham, HL Debs., 3 July 1996, cols. 1465–7; F Klug and K Starmer, "Incorporation through the Back Door?" [1997] *PL* 223 at 224–5.

[65] At one time, certain judges held the view that the Convention could be used as an aid to construction even in the absence of ambiguity in national legislation (see, *e.g.*, *Ahmad* v. *Inner London Education Authority* [1978] QB 36, *per* Scarman LJ). However, it later became clear that, in the absence of legislative incorporation, ambiguity was necessary to trigger recourse to the Convention as an aid to construction: *R* v. *Secretary of State for the Home Department, ex parte Brind* [1991] 1 AC 696. This was consistent with the general approach to unincorporated treaties: *Salomon* v. *Commissioners of Customs and Excise* [1967] 2 QB 116.

[66] *Attorney-General* v. *British Broadcasting Corporation* [1981] AC 303 at 352, *per* Lord Fraser. See also *Derbyshire County Council* v. *Times Newspapers Ltd.* [1992] QB 770; *Rantzen* v. *Mirror Group Newspapers (1986) Ltd.* [1994] QB 670.

[67] See *Attorney-General* v. *Guardian Newspapers Ltd.* [1987] 1 WLR 1248.

[68] See *R* v. *Khan (Sultan)* [1997] AC 558 (although *cf Khan* v. *United Kingdom, The Times*, 23 May 2000).

[69] Case 11/70, *Internationale Handelsgesellschaft mbH* v. *Einfuhr- und Vorratsstelle für Getreide und Futtermittel* [1970] ECR 1125 at 1134.

[70] Case 4/73, *Nold KG* v. *Commission of the European Communities* [1974] ECR 491 at 507.

Rights Act, that, in areas regulated by EU law, "we already enjoy a full Bill of Rights: the Convention is directly enforceable in our courts".[71]

Against this backdrop of broad judicial willingness to take account of the ECHR, the general reluctance of the courts to require decision-makers to exercise their discretionary power in accordance with Convention standards was striking.[72] A good illustration of this judicial attitude is supplied by the decision of the House of Lords in *R v. Secretary of State for the Home Department, ex parte Brind*.[73] The Home Secretary had made regulations imposing certain restrictions on the broadcasting of interviews with representatives of proscribed terrorist organisations. The applicants sought a declaration that the regulations were unlawful *inter alia* on the ground that they contravened their right of free expression under Article 10 of the ECHR.

Relying on the established principle that ambiguities in municipal legislation may be resolved by reference to a presumption that Parliament intends to legislate consistently with the UK's international obligations, counsel argued that ambiguity necessarily inheres in any statutory provision which creates discretionary power, given that the myriad principles of good administration which condition its exercise are not explicitly enumerated. This ambiguity, it was submitted, should be resolved by recourse to the ECHR, thereby securing the limitation of discretionary power by reference to the Convention norms. Any exercise of discretionary power which engaged a Convention right would thus have to be justified objectively, and it would be a matter for the courts' judgment whether sufficient justification had been furnished. This argument, however, was rejected. Lord Bridge said that:

> where Parliament has conferred on the executive an administrative discretion without indicating the precise limits within which it must be exercised, to presume that it must be exercised within Convention limits would be to go far beyond the resolution of an ambiguity. It would be to impute to Parliament an intention not only that the executive should exercise the discretion in conformity with the Convention, but also that the domestic courts should enforce that conformity by the importation into domestic administrative law of the text of the Convention and the jurisprudence of the European Court of Human Rights in the interpretation and application of it.[74]

Thus the House of Lords firmly signalled that the rights set out in the ECHR could not be considered as implicit limits on the decision-making power of officials. Taken at face value, this case appears to indicate that administrative law was entirely insulated from human rights considerations. However, as Lord Bridge himself pointed out,[75] the effect of *Brind* was not quite so stark. Indeed,

---

[71] Lord Browne-Wilkinson, "The Infiltration of a Bill of Rights" [1992] *PL* 397 at 401.

[72] Although *cf* early cases like *R v. Secretary of State for the Home Department, ex parte Bhajan Singh* [1976] QB 198 which disclosed a greater judicial willingness to allow Convention norms to permeate administrative law.

[73] [1991] 1 AC 696.

[74] *Ibid.* at 748. Lord Templeman's reasoning (at 751) was closer to the Strasbourg system of human rights review, but other judges were reluctant to follow it.

[75] *Ibid.* at 748–9.

it is possible to discern three distinct methodologies which the courts employed in order to impose some rights-based constraints on the discretionary power of decision-makers in the absence of incorporation. Each of these judicial initiatives will be considered in turn, but it will be argued that they did not (either individually or collectively) give rise to a comprehensive human rights jurisdiction.[76]

2.3.2. *Judicial review generally*

First, the contribution made by the courts' traditional powers of judicial review to the protection of human rights should not be underestimated. By requiring decision-makers to treat citizens fairly and reasonably, the courts uphold important individual rights. However, as observed above,[77] judicial review has historically been concerned more with the process by which decisions are reached than with their content and effect. As Lord Irvine observed, review has traditionally involved

> something akin to the application of a set of rules. If the rules are broken, the conduct will be condemned. But if the rules are obeyed (the right factors taken into account, no irrelevant factors taken into account, no misdirection of law and no out and out irrationality) the decision will be upheld, usually irrespective of the overall merits of the policy.[78]

This emphasis on process clearly inhibited the judicial review jurisdiction from furnishing a fully comprehensive system of human rights protection.

2.3.3. Wednesbury *unreasonableness and human rights*

However, it would be misleading to suggest that administrative law was historically concerned solely with process. In particular, the doctrine of *Wednesbury* unreasonableness,[79] which is directed towards the content of decisions rather than the process by which they are reached, can be used as a tool for the protection of substantive norms, since it is clearly possible to stigmatise as irrational a decision which flagrantly abrogates fundamental rights for no good reason.

---

[76] This conclusion is consistent with the empirical study of F Klug and K Starmer, "Incorporation through the Back Door?" [1997] *PL* 223 which found that, although numerous English cases referred to the ECHR, it had little practical impact prior to incorporation.

[77] At 203–4.

[78] Lord Irvine, "The Development of Human Rights in Britain under an Incorporated Convention on Human Rights" [1998] *PL* 221 at 235.

[79] See *Associated Provincial Picture Houses Ltd. v. Wednesbury Corporation* [1948] 1 KB 223. For recent analyses of the *Wednesbury* principle, see P Walker, "What's Wrong with Irrationality?" [1995] *PL* 556 and "Unreasonableness and Proportionality" in M Supperstone and J Goudie (eds.), *Judicial Review* (London: Butterworths, 1997); F Donson, "Civil Liberties and Judicial Review: Can the Common Law Really Protect Rights?" in P Leyland and T Woods (eds.), *Administrative Law Facing the Future: Old Constraints and New Horizons* (London: Blackstone Press, 1997); Sir John Laws, "*Wednesbury*" in C F Forsyth and I C Hare (eds.), *The Golden Metwand and the Crooked Cord* (Oxford: Clarendon Press, 1998).

Indeed the rationality doctrine's capacity for rights protection has been emphasised by the courts in recent years: judges have announced their willingness to subject decisions touching on fundamental rights to "the most anxious scrutiny",[80] so that courts are:

> perfectly entitled to start from the premise that any restriction of the right to freedom of expression requires to be justified and that nothing less than an important competing public interest will be sufficient to justify it.[81]

At first glance, this methodology bears striking similarity to the human rights jurisdiction exercised by the European Court of Human Rights in cases concerning Articles 8–11 of the Convention.[82] This approach centres on the justification of rights infractions: having established that a Convention right has been infringed, the Court requires the defendant state to demonstrate that the violation occurred in pursuit of a legitimate aim, and that the magnitude of the infringement was proportionate to the objective being pursued.[83] However, for two reasons, the level of review which English courts traditionally adopted in human rights cases fell considerably short of this approach.[84]

First, the dominant view was that, in human rights cases, English courts could not "lower 'the threshold of unreasonableness'".[85] Consequently, although cases involving human rights attracted a "more intensive review process and a greater readiness to intervene than would ordinarily characterise a judicial review challenge",[86] the standard of justification required to avoid a finding of unreasonableness remained constant. The courts simply reviewed the decision more thoroughly, applying the usual test with greater rigour.

Secondly, in *Brind*, Lord Bridge attached an important qualification to his statement of principle concerning review of decisions which affect human rights:

> The primary judgment as to whether the particular competing public interest justifies the particular restriction imposed falls to be made by the Secretary of State to whom Parliament has entrusted the discretion. But we are entitled to exercise a secondary judgment by asking whether a reasonable Secretary of State, on the material before him, could reasonably make that judgment.[87]

---

[80] *R v. Secretary of State for the Home Department, ex parte Bugdaycay* [1987] AC 514 at 531, *per* Lord Bridge.

[81] *R v. Secretary of State for the Home Department, ex parte Brind* [1991] 1 AC 696 at 748–9, *per* Lord Bridge.

[82] On which see generally D J Harris, M O'Boyle and C Warbrick, *Law of the European Convention on Human Rights* (London: Butterworths, 1995), ch. 8.

[83] This is consistent with the definition of human rights review advanced above at 203–4.

[84] See generally F Klug and K Starmer, "Incorporation through the Back Door?" [1997] *PL* 223, at 228–32.

[85] *R v. Secretary of State for the Home Department, ex parte Brind* [1991] 1 AC 696 at 767, *per* Lord Lowry; *R v. Secretary of State for the Environment, ex parte National and Local Government Officers' Association* (1992) 5 Admin. LR 785 at 797, *per* Neill LJ; *R v. Ministry of Defence, ex parte Smith* [1996] QB 517 at 538, *per* Simon Brown LJ.

[86] *R v. Ministry of Defence, ex parte Smith* [1996] QB 517 at 538, *per* Simon Brown LJ.

[87] *R v. Secretary of State for the Home Department, ex parte Brind* [1991] 1 AC 696 at 749.

The profound implication of this is that review of decisions which touch fundamental rights was rendered parasitic on the rationality doctrine. Consequently
English courts were precluded from reviewing such decisions with the same
intensity as the European Court of Human Rights, which deploys the much
sharper tools of objective justification and proportionality.[88]

This point is most readily apparent from the decisions of the Divisional Court
and the Court of Appeal in R v. *Ministry of Defence, ex parte Smith*.[89] The
applicants sought to establish the illegality of the Government's administrative
policy precluding persons of homosexual orientation from serving in the armed
forces.[90] The challenge was made, *inter alia*, on the ground that it was irrational
and contrary to Article 8 of the ECHR, which requires respect for private and
family life. The judgment of Simon Brown LJ in the Divisional Court usefully
illustrates the approach adopted by English reviewing courts in fundamental
rights cases prior to incorporation. His Lordship explained that he had to
approach the case:

> on the conventional *Wednesbury* basis adapted to a human rights context and ask: can
> the Secretary of State show an important competing public interest which he could
> reasonably judge sufficient to justify the restriction [of the applicants' rights]? The pri-
> mary judgment is for him. Only if his purported justification outrageously defies logic
> or accepted moral standards can the court, exercising its secondary judgment, prop-
> erly strike it down.[91]

Crucially, Simon Brown LJ came to the conclusion that, even though, objectively speaking, the policy was not justifiable, the court could not strike it down:

> The real question becomes: is it reasonable for the Secretary of State to take the view
> that allowing homosexuals into the forces would imperil [the delivery of an opera-
> tionally efficient and effective fighting force] . . . ? Is that, in short, a coherent view,
> right or wrong? . . . [In] my own opinion that is a wrong view, a view that rests too
> firmly upon the supposition of prejudice in others and which insufficiently recognises
> the damage to human rights inflicted. But can it properly be stigmatised as irrational?
> . . . I have come finally to the conclusion that, my own view of the evidence notwith-
> standing, the minister's stance cannot properly be held unlawful. His suggested justi-
> fication for the ban may to many seem unconvincing; to say, however, that it is
> outrageous in its defiance of logic is another thing. There is, I conclude, still room for
> two views. Similarly it is difficult to regard the policy as incompatible with 'accepted

---

[88] In R v. *Lord Saville of Newdigate, ex parte A* [1999] 4 All ER 860 at 870–1 the Court of Appeal
confirmed that the reasonableness doctrine, albeit adapted to the human rights context, remained
the correct standard of review prior to incorporation.

[89] [1996] QB 517.

[90] The prohibition has now been lifted following the decision of the European Court of Human
Rights (discussed below at 212) that it was unlawful. It has been replaced with an Armed Forces
Code of Social Conduct which recognises that gays and lesbians may lawfully serve in the armed
forces, and which sets out a code of behaviour applying to all service personnel, irrespective of their
sexual orientation.

[91] [1996] QB 517 at 540.

moral standards'. There is no present uniformity of outlook on this issue: not every-one would condemn the ban on moral grounds . . .[92]

The Court of Appeal upheld Simon Brown LJ's conclusion that the policy was lawful, although it expressed no opinion concerning the justifiability (as distinct from the rationality) of the policy.[93]

The distinction between the level of intervention which English courts embraced and that which courts exercising a full human rights review jurisdiction adopt is made particularly evident by the judgments of the European Court of Human Rights in *Smith and Grady* v. *United Kingdom*[94] and *Lustig-Prean and Beckett* v. *United Kingdom*,[95] both of which arose from the decisions of the domestic courts in *Ex parte Smith*. First, applying a test of proportionality, the Strasbourg Court found that the applicants' Article 8 rights had been infringed: this was unsurprising, given that the English judges had indicated that, had they been applying the proportionality test, they too would have concluded that the Ministry of Defence's policy was unlawful. Secondly, it was held that the English courts' insistence that they could not go beyond *Wednesbury* review meant that the applicants had been denied an effective remedy, contrary to Article 13 of the ECHR.

This supplies a particularly clear illustration of the limits of the rationality doctrine as a vehicle for the protection of fundamental rights and explodes the myth which had begun to develop that *Wednesbury* review is capable of pro-viding the same level of human rights protection as the self-evidently more rigorous proportionality doctrine.[96] On this basis it is clear that, prior to incor-poration, judicial review in English law fell some way short of full human rights review. The reasons underlying this state of affairs are explored below. First, however, it is necessary to address one further method by which the judges sought to safeguard human rights prior to incorporation.

2.3.4. Common law constitutional rights

The common law has long attached special weight to certain fundamental inter-ests, such as life, liberty and property. This ethos most commonly finds expres-sion in the context of statutory construction, according to which the courts, wherever possible, strive to interpret legislation in a manner which is consistent with those interests which the common law holds to be particularly important.

For example, the common law's respect for the liberty of the individual dic-tates that "a statute will not be construed to give retroactive force to criminal

---

[92] *Ibid.* at 540–1.
[93] Indeed, Henry LJ, *ibid.* at 564, strongly disapproved of speculation about how the court would have reacted had the ECHR been part of municipal law. The approach in *Smith* was followed in sub-sequent cases, including *R* v. *Secretary of State for the Home Department, ex parte Canbolat* [1997] 1 WLR 1569; *R* v. *Secretary of State for the Home Department, ex parte Launder* [1997] 1 WLR 839.
[94] *The Times*, 11 October 1999.
[95] (1999) 7 Butterworth's Human Rights Cases 65.
[96] See further I C Hare, "Privacy and the Gay Right to Fight" (2000) 59 *CLJ* 6 at 8.

provisions unless it clearly does so in express words or by necessary implication".[97] Similarly it has been held that provisions in the Immigration and Asylum Act 1996 inhibiting certain categories of asylum-seekers from claiming welfare payments—a policy which, according to Simon Brown LJ in an earlier case, "no civilised nation can tolerate"[98]—must be strictly construed, because of the weight which the common law attaches to the fundamental right to life.[99]

For present purposes it is significant that, prior to incorporation, and in contrast to the courts' pre-incorporation attitude to the ECHR rights *per se*, some of these common law rights were translated into limits on the discretionary powers of administrators. This occurred to greatest effect in the field of access to justice.

A long line of authorities affirms the pre-eminent status which the common law accords to the right of access to the courts. As well as narrowly construing legislative provisions which appear to inhibit access to justice,[100] the judges have struck down secondary legislation which has had this effect.[101] The methodology by which the common law right of access to the courts is given expression in the administrative law field is of considerable interest, and the decision in *R v. Lord Chancellor, ex parte Witham*[102] is particularly illuminating.

The Lord Chancellor had attempted to repeal, by means of secondary legislation,[103] a provision of an earlier statutory instrument[104] which had relieved persons receiving income support of the obligation to pay court fees. The applicant—a recipient of income support—contended that this had the effect of precluding him from instituting proceedings in defamation because, in light of his financial circumstances, the cost was prohibitive. He therefore sought to impugn the amendment as ultra vires, arguing that the power on which the Lord Chancellor had relied[105] did not, properly construed, confer any competence to interfere with individuals' constitutional right of access to the courts. Laws J, giving the leading judgment, accepted the applicant's submissions; however, it is the reasoning by which he reached that conclusion which is of particular interest.

It has already been noted that, prior to the entry into force of the Human Rights Act, the usual way in which the courts sought to impose substantive

---

[97] *Waddington v. Miah* [1974] 1 WLR 683 at 688, *per* Stephenson LJ.

[98] *R v. Secretary of State for Social Security, ex parte Joint Council for the Welfare of Immigrants* [1997] 1 WLR 275 at 292.

[99] *R v. Hammersmith and Fulham London Borough Council, ex parte M* [1996] TLR 556 at 557, *per* Collins J.

[100] See, *e.g.*, *Anisminic Ltd. v. Foreign Compensation Commission* [1969] 2 AC 147; *R v. Secretary of State for the Home Department, ex parte Fayed* [1998] 1 WLR 763.

[101] See, *e.g.*, *Chester v. Bateson* [1920] 1 KB 829; *Commissioners of Customs and Excise v. Cure and Deeley Ltd.* [1962] 1 QB 340; *Raymond v. Honey* [1983] 1 AC 1, *per* Lord Bridge; *R v. Secretary of State for the Home Department, ex parte Anderson* [1984] QB 778; *R v. Secretary of State for the Home Department, ex parte Leech* [1994] QB 198; *R v. Lord Chancellor, ex parte Witham* [1998] QB 575.

[102] *Ibid.*

[103] Supreme Court Fees (Amendment) Order 1996, SI 1996/3191.

[104] Supreme Court Fees Order 1980, SI 1980/821.

[105] Supreme Court Act 1981, s. 130(1).

limits on the exercise of discretionary power was through the rationality doctrine adapted to the human rights context. However, as *Smith*[106] vividly illustrates, this approach was of limited utility because the administrator's decision was immune from review provided that it remained within the range of responses open to a reasonable decision-maker; in this manner, the reasonableness principle generally creates a zone of discretion which is wider than that permitted by the proportionality test.

In *Witham* counsel for the respondent argued that the legality of the amendment order should have been assessed by reference to the reasonableness standard: only if the Lord Chancellor had acted unreasonably should the delegated legislation have been impugned. Laws J roundly rejected this contention.[107] The fact that the case touched a common law constitutional right meant that the Lord Chancellor's action fell to be tested not against the generous rationality standard: rather, the matter was a vires issue. The court therefore had to determine whether the enabling legislation conferred any power to inhibit access to justice. This was a hard-edged question which, once answered in the negative, precluded any delegated legislation which reduced access to the courts, irrespective of the rationality of such legislation. *Witham* must therefore be distinguished from *Brind* and *Smith* because the human right of access to justice took effect as a direct fetter on the executive's authority, rather than as an indirect limit mediated—and, therefore, diluted—by the rationality principle.

Judicial recognition of the right of access to the courts as an independent and direct limitation on the power of decision-makers has important implications. It is particularly significant that, according to the case law, recognition of access to justice as a common law right meant that, even prior to the activation of the Human Rights Act, it was insufficient for the decision-maker simply to establish the rationality of action which impacted upon that right. Instead, the administration was required, by the courts, to satisfy a stricter test, showing that its action was objectively justified by reference to a legitimate aim. This point is illustrated most clearly by the *Leech* case.[108]

The applicant challenged the legality of the Prison Rules 1964, rule 33(3), arguing that, to the extent that this provision permitted the censoring of a prisoner's correspondence with his legal adviser concerning legal proceedings not yet commenced, it was ultra vires the Prison Act 1952, section 47(1). Giving the judgment of the Court of Appeal, Steyn LJ held that the rule was sufficiently broadly drafted to permit this form of interference. This, his Lordship held, meant that the rule constituted a fetter on prisoners' access to the courts. In an important passage Steyn LJ asked "whether a demonstrable need for an unrestricted power to read and examine letters, and for a qualified power to stop letters on the ground of objectionability, have been established".[109] Reliance on

---

[106] [1996] QB 517.
[107] [1998] QB 575 at 586.
[108] R v. *Secretary of State for the Home Department, ex parte Leech* [1994] QB 198.
[109] *Ibid.* at 213. The court held that no such justification had been established.

such concepts as "demonstrable need" indicates that the court was exercising a primary judgment regarding the *justifiability* of the provision, rather than limiting itself to a secondary assessment of the provision's *rationality*.

Taken together, *Witham* and *Leech* show that, in relation to access to justice, the courts crossed the line which the House of Lords drew, in relation to freedom of expression, in *Brind*, by holding access to the courts to be a substantive implied limit on discretionary power, such that any infraction of that right—if it is to escape judicial condemnation—must not merely be rational but must also be objectively justified to the satisfaction of the court.

Although this pre-incorporation willingness to infuse administrative law with the sort of rigorous, high-intensity scrutiny which is one of the hallmarks of human rights review was most apparent in the field of access to the courts, it was evident, to some extent, in certain other spheres. For instance, the importance which the common law attaches to the liberty of the individual, which usually finds expression in the narrow construction of penal statutes, was also used to limit discretionary power prior to the activation of the Human Rights Act. Thus, in *R v. Secretary of State for the Home Department, ex parte Pierson*,[110] the Home Secretary effectively increased the penal element (that is, the minimum period of detention before release could be considered) of the applicant's mandatory life sentence. By a majority the House of Lords held that the Home Secretary had acted unlawfully. As is particularly clear from Lord Steyn's reasoning this conclusion was reached on the basis of a rights-based limit on the Home Secretary's power:[111]

> . . . a general power to increase tariffs duly fixed is in disharmony with the deep rooted principle of not retrospectively increasing lawfully pronounced sentences. In the absence of contrary indications it must be presumed that Parliament entrusted the wide power to make decisions on the release of mandatory life sentence prisoners on the supposition that the Home Secretary would not act contrary to such a fundamental principle of our law. There are no contrary indications.[112]

Thus *Pierson* indicates a willingness, incorporation aside, to impose direct, rights-based limits on discretionary power in support not only of the individual's access to justice but also, more broadly, his liberty. More recently, in *R v. Secretary of State for the Home Department, ex parte Simms*,[113] the House of Lords subjected a decision which affected the applicant's freedom of expression to a standard of review which at times appeared to verge on proportionality. However, the reasoning was somewhat opaque,[114] and there was little attempt

---

[110] [1998] AC 539.

[111] Lord Steyn's analysis in *Pierson* echoed his judgment in *Leech* and foreshadowed his speech in *Simms*. Indeed, Lord Steyn has been a particularly enthusiastic exponent of the common law rights approach (which he terms the "doctrine of legality", given the manner in which human rights are conceptualised as direct limits on the vires of decision-makers).

[112] [1998] AC 539 at 590.

[113] [1999] 3 WLR 328.

[114] Unsurprisingly, Lord Steyn's approach was consistent with the common law rights model: thus he conceptualised free speech as a limit on the power of the decision-maker and appeared to

to discuss openly the standard of review being applied. It is also arguable that *Simms* actually forms part of the line of case law which appears to confer a particularly high level of protection on access to justice, given that the applicant in *Simms* was seeking to exercise his right of free speech in order ultimately to prompt his criminal conviction to be referred back to the Court of Appeal.[115]

In any event, it is clear that this rigorous pre-Human Rights Act approach was certainly not applied consistently. For instance, *Simms*, on one reading, seems to cast free speech as a constitutional right in the *Witham* sense, capable of protection by means of a proportionality test (in substance if not in name), yet it fails to explain why, in other House of Lords cases such as *Wheeler* v. *Leicester City Council*[116] and *Brind*,[117] free speech could be protected only by reference to established principles (specifically the *Wednesbury* test, albeit adapted to the rights context). Similar ambiguity is evident in the pre-incorporation case law on the right to life. In *R* v. *Cambridge Health Authority, ex parte B* the applicant challenged the decision of a health authority to withhold, on economic grounds, potentially life-saving treatment.[118] In the Divisional Court Laws J allowed the applicant's claim and quashed the authority's decision to refuse treatment. His reasoning was rather opaque. At times it appears that he envisaged the right to life as a direct limit on the respondent's power, entertaining "the greatest doubt whether the decisive touchstone for the legality of the respondents' decision was the crude *Wednesbury* bludgeon. It seems to me that the fundamental right, the right to life, was engaged in the case."[119] He also spoke of the necessity of "justification . . . on substantial, objective grounds".[120] Such reasoning seems to mirror the common law rights approach adopted in such cases as *Leech* and *Witham*. Ultimately however, Laws J, on the authority of *Brind*, acknowledged that "The court's role is secondary".[121] In any event, the Court of Appeal reversed Laws J's decision on the ground (*inter alia*) that he had adopted too intrusive a level of review by requiring justification of the refusal by reference to detailed financial information.[122]

---

apply a proportionality test in determining the legality of the infraction of that right, although he also thought that the policy in question was unreasonable. Similarly, Lord Hobhouse considered that the policy was both unreasonable and disproportionate. Given judicial reliance on both proportionality and unreasonableness, it is difficult to argue that *Simms* clearly establishes proportionality as an independent ground of review, distinct from *Wednesbury*.

[115] See further M C Elliott, "Human Rights in the House of Lords: What Standard of Review?" (2000) 59 *CLJ* 3.

[116] [1985] AC 1054. Browne-Wilkinson LJ in the Court of Appeal adopted a rights-based approach similar to that which the doctrine of common law constitutional rights embodies. The House of Lords, however, rejected that reasoning, preferring instead to decide the case on established administrative law grounds.

[117] [1991] 1 AC 696.

[118] (1995) 25 Butterworth's Medico-Legal Reports 5 (QBD); [1995] 1 WLR 898 (CA).

[119] (1995) 25 Butterworth's Medio-Legal Reports 5 at 11.

[120] *Ibid.* at 12 and 17.

[121] *Ibid.* at 12.

[122] [1995] 1 WLR 898 at 906, *per* Sir Thomas Bingham MR.

2.3.5. Conclusions

What conclusions can be drawn from the leading cases, considered above, which illustrate the role which human rights occupied in English administrative law prior to the activation of the Human Rights Act?

The overall impression which the case law generates is one of confusion. On the one hand a very clear, orthodox line was authoritatively established by decisions such as *Brind* and *Smith*. That line of authority indicated that—pending legislative intervention, through incorporation of the ECHR or otherwise—the role of the courts was secondary: *Wednesbury* demarcated the courts' jurisdiction in public law proceedings, and the deployment of more intrusive tools such as proportionality was inappropriate. On the other hand it was self-evident that the courts wished to confer greater protection on human rights than was possible under *Brind* and *Smith*. As a result the doctrine of common law constitutional rights emerged, which conceptualises some fundamental rights as direct fetters on administrative power, and which appears to evaluate the legality of rights infractions by means which are more intensive than those which are provided for by the *Wednesbury* principle, even when it is adapted to the human rights context.

However, a number of factors indicate that the doctrine of common law rights did not amount to a full, pre-incorporation human rights review jurisdiction (according to which a broad range of fundamental rights are conceptualised as limits on discretionary powers whose transgression falls to be evaluated by reference to rigorous methodologies such as proportionality and objective justification). For instance, the scope of the common law rights doctrine is ambiguous: it evidently operates in the field of access to justice, but it is unclear how much further it extends. Moreover, the extent to which review could, under the common law rights approach, transcend *Wednesbury* protection is uncertain. Although decisions such as *Leech* and *Simms* seemed implicitly to assume that proportionality-style protection was available prior to incorporation, this raised substantial problems in itself. In particular, the *Brind/Smith* line of case law, which—in extremely clear terms—confined reviewing courts to a secondary role based on the rationality doctrine, was not overruled. Thus, as Laws LJ remarked prior to the activation of the Human Rights Act:

> As our law presently stands he [the Secretary of State] is the first judge of the facts, as to which he is only to be reviewed on *Wednesbury* grounds. Any contention that . . . a more intrusive review [is possible, which] . . . requires the court to judge the Secretary of State's decision as if for all the world it were sitting at Strasbourg, would be contradicted (at least until the [Human Rights] Act comes into force: and then we must see how the courts work out their duty [to take account of Strasbourg jurisprudence] under s. 2) by binding authority of their Lordships' House in Brind's case.[123]

---

[123] R v. *Director of Public Prosecutions, ex parte Kebilene* [1999] 3 WLR 175 at 200.

Perhaps the most that can be said is that, before the Human Rights Act's entry into force, the attitude of English administrative law to human rights was somewhat schizophrenic. Judges were (as they still are) enthusiastic about requiring the administration to respect fundamental rights and, to that end, they pursued certain initiatives of which the doctrine of common law constitutional rights is the most notable example. At the same time, however, decisions like *Brind* and *Smith* evidence an acute judicial awareness that to have pushed forward by unilaterally creating a comprehensive system of human rights review would have been inappropriate. It therefore becomes necessary to ask why there arose this curious paradox of a judiciary which was "straining at the leash"[124] to uphold fundamental rights but which was, in many respects, reticent to do so within the administrative law context. In other words, why did the courts apparently feel that they had to await legislative intervention before engaging fully in human rights review?

2.4. The Human Rights Act as a Constitutional Warrant

2.4.1. The dualist tradition of English law

The answer which the courts most commonly provided to that question was based on the principle of dualism, according to which "a treaty is not a part of English law unless and until it has been incorporated into the law by legislation".[125] On this basis, the courts refused to give full effect to the ECHR in the absence of statutory incorporation. The dualism principle is traditionally justified on the ground that, to allow the executive, through its treaty-making prerogative, unilaterally to change domestic law would run contrary to the separation of powers and would undermine the constitutional role of Parliament.

Brind, which pre-eminently established the limited relevance of the Convention in English law, is imbued with such thinking. Lord Ackner said that to embrace the ECHR as a direct limit on the power of decision-makers would "inevitably . . . result in incorporating the Convention into English domestic law by the back door".[126] Lord Bridge thought that this would be constitutionally unacceptable, and emphasised the necessity of legislative intervention if Convention rights were to be justiciable in national courts:

> When Parliament has been content for so long to leave those who complain that their Convention rights have been infringed to seek their remedy in Strasbourg, it would be surprising suddenly to find that the judiciary had, without Parliament's aid, the means to incorporate the Convention into such an important area of domestic law [*viz.*

---

[124] M J Beloff and H Mountfield, "Unconventional Behaviour: Judicial Uses of the European Convention in England and Wales" [1996] *European Human Rights Law Review* 467 at 495.

[125] *J H Rayner (Mincing Lane) Ltd. v. Department of Trade and Industry* [1990] 2 AC 418 at 500, *per* Lord Oliver.

[126] *R v. Secretary of State for the Home Department, ex parte Brind* [1991] 1 AC 696 at 762.

administrative law] and I cannot escape the conclusion that this would be a judicial usurpation of the legislative function.[127]

Some writers, such as Hunt[128] and Beyleveld,[129] argue that dualist tradition should yield in the particular context of international human rights instruments. For present purposes, however, it is sufficient simply to observe that dualism cannot, in any event, furnish an adequate explanation for English courts' pre-incorporation reluctance to engage fully in human rights review. Even if the dualism principle did prevent the inception of a human rights jurisdiction based on the ECHR, it could not logically have blocked the development of a wholly domestic review jurisdiction based on an indigenous set of fundamental rights: dualism would have been irrelevant to such an endeavour. Moreover, an argument based only on dualism fails to explain why the courts appeared to be willing to allow the Convention rights to influence other areas of English law to a greater extent than they permitted them to infiltrate administrative law. It is therefore necessary to look elsewhere in order to understand why the courts considered it constitutionally proper to await legislative intervention before exercising a human rights review jurisdiction in the full sense of that term.

2.4.2. Legitimacy in two contexts

Prior to incorporation there was a good deal of discussion concerning the desirability or legitimacy of judicial adjudication on human rights matters. In fact, there are two separable issues at stake in this area. One question is whether the *exercise* of a human rights review jurisdiction is an appropriate matter for the courts; the answer to this question turns on perceptions of the proper role of the judiciary and its suitability to determine the type of issues which human rights review raises. However, a logically prior question concerns how, legitimately, the courts may *acquire* such jurisdiction in the first place. By reference to this distinction it is possible to make sense of the pre-incorporation position of the English courts. Their enthusiasm for human rights, coupled with a measure of reluctance to embrace them as administrative law controls, suggests that they felt that the exercise of a human rights review jurisdiction was a desirable and appropriate judicial task, but that such jurisdiction could not legitimately be seized unilaterally by the judiciary.

Two principal factors appear to have underpinned this attitude, each of which centrally relates to the role of the courts within a constitution which embodies a separation of powers ethos. In the first place, it is arguable that the arrogation of a human rights review jurisdiction would have been an improper exercise in judicial law-making in an area which is properly the province of the *legislature*.

---

[127] *Ibid.* at 748.
[128] M Hunt, *Using Human Rights Law in English Courts* (Oxford: Hart Publishing, 1997).
[129] D Beyleveld, "The Concept of a Human Right and the Incorporation of the European Convention on Human Rights" [1995] *PL* 577.

Secondly, full human rights review, bearing in mind the intrusiveness of the juridical tools by which it is effected, substantially increases judicial control of the *executive*, thereby significantly altering the constitutional balance of power between courts and government. It is necessary to address each of these points in turn.

2.4.3. The judiciary and the legislature

It has already been noted that, in light of the dualist tradition of the British constitution, the courts felt that a unilateral decision by the judiciary to enforce the ECHR would have usurped Parliament's role. However, it is possible to argue that, even if the assertion by the courts of a rights-based review jurisdiction had not been based on the Convention, thus involving no breach of dualist theory, such a step would still potentially have amounted to judicial interference in an area which falls properly within Parliament's sphere.

Lord Diplock famously said that "it cannot be too strongly emphasised that the British constitution, though largely unwritten, is based firmly upon the separation of powers; Parliament makes the laws, the judiciary interpret them".[130] This conceptualisation of the role of separation of powers theory in the UK is at once both simplistic and exaggerated, but it does at least capture the idea that primary law-making responsibility rests with Parliament. The courts' reluctance unilaterally to create a human rights review jurisdiction was clearly based, at least in part, on precisely such thinking: in particular, it appears that the identification of which substantive human rights were sufficiently important to be afforded legal protection was felt to be a function falling within the province of Parliament, not the courts, under the constitutional separation of powers.

However, although the case law indicates that this view commanded a good measure of judicial support, Sir John Laws did not share it. Writing prior to the entry into force of the Human Rights Act, he identified two particular arguments which, if accepted, imply that it would have been legitimate for the courts to assume a full human rights review jurisdiction without waiting for a legislative warrant. It is helpful to consider each of his arguments in turn.

Laws built the first aspect of his thesis on *the distinction between negative and positive rights*. Respect for the former—such as the rights to life, free expression and privacy—requires that they should not be interfered with except where this is adequately justified by reference to a competing interest. Positive rights, on the other hand, require pro-active steps to be taken if they are to be upheld: the right to a decent education and adequate health care fall into this category. Such rights, says Laws, are "the stuff of political debate . . . [C]onstitutional responsibility [for upholding them] rests on the shoulders of our elected politicians. It is not the domain of the judges . . .".[131] In contrast, it is the "constitutional role of the courts" to act as the "guardians" of negative rights.[132]

---

[130] *Duport Steels Ltd.* v. *Sirs* [1980] 1 WLR 142 at 157.
[131] Sir John Laws, "The Constitution: Morals and Rights" [1996] *PL* 622 at 629.
[132] *Ibid.*

Having set out this familiar distinction, Laws uses it to support the proposition that there is a self-selecting class of human rights which are, without more, proper candidates for judicial protection. On this argument, the enforcement of negative rights is not preceded by any improper activism or law-making: the judges have not given vent to their social or political mores in deciding which rights should be upheld and which should not, because the distinction between rights which can and cannot be protected by judges inheres in the very nature of human rights themselves.

This thesis relies heavily on two implicit premises. First, in empirical terms, it must be possible to draw a clear distinction between positive and negative rights since, on Laws's own argument, it is constitutionally imperative that judges deal only with the latter. Secondly, in normative terms, it must be the case that the dividing line between negative and positive rights truly marks the boundary between those matters with which the courts should and should not be concerned. In reality, neither of these propositions can easily be substantiated: the distinction between negative and positive rights is neither a feasible nor a satisfactory criterion by which to delimit the proper role of the courts in the human rights arena.

The empirical premise is problematic because it is broadly accepted that the division between negative and positive rights is so nebulous that it "often becomes blurred".[133] For example, "Some may see the right to a good education as a positive right; others may claim that it is an essential component of, say, the right to freedom of speech [which is a negative right], since without education, we are disabled from communicating our opinions to others effectively".[134] And, as the jurisprudence of the European Court of Human Rights indicates, ostensibly negative rights may well conceal positive elements.[135]

Moreover, not only is it very difficult to distinguish clearly between positive and negative rights in practice: the distinction does not make sense in principle as the criterion by which to delimit the role of the courts in this field. Even an instrument as modest as the ECHR embodies positive as well as negative rights. For example, Article 5 imposes extensive positive duties on the state in the field of criminal procedure. Article 6 does the same *vis-à-vis* the criminal trial process and access to the courts. Furthermore, when apparently negative rights are scrutinised through the forensic process they are often found to be composites of both positive and negative obligations:[136] in English law, the right to life has

---

[133] Lord Irvine, "Response to Sir John Laws 1996" [1996] *PL* 636 at 638. See also R Singh, *The Future of Human Rights in the United Kingdom* (Oxford: Hart Publishing, 1997) at 51–8; F Donson, "Civil Liberties and Judicial Review: Can the Common Law Really Protect Rights?" in P Leyland and T Woods (eds.), *Administrative Law Facing the Future: Old Constraints and New Horizons* (London: Blackstone Press, 1997) at 362–4.

[134] Irvine, above n. 133, at 638.

[135] See, *e.g.*, *Marckx v. Belgium* (1979) Series A, vol. 31; *X and Y v. Netherlands* (1985) Series A, vol. 91. See further D J Harris, M O'Boyle and C Warbrick, *Law of the European Convention on Human Rights* (London: Butterworths, 1995) at 19–22.

[136] See above, n. 135.

been held to comprise a positive duty to provide financial support,[137] and Laws J himself held that it can require the provision of medical treatment.[138] It is thus clear that it makes no sense to argue that only negative rights are suitable for judicial protection. In practice, courts—in Britain and elsewhere—enforce both positive and negative rights, and it is misleading to suggest that positive rights are *per se* non-justiciable.

It therefore becomes clear that rights cannot and should not be placed in separate compartments labelled "positive" and "negative". It is even clearer that this putative distinction cannot bear the strain which Laws places on it. It follows that, if those rights which ought to qualify for judicial enforcement are not set apart by virtue of their negative character, any judge-made human rights regime must be the fruit of judicial choice. This is significant, given that Laws readily concedes that judicial decision-making *vis-à-vis* positive rights would be constitutionally improper:

> [T]here will always be hard choices about which . . . decent and honourable people will disagree. At the level of political decision-making such choices find expression as rival policies. Indeed, the very concept of a policy imports the existence of a potential argument as to how competing priorities should be ordered . . . [The judges] have no commanding voice in such matters. In relation to positive rights, Parliament is necessarily and rightly supreme.[139]

Once it is recognised that rigid separation of positive and negative rights is highly problematic, it becomes apparent that the legitimacy of a judge-made human rights system cannot be established by reference to a self-selecting class of negative rights. This, in turn, helps to explain the attitude of English courts prior to incorporation. Any movement towards full human rights review—embracing rigorous enforcement of a broad range of substantive rights—necessarily required prior evaluation of which rights were to be protected. This reflects the fact that the catalogue of legally enforceable human rights which any society adopts is necessarily the product of political and cultural forces which are rooted in contemporary morality—and, the further one moves into the territory of substantive rights review, the more divisive are the moral choices which fall to be made in selecting the rights which are to be protected. Judicial caution in this field was therefore well founded.

Writing more recently, Laws has advanced a second argument which is relevant to the present discussion. In an effort to defend rights adjudication from the charge that it inevitably involves judicial subjectivity, he argues that *fundamental rights are legal, not moral, constructs.*[140] Hence judicial enforcement of the ECHR:

---

[137] *R* v. *Hammersmith and Fulham London Borough Council, ex parte M* [1996] TLR 556; *R* v. *Secretary of State for Social Security, ex parte Joint Council for the Welfare of Immigrants* [1997] 1 WLR 275.

[138] *R* v. *Cambridge Health Authority, ex parte B* (1995) 25 Butterworth's Medico-Legal Reports 5 (QBD) (reversed [1995] 1 WLR 898 (CA)).

[139] Sir John Laws, "The Constitution: Morals and Rights" [1996] *PL* 622 at 629.

[140] See Sir John Laws, "The Limitations of Human Rights" [1998] *PL* 254 at 255–6.

will not be to vindicate a higher morality. Rather it will be to determine the reach of a strictly legal right conferred by the Convention against the background of the case's specific facts . . . [This approach] is an important intellectual armoury in the judicial task of dealing with the Convention as law and not as moral idealism, upon which the judges have no special voice.[141]

Although he seeks, in this manner, to distinguish between morals and rights, Laws acknowledges that there exists an essential relationship between the two concepts, because the notion of legal rights springs from a higher framework of morality. Thus, rather than being an end in themselves, rights are simply a legal manifestation of that higher morality.[142] It is for this reason that Laws refers to the "secondary nature of rights" in order to express both their derivation and distinction from morals.[143] This prompts two comments.

First, it is difficult to see how judges can give meaning and force to fundamental rights without some recourse to the moral philosophy which underpins and gives rise to them. However feasible it may be to express rights in legalistic, rather than moralistic, terms, it is impossible to explore their content and limits without regard to the morality in which they are founded. Consequently the meaning and nuances of any right can be determined only by locating it within precisely that framework of morality from it sprang in the first place.

Secondly, in advancing his thesis, Laws's primary objective is to argue that enforcement of human rights is an appropriate task for the judiciary. In this sense, the argument is directed towards the legitimacy of the judiciary's *exercising* a human rights jurisdiction, rather than the prior question of how such jurisdiction is *acquired* in the first place. Nevertheless, his argument is clearly relevant to the latter issue as well. In fact, the connection between rights and morality which Laws correctly identifies has important implications for the propriety of any judicial arrogation of a substantive human rights jurisdiction. Even if, in enforcing human rights, the judges are able to avoid making "moral" decisions, the same cannot be true of the logically prior task of identifying those rights which are to be protected. If rights spring from a higher moral framework, any human rights jurisdiction which the judges themselves fashion must derive from whichever conception of morality they choose to adopt. Lord Irvine observes that:

The central difficulty [of a judge-made human rights system] . . . is that, whilst the fundamental importance of individual rights is almost universally recognised, the nature and content of those rights is not . . . However great a consensus there may be about the primacy of individual . . . rights in general, there is no consensus as to which particular rights are fundamental; what their content is; when they may be overridden; and what hierarchy, if any, should exist among them.[144]

---

[141] *Ibid*. at 257.
[142] Sir John Laws, "The Constitution: Morals and Rights" [1996] *PL* 622 at 622–7.
[143] Above n. 140, at 257.
[144] Lord Irvine, "Response to Sir John Laws 1996" [1996] *PL* 636 at 638.

He therefore goes on to argue that "the protection of human rights can only be secured effectively if these rights are crystallised in a democratically validated Bill of Rights"[145] because "judicial determination of which rights are sufficiently fundamental to qualify for legal protection would create [at least] the appearance of judicial law-making in the sphere allocated to an elected Parliament".[146] Similarly, writing before the Human Rights Act was passed, Singh acknowledged that "a Bill of Rights . . . enacted by Parliament . . . would give democratic legitimacy to the efforts being tentatively made by some judges to develop human rights in the common law. It would give the judges a clear idea of which rights are to be treated as fundamental in our society."[147] These sensitive issues of demarcation which arise at the interface between legislative and curial power—which unilateral judicial assertion of a human rights review jurisdiction would inevitably have raised—help, at least in part, to explain the reluctance of the courts to assert such jurisdiction in the absence of legislative intervention.

It is worth noting, in passing, that these considerations of constitutional principle are complemented by a closely related factor which is more pragmatic in nature. Experience indicates that human rights initiatives enjoy much greater success if they command widespread support across government and within society.[148] The Canadian Bill of Rights, enacted in 1960, achieved very little, and neither judges nor administrators demonstrated any real commitment to its enforcement.[149] In striking contrast, the Canadian Charter of Rights and Freedoms, adopted in 1982, has had a very substantial impact, significantly advancing the status of human rights in Canada.[150] Doubtless there are many factors which explain the divergent fortunes of the two initiatives; but, as Professor Harry Arthurs has commented, the failure of the 1960 Bill of Rights was at least partly due to its lack of broadly based support: "Only when the Bill begins to command the loyalty of individuals—judges, politicians, policemen, bureaucrats, ordinary citizens—will its aspirations be translated into reality".[151]

Thus the Canadian experience—as well as common sense—suggests that the wider the support for a human rights system, the more likely it is to succeed in engendering a human rights culture. Such considerations suggest that unilateral

[145] *Ibid.*

[146] Lord Irvine, "Constitutional Change in the United Kingdom: British Solutions to Universal Problems" (the 1998 National Heritage Lecture, delivered at the Supreme Court in Washington DC, USA, March 1998).

[147] R Singh, *The Future of Human Rights in the United Kingdom* (Oxford: Hart Publishing, 1997) at 17.

[148] See generally M Zander, *A Bill of Rights?* (London: Sweet and Maxwell, 1997) at 126–32.

[149] See E A Driedger, "The Meaning and Effect of the Canadian Bill of Rights: A Draftsman's Viewpoint" (1977) 9 *Ottawa Law Review* 303; J Black-Branch, "Entrenching Human Rights Legislation under Constitutional Law: The Canadian Charter of Rights and Freedoms" [1998] *European Human Rights Law Review* 312 at 315–19.

[150] For an overview see R Penner, "The Canadian Experience with the Charter of Rights: Are there Lessons for the United Kingdom?" [1996] *PL* 104.

[151] H Arthurs in "Minutes of Evidence taken before the Select Committee on a Bill of Rights" (London: TSO, 1977).

judicial assertion of a fundamental rights jurisdiction would not only have affronted the constitutional balance between legislature and judiciary, but would also, by excluding the democratically-elected legislature from the enterprise, have inhibited the resultant human rights regime's capacity to effect a genuine change in legal culture. In this sense, the necessary pervasiveness of human rights initiatives requires that they rest on a foundation which is broader and more inclusive than judicial activism.

2.4.4. *The judiciary and the executive*

The reticence of English judges to embrace full rights-based review prior to incorporation can also be traced, in part, to their perception of its implications for the relationship between the courts and the executive. In particular, they recognised that movement along the continuum, from a largely process-oriented conception of review towards a regime embracing high-intensity review on substantive human rights grounds, would necessarily change the character and increase the intrusiveness of the review jurisdiction. Such considerations evidently weighed heavily on Simon Brown LJ in the *Smith* case:

> If the Convention . . . were part of our law and we [the judges] were accordingly entitled to ask whether the policy answers a pressing social need and whether the restriction on human rights involved can be shown proportionate to the benefits, then clearly the primary judgment (subject only to a limited 'margin of appreciation') would be for us and not others: *the constitutional balance would shift*.[152]

This is consistent with Lord Irvine's assessment of the operation of judicial review under the Human Rights Act. Writing before its entry into force, he observed that "a more rigorous scrutiny than traditional judicial review will be required" because "there is a profound difference between the Convention margin of appreciation and the common law test of rationality".[153] Thus he acknowledges that cases like *Brind* may well have been decided differently had the courts possessed a human rights jurisdiction at the relevant time.[154] The increase in the intensity of review which attends movement towards a full human rights jurisdiction therefore impacts substantially on the balance of power between the executive and the courts, thereby producing important implications for the traditional conception of the separation of powers.

Barendt has observed that British commentators "have paid relatively little attention" to the doctrine of the separation of powers.[155] It is true that there exists a perception that the British constitution does not embody any meaningful conception of that principle. This arises largely because of the numerous

---

[152] R v. *Ministry of Defence, ex parte Smith* [1996] QB 517 at 541 (emphasis added).
[153] Lord Irvine, "The Development of Human Rights in Britain under an Incorporated Convention on Human Rights" [1998] PL 221 at 234.
[154] *Ibid*. at 227–8.
[155] E Barendt, "Separation of Powers and Constitutional Government" [1995] PL 599 at 599.

technical "breaches" of the doctrine which occur.[156] De Smith thus remarked that the separation of powers doctrine is regarded as "an irrelevant distraction for the English law student and his teachers".[157]

This, however, is based on a rather narrow view of the separation of powers, and overlooks the fact that it may—and, properly, should—be regarded as an ethos rather than as a prescriptive rule.[158] As James Madison recognised in his seminal work on the subject, it does not direct that the institutions of government "ought to have no *partial agency* in, or *control* over, the acts of each other". Rather, it provides that "where the *whole* power of one department is exercised by the same hands which possess the *whole* power of another department, the fundamental principles of a free constitution are subverted".[159] Similarly Barendt explains that the doctrine "should not be explained in terms of a strict distribution of *functions* between the three branches of government, but in terms of a network of rules and principles which will ensure that power is not concentrated in the hands of one branch".[160] It is this conception of the separation of powers which is arguably evident in the British constitution. Thus, as Munro remarks, "The separation in the British constitution, although not absolute, ought not to be lightly dismissed".[161]

In seeking to ensure that the executive does not exceed the scope of its legal powers, judicial review of administrative action is an important mechanism by which the separation of powers is upheld in the UK. However, the courts are required, in this context, to strike a delicate balance. If review extends too far, it ceases to be a legitimate check on the use of executive power, and becomes an improper usurpation which, far from promoting the separation of powers, seriously undermines it. It is for this reason that the English courts have exercised caution in their development of judicial review, seeking to tread a careful line between promoting and undermining the separation of powers through a combination of self-restraint and intervention. As Michael Fordham comments, "It is faithfulness to these dual concerns of vigilance and restraint which produces that unique 'supervisory' jurisdiction . . . by which the courts decide when it is appropriate to interfere with public decision making."[162]

---

[156] See generally A W Bradley and K D Ewing, *Constitutional and Administrative Law* (London: Longman, 1997) at 92–7.

[157] S A de Smith, "The Separation of Powers in New Dress" (1966) 12 *McGill Law Journal* 491 at 491. See also O Hood Phillips, "A Constitutional Myth: Separation of Powers" (1977) 93 *LQR* 11.

[158] See C R Munro, "The Separation of Powers: Not Such a Myth" [1981] *PL* 19; C R Munro, *Studies in Constitutional Law* (London: Butterworths, 1999), ch. 9.

[159] J Madison, A Hamilton and J Jay, *The Federalist Papers* (I Kramnick, ed.) (Harmondsworth: Penguin Books, 1987) at 304 (original emphasis).

[160] E Barendt, "Separation of Powers and Constitutional Government" [1995] *PL* 599 at 608–9 (original emphasis).

[161] C R Munro, *Studies in Constitutional Law* (London: Butterworths, 1999) at 332.

[162] M Fordham, "Surveying the Grounds: Key Themes in Judicial Intervention" in P Leyland and T Woods (eds.), *Administrative Law Facing the Future: Old Constraints and New Horizons* (London: Blackstone Press, 1997) at 186.

The sensitive nature of this exercise is highlighted by *R* v. *Secretary of State for the Home Department, ex parte Fire Brigades Union*.[163] The Criminal Justice Act 1988 provided for a new statutory criminal injuries compensation scheme,[164] to take effect "on such day as the Secretary of State may . . . appoint".[165] Having decided, before it was ever activated, that this scheme would be too expensive to operate, the Home Secretary used his prerogative powers to introduce a cheaper alternative. The House of Lords held that this contravened the minister's implied statutory duty to keep under active consideration the question when, if at all, to invoke the statutory scheme, and also entailed an abuse of his prerogative power which, it was held, he could not properly use in a manner which involved a breach of statutory duty.

This factual matrix raised particularly sensitive issues concerning the separation of powers, and the interest, for present purposes, lies in the different approaches adopted by the minority and the majority. On the one hand, Lord Mustill, in his dissenting speech, felt that the case raised a matter which was essentially for Parliament and the executive to resolve, so that by reviewing the decision the court would be intervening in an area lying outwith its constitutional province:

> Absent a written constitution much sensitivity is required of the parliamentarian, administrator and judge if the delicate balance of unwritten rules [of judicial review] evolved . . . in recent years is not to be disturbed, and all the recent advances undone . . . [S]ome of the arguments addressed [to the court in this case] would have the court push to the very boundaries of the distinction between court and Parliament . . .[166]

In contrast, the majority invoked the separation of powers in order to justify judicial review. This line of reasoning turned on the fact that the minister, by *de facto* repealing legislation by executive fiat, was usurping a function which was properly Parliament's; by intervening, the courts would uphold the separation of powers by preventing the executive from transgressing beyond its proper sphere. Thus Lord Browne-Wilkinson opined that:

> [I]t would be most surprising if, at the present day, prerogative powers could be validly exercised by the executive so as to frustrate the will of Parliament expressed in a statute . . . It is not for the executive . . . to state . . . that the provisions in the Act of 1988 "will accordingly be repealed when a suitable legislative opportunity occurs". It is for Parliament, not the executive, to repeal legislation.[167]

This case demonstrates acute judicial awareness of the importance of evaluating the legitimacy of judicial review by reference to the proper role of the courts within the unwritten constitutional order; and, although it shows that there is clearly scope for disagreement on this matter, it is evident that a broader

---

[163] [1995] 2 AC 513.
[164] See ss. 108–17 and scheds. 6 and 7.
[165] S. 171(1).
[166] [1995] 2 AC 513 at 567–8.
[167] *Ibid.* at 552.

consensus permeated judicial thinking in the field of human rights review. That thinking held that, according to the division of functions within the British constitution, it would not be appropriate for the courts to institute a judicial review jurisdiction based on substantive fundamental rights. Given the considerable expansion of judicial power and the consequent reduction in executive freedom which would attend such a development, the judges acknowledged that it would involve a fundamental alteration in the constitutional distribution of power. Thus they considered that it would be inappropriate for them unilaterally to bring about such a change, as Simon Brown LJ explained in *Smith*:

> The protection of human rights is, [counsel for the applicants] submits . . . , a matter with which the courts are particularly concerned and for which they have an undoubted responsibility. So they do. *But they owe a duty too to remain within their constitutional bounds and not trespass beyond them.* Only if it were plain beyond sensible argument that no conceivable damage could be done to the armed forces as a fighting unit would it be appropriate for this court now to remove the issue entirely from the hands both of the military and of the government.[168]

Lord Irvine has also emphasised the important role of the separation of powers in moulding the proper role of reviewing courts. He points to the intention of Parliament that executive agencies, not judges, should exercise administrative discretion; the judiciary's lack of expertise in such matters, and the desirability of public power being exercised by those who are democratically accountable. These three factors, all based to some extent on the separation of powers, reduce to a "constitutional imperative of judicial self-restraint" in the field of public law.[169] Thus, speaking before the activation of the Human Rights Act, he concluded that, "Although they clearly wish to give effect to a substantive theory of the rule of law by affording direct protection to fundamental rights, the courts are ultimately deterred from doing so by a concern to avoid transgressing the bounds of their allotted constitutional province".[170]

It might be retorted that the courts exhibited greater willingness to invoke human rights considerations—based on the ECHR—in a variety of other contexts, such as the exercise of *judicial* discretion[171] and the development of *private* law.[172] However, the fact that the courts felt able to apply human rights in these areas while, at least to an extent, insulating administrative law from that trend, is not incompatible with the rationalisation of the courts' jurisprudence

---

[168] *R v. Ministry of Defence, ex parte Smith* [1996] QB 517 at 541 (emphasis added).

[169] Lord Irvine, "Judges and Decision-Makers: The Theory and Practice of *Wednesbury* Review" [1996] PL 59 at 60–1.

[170] Lord Irvine, "Constitutional Change in the United Kingdom: British Solutions to Universal Problems" (the 1998 National Heritage Lecture, delivered at the Supreme Court in Washington DC, USA, March 1998).

[171] See, e.g., *R v. Khan (Sultan)* [1997] AC 558, in which the ECHR was taken into account by the court in exercising its discretion whether to exclude evidence in a criminal trial.

[172] See, e.g., *Derbyshire County Council v. Times Newspapers Ltd.* [1992] QB 770, in which the Court of Appeal relied on the ECHR in holding that local authorities may not institute defamation proceedings.

which is being suggested. When a court takes Convention or any other substantive rights into account in non-administrative law contexts, this has little impact on the separation of powers since it entails no judicial attempt to assert power over and impose norms on the executive branch. The same is not true of administrative law. Although, through judicial review, the courts have traditionally exercised considerable supervisory power over the executive, they were evidently aware that movement towards a more substantive system of human rights review would involve a significant shift in the balance of power between the judiciary and the executive which is not entailed in other applications of human rights law by the courts.

This approach can transparently be seen in the reasoning of McCullough J in *R v. Radio Authority, ex parte Bull*.[173] Counsel urged that a discretionary power should be read as being subject to Article 10 of the ECHR, which protects freedom of expression. He relied, *inter alia*, on certain dicta in *Attorney-General* v. *Guardian Newspapers (No. 2)*[174] to the effect that English law and the Convention are of a piece in the field of free speech. McCullough J rejected the analogy, pointing out that "unlike that case . . . we are not here in the realm of the common law; we are interpreting [the scope of the discretionary power granted by] a statutory provision".[175] In other words, while judges were comfortable with allowing the ECHR to influence some areas of law, they were markedly less willing to allow it to permeate administrative law. Thus it is, at least in part, the peculiar sensitivity of administrative law *vis-à-vis* the separation of powers which led the courts to exercise particular self-restraint in this area prior to legislative incorporation.

2.5. Human Rights Review and the Traditional Law of Judicial Review

The conclusion reached thus far—that the courts generally considered it constitutionally improper unilaterally to assert a human rights jurisdiction, within which they would require discretionary power to be exercised consistently with substantive norms and would demand objective justification of any rights infractions—begs an obvious question. If, as appears to be the case, the courts were reluctant to engage fully in human rights review without a legislative warrant, why—given the absence of any explicit warrant—have they never considered it similarly inappropriate to review administrative action on the traditional grounds? This matter can best be addressed by revisiting the factors, identified above, which largely inhibited the courts from engaging in full human rights review, and considering their relevance to the traditional law of review.

---

[173] [1996] QB 169 (upheld [1998] QB 294 (CA)).
[174] [1990] 1 AC 109 at 283–4, *per* Lord Goff.
[175] [1996] QB 169 at 192.

2.5.1. The judiciary and the legislature

First, it was noted that the more substantive is the system of review which judges fashion, the more morally difficult and divisive are the choices which they must make as they determine which particular values are deserving of legal protection. Consequently, the further one moves along the continuum from process- to substance-oriented review, the identification of the norms which are to be upheld increasingly becomes a task to which legislators are better suited than judges. Conversely, on that part of the continuum which is concerned mainly with questions of process, which is where judicial review has traditionally stood in English law, the issues that arise in identifying the values which are to be protected are more self-evidently matters for judges. The point is expressed clearly by Sir John Laws. Referring to English law, he observes that:

> It is no accident that anything approaching absolute rights is largely confined to the means by which disputes are adjudicated. Rights of that kind *are not divisive, do not represent an isolated morality.* They constitute, very obviously, an essential condition in a civilised state for the resolution of claims between man and man and between man and state . . . [R]ights of due process . . . possess in principle *a settled, overarching quality.*[176]

Professor Jeffrey Jowell similarly characterises principles of due process:

> . . . the tenets of procedural fairness do not require an utilitarian evaluation of preferred outcomes. They are not therefore based upon policy evaluations best suited to elected officials or their agents in a democracy . . . [I]t is not seriously contended that the imposition of procedural norms is beyond the constitutional capacity of judges, who aim thereby not to achieve any particular social or economic objective but to ensure only that the decision was fairly arrived at.[177]

Progress along the continuum from process- to substance-oriented judicial review thus reveals a related shift in constitutional and institutional competence from the judge to the legislator.[178] The position is therefore arrived at that the further one moves along the continuum the greater is the risk that the courts will intervene in an area which is not constitutionally theirs. No-one would sensibly contend that the dividing line between proper and improper judicial activity in this field is clearly demarcated. Nevertheless, the awareness that there exist areas in which judicial intervention is less justifiable quite properly shaped the judiciary's attitude to human rights review, and provides at least a partial explanation of why the courts have long considered themselves constitutionally justified in unilaterally applying process-oriented principles of review without any explicit legislative warrant, while exhibiting less willingness, in the absence of

[176] Sir John Laws, "The Limitations of Human Rights" [1998] *PL* 254 at 259–60 (emphasis added).
[177] J Jowell, "Of Vires and Vacuums: The Constitutional Context of Judicial Review" in C F Forsyth (ed.), *Judicial Review and the Constitution* (Oxford: Hart Publishing, 2000) at 331.
[178] *Ibid.*

such a warrant, to propel judicial review towards that part of the continuum which embraces a wide range of substantive rights.

2.5.2. *The judiciary and the executive*

Secondly, it was observed that, prior to the entry into force of the Human Rights Act, judges tended to desist from engaging in high-intensity substantive rights adjudication because they wished to avoid undue interference with the executive, given the reduction in administrative autonomy which would attend the institution of such review.

Again, the caveat must be entered that the question is ultimately one of degree; nevertheless, it is undeniable that, as one moves along the continuum from process-oriented to substantive rights-based review, and from low-intensity modes of protection like *Wednesbury* to high-intensity devices such as proportionality, one necessarily witnesses an incremental reduction in executive autonomy as the courts' supervision grows ever more intrusive. To a large extent, the traditional principles of administrative law leave the ultimate discretion of decision-makers intact, given that they are concerned generally, albeit not exclusively,[179] with *how* decisions are made, rather than with *what* decisions are made. However, embracing substantive principles of review and the high-intensity tools by which they are protected changes the position. Although it is highly unlikely that, under the Human Rights Act, courts of supervisory jurisdiction will be transformed into appellate tribunals (given that administrators will no doubt still be accorded some margin of freedom[180]) a significant change will certainly take place in terms of the nature and intensity of review which, in turn, will impact upon the relationship and balance of power between the courts and the executive.

It is clear, therefore, that the willingness of the courts to apply the traditional principles of review without any legislative warrant, and their unwillingness to engage in substantive review in the absence of such a warrant, can be explained (partly, at least) by reference to the implications for agency autonomy. A regime which embraces and protects a broad range of substantive values by means of high-intensity tools of review leaves decision-makers with a smaller margin of freedom than the traditional model of review which is largely preoccupied with matters of due process. The implications, so far as the balance of power between judges and decision-makers is concerned, are self-evident.

---

[179] Clearly, some traditional principles of review, such as jurisdictional error and *Wednesbury* unreasonableness, impact upon the substantive freedom of the decision-maker. However, it is undeniable that the general concentration of the classic principles of review on decision-making rather than decisions tends to preserve ultimate administrative autonomy.

[180] See *R v. Director of Public Prosecutions, ex part Kebilene* [1999] 3 WLR 972 at 993–4, *per* Lord Hope, for discussion of the "discretionary area of judgment" under the Human Rights Act.

2.5.3. Conclusion

It would be unduly simplistic to say that the traditional law of judicial review, with its focus largely (but not, of course, exclusively) on process, enjoyed inherent constitutional legitimacy, whereas human rights review could be legitimated only through the provision of an explicit legislative warrant. Just as there is no clear distinction between process and substance, or between low-intensity and high-intensity review, so there is no simple division between "traditional review", which occurred without any explicit warrant, and "human rights review", in which the courts were unwilling fully to engage until such a warrant was supplied.

The differences which exist in these areas are, in truth, differences of degree. The further one moves along the continuum from process- to substance-oriented review, and from low-intensity to high-intensity modes of judicial intervention, the less evident it becomes that the activities in which the courts are involved lie squarely within their constitutional province as it has traditionally been perceived. It was the judiciary's awareness of precisely this point which tended to exert a braking effect on the development of English public law. Lacking a written constitution on which to rely, the courts sought to confine themselves to those areas of activity which they felt could be justified by reference to the unwritten constitutional order and the separation of powers ethos which it embodies. For the reasons advanced above, the closer the courts approached full human rights review, the less apparent it became that it was consistent with that ethos. It is for this reason that the Human Rights Act has proved necessary as a constitutional warrant for rights-based, high-intensity judicial review. It supplies the courts with a legislative signal that society has ordained that, henceforth, such review *is* constitutionally acceptable, notwithstanding that this entails a reordering the constitution in terms of the manner in which the three branches of government interrelate.

Forsyth has written that:

> [I]n any democratic polity change in the constitutional order must—or at any rate should—come about through the democratic process. And the judiciary, as important as its independence is to the rule of law, is a non-elected part of the constitutional order. How can some judges suppose they are entitled to change the fundamentals of the constitution without reference to the elected elements of that constitution? It may very well be a good thing if the judges were to have the task of protecting democracy and fundamental rights . . . but they should be given that task by the people; it is unseemly that they should seize it for themselves.[181]

The courts' jurisprudence in the human rights context shows that they recognise the force of such reasoning. In turn, this discloses a healthy judicial awareness of constitutional principle and of the proper mode of constitutional change in a

---

[181] C F Forsyth, "Of Fig Leaves and Fairy Tales: The Ultra Vires Doctrine, the Sovereignty of Parliament and Judicial Review" (1996) 55 *CLJ* 122 at 140.

democratic polity which embraces the ethos—albeit not a rigid doctrine—of the separation of powers.

Having explored why the courts awaited legislative intervention in the present sphere, it is necessary to turn to the more technical question of the legal basis of the system of human rights review which the Human Rights Act has instituted. Three specific points are considered. Section 3.1 evaluates an approach to the legal basis of human rights review which places it on a straightforward footing and which renders recourse to construction-oriented methodology—which forms the conceptual justification for the application of the traditional grounds of review—unnecessary so far as review on Convention grounds is concerned. However, the argument is advanced that this methodology raises substantial constitutional problems, and a vires-based alternative is therefore set out in section 3.2. The implications of adopting the latter model are then explored in section 3.3.

3.1. Human Rights as Substantive Rules of Good Administration

3.1.1. A rule-based approach to human rights review?

As Chapter 2 explains, dissatisfaction with the orthodox ultra vires principle as the justification for the traditional law of judicial review has led many commentators to urge its abandonment in favour of a doctrine based on autonomous common law rules of good administration. We have seen that this approach possesses many advantages, not least its openness and simplicity, but that it also encounters fundamental constitutional problems.

At first glance, it appears that the Human Rights Act prescribes an approach to human rights review which is substantially similar to the model founded on autonomous rules of good administration. The foundation for a simple rule-based approach, which seems to obviate the need to have recourse to the ultra vires theory's construction-based methodology, is apparently supplied by section 6(1) of the Act. It provides that: "It is unlawful for a public authority to act in a way which is incompatible with a Convention right". By setting out such a clear duty to respect human rights, this provision ostensibly places rights-based review on an altogether different and more straightforward footing than the traditional grounds of review. It seems that the courts are not required to characterise review under the Human Rights Act as an exercise in interpretation; instead, they are simply to be regarded as enforcing a set of rules based on respect for human rights which decision-makers are obliged to obey.[182]

---

[182] Unless the enabling provision necessarily requires the infringement of human rights: see s. 6(2).

This rule-based conception of human rights review carries with it a further advantage. The ultra vires doctrine's reliance on statutory implication means that it is unable to supply the conceptual foundation for judicial review of non-statutory powers: if no relevant statute exists, then self-evidently the controls applied by the courts cannot be regarded as implied statutory terms.[183] The same difficulty would not confront human rights review if it were rationalised—as section 6(1) appears to suggest it should be—as a straightforward duty to respect fundamental rights which is incumbent upon all public authorities, irrespective of whether their authority derives from statute. Since the section 6(1) approach does not characterise human rights as implied fetters on derived statutory powers, it supplies an all-encompassing juridical foundation which secures rights protection for individuals as they interact with all types of decision-maker.

3.1.2. Rule-based review, entrenchment and sovereignty

In order to evaluate this conceptualisation of the juridical basis of human rights review, it is necessary to revisit the distinction, set out in earlier chapters, between *vires-based* and *rule-based* models of review.

It will be recalled that the *vires-based* model presents the principles of review as interpretative constructs: in other words, it characterises them as limits which are internal to the scope of any given discretionary power. Consequently, in review cases, the courts are engaged in identifying the contours and reach of conferred power and policing the limits which they find.[184]

In contrast, the principles of review within the *rule-based* model are unrelated to the scope of the discretionary power as it is determined by enabling legislation. Rather, they exist as free-standing rules which make it unlawful to exercise discretionary power in a manner which is unreasonable, unfair, and so on. They do not represent the limits on power which Parliament is taken to have intended to apply: instead, they are wholly external to the scope of the power and independent of the intention of Parliament. In practice, they cut down the scope of discretionary power by rendering unlawful certain exercises of such power.[185]

Thus the essential difference between rule- and vires-based review is that the latter involves the courts' policing that perimeter of discretionary power which Parliament is taken to have ordained, whereas the former entails the application of external rules which dictate how such power can be exercised.

Chapter 3 argues that constitutional impropriety inheres in any attempt to rationalise the traditional law of judicial review, as it applies to statutory power, in rule-based terms: such an approach contradicts sovereignty theory, given that

---

[183] Although it was argued above that it is nevertheless possible to provide a justification for review of all forms of power which is globally coherent, notwithstanding that different contexts require the articulation of appropriate theoretical foundations: see Ch. 4, section 4.3, and Ch. 5.

[184] See Fig. 1, above at 39.

[185] See Figs. 2 and 3, above at 39–40.

it logically involves setting up common law rules of good administration against the legislative scheme established by Parliament. However, conceptualising the new grounds of review introduced by the Human Rights Act in rule-based terms would not suffer from the same shortcoming. The "rules" which would exist within that model would be statutory, having their basis in legislation—*viz.* section 6(1) of the Human Rights Act—rather than the common law. There is, therefore, no question that rule-based review on Convention grounds would involve the setting up of the common law against the sovereign will of Parliament. Nevertheless, a rule-based approach founded on section 6(1) still raises considerable constitutional problems. It is necessary to substantiate this proposition in two stages by considering the *analytical* and then the *constitutional* implications of adopting section 6(1) as the foundation of a rule-based approach to human rights review.

The *analytical* implications of the rule-based approach to review under the 1998 Act are identical to the analytical consequences of conceptualising the traditional grounds of judicial review as common law rules. If human rights find expression as straightforward statutory rules which decision-makers must obey, rather than as interpretive principles which shape the contours of discretionary powers, then, just as with common law rules of good administration, they must be viewed as cutting down the scope of decision-making powers and, therefore, as removing from administrators powers which Parliament initially granted to them.

Once this is recognised, it becomes necessary to analyse the *constitutional* implications which follow. In order to do so, a distinction must be made between judicial review of the exercise of statutory discretionary power created *before* and *after* the enactment of the human rights legislation.

First, consider a piece of legislation enacted in, say, 1990, which creates a particular decision-making power. The rule-based approach to judicial review provides that, properly interpreted, the agency's power is not subject to any implied conditions requiring it to be exercised compatibly with the Convention rights. (After all, if such implied limits existed, the application of rules would be pointless, since they would simply replicate the duty to respect the Convention rights which, by virtue of its implicitly limited powers, would already be incumbent upon the agency.) However, within the rule-based model, section 6(1) demands adherence to the Convention rights and, subject to section 6(2), renders "unlawful" any use of the discretionary power which is "incompatible with a Convention right". There therefore arises a discrepancy between the Acts of 1990 and 1998. The former vests a broad competence in the agency to exercise its discretion in a manner which need not be compatible with Convention rights, while the latter directs that it is unlawful to use the discretionary power in such a way. In this situation, orthodox theory provides that the later legislation should prevail, so that, according to a rule-based analysis, the Human Rights Act 1998 operates so as to remove from decision-makers powers which earlier enabling legislation, properly interpreted, conferred upon them.

This raises two points. On the one hand, the rule-based analysis does not, in relation to human rights review of discretions created before the enactment of the Human Rights Act, raise any constitutional problem, since it is perfectly clear that later legislation can prevail over earlier legislation. On the other hand, however, it is apparent that this is emphatically not the approach which the promoters of the Human Rights Act had in mind. The White Paper stated that:

> It has been suggested that the courts should be able to uphold the [Convention] rights in preference to any provisions of earlier legislation which are incompatible with those rights. This is on the basis that a later Act of Parliament takes precedence over an earlier Act if there is a conflict. But the Human Rights Bill is intended to provide a new basis for judicial interpretation of all legislation, not a basis for striking down any part of it.[186]

Consequently the Act provides that the courts' duty to attempt to interpret enactments consistently with human rights and their power to issue declarations of incompatibility when this proves impossible shall have no impact upon the "validity, continuing operation or enforcement" of primary legislation.[187] Although these provisions of the Act and of the White Paper are primarily intended to demonstrate that judges should not, under the new law, possess the power to strike down legislation, it nevertheless follows that the implication of the rule-based analysis identified above—according to which the Human Rights Act would remove from administrators powers which earlier statutes had conferred upon them—is inconsistent with this ethos. Hence, in the context of human rights review of pre-Human Rights Act discretions, it can be said that the rule-based model, while constitutionally workable, is certainly incompatible with the philosophy on which the 1998 Act is founded.

Adherence to the rule-based model raises more profound constitutional difficulties in respect of judicial review, on human rights grounds, of discretionary powers created *after* the enactment of the Human Rights Act. Consider an enactment of, say, 2001 which creates, in broad terms which make no reference to respect for human rights, a certain discretion. According to the rule-based analysis, the scope of that discretion, properly interpreted, would not be subject to any implied obligation to observe human rights standards:[188] as discussed above, if the position were otherwise, no "rules" would be needed. Consequently it would be necessary to argue that the earlier 1998 Act rendered unlawful (by operation of section 6(1)) something which, according to the later enabling legislation, would not be unlawful. The Act of 1998 would therefore

---

[186] Cm 3782, *Rights Brought Home: The Human Rights Bill* (London, 1997) at 10.

[187] Human Rights Act 1998, ss. 3(2)(b) and 4(6)(a).

[188] It would, of course, be difficult to justify reading the legislation thus if a ministerial statement had been made under the Human Rights Act s. 19 to the effect that the legislation was thought to be compatible with respect for ECHR rights. In light of s. 19, it would be much more natural to hold that provisions creating discretionary powers were intended to be implicitly limited by reference to Convention standards. This is one reason why the vires-based model, set out below in section 3.2, is to be preferred over the rule-based model presently under discussion.

purport to take away from the agency a power which, properly interpreted, the Act of 2001 conferred upon it. For this to be possible the Human Rights Act would have to be an entrenched enactment, capable of prevailing over later legislation which—positively or by omission, expressly or implicitly—was inconsistent with the 1998 Act's policy of securing respect for human rights. Although the European Communities Act 1972 has arguably been entrenched in this manner,[189] it is clear from the provisions of that Act that it was intended to have such effect: hence it provides that Community law is to take priority over any legislation "passed or to be passed".[190] However, it is very clear that the Human Rights Act does not purport to be entrenched in this way: the White Paper confirms this conclusion in terms,[191] and there exists no provision in the Act which suggests otherwise.

This analysis discloses a striking symmetry between the constitutional consequences of adopting a rule-based approach in relation to the traditional grounds of review and the new substantive principles of review. Just as it is impossible to set up the common law against legislation, so it is not possible for earlier legislation (in the form of the Human Rights Act) to cut down or take away powers granted by later legislation (in the form of enabling provisions giving rise to discretionary power which, unless an interpretative approach is adopted, will not be subject to any internal rights-based limits). In each instance the same reasoning explains the result: within the British hierarchy of legal norms, the common law is inferior to legislation, just as earlier legislation cannot be set up against later legislation. Both of these propositions are logical functions of the doctrine of parliamentary sovereignty, according to which the contemporary will of Parliament is the ultimate source of law in the constitution, prevailing over the common law and earlier legislation alike.

In light of this, it may be thought that the Human Rights Act creates a background against which future grants of discretionary power should be interpreted as being subject to internal limits based on human rights,[192] in which case the application of substantive norms in the administrative law context would reveal no conflict between the 1998 Act and later legislation. The following section argues that this is indeed so. However, far from rescuing the rule-based model from constitutional unworkability, such an approach necessarily entails the rejection of that model. If the Human Rights Act is viewed as giving rise to such an interpretative backdrop, thereby leading to the implied limitation of future grants of discretionary power on rights-based grounds, this reflects an altogether different approach, based on interpretation. Indeed, it takes us back to the familiar implication-based methodology of the ultra vires principle, to which we now turn.

---

[189] See above at 80–3.
[190] European Communities Act 1972, s. 2(4).
[191] Cm 3782, *Rights Brought Home: The Human Rights Bill* (London, 1997) at 9–11.
[192] As discussed in section 3.2 below, such an argument would be founded principally on ss. 3 and 19.

3.2. Human Rights as Interpretative Constructs

3.2.1. A vires-based, not a rule-based, model of judicial review

Having rejected a rule-based conceptualisation of judicial review under the Human Rights Act in light of the constitutional difficulties which it raises, it is necessary to articulate a theory which gives effect to fundamental rights in the administrative law sphere in a manner which is consistent with the non-entrenched status of the Act.

The solution to this conundrum is clear. The Convention rights, as they apply to the administrative decision-making process, must be rationalised as interpretive constructs which shape the internal contours of enabling provisions, thereby ensuring that the courts, in effecting judicial review on rights-based grounds, enforce the limits of discretionary powers which enabling legislation—properly interpreted—sets, rather than cutting down the scope of such powers and thereby giving rise to the problems, identified above, which inhere in the rule-based approach. The Human Rights Act, in section 3(1), supplies the foundation for precisely this methodology. It provides that, "So far as it is possible to do so, primary and subordinate legislation must be read and given effect in a way which is compatible with the Convention rights".

The first point to note is that the Act provides no indication of how sections 3(1) and 6(1) relate to one another. At first glance, the most likely answer is that section 6(1) deals specifically with administrative law, placing public decision-makers under a simple, direct obligation to respect human rights: in other words, a rule-based approach to judicial review on Convention grounds. Within this framework, section 3(1) would relate to areas other than administrative law, imposing upon the courts a broad obligation to adopt, where possible, a rights-oriented construction of legislation generally. This approach is attractive, at least superficially: not only does it place judicial review on a straightforward footing which avoids interpretive methodology; it also allots clear, distinct roles to sections 3(1) and 6(1), thereby helping to make sense of the structure of the Act.

However, it has already been established that this model cannot be adopted. For this reason, the focus, in the administrative law field, must be on section 3(1) rather than section 6(1). Since it is not constitutionally possible to conceptualise human rights as rule-based limits, rights-oriented review must instead be facilitated by reliance on the familiar methodology of ultra vires. In this manner fundamental rights must be internalised: they must be given effect interpretatively rather than directly. Section 3(1) must therefore be relied upon as an interpretive tool so that all discretionary power—whether created before or after the entry into force of the Human Rights Act—is read as being inherently limited by reference to human rights norms.[193]

---

[193] The justifiability of interpreting post-Human Rights Act legislation in this way is buttressed by the fact that such legislation is (almost inevitably) accompanied by a ministerial statement of compatibility, pursuant to s. 19 of the Human Rights Act. Such statements provide that, in the minister's view, the legislation is consistent with the Convention rights.

There therefore exists an important distinction between the rule- and vires-based models. Whereas the rule-based approach involves the taking away (by the Human Rights Act) of power which is conferred by enabling legislation, the vires-based model holds that grants of discretionary power never, in the first place, confer upon decision-makers any vires to breach the Convention rights. It follows from this that—unlike the rule-based method—the vires-based model is able to reconcile judicial review on human rights grounds with the non-entrenched status of the Human Rights Act since, within that model, there is no attempt to use the Act in order to remove power which was conferred by enabling legislation. This, in turn, is consistent with the stated objective of the White Paper and the ethos of the Act itself.

The vires-based model therefore raises no constitutional difficulties. It is well established that earlier legislation can contribute to the interpretive framework within which later legislation is construed. The Interpretation Act 1978 is a good example of this. Provided that earlier legislation does not seek to override later legislation, no problems arise: subsequent legislation must therefore prevail if it is not possible to give effect to it in a manner which is consistent with the interpretive direction contained in the earlier measure. Thus, in the present context, later legislation must be given effect to when it clearly confers on decision-makers the power to act in a manner which involves a breach of human rights. Precisely this approach is embodied in the Human Rights Act through its qualification of the interpretative obligation in section 3(1) by the caveat "so far as it is possible to do so".

In this sense, the Human Rights Act is not, in itself, the straightforward legal basis of human rights review. Instead, all enabling provisions which create discretionary power constitute the legal bases of this new form of review. When such provisions are properly interpreted—which, *inter alia*, means construed pursuant to the direction in section 3(1) of the Human Rights Act—it can be seen that it is those enabling provisions, rather than the 1998 Act, which withhold from administrators the competence to infringe Convention rights.

3.2.2. *The vires-based model and the relationship between sections 3(1) and 6(1)*

It is clear from the foregoing that, within the vires-based model, section 6(1) of the Human Rights Act is not directly in play when the courts are involved in reviewing, on Convention rights grounds, the exercise of statutory discretions. This does not, however, mean that section 6(1) is redundant; indeed, it serves two crucial functions.

First, it elucidates the meaning of section 3(1). It was explained above that, in the *Brind* case,[194] counsel urged that, even without statutory incorporation of the ECHR, discretionary powers should, in the absence of specific contrary

---

[194] R v. *Secretary of State for the Home Department, ex parte Brind* [1991] 1 AC 696.

provision, be interpreted as containing implied limits requiring adherence not only to the established principles of good administration but also to the substantive guarantees contained in the Convention. For the reasons considered above, this argument failed. However, reading sections 3(1) and 6(1) together, it becomes clear beyond any doubt that, now that the Human Rights Act is in force, the interpretation of statutory provisions giving rise to discretionary powers will reveal the existence of implied limits relating to *both* the traditional grounds of judicial review *and* the substantive rights which are enshrined in the ECHR. Section 6(1) therefore confirms that the interpretive duty contained in section 3(1) extends to the discovery of implied rights-based limits in legislative provisions which create discretionary powers, thereby effectively reversing the House of Lords' decision in *Brind*.

Section 6(1) serves a second, equally important purpose. Although considerations of constitutional propriety require the Convention rights to be conceptualised as interpretative constructs in the context of rights-based review of statutory discretions, such an approach would be inappropriate in relation to review, on Convention grounds, of non-statutory powers. In the absence of a statute to construe, the Convention rights cannot take effect interpretatively. Thus, whereas judicial review of statutory powers under the Human Rights Act is underpinned by section 3(1) (read in conjunction with section 6(1)), review of non-statutory powers is founded on section 6(1) alone. The absence, in the sphere of non-statutory powers, of any difficulties concerning sovereignty and entrenchment permit the Convention rights to take effect directly rather than interpretatively. This, in turn, is consistent with the way in which the juridical basis of review of non-statutory powers on traditional grounds was conceptualised in Chapter 5.[195] Moreover, as with the traditional grounds of review, no difficulty is presented by this approach: the substantive principles of review are identical in all the spheres in which they operate and share a common normative foundation in the Human Rights Act; this is not contradicted by acknowledging that the way in which their application is rationalised must take account of the constitutional and conceptual differences between the various types of decision-making power to which judicial review extends.

3.3. Further Implications of the Vires-Based Model

Having set out the vires-based model by reference to which review, under the Human Rights Act, of statutory discretionary power must be rationalised, it is worth considering three particular implications of that model.

---

[195] However, for the reasons advanced above at 175–82, human rights should be conceptualised as *a priori* determinants of the scope of prerogative power. In contrast, they represent rule-based fetters on *de facto* powers of government. This scheme is consistent with that which was articulated in Ch. 5 in relation to the supervision, on pre-Human Rights Act grounds, of prerogative and *de facto* powers. It will be recalled that Ch. 5 advocated a vires-based (albeit not an interpretation-based) approach in the context of the prerogative, and a rule-based model in relation to non-statutory powers.

3.3.1. *Vires-based human rights review and the modified ultra vires principle*

It is unnecessary to revisit the reasons why, in the context of judicial review of statutory power on traditional grounds, the essence of the ultra vires doctrine remains crucial. It is, however, appropriate at this point to make two specific comments about the relationship between the vires-based approach to human rights review, set out above, and the modified ultra vires principle.

First, far from demonstrating the redundancy of ultra vires methodology as we move into a new, rights-based legal culture, the construction-oriented approach of ultra vires is essential to the human rights legislation's compatibility with the constitutional framework. As the foregoing analysis demonstrates, it is only by embracing human rights as interpretative constructs, rather than as free-standing legal obligations, that the vindication of such rights can be secured in a manner which is sensitive to the axiom of parliamentary sovereignty.

Secondly, the relationship between the modified ultra vires principle and the Human Rights Act is, in a sense, reciprocal. Not only does the ultra vires doctrine strengthen—or, more accurately, facilitate the operation of—the legislation; the Act also confirms—if such confirmation is needed—the centrality of the ultra vires doctrine. There is a clear symmetry between the approach of the Human Rights Act and the conception of ultra vires presented in this work. Both begin from the premise that it is the courts' duty to uphold the rule of law. The traditional law of judicial review derives from a process-oriented conception of the rule of law, which is vindicated by the courts by means of statutory construction. The Human Rights Act complements that approach. It adds a substantive element to the rule of law, thereby transforming the constitutional setting within which legislation is interpreted and discretionary power limited. This point is clearly taken by David Feldman who has written that:

> . . . the Human Rights Act 1998 will generate new developments in substantive review which all have either express or clearly implied authority from Parliament . . . So far as the Convention rights open a new direction for judicial review, the path-finding judges will be able to legitimate their creativeness by reference to a sound foundation in the classical doctrine of ultra vires.[196]

In this way the ideal of the rule of law is translated into enforceable legal principle in a manner which accommodates the theory of legislative supremacy: in relation to all the grounds of judicial review, procedural and substantive, old and new, this is made possible by recourse to the interpretive doctrine of ultra vires.[197]

---

[196] D Feldman, "Convention Rights and Substantive Ultra Vires" in C F Forsyth, *Judicial Review and the Constitution* (Oxford: Hart Publishing, 2000) at 266.

[197] It is particularly convenient that the existing and new grounds of review rest on the same theoretical foundation given that there is an inevitable degree of overlap between the matters covered by the Convention rights and the principles traditionally embraced by English administrative law.

3.3.2. Preclusive provisions

It was observed in Chapter 4 that, so far as narrow interpretation of preclusive provisions is concerned, the modified ultra vires principle places the courts in a much stronger position than the rule-based methodology of the common law model. The reasons for this conclusion are set out at length above and it is unnecessary to repeat them here.[198] It is sufficient to note that the contrast, *vis-à-vis* ouster clauses, between the modified ultra vires and common law theories is precisely mirrored, in the present context, by the distinction between the vires-based and rule-based conceptions of human rights review.

If the new, rights-based grounds of review were conceptualised as taking effect in rule-based terms (under section 6(1)) rather than interpretatively (pursuant to section 3(1) understood in light of section 6(1)) then the Convention norms would not form an internal fetter on the discretionary power of executive agents. Consequently a decision contradicting one or more of those norms would not be outwith the power conferred by the enabling legislation. For the reasons advanced in Chapter 4, this would substantially undermine the courts' ability to vouchsafe the rule of law by reading preclusive provisions narrowly.

This would lead to the strange position that standard ousters would preclude human rights review, but not review on traditional, process-oriented grounds (which would continue to be rationalised through the ultra vires doctrine and to which, therefore, the logic of *Anisminic*[199] reasoning would continue to apply). Such a perverse result surely cannot have been intended by the framers of the Human Rights Act. It is therefore important to appreciate that, so far as its operation in the field of judicial review of statutory power is concerned, ultra vires theory lies at the heart of the Human Rights Act, as sections 3(1) and 6(1), properly understood, demonstrate. Embracing human rights as interpretative constructs thus ensures that the constitutional logic exposed by the *Anisminic* case can be deployed in order to minimise the impact of preclusive provisions on the operation of the new rights-based review jurisdiction.

3.3.3. Collateral challenge

Chapter 4 suggests that a further pragmatic reason for retaining ultra vires theory is that it secures the availability of collateral attack by ensuring the voidness of executive action which breaches the existing principles of administrative law. The reasons underlying that conclusion are set out in detail in Chapter 4,[200] but they essentially reduce to the fact that there exists an ineluctable connection between the concepts of ultra vires, voidness and collateral impeachability.

In contrast, if administrative law is conceptualised in rule-based terms, such that the concept of excess of power is no longer considered to be central, then

---

[198] See above at 145–57.
[199] *Anisminic Ltd. v. Foreign Compensation Commission* [1969] 2 AC 147.
[200] See above at 157–61.

logic no longer dictates that executive action which breaches the rules of good administration must be regarded as void. Crucially, if such action is not void, then it is valid unless and until a court of public law jurisdiction quashes it, with the consequence that collateral attack ceases to be available. Precisely these considerations led the House of Lords, in *Boddington* v. *British Transport Police*,[201] to reassert that the ultra vires doctrine is the basis of the traditional law of judicial review and that, as a logical consequence, executive action which breaches any of the principles of administrative law is void and collaterally impeachable (unless, of course, primary legislation directs to the contrary).

It is worth emphasising that the consequences of a rule-based conceptualisation of the traditional principles of administrative law, which were felt to be so undesirable in *Boddington*, would logically attend the adoption of a rule-based model of human rights review. The reasoning is precisely the same: if the Convention norms are not inherent limits on discretionary powers, then their breach does not necessarily constitute an excess of power; consequently, action committed in breach of the Convention need not be regarded as void, in which case it would not be vulnerable to collateral attack. In *Boddington*, speaking in the context of the traditional principles of administrative law, Lord Steyn remarked that such a situation would be fundamentally repugnant to the rule of law. This would equally be true if rule-based reasoning defeated collateral impeachability in relation to the Convention rights. Given that the central purpose of the Human Rights Act is to strengthen the rule of law, such an outcome would be ironic, to say the least; it is appropriate, therefore, that the operation of human rights review is rationalised in conceptual terms which secure the collateral impeachability of executive action which breaches the Convention.

It may be thought that there exists a fairly obvious retort to this line of argument. Section 7(1)(b) of the Human Rights Act permits an individual to "rely" on a breach of Convention rights "in any legal proceedings". At first glance, it may seem that this statutorily guarantees the availability of collateral challenge in cases where Convention rights have been infringed, so that such challenge would be possible irrespective of whether a vires-based or rule-based model was used to explain human rights review. However, such reasoning is faulty. Notwithstanding section 7(1)(b), it is necessary to retain the concepts of vires and voidness if collateral attack is to be possible on Convention grounds. An example will help to demonstrate why this is so.

Assume that an individual is prosecuted, in a magistrates' court, for breaching a byelaw. The defendant wishes to argue, in his defence, that the relevant byelaw was made in breach of one or more of the Convention rights. He will, therefore, bring this matter to the attention of the magistrates, as he is entitled to do under section 7(1)(b). If the magistrates are satisfied that there has been a breach of the Convention, it becomes necessary to determine precisely what, if

---

[201] [1999] 2 AC 143.

anything, they may do in response. It is at this point that the distinction between the vires-based and rule-based models becomes crucial.

If it is acknowledged that human rights take effect as interpretive constructs, so that they represent inherent limits on statutory powers, no problem arises. The byelaw is ultra vires and hence void. The defendant can therefore successfully raise the breach of Convention rights, and can escape conviction on the ground that the byelaw under which he was charged is without legal effect. The reasoning in *Boddington* which secures this outcome in cases concerned with the traditional principles of administrative law would apply with precisely the same force to a case involving breach of the Convention rights, given that, within the vires-based model, all of the principles of public law, old and new, are species of ultra vires.

However, if human rights are free-standing rules which have nothing to do with the internal contours of statutory powers, the position is very different. Notwithstanding that section 7(1)(b) allows the defendant to rely on his Convention rights, there is nothing which the magistrates' court can do in response to such reliance. The reasoning is as follows. Within the rule-based model, the byelaw is not ultra vires and therefore need not be conceptualised as void; instead, it may be voidable, in which case it will be valid and legally effective unless and until it is quashed by a court of competent jurisdiction. The difficulty is that a magistrates' court does not have the power to quash unlawful administrative action. Moreover, section 8(1) of the Human Rights Act is of no avail here, since it merely allows a court to "grant such relief or remedy" as is "within its powers": certiorari is quite clearly outwith the powers of a magistrates' court. As a result the byelaw, which has been made in breach of the Convention, remains valid unless it is quashed on judicial review.

It may be argued that it is implicit in section 7(1)(b) that there exists a power, in cases of collateral challenge, to quash executive action which is in breach of Convention rights. However, this would represent a very strained construction of the Act. The most natural interpretation is to accept that the reliance which section 7(1)(b) allows litigants to place on Convention infringements presupposes—in line with orthodox administrative law reasoning—that executive action which is unlawful for breach of the Convention is ultra vires and therefore void. Adopting this approach carries the dual benefits that section 7(1)(b) can be accorded a natural construction, while litigants are truly able to rely on their Convention rights collaterally as well as directly. Once again, it becomes apparent that the theory of ultra vires is central to the effective functioning of the Human Rights Act.

4. CONCLUSION

One of the hallmarks of modern administrative law is its vibrancy and its ability to adapt to changing circumstances. This is particularly evident from the way in which it has responded to the general decline in the ability, or willingness, of Parliament to act as an effective check on the executive. However, this expansionist tendency is sometimes accompanied by a reluctance to pay sufficient attention to the underlying questions of constitutional propriety which the growth of administrative law inevitably raises. We have already seen one example of this in the context of judicial review of *de facto* power. As techniques of governance have changed, it has become increasingly necessary for the courts to assert supervisory jurisdiction over non-legal governmental powers; yet this has occurred with little accompanying explanation in terms of constitutional justification. The subjugation of issues of constitutional legitimacy in the face of a desire to secure ever more rigorous forms of judicial control of the executive is also apparent in the human rights context in two particular respects.

First, many writers urged the British courts unilaterally to assert a substantive rights-based jurisdiction. However, as section 2 explained, the adoption of such a course of action by the courts would have had fundamental implications in terms of their relationship with the other branches of government. For this reason it was argued that the courts were right to await legislative intervention in order to legitimate the exercise of a rights-based review jurisdiction.

Secondly, it has long been fashionable, in the field of judicial review, to eschew the idea of statutory implication in favour of straightforward rules requiring adherence to a set of principles of good administration. This approach has been promoted in the context of the traditional grounds of judicial review, and its attractions appear, at first glance, to apply equally to the new, rights-based principles of review which the Human Rights Act creates. In both instances, however, constitutional propriety precludes this approach from being adopted, and points, instead, towards construction-oriented methodology.

Thus, notwithstanding the widely held view that human rights review is a positive development, underlying considerations of constitutional legitimacy suggested that it was appropriate for the courts to await legislative intervention before asserting such jurisdiction; and, now that a human rights jurisdiction exists, the constitutional order requires that its operation be rationalised in terms which render it consistent with the principle of parliamentary sovereignty and the non-entrenched nature of the Human Rights Act. It therefore becomes apparent that the ultra vires doctrine is the central principle of administrative law not only in the traditional area of process-oriented review: it is also vital to the new, rights-based approach to judicial review which is now beginning to take shape. This is unsurprising. It is the deep foundations of constitutional logic on which the ultra vires principle rests—and, in particular, its recognition of the need to reconcile respect for individuals' rights, whether procedural or substantive, written or unwritten, with the constitutional framework—which explain its ubiquitous relevance to both the long history of English administrative law and the new dawn of constitutionalism which is now breaking.

7

The Constitutional Foundations of Judicial Review

1. INTRODUCTION

THE DEVELOPMENT of the modern public law supervisory jurisdiction forms a key element of the twentieth century's legal heritage. By enforcing principles of good administration of an increasingly rigorous nature over an ever broader range of decision-making powers, English judges have fashioned a potent mechanism for the control of public power and the prevention of its abuse.

Against this background, it has been the purpose of this book to examine the constitutional foundations upon which the superstructure of modern English administrative law rests. Such an inquiry is necessary quite simply because Britain is a democracy based on a constitutional separation of powers and on the rule of law. Claims of power by the different institutions of government must be scrutinised in order to ensure that they are legitimate and do not exceed the limitations which the unwritten constitution prescribes. The courts are no exception in this regard. Their assertion of powers of judicial review raises particularly significant and sensitive issues of legitimacy in light of the fact that it both attenuates executive autonomy and assumes primary responsibility for a supervisory function that has traditionally belonged to the legislature.

The foregoing chapters have addressed the question of legitimacy in relation to review of statutory, prerogative and de facto governmental powers, as well as examining the foundations of the new, rights-based principles of review which the Human Rights Act 1998 introduces. No attempt will be made here to summarise the detailed conclusions reached on those matters. Instead, some of the overarching themes which have emerged from this investigation will be underscored by way of conclusion. The first of these is the importance of distinguishing between what may be called *constitutional justification* and *normative justification* in the field of judicial review.

2. CONSTITUTIONAL JUSTIFICATION AND NORMATIVE JUSTIFICATION

Chapter 1 explains that, as the scope and significance of judicial review have steadily expanded, the concern of the courts—and, generally speaking, of academic commentators—has been with the normative worth of such curial innovation. Attention has thus tended to focus on whether it would be desirable, from a policy standpoint, to apply or develop judicial review—or certain aspects of review—in particular contexts. This attitude, it has been observed, was especially apparent in those cases which extended judicial review beyond the control of statutory power.[1]

Such normative evaluation of the courts' case law is absolutely crucial, and it is right that judges, in developing the law, and academics, as they evaluate it, pay careful attention to this matter. However, at a logically prior stage, the question of constitutional justification arises. This matter is distinct from the desirability, in normative or policy terms, of any given extension of judicial review (*vis-à-vis* either its scope or the grounds of challenge which it encompasses). Determination of whether judicial review in a certain context or on a certain ground is beneficial in a normative sense must be preceded by consideration of the constitutional foundations of such review. Only if a satisfactory constitutional basis exists may an extension of judicial review enjoy constitutional legitimacy.[2] For instance, although, prior to the introduction of the Human Rights Act there was broad agreement that the *exercise* of a human rights jurisdiction is, normatively speaking, an appropriate judicial task, a prior, and equally important, question arose concerning the constitutional legitimacy of the judiciary's unilaterally *asserting* such jurisdiction. Similarly the desirability, from a normative, or policy-oriented, perspective, of subjecting the exercise of statutory power to judicial control does not obviate the need to address how such review may be rationalised in constitutional terms, thus engaging with the debate concerning parliamentary sovereignty, the ultra vires principle, and so on.

It has been suggested that the notion of constitutional legitimacy can, in the present context, be resolved into two principal components.[3] The requirement that the courts must possess an adequate *constitutional warrant* reflects the fact that their supervisory endeavour must be capable of justification by reference to the nature of the constitutional order and to the courts' position within it. The second element of legitimacy, that judicial review of any given type of power must rest on a satisfactory *legal basis*, derives from a concern to ensure that curial supervision is juridically rationalised in a manner which is capable of recon-

---

[1] See above at 6–9.

[2] It must be emphasised that an enquiry into the constitutional justification for judicial review in any given area is itself normative, in the sense that it engages with the principles on which the constitutional order is founded and asks whether review is consistent with those principles. This, however, is a rather different enquiry from one which is concerned solely with the inherent policy-based merit of invoking judicial review in a given context. It is the difference between those two modes of enquiry which the terms "normative justification" and "constitutional justification" are intended to reflect.

[3] See further above at 10–12.

ciliation with the constraints which the constitutional framework imposes[4] and in a way which is legally coherent.[5]

Of course, to attempt to draw a bright-line distinction between questions of normative worth and constitutional justification is ultimately futile. The normative value of a particular innovation may clearly impact upon whether it is a constitutionally appropriate—or justifiable—task for the courts to undertake. However, the fact that the dividing line between normative and constitutional considerations is not watertight does not obviate the need to address both of these issues: the desirability of judicial review does not detract from the importance of examining its underlying constitutional basis. This book has pointed out that the former has tended to obscure the latter, and has therefore attempted to redress that balance by exploring the constitutional foundations on which review rests.

The importance of paying due regard to questions of constitutional justification crystallises with particular clarity in the context of ultra vires. The question whether this principle furnishes an adequate basis for judicial review is one of the most keenly debated theoretical issues in contemporary English public law. One of the principal factors which is perceived by many as militating in favour of its abandonment is the desirability of articulating a theory of review which, unlike the superficial fiction of legislative intention upon which accounts of ultra vires are traditionally based, fully embraces the normative worth and constitutional resonance of the values which the courts uphold through the supervisory jurisdiction. This creates a strong impetus for a fresh approach in this area.

In spite of this, it has been argued that the implication-based essence of ultra vires must be retained as part of the justification for review of statutory power. To discard completely the methodology of ultra vires is to over-emphasise arguments based on the (self-evident) inherent normative worth of the principles of public law at the expense of furnishing an account of judicial review which secures its compatibility with the constitutional order. Valuable though many of their contributions have been, it is this point which many critics of ultra vires have tended to overlook. To rely on the normative value of the principles of judicial review as sufficient to establish the constitutional legitimacy of the supervisory jurisdiction is to conflate to an unacceptable degree the related but separable issues of constitutional and normative justification.

In terms of both common sense and policy, the desirability of the courts' supervisory endeavour speaks for itself. However, to assume that this supplies

---

[4] See, *e.g.*, Ch. 3 and Ch. 6, section 3, on the importance of constructing the legal bases of review of statutory power on existing and rights-based grounds so as to secure compatibility with the doctrine of parliamentary sovereignty.

[5] See, *e.g.*, the distinction, advanced in Ch. 5, between the vires-based approach to review of prerogative power and the rule-based model applied to review of *de facto* governmental power. The differences between these two types of power dictated divergent conceptualisations of the legal bases (or locations) of the principles of good administration enforced by reviewing courts. Only by adopting such an approach was it possible to furnish a legally coherent rationalisation of review in those areas.

sufficient justification from a constitutional perspective is to indulge in constitutional insouciance. Although the good sense inherent in curial scrutiny of the
executive is self-apparent, so, too, is the need to rationalise the discharge of this
crucial judicial function in a manner which accords with, rather than ignores,
the established order of the constitution. It was for this reason that the argument
was advanced above that judicial review of statutory power must be constitutionally justified in a way which conceptualises the principles of good administration as interpretative constructs while, at the same time, acknowledging that
the grounds of review owe their existence to a process of judicial creativity
which has drawn upon the fundamental norms on which the constitution is
founded.

3. A CONTEXT-SENSITIVE APPROACH TO CONSTITUTIONAL JUSTIFICATION

While it is crucial to recognise the significance of constitutional principle and the
importance of justifying judicial review by reference to it, it is equally necessary
to avoid exaggerating the compass of particular doctrines. The point advanced
in the previous section, that review must be justified constitutionally, as well as
evaluated normatively, can therefore be refined: it must be justified by reference
to *relevant* constitutional principles.

For example, while the axiom of legislative supremacy exerts a profound
influence on the approach which must be adopted to justifying review of statutory power on both conventional[6] and rights-based grounds,[7] it is of little relevance in the fields of prerogative and *de facto* governmental power. In this sense
it is futile to attempt to articulate an overarching constitutional justification for
judicial review, because to do so is to overlook the fact that the justificatory
issues raised by various forms of governmental power are distinct and must be
dealt with context-specifically. Different types of power thus raise different
challenges of justification.

Once this is recognised it becomes possible to justify judicial review of distinct forms of power in a more coherent and intellectually honest fashion. Thus
the worth—and, indeed, necessity—of the ultra vires doctrine can be acknowledged while recognising that any attempt to apply its logic outside the ambit of
statutory power would be to stretch a central constitutional principle beyond
breaking point. Similarly, as was noted in Chapter 5, the relevance of parliamentary intention to the review of statutory power should not lead the courts
artificially to restrict the scope of review of non-statutory powers by adopting a
test of amenability based on whether they think Parliament would intervene in
the absence of a non-statutory agency. The importance of context also pervaded
the argument, advanced in Chapter 5, that the justification of review of non-

---

[6] See Chs. 3–4.
[7] See Ch. 6, section 3.

statutory powers must be predicated on the essential differences between prerogative power and the residual liberties whose exercise gives rise to *de facto* powers of governance. In this manner it became apparent that review of the former must logically be rationalised in terms of a vires-based regime, whereas control of the latter entails the application of a set of free-standing common law rules.

It is, therefore, crucial to take account of important constitutional principles—such as the doctrines of parliamentary sovereignty and ultra vires—where they are relevant, while recognising the limits of their influence and embracing the diffuse justificatory considerations which arise in different contexts.

4. IMPETUS AND IMPLEMENTATION

However, arguing that judicial review must be justified in ways which are appropriate to the different fields in which it now operates need not lead inevitably to the untenable conclusion that there exist a number of disjointed supervisory jurisdictions resting on wholly distinct constitutional foundations. Such an approach would be wholly unrealistic, since it would fail to explain why the same grounds of review apply to all exercises of governmental power, irrespective of whether the source is statutory, prerogative or *de facto*.

Acknowledgment of the need to fashion context-specific justifications for judicial intervention need not occur at the expense of recognising that judicial review constitutes a coherent approach to the control of public power. Underpinning review of the various kinds of governmental power there exists a common impetus. As Jowell has rightly observed, "Administrative Law is the implementation of the constitutional principle of the Rule of Law".[8] Thus it is a desire to confine governmental action within the limits prescribed by that constitutional principle which underlies judicial review in all its guises.[9] A similar point is made by Sir John Laws, who writes that the principle that the law "will not permit abuse of power" forms "the basis of judicial review".[10] It is this commonality of purpose which connects judicial review of all forms of governmental power and which explains why the same principles of good administration are applied to different types of power.[11] In all instances, the courts' ultimate

---

[8] J Jowell, "The Rule of Law Today" in J Jowell and D Oliver (eds.), *The Changing Constitution* (Oxford: Clarendon Press, 1994) at 73.

[9] Indeed, a modern literature is developing which argues that the values to which judicial review gives effect in the public law context are also of relevance in the field of private law. See D Oliver, "Common Values in Public and Private Law and the Public/Private Divide" [1997] *PL* 630, "The Underlying Values of Public and Private Law" in M Taggart (ed.), *The Province of Administrative Law* (Oxford: Hart Publishing, 1997) and "Review of (Non-Statutory) Discretions" in C F Forsyth (ed.), *Judicial Review and the Constitution* (Oxford: Hart Publishing, 2000); Sir John Laws, "Public Law and Employment Law: Abuse of Power" [1997] *PL* 455.

[10] Laws, above n. 9, at 464.

[11] Subject, of course, to considerations *other than* the source of the power, such as the context in which the power is used and the justiciability of the governmental function in question.

purpose is to vindicate the rule of law in order that individuals may be protected from executive abuse.

The impetus for judicial review is therefore constant, being based on the rule of law doctrine which abhors the abuse of power. The manner in which this policy is implemented is a distinct issue, and it is this question of effectuation which must be dealt with in ways which are appropriate to the different fields in which judicial review occurs. Only by recognising this distinction between the common stimulus underlying curial supervision and the diffuse mechanisms by which its practical implementation is secured is it possible to ensure the application of standards of good administration in a manner which is constitutionally and conceptually coherent.

5. CONCLUSION

The impetus for this book was never the question *whether* judicial review could be legitimated in constitutional terms. A constitution which could not accommodate a judicial regime of governmental accountability would, to say the least, be defective. This would be especially so if it were true of the British constitution, given the clear need for judicial review following the decline of political modes of executive accountability, and in light of the fact that one of the claimed strengths of the informal British constitution is its ability to adapt to precisely such changing circumstances. The interesting question, therefore, has always been *how* judicial review may be justified. The response to that question which is supplied in this book is implicit in its title. The notion that judicial review rests on a *set of constitutional foundations*, rather than on a *single foundation*, captures two central truths about the juridical underpinnings of the supervisory jurisdiction.

In the first place, it emphasises that the ethos lying at the heart of orthodox ultra vires theory—that judicial review is based solely on the intention of the legislature—is fundamentally incorrect. In truth, judicial review's legitimacy is secured, and its ambit determined, by the rich set of constitutional principles—most notably the rule of law, the separation of powers and the sovereignty of Parliament—on which the constitution is founded. It is in the interaction of those constitutional fundamentals, rather than in the legislative command of the sovereign, that the justification for judicial review is to be found. Secondly, the pluralism which inheres in the notion of constitutional foundations reflects the fact that judicial review must be justified in ways which are appropriate to the diverse areas within which it now operates. The search for a single doctrine capable of furnishing a juridical rationalisation of all judicial review is futile—albeit that this conclusion emphatically does not detract from the fact that review in all its contexts rests on a common normative basis.

English public law presently stands at the dawn of a new era of constitutionalism. The constitutional reform programme significantly emphasises and enhances the constitutional role of the judiciary. In particular, the devolution and human rights schemes mean that the courts are now, for the first time, exercising a constitutional jurisdiction properly so called. Just as the growth of the state and the decline of political accountability prompted changes which fundamentally reshaped the landscape of administrative law over the last 100 years, so public law is set for a transformation of at least equal proportions during the opening years of the new century.

Against the background of such developments, it may seem that the traditional law of judicial review and the debate concerning its constitutional foundations are of diminishing significance. Such a conclusion would not, however, be wholly justified. The established regime of judicial review is the anvil on which contemporary British public law has been formed, and only by attempting to understand its theoretical foundations is it possible to begin to rationalise the juridical implications of the constitutional changes which are now in motion.[12] The constitution has supplied firm, if sometimes unarticulated, foundations for the established law of judicial review; and the new, rights-based regime of judicial review rests on an equally secure basis. However, as the inevitable evolution of administrative law continues, it will serve us well to remember the central importance of evaluating its legitimacy by reference to the constitutional order. That way lies the strongest possible foundation for English public law in the twenty-first century.

---

[12] As Ch. 6 (see especially section 3) sought to demonstrate in the context of fundamental rights adjudication under the Human Rights Act 1998.

Index

Printed in the United Kingdom
by Lightning Source UK Ltd.
104756UKS00001B/82